KT-225-419

FACT FILE

Sport

Peter Brooke-Ball

WHSMITH

EXCLUSIVE
· BOOKS ·

Editor	Rachel Pilcher
Assistant editor	Lee Simmons
Designers	Michèle Arron
	Branka Drobac
	Cathy Tincknell
Illustrators	John James
	Hayward Art Group
	Marion Appleton

First published in 1991 by
Grisewood & Dempsey Ltd
Elsley House
24–30 Great Titchfield Street
London W1P 7AD.

10 9 8 7 6 5 4 3 2 1

© Grisewood & Dempsey Ltd 1991

All rights reserved. No part of this
publication may be reproduced, stored in a
retrieval system, or transmitted, in any form
or by any means, electronic, mechanical,
photocopying, recording or otherwise,
without the prior permission of the
publishers.

Printed and bound in Spain

ISBN 0 906279 60 7

The publishers would like to thank the following for their assistance in the preparation of the text:

All England Netball Association; Amateur Boxing Association of England; Amateur Fencing
Association; Amateur Swimming Association; Badminton Association of England Limited;
Billiards & Snooker Control Council; British Aikido Board; British Amateur Gymnastics Associ-
ation; British Amateur Weight Lifters' Association; British Bobsleigh Association; British Canoe
Union; British Cycling Federation; British Cyclo-cross Association; British Gliding Association;
British Hang Gliding Association; British Harness Racing Club; British Ice Hockey Association;
British Motorcycle Sport; British Orienteering Federation; British Pétanque Association; British
Surfing Association; British Tenpin Bowling Association; British Water Ski Federation; Cyclists'
Touring Club; English Basket Ball Association; English Crown Green Bowling Association; English
Curling Association; English Darts Organization; English Golf Union; English Lacrosse Union;
English Olympic Wrestling Association; English Table Tennis Association; English Volleyball
Association; Federation of Ice Skating Ltd; Grand National Archery Society; Hurlingham Polo
Association; J & D Jelley; Martial Arts Commission; National Small-bore Rifle Association; Royal
and Ancient Golf Club; Rugby Football Union; Scottish Triathlon Association; Squash Rackets
Association; Tennis and Rackets Association; The British Balloon and Airship Club; The British
Show Jumping Association; The British Ski Federation; The Clay Pigeon Shooting Association;
The Cricket Council; The Croquet Association; The Cycle Speedway Council; The Football Associ-
ation; The Hockey Association; The Jockey Club; The Lawn Tennis Association; The Modern
Pentathlon Association of Great Britain; The RAC Motor Sports Association Limited.

FACT FILE

FILE

Sport

CONTENTS

FEATURES OF THIS BOOK

Factfile Sport is a book for everyone interested in sport, whether regular participators, spectators or those who simply enjoy watching sport on the television. It aims to provide all the essential information on the world's major sports, delving into histories, unravelling rules, explaining obscure technical terms and revealing the backgrounds of outstanding individuals and teams. Hundreds of illustrations and photographs bring the information to life. *Factfile Sport* will help settle those niggling family disputes, introduce people to new activities and make sport even more enjoyable.

AIMS OF THE GAME explain the objectives and basic rules of each sport in a clear and concise way.

INTRODUCTIONS explore the history and development of each sport and describe fascinating details of the modern game.

HUNDREDS OF ILLUSTRATIONS help to bring each sport to life. In addition to the many action shots, informative diagrams portray positions, pitches and equipment.

EXCITING PHOTOGRAPHS have been chosen to complement the text and illustrations.

228

ICE HOCKEY

The fastest of all team games is ice hockey — usually just called 'hockey' in North America where field hockey is seldom played. The sport is thought to have originated in Canada during the winter of 1860 when English garrison soldiers introduced a disc-shaped 'puck', instead of a ball, whilst playing bandy (see page 218) on frozen lakes. It was soon taken up by players in the United States, USSR, and the Scandinavian countries, all of which had natural ice on which to participate.

Today ice hockey is played by amateurs and professionals on indoor and, when it is cold enough, outdoor rinks. It is an exciting, fast, and occasionally violent sport. It is rapidly gaining, or regaining, popularity in Britain, where dozens of clubs — and a professional league — have been established.

The ruling body is the International Ice Hockey Federation (IIHF) which was founded in 1908 and is based in London. The professional game, as played by North American club teams, is ruled by the National Hockey League (NHL) which was established in 1917. For amateurs, the premier events are the Winter Olympic Games, the annual World Championships and the European Championships.

▼ Standard ice rinks are usually painted white with the blue and red lines added. A sheet of clear ice covers the surface.

AIMS OF THE GAME

COMPETITION
● The game is played on ice between two 6-a-side teams. Substitutions are allowed. Each team tries to score goals by manoeuvring a puck about the rink using 'sticks'.
● For major competitions, the rink must be 56-61 m (61-68 yd approx.) long and 26-30 m (28-33 yd approx.) wide. In junior competitions, smaller rinks are permitted.
  The corners of the rink have to be rounded and the entire playing area has to be surrounded by a barrier that stands 1.22 m (4 ft) high. Markings and features on the rink include
  - 2 'goal' lines, marked in red at each end, sited 4 m (13 ft) from the edges of the rink;
  - 2 'zone' lines, marked in blue, dividing the rink into 3 equal areas — 2 'end zones' and a 'central zone';
  - a red 'centre' line dividing the rink into halves;
  - a 'centre spot', in the middle of the centre line surrounded by a blue 'centre circle' 4.5 m (15 ft approx.) in diameter

SKILLS describe the particular skills and talents required for each sport.

EQUIPMENT gives detailed information on the equipment needed.

TABS provide easy access around the book. Sports which share common ground are grouped together into chapters, identified by the tabs running down each page.

230

GOAL SPORTS

another from one zone to another but the ultimate aim is to get the puck into the opposition's goal. Players can 'check' (tackle) for the puck by directly, and physically, going for the man who has it or by intercepting passes

• Fouls and minor infringements occur all the time in ice hockey. When this happens, it is usual for face-offs to be taken in the nearest face-off spot. However a referee will play advantage to the team offended against until the offending team gains possession. If the offended team scores during such 'delayed penalties', the offence is forgotten. Players that foul the opposition are sent to the 'sin bin' — a side bench — for a period of time. For minor offences (like hooking another player's stick), a 2-min penalty is usual; major offences (outright violence or abusing the referee) penalties can run from 5 to 10 mins. When a player is in the sin bin, a team plays 'one short' and substitution is not allowed. On minor penalties, if the opposition scores, then the offending player immediately rejoins the action.

Individual points are awarded for goals and assists. A goal is scored when the puck crosses the goal line and goes into the goal; assists are given by the referee to players who begin an attacking movement before a goal is scored. Both goals and assists equal 1 point.

Ice hockey games are divided into three 20-min 'periods'. The team scoring most goals is the winner.

Ice hockey is a fast and furious game. Players should constantly keep their heads up as they play at top speed, even when controlling the puck. In this way they see opportunities for attack.

229

within

(15 ft
end zone
sited in

naturally
each end,
1.83 m
at are not
x.) deep. In
is a shallow

referee drops
-off players at
ve to gain
ayers must be
centre circle.
soft, team
e puck amongst
er of rules
ayer can pass to

ll the net for the
orwards try to get
s it to their centre
al. Defenders can
y starting an attack
ir own goal.

SKILLS

• Ice hockey players have to be able to skate in all directions, including backwards. At the same time they must also be able to control a puck. Most teams contain:

- a net minder (goalie) whose job it is to keep the puck out of the goal;
- defencemen who specialize in tackling and defending;
- wingers who are fast skaters who patrol the perimeters of the rink with the aim of either scoring or passing to the centre who is invariably an all-round player with a talent for scoring goals.

• Ice hockey is a frantic and gruelling sport, so many substitutions and re-substitutions may take place during a game — 18 players plus 2 net minders are permitted per team.

• A team coach decides when his players should come off and when a fresh one should go on. He is also responsible for relaying tactics to his team members.

EQUIPMENT

• Most ice hockey sticks are made from laminated wood although some synthetic materials are permitted. A stick may not measure more than 147 cm (32 in) in length. The blades on net minders' sticks can be slightly longer and broader than those for other players, but no blade can be longer than 39 cm (15 in approx.).

• The black puck is made of vulcanized rubber and has a diameter of 7.63 cm (3 in), a thickness of 2.54 cm (1 in) and a weight of around 170 g (6 oz).

• In addition to superficial gear, all players wear helmets, gloves, and pads on the shins and elbows. The skates used are specially designed and do not carry rasps on the leading edges. Net minders wear heavy pads, chest protectors, gauntlets, face protectors, and special boots and skates.

TECHNICAL TERMS

poke check when one player stops another by blocking the puck

slap shot a full-blooded hit of the puck; neither a flick nor a push

FOR THE RECORD

The National Hockey League is fought out between 21 North American teams which are divided into 2 'conferences' - the Wales Conference and the Campbell Conference. Each conference has 2 divisions. The top teams in each division play off for the Stanley Cup each year. A best-of-seven series of games is played in the finals. New franchises have been awarded recently enabling new teams to join the NHL.

231

GOAL SPORTS

PERSONALITY PROFILE

Wayne Gretzky
Without doubt the greatest ice hockey player of all time is Wayne Gretzky, who has earned more points for his teams than any other professional in the sport — nearly 2000 in 850 games. He also has broken virtually every scoring record there is — goals in a season, points in a season, assists in a season etc. Gretzky even won the trophy for the NHL's 'most gentlemanly player' in 1980.

Gretzky was born in Brantford, Canada, in 1961 and after a precocious start with amateur teams, he joined the Indianapolis Racers before transferring to the Edmonton Oilers in 1977. In 1988, he led the Oilers to a fourth victory in the Stanley Cup before signing up with the Los Angeles Kings for a record fee of $15 million.

Quiet and unassuming both on the ice and off it, Gretzky does not behave like most 'superstars'. He is always able to 'read' a game like no other — in the right place at the right time, ready to pass as well as shoot. He is a true hockey genius.

TECHNICAL TERMS and special or obscure words, peculiar to a sport, are clearly explained.

FOR THE RECORD highlights interesting facts about particular teams, events and competitions. These are complemented by **DID YOU KNOW?** boxes giving nuggets of strange-but-true information.

PERSONALITY PROFILES reveal the background and accomplishments of leading sportsmen and sportswomen.

COMBAT SPORTS

The origins of many combat sports date back centuries — martial arts were recorded as far back as 2000 BC and the Ancient Greeks and Romans certainly wrestled and jousted. Some sports, such as sumo, have changed little over the years but others have evolved to become so-called 'modern' sports with strict rules and codes of conduct. The combat sports are all essentially ways of fighting, where one competitor tries to overwhelm his opponent, using a combination of skill, strength and guile.

DID YOU KNOW?

Before the modern rules of Greco-Roman wrestling came into being, Anders Ahlgren of Sweden and Ivar Bohling of Finland fought for 9 hr in the Light-heavyweight Olympic final of 1912. Officials finally called the contest a draw but the men were not given gold medals. This was because the existing rules stated that a champion actually had to defeat his opponent. Ahlgren and Bohling had to settle for silver medals.

AMATEUR WRESTLING

Wrestling is one of the oldest of all sports. It was a popular spectator sport for the Jews of biblical times and the Ancient Greek, Milo, is reputed to have won six Olympic titles. Variations now exist in countries as far apart as Mongolia, England and Iran but only two styles are competed at international level — Greco-Roman and freestyle. Together they are known as Olympic wrestling.

In Greco-Roman wrestling, combatants are not allowed to seize each other below the waist nor

▶ *The techniques and codes of modern wrestling had become established by the beginning of the 20th century, as this etching from 1903 shows.*

are they permitted to grip with their legs. Before rules were laid down for the sport, bouts could last for hours as some champions were so skilled at staying on their feet that they were virtually impossible to topple.

Because Greco-Roman wrestling appeared boring to European spectators in the last century, freestyle wrestling came into being. In freestyle, the legs are allowed to be used and trips, sweeps and dives to the legs are all legitimate moves. This makes it a more lively and entertaining sport to watch, but devotees of Greco-Roman wrestling still maintain that the older sport is more skilful.

Since the first modern Olympic Games held in Athens in 1896, both Greco-Roman and freestyle wrestling events have been included. Second to the Olympics in importance come the annual World Championships. The ruling body of amateur wrestling is the Fédération Internationale de Lutte Amateur (FILA) and the countries with the strongest traditions in wrestling include the Soviet Union, Bulgaria, Iran and the United States.

DID YOU KNOW?

Amateur wrestling is popular in several rural areas of Britain. Various regional styles have evolved, including the Cornish and the Lancashire. Perhaps the best known is the Westmorland style in which 2 competitors hug each other with their arms clasped around one another's bodies. To win a contest a wrestler must either throw his opponent to the ground or force him to lose his balance.

▶ *Points are awarded for pinning an opponent down as well as for successful holds, such as an armlock.*

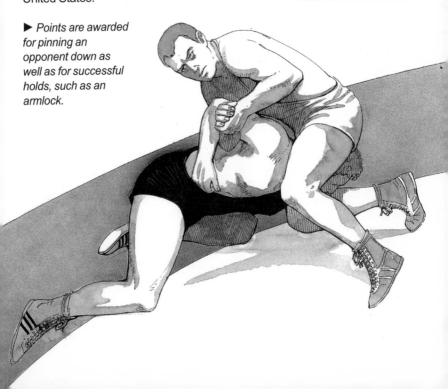

AIMS OF THE GAME

COMPETITION

• Contestants are divided into 10 weight categories to make fights more even. The divisions are the same for both types of wrestling. A limit to the highest category helps ensure that extra weight should not decide a bout.

• At international events both Greco-Roman and freestyle competitions take place on a raised platform with sloping sides. There are no ropes but in the middle of the platform, there is a marked circle 3 m (10 ft) in diameter where the bout actually takes place. The 'passivity zone' — a red band 1 m (3 ft) wide inside the circle — shows wrestlers when they are approaching the limits of the wrestling area.

• Four officials control a bout: a mat chairman who supervises the contest from outside the area, a referee, a judge who can give a second opinion to the referee's decisions and a timekeeper.

• Bouts comprise one 5-min round.

• The system of scoring is identical for Greco-Roman and freestyle wrestling but in Greco-Roman no holds may be made below the hips and the use of the legs is prohibited.

• Points are awarded by the referee for successful holds, positions of advantage and near-throws.

• Fouls include pulling an opponent's leotard, hair or ears, and bending his arm behind his back more than 45°.

• A bout is won when a wrestler pins his opponent's shoulders to the ground for 1 sec or when he has achieved a clear 15-point lead.

• There are specific rules to lessen the chance of serious injury. For example, to lessen the impact, a wrestler must drop to one knee when completing a throw.

SKILLS

• One of the classic moves that all wrestlers attempt to master is called bridging. In this, a wrestler who is in danger of having his shoulders pinned to the mat, arches his back and balances on his head and toes. It requires phenomenal strength but can be a match-winning tactic. It was used spectacularly by the 1984 Olympic gold medallist Pasquale Passarelli from West Germany who spent the last 96 sec of his final bout with World Champion Masaki Eto (Japan) in a body arch. This defensive tactic staved off the danger of being pinned and allowed him to preserve his lead in points.

• In Greco-Roman, opponents grab each other around the chest or lock arms and try to throw each other to the ground. This requires great strength in the torso.

• Sudden moves to unbalance an opponent are often the key to success but many exponents are adept at evasion techniques and can be hard to throw.

• To make it difficult to be thrown, a defender will try to keep his body low to the ground and he will crouch with his legs spread wide apart; a wrestler who stands up tall is comparatively easy to topple.

• Strength also plays a big part in a wrestling match as some techniques involve levering an opponent backwards onto the mat.

• In freestyle wrestling, where the legs can be used, some wrestlers have adopted throwing techniques. Dives to the legs are also common in freestyle wrestling. Freestyle throwing techniques have been adopted by many martial arts sportsmen. They are used to good effect in judo and ju-jitsu in particular.

◀ *The leotard used in amateur wrestling leaves the shoulder bare. Competitors are not allowed to grab an opponent's clothing in order to gain extra leverage.*

▲ *Tall, lightweight boots are worn by both Greco-Roman and freestyle wrestlers. The soles are thin and have no heels; the sides provide important ankle support.*

FOR THE RECORD

WEIGHT CATEGORIES

Light flyweight to	48 kg (106 lb)
Flyweight to	52 kg (115 lb)
Bantamweight to	57 kg (126 lb)
Featherweight to	62 kg (137 lb)
Lightweight to	68 kg (150 lb)
Welterweight to	74 kg (161 lb)
Middleweight to	82 kg (180 lb)
Light-heavyweight to	90 kg (198 lb)
Mid-heavyweight to	100 kg (220 lb)
Heavyweight min	100 kg (220 lb)
max	130 kg (285 lb)

EQUIPMENT

● The standard piece of equipment for Greco-Roman and freestyle wrestlers is a leotard which leaves the upper chest and shoulders bare. In competition, one wrestler wears a red leotard, the other blue so that they are easily identifiable to spectators and officials.
● Light wrestling boots are also usually worn.
● Unlike in some other forms of wrestling, combatants are not allowed to smear oil or grease over their bodies prior to a bout.

TECHNICAL TERMS

fall when a wrestler pins his opponent's shoulders to the mat for 1 sec
passivity zone the red band inside the circle which warns wrestlers that they are nearing the edge
take-down a skill when a competitor gradually forces his opponent from a standing position down onto the mat. It requires considerable strength

12

DID YOU KNOW?

Sumo wrestlers prepare for battle by slamming their bodies and arms against wooden pillars — a training method known as teppo.

SUMO

The first sumo wrestling match was recorded in 23 BC in Japan. The loser was killed. As centuries rolled by, sumo became a more refined sport and was adopted by samurai warriors as a training method for unarmed combat. It ultimately led towards the foundation of ju-jitsu.

While the samurai perfected the arts of self-defence, a more elaborate form of sumo wrestling came into being. Between 1603 and 1867 sumo wrestling was organized as a professional sport under the patronage of the emperors. Little has changed since then.

Sumo wrestlers are traditionally extremely large, obese characters. They put on weight by eating high-protein stew. They are, however extremely fit. Every wrestler belongs to a sumo 'stable', which is usually governed by an ex-wrestler. There are currently about 40 stables in Japan; they double as gymnasia and hostels. Within each stable, a strict hierarchy is observed: juniors cook, clean and dote on their superiors, earning virtually no wage at all; senior wrestlers lead a life of luxury.

In Japan, sumo is revered almost as a religion. Ritual is an important part of the sport. There are just six 15-day annual tournaments and seats for each of them are sold out months in advance. The ruling body of this uniquely Japanese sport is the Japan Sumo Association.

▼ *In the first move of a contest, wrestlers lunge forwards towards each other in a sudden and powerful attack.*

AIMS OF THE GAME

COMPETITION
● Sumo bouts take place in a ring 4.6 m (5 yd) in diameter. It is surrounded by 20 small bales of rice straw. The ring is centred on a raised platform of clay which is blessed by shinto priests before each tournament.
● There are no weight categories. Bouts are won by the wrestler who forces his opponent out of the ring or makes him touch the ground with any part of his body apart from the soles of his feet. Punches, hair-pulls and kicks are forbidden. Bouts can end very quickly, sometimes in seconds, but there are no time limits.
● Five judges and a referee survey a bout.

SKILLS
● Over 200 techniques are available, but in practice only 20 are ever used. These can be divided up into 2 groups — pushing and holding.
● Pushing techniques often incorporate hand-slapping movements.
● Holding skills are used less often. Usually, one man tries to lift his opponent up by his belt.

FAMOUS NAMES

Konishiki, otherwise known as 'Dump Truck', is currently one of the most famous sumo wrestlers in the world. He was born in Hawaii of Samoan parents and has risen to the top echelons of the sport. He is also the heaviest wrestler of modern times — 250 kg (550 lb).

In Japan, **Chiyonofuji,** the 'Wolf', who weighs a meagre 122 kg (270 lb), is considered the greatest of all champions.

▲ *Sumo contests take place within the inner circle of the clay ring. The boundary of the clay ring is marked with bales of rice straw.*

EQUIPMENT

● A loincloth, measuring 10 m (11 yd) is wrapped around the waist and between the legs.
● A buckle, bearing 19 starched silk threads, is worn inside the loincloth by senior wrestlers.
● No footwear is ever worn.

TECHNICAL TERMS

basho sumo tournament
beya stable of wrestlers
chanko-nabe protein-rich stew, which is the staple diet of sumo wrestlers
dohyo sumo ring for bouts
rishiki wrestler
sumotori sumo student

FOR THE RECORD

SUMO GRADINGS
Yokozuna	grand champion
Ozeki	champion
Sekiwake	junior champion
Komusubi	2nd grade junior champion
Maegashira	senior
Juryo	contender
Makushita	leading junior
Sandamne	lower junior
Jonidan	qualified
Jonokuchi	novice

KUNG-FU AND MISCELLANEOUS MARTIAL ARTS

The first martial arts almost certainly originated in India more than two thousand years ago and gradually spread to China, Japan and other countries in the Far East. Different countries and sects evolved their own techniques and styles and today there are hundreds of martial arts.

INDIA

Muki boxing is one of India's oldest sports but has almost become extinct due to the popularity of Western boxing. However, annual duels are held at the holy city of Varanasi and maiming and death are not uncommon. There are virtually no rules in muki. A skilled boxer is supposed to be able to crack stones with his bare fists.

CHINA

The term 'kung-fu' means 'the fist way' but it is commonly used to describe any of the many Chinese martial arts.

Shaolin Temple boxing was supposed to have been taught to monks at the Shaolin Temple in Honan Province by a Zen master. Several of the different styles of temple boxing have developed

DID YOU KNOW?

Nin-jitsu, the art of invisibility, was practised by the ninja who were secret agents and assassins hired by feudal Japanese lords. As well as being skilled in camouflage techniques, the ninja were experts in using poisons, bombs and knives. Nin-jitsu has received much publicity in the West in recent years.

▶ Taekwondo is the national sport of South Korea, and is thought to have developed from the ancient martial art of t'aekyon. Flamboyant kicks, stylized punching techniques, and special chopping moves distinguish it from most of the other martial arts. The flying kick to the head is a typical taekwondo move.

▼ *Supple limbs and flexible joints are crucial in Thai boxing.*

and now resemble acrobatic gymnastics rather than methods of self-defence.

Tai-chi-ch'uan is the most famous style of Shaolin Temple boxing and is the most popular martial art in China. Tai-chi-ch'uan is characterized by majestic, flowing movements. It is occasionally practised with swords, but essentially it is a contemplative martial art which aims to foster inner peace rather than aggression.

KOREA

High-flying kicks and flamboyant punches are hallmarks of taekwondo, an amalgamation of karate and traditional Korean martial arts. Experts are supposed to be able to crack blocks of wood and bricks with their bare limbs. It entered the Olympic Games programme, fittingly enough at Seoul, South Korea, in 1988, as a demonstration sport.

THAILAND

Thai boxing has, quite rightly, earned a reputation for being a truly devastating sport. Unlike in Western boxing, the fists only play a minor role in Thai boxing — kicks and the use of the elbows and knees are more important. A Thai boxing match usually ends with one competitor knocked senseless or unable to continue.

PERSONALITY PROFILE

Bruce Lee

Bruce Lee (originally named Lee Yuen Kam) was largely responsible for making kung-fu popular in the West. He was born in Hong Kong in 1943 and became a master at 'wing chun', a form of Shaolin Temple boxing. Lee subsequently established a style of his own (Jeet-kune-do) and moved to California where he became an actor, using his skills to great effect in films such as *Enter The Dragon.*

Lee died mysteriously in 1973. Among his pall bearers was Hollywood star James Coburn.

DID YOU KNOW?

Some of the throws and holds of ju-jitsu have been adopted by other sports. Judo is wholly derived from ju-jitsu, with the more aggressive techniques removed so that it could be taught in Japanese schools. In addition, some of the more practical and simple self-defence techniques are taught to ordinary men and women who want to learn how to defend themselves.

JU-JITSU

The 'art of flexibility', or ju-jitsu, is a generic term for a whole host of martial arts systems that originated in Japan. Centuries ago, the samurai (Japanese warriors) developed grappling and striking skills that enabled them to defend themselves when they were unarmed or only partially armed. Many of the techniques were based on old Chinese martial arts but the samurai also injected some skills of their own. Over the years several schools of ju-jitsu sprang up and hundreds of different styles came into being. Some teachers favoured hitting and kicking; others relied heavily on using sticks, swords and thrown objects. Ju-jitsu has never had a ruling body in Japan to decide what skills should be included or excluded, but nevertheless it has had a huge influence on other combat sports. As with most martial arts, coloured belts are worn by players to denote proficiency. However, as there are so many schools, there are no hard and fast rules as to what the colours actually signify — different schools issue different colours.

Ju-jitsu was one of the first martial arts to be taught in the West — arriving in Britain and the United States in the 1870s. Various techniques and skills have been passed onto police forces throughout the world in their bid to overcome hoodlums and muggers.

▼ *This highly effective armlock would immobilize an attacker.*

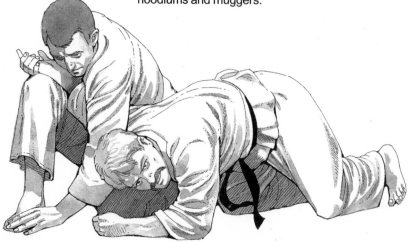

AIMS OF THE GAME

● Ju-jitsu is not a competitive sport — it is a way of self-defence. But it follows the credo that attack is sometimes the best form of defence. As well as using throwing, punching and grappling techniques that are familiar to exponents of judo and karate, it also uses some holds and techniques that have been outlawed in other martial arts competitions — for example, kicks to the groin and kneecaps.
● The techniques taught in most ju-jitsu schools enable a person to fight off an assailant in the most efficient and devastating way.
● Defensive moves include methods of disarming a gunman and parrying a knife attack. More aggressive skills are used to incapacitate an attacker or even maim him. Holds often apply pressure to nerve centres.

▲ *A quick punch from the attacker on the right is blocked by his opponent's hand.*

● Although ju-jitsu is an openly aggressive sport, codes of conduct at modern dojos, or schools, are nevertheless maintained. Physical restraint is vital. Teachers and pupils are taught to respect one another and it is usual to wear a traditional martial arts suit, or gi, when practising. The terminology used is also based on samurai traditions and is similar to that used in judo.

EQUIPMENT

● For practice, and in exhibition matches, a gi or martial arts suit of white cotton is essential. Ju-jitsu gi are usually lighter than those worn by judo players.

DID YOU KNOW?

Yukio Mishima, the Japanese author of many outstanding novels including *Confessions of a Mask* and *The Sailor Who Fell from Grace with the Sea,* was obsessed by the cult of the samurai and was a master at kendo. He founded a private army, the so-called Association of Shields, but committed suicide in 1970 by ritual disembowelment by the sword, or hara-kiri.

KENDO

The craftsmen who made the double-handed swords for Japanese samurai warriors during the Middle Ages became so skilled in their work that the weapons they produced could cut through virtually anything, including iron. It is small wonder then that the samurai themselves declined to use these swords while practising their devastating skills. Instead they devised a sport, kendo, which means 'the way of the sword'.

As a training method for swordsmanship, kendo incorporated all the deadly swipes and stabs of a sword but instead of wielding a real weapon, the samurai used bamboo poles. Ken-jitsu means 'sword techniques', and 'live' swords are used. Iaido is practised by a solitary person, using a real sword. It is a series of stylized techniques, to enhance skill and develop spirit.

In Japan, it is compulsory for some students to learn kendo and it is widely practised by the police and military groups. Elsewhere it is governed by the International Kendo Federation, which has a membership of 15 countries including Brazil, Canada, the United States and Britain. World Championships began in 1970 and are held every three years. No country has yet challenged the supremacy of the Japanese.

◀ *Speed and accuracy in wielding the shinai, and swift footwork, lie at the heart of kendo.*

AIMS OF THE GAME

COMPETITION

● Matches take place in a wooden arena measuring between 9 and 11 m (10 and 13 yd) square.

● Points are awarded when a combatant strikes a blow with the 'sharp' edge of his sword to a target area. For a blow to be valid, an attacker must shout out the name of the target area. Target areas include: the left, right and top of the head, the right or left wrist, and the right and left of the trunk. A point can also be scored with a stab to the throat.

● A match is won by the first combatant to score 2 points which have been verified by the referee.

SKILLS

● The moves and techniques in kendo are formal and have to be delivered in a specific way. For this reason, it is possible for a defender to identify an attack before it is delivered. From an attacker's point of view, this makes speed very important if he is to strike his target.

● The sword is usually held with both hands and great technique is needed to wield it swiftly, especially in attack.

● The code of practice that goes hand-in-hand with fighting is very important to kendo.

● Self-discipline and patience are emphasized in a bid to overcome fear, doubt, surprise and confusion.

EQUIPMENT

● Most important is the shinai, or sword, which is made from 4 strips of bamboo bound with waxed cord. It can be up to 118 cm (47 in) long. A bokuto is a wooden practice sword; the samurai version is the katana.

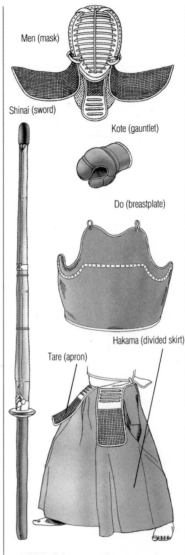

Men (mask)

Shinai (sword)

Kote (gauntlet)

Do (breastplate)

Hakama (divided skirt)

Tare (apron)

▲ *Combatants wear traditional protective garments derived from samurai fighting outfits.*

● The protective clothing includes a uwagi (jacket), hakama (long, divided skirt), tare (waist protector), do (chest protector), men (mask) and kote (padded gloves).

DID YOU KNOW?

Fencing can be a dangerous sport, even for the experts. In 1982, the Olympic foil champion, Vladimir Smirnov, was defending his world title against Matthias Behr of West Germany when his opponent's sword broke, went straight through his mask and into his skull. Tragically Smirnov died soon afterwards.

FENCING

Duelling with swords is as old as the sword itself. Ancient Egyptians used swords in personal combat as did gladiators of Ancient Rome. During Europe's Middle Ages, the rapier was invented. This was a sword with a thin blade and a sharp point. It had no cutting edge but was nevertheless an extremely effective weapon and lethal in one-to-one combat. Using a rapier effectively became such an art form that it was adopted by the aristocrats of European society to settle matters of honour. To practise for impending rapier duels, the well-to-do of the 18th century took to using foil swords which had no edge, were light, and had blunted tips at the end of a long, flexible blade. Fencing with foils became a popular sport and by 1780 combatants were wearing protective masks and jackets. Women's fencing is usually confined to duelling with the foil.

▼ *The lunge, demonstrated by the fencer on the left, is the classic aggressive action. It is best defended by parrying the attacker's sword before it registers a hit.*

The épée, the second sword in weight in contemporary fencing, is more akin to the actual duelling swords of the last century. It has a stiffer blade and a larger hilt than the foil. The sabre, the heaviest of fencing weapons, has a blade with two cutting edges as well as a point.

Fencing is governed by the Fédération Internationale d'Escrime (FIE), which was founded in 1913. Fencers follow a strict amateur code and there is no professional organization. In major competitions, of which the Olympic Games and the annual World Championships are the most important, fencers from continental Europe tend to win most of the medals.

▼ *In foil fencing (1) the legitimate target area is limited to the back and front of the torso. This player is in the 'salute' position, adopted at the beginning of a contest.*

▶ *In foil and épée, only the tips of the swords can be used for scoring; in sabre the whole blade can register hits.*

▼ *The target area in épée (2) is the whole of the body. This player is in the 'on guard' position, poised to start or resume after a point has been scored.*

▼ *With sabre fencing (3), the whole of the body above the hips is the target area. This player shows the importance of balance in lunging.*

Foil

Sabre

90 cm (3 ft)

90 cm (3 ft)

88 cm (2 ft 11½ in)

Épée

1

Foil

Target area

2

Épée

Target area

3

Sabre

Target area

AIMS OF THE GAME

COMPETITION
● Fencing is confined to a narrow strip of mat which is 14 m (46 ft) long and 2 m (6 ft approx.) wide. This mat is marked at each end with a series of lines: the 'on guard' line, the 'rear limit' line, and up to 2 'warning lines'. The on guard lines mark where fencers start at the beginning of a bout (fencing contest) or where they must return to after a hit has been scored. The warning lines are spaced in from the ends of the mat and are intended to warn a fencer that he is in danger of backing into the rear limit.

● Although different styles are adopted in the 3 fencing categories (foil, épée and sabre), the scoring system is similar in them all. Bouts are fought to a specified number of hits within a given time period.

● Time periods for the contest vary from 6 to 12 mins. If extra time is required, the first fencer to hit wins the bout.

Rules for foil
The basic rules for foil date back 200 years and developed from the codes of honour employed by the wealthy to settle their disputes. Foil is the only fencing style fought by both sexes, and these competition rules apply to both men and women.

● The target area is the whole of the trunk (both back and front). Hits to the arms, legs and head do not score in foil bouts.

● A valid hit must strike the target with such force that it depresses the spring-loaded top to a force of 500 g (1 lb approx.). In major competitions, fencers are 'wired up' to monitoring consoles — a mis-hit is registered by a white light and a hit by a red or green light.

● The fencer who first threatens his opponent on target with a straight arm is deemed the 'attacker'. The 'defender' only has the right to hit once he has parried an attack or the attacker has mis-hit. Should the fencers score hits at the same time, the attacker alone scores.

● After a valid hit, both fencers return to their on guard lines.

● A president judges a foil bout.

Rules for épeé
● As with foil, hits are scored only by the point, which must be depressed to a pressure of 750 g (1.5 lb approx.).

● The whole body is the target area and any hit counts. Should fencers hit simultaneously, both are taken into account.

● A president, as in foil, rules over an épée contest.

Rules for sabre
● Hits are recorded by cuts or slashes with the leading edge of the blade or with the first third of the back edge nearest the point. The point can also be used for scoring.

● The whole of the body above the hips is the target area.

● As with foil, the attacker is the first fencer to threaten his opponent with a straight arm.

● Electronic apparatus is used for recording hits and a president controls the bout.

SKILLS
Fencing is extremely fast — and an attacker can be quickly forced back into defence — making it exciting to watch.

● Fencers always try to stand sideways on to each other so that the presented target areas appear smaller. They often keep their balance by holding an arm out behind them.

- Being able to judge distance accurately is crucial to a fencer: a lunge too far forward and he is open to counter-attack; not far enough and he will not score a hit.
- Deception is all part of the sport. A series of elaborate moves can precede a decisive, lightning-quick attack.

EQUIPMENT

Special protective equipment is necessary in fencing — even blunt swords can be dangerous.
- The chest and trunk are protected by a sturdy undergarment called a plastron. A white canvas jacket is worn over the plastron and knee-length canvas breeches protect the legs.
- A mask with a wire grille at the front protects the face and head.
- A soft leather glove is worn on the fencing hand.
- For foil and sabre competitions, a metallic jacket is worn so that valid hits will register on the electronic equipment. This is not necessary with épée, as valid hits can be scored on the whole body.

TECHNICAL TERMS

bout a contest between 2 fencers
compound attack an attack which uses several feints
feint a false attack, designed to confuse an opponent
lunge an attacking move when an attacker thrusts forwards
parry a defensive action when a defender deflects his opponent's sword
piste the mat on which a bout takes place
riposte an attack which follows a defensive action
Touché! the exclamation used when an attacker scores a hit

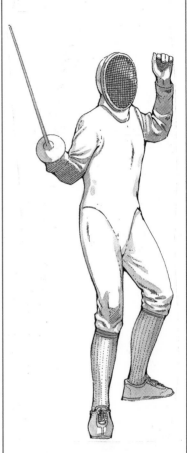

▲ *Tough protective clothing is worn by all fencers. It must be white and free from buckles, straps and openings that could cause a sword to snag.*

FOR THE RECORD

MAJOR FENCING NATIONS
France
Germany
Italy
USSR
Hungary
Poland

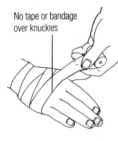

No tape or bandage over knuckles

▲ *Boxers wind long bandages around their hands before they put on gloves. These bandages help to protect the thumbs and wrists from being dislocated or sprained.*

BOXING

Organized fist fighting originally became a popular spectator sport over 2000 years ago. An Ancient Greek king named Theseus instructed gladiators to sit on stone benches and slug each other with their hands bound with leather thongs. Metal studs and spikes were later added to the thongs. The victor was the man who smashed his opponent to death. The Roman Empire made boxing a major entertainment. The Romans called the studded thongs *cesti*; like the Greeks, Roman gladiators fought to the death.

With the fall of the Roman Empire, boxing as a sport became virtually extinct for hundreds of years. It was resurrected by the English in the 17th century when matters of honour were settled by fisticuffs. These fights drew large crowds, and during the 18th century a special boxing 'ring' was constructed in Hyde Park in London. In those days bouts were fought bare-fisted and the rules were haphazard. Fights could last for nearly a day — one is reputed to have taken over seven hours.

'Bare-knuckle' fighting remained a popular spectator, as well as participatory, sport in Europe, Australia and North America until the Marquess of Queensberry introduced new rules in 1867. The so-called Queensberry Rules stated that boxers should wear gloves that were not less than 170 g (6 oz); that a bout should last for 20 three-minute rounds; and that if a boxer was knocked down for more than 10 seconds the contest was over. In addition, Queensberry suggested that should a bout last the allocated number of rounds, a winner should be declared on a point-scoring basis. The Queensberry Rules have been modified slightly over the years, but it is entirely thanks to them that boxing has developed into a comparatively safe and humane combat sport. Until the Marquess intervened, death and maiming in the ring were commonplace.

Contemporary boxing is divided into amateur and professional versions of the sport. Different rules apply to each version, although the ulti-mate aim is the same: to win, preferably by

DID YOU KNOW?

One of the most famous bare-fist fighters of the last century was Bendigo Johnson, who came from Nottingham. After a mystical revelation, Johnson gave up fighting and became a travelling evangelist. He went to Australia, where the town of Bendigo was named after him.

stopping the opponent inside the distance, that is, before the allocated number of rounds.

Boxing has come under fire in recent years for being an unnecessarily dangerous sport, despite the presence of medical personnel at all contests. However, an alternative lobby maintains that boxing instils discipline into boys and men who lack direction and ambition. Indeed, many great champions were born into poverty but rose to the top — Britain's Henry Cooper and the United States' Mike Tyson are just two examples.

The two paramount amateur competitions are the Olympic Games and the World Amateur Championships. Professional bouts are arranged by managers, agents or promoters as and when suitable contenders are available. Of all the professional sports, boxing is one of the most lucrative for the talented.

▼ *Protective clothing is worn by all boxers to minimize injury. Head guards are used in most amateur fights.*

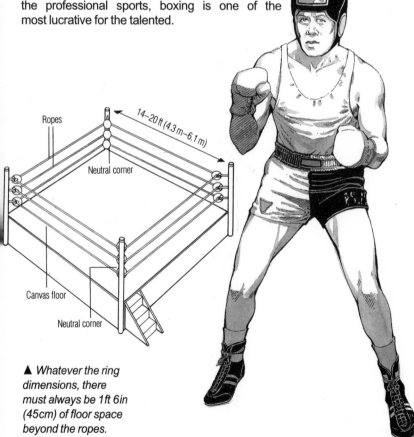

Ropes

14–20 ft (4.3 m–6.1 m)

Neutral corner

Canvas floor

Neutral corner

▲ *Whatever the ring dimensions, there must always be 1ft 6in (45cm) of floor space beyond the ropes.*

AIMS OF THE GAME

COMPETITION — AMATEUR BOXING
● The 3-roped ring for amateur contests measures between 14 and 20 ft (4.27 and 6.1 m) on each side. The floor is covered with tough canvas laid over a layer of felt or rubber and the corner posts are padded.
● The officials include a referee who rules the bout from within the ring, up to 5 judges around the edge of the ring, and a timekeeper.
● A boxer can fight only against an opponent of similar weight, and both contestants have to be inside their weight limit on the morning of their bout. Boxers also have to be checked by a doctor before a contest.
● At the beginning of a bout, the boxers are called to the centre of ring by the referee where they shake hands (touch gloves) before returning to their allocated corners which are diagonally opposite each other. On the sound of a bell the first round starts.
● The 3 rounds for an amateur bout each last between 1½ and 3 min (depending on the type of contest) with 1 min between each round. The beginning and end of each round is signalled by the bell. At the end of each round, the boxers return to their corners where they can sit down and be tended by their 'seconds'.
● A boxer can win a bout by:
- knocking his opponent out (counted out for 10 sec or stopped from continuing by the referee);
- outpointing his opponent (points are scored by blows struck with the knuckle part of the glove to target areas — any part of the sides or front of the head or body above the belt). In amateur boxing 20 points are awarded to the winner of a round and proportionally fewer are given to the loser;
- wearing down his opponent to such a degree that he can no longer fight (technical knockout);
- his opponent being disqualified (such as butting with his head, punching below the belt);
-forcing his opponent to retire.
● Draws are not given in amateur contests.

COMPETITION — PROFESSIONAL BOXING
The rules of professional boxing are governed by several organizations, each of which has slightly different codes. There are also some differences in the rules applied by the governing bodies of different countries or even different US states. However, most of the essential rules are similar to those of amateur boxing. The main differences are as follows:
- rounds last 3 mins but up to 15 rounds are permitted.
- three judges give points, one of which is usually the referee. In some countries the referee alone decides the winner.
- scoring usually follows a so-called 10-point rule which states that at the end of each round, each judge is obliged to award 10 points to the winner of the round and proportionally fewer to the loser.
- a drawn verdict can be given at the end of a contest.

SKILLS
'Anybody can fight but only a few can box' is an old and true saying. Boxing requires strength, skill, stamina and courage.
● All boxers have a 'lead' arm, which they use to jab their opponent; usually this is the left arm (orthodox boxer). The right arm is used more for punches that take longer to deliver. When the

right arm is not punching, it is used to fend off blows and to protect the head. Left-handed boxers lead with their right arm, and are sometimes known as 'southpaws'.

● There are 4 basic blows in boxing: the uppercut, the left or right hook, the straight right or left and the jab.

● Fast footwork and manoeuvrability are important in boxing, especially in the lower weight categories, where punches are not so heavy. Quick feet can get a boxer out of trouble and can lead into an attack.

EQUIPMENT

Boxing at either professional or amateur level requires special safety equipment, much of it unseen by a spectator.

● The essential piece of attire for any boxer is gloves. These are made of padded leather and must usually weigh between 227 and 280 g (8 and 10 oz).

● To protect his hands further, a boxer wraps surgical bandages around the wrists and thumbs — these bandages are not allowed to cover the knuckles.

● All boxers wear lightweight boots and shorts (the shorts must have a clear 'belt line' — a line between the hips and the navel).

● Underneath the shorts, abdominal guards are essential.

● In amateur contests, a sleeveless vest is compulsory.

● A gumshield prevents severe damage to the teeth.

● For training, boxers use:
- a speed ball (a stuffed leather bag suspended from a low ceiling on a strong spring) to sharpen reflexes; this is punched in a rhythmic fashion;
- a punch bag (a large, leather bag filled with sand and hung on a rope) for practising heavy punches;

- a skipping rope (similar to the sort used in playgrounds the world over) to quicken foot movements;
- head guards (protective caps worn by sparring partners while practising for a bout). Head guards are required for all amateur bouts.

▲ *The left jab is a quick punch in every right-handed boxer's repertoire. Left-handed boxers use an equivalent right jab.*

▼ *A boxer 'blocks' punches by crouching forwards and protecting his head with raised fists.*

FOR THE RECORD

Boxing's major ruling bodies

AMATEUR
International Amateur Boxing
Association

PROFESSIONAL
World Boxing Association (WBA)
World Boxing Council (WBC)
International Boxing Federation (IBF)
World Boxing Organization (WBO)

In addition to the international organizations listed above, individual countries have powerful ruling bodies, which can dictate how a bout should be held within their jurisdiction. Safety is a chief concern. For example, the British Boxing Board of Control does not allow boxers who have suffered severe damage to their eyes such as detached retinas, to box within the United Kingdom.

FOR THE RECORD

WEIGHT DIVISIONS

	Maximum Weight
Mini-flyweight	47.6 kg (105 lb)
Light flyweight	48.0 kg (106 lb)
Flyweight	51.0 kg (112 lb)
Super-flyweight	52.0 kg (115 lb)
Bantamweight	54.0 kg (119 lb)
Super-bantamweight	55.3 kg (122 lb)
Featherweight	57.0 kg (126 lb)
Super-featherweight	59.0 kg (130 lb)
Lightweight	60.0 kg (132 lb)
Light-welterweight	63.5 kg (140 lb)
Welterweight	67.0 kg (148 lb)
Light-middleweight	71.0 kg (156 lb)
Middleweight	75.0 kg (166 lb)
Super-middleweight	76.2 kg (168 lb)
Light-heavyweight	81.0 kg (179 lb)
Cruiserweight	88.5 kg (195 lb)
Heavyweight	91.0 kg (201 lb) plus
Super-heavyweight	91 kg (201 lb) plus (amateur only)

Note. Not all the categories listed above, or the weights that have been applied to them, are universally recognized by all boxing associations and ruling bodies. Minor discrepancies between organizations.

FAMOUS NAMES

SUGAR RAY ROBINSON (US)

Middleweight	1951-1953 (undisputed)
	1955-1957 (undisputed)
	1958-1960 (undisputed)
Welterweight	1946-1951 (undisputed)

Robinson took the middleweight title from Jake La Motta at the beginning of 1951 only to lose it to Britain's Randolph Turpin a couple of months later. Towards the end of the year, Turpin's brief reign as champion came to an end — Robinson stopped him in a classic fight held in New York.

SUGAR RAY LEONARD (US)

Light-welterweight	Olympic gold 1976
Welterweight	1979-1980 (WBC) 1980-1983 (WBC)
Light-middleweight	1981 (WBC)
Welterweight	1981-1985 (undisputed)

| Middleweight | 1987-1988 (WBC) |
| Super-middleweight | 1988-1991 (WBC) |

Sugar Ray Leonard became the first boxer to win professional world titles at 5 different weight levels.

TEOFILIO STEVENSON (CUBA)

Heavyweight	Olympic gold 1972
	Olympic gold 1976
	Olympic gold 1980

Probably the greatest heavyweight amateur of them all, Teofilio Stevenson refused an offer of $2 million to turn professional, preferring to live and work in his native Cuba, boxing only in amateur competitions. In the semi-finals of the 1980 Moscow Games, Istvan Levai of Hungary was so terrified of Stevenson he spent the 3 rounds running around the edge of the ring.

▼ *Hearns versus Medal in 1986.*

MUHAMMAD ALI (US)

Light-heavyweight	Olympic gold 1960
Heavyweight	1964-1967 (undisputed)
	1974-1978 (undisputed)
	1978-1979 (WBA)

Muhammad Ali is the only man to have won the heavyweight title 3 times. He was stripped of his world title in 1967, after refusing to fight in the Vietnam War on religious grounds, but he regained it in 1974. Tragically, Ali suffers from an incurable disease which affects his speech.

MIKE TYSON (US)

| Heavyweight | 1986-1990 (WBC) |
| | 1987-1990 (undisputed) |

Tyson became the youngest heavyweight champion ever when he knocked out Trevor Berbick in 1986 to win the WBC title at the age of 20.

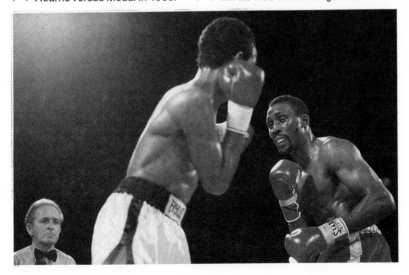

DID YOU KNOW?

The only man to have been awarded a 12th dan white belt is Dr Jigoro Kano, the founder of judo. Nobody has come close to challenging his superiority, but 13 men have been awarded 10th dan red belts.

JUDO

Judo means 'the gentle way' in Japanese. Dr Jigoro Kano established the first judo school, the Kodokan, in 1882 at Shitaya. His aim was to bring together what he considered to be the best techniques and philosophies from ju-jitsu to form a new sport. His phrase 'maximum effect with minimum effort' sums up his intentions.

In 1886, Kano's new sport gained local recognition when his Kodokan Club overwhelmed a large ju-jitsu club in a tournament organized by the Tokyo police. From then on, judo became one of the most popular sports in Japan and, with sumo, it is acknowledged to be one of the Japanese national sports.

Judo was taken to the United States by a student of Kano's in 1902, but it remained an unknown sport in Europe until 1918, when the Budokwai Club opened in London. Today over eight million people take part in judo worldwide. It is an international sport, governed by the International Judo Federation which was founded in 1951 — the same year that the first European Championships were held. Strictly an amateur sport, the main arenas for competitive judo are the biennial World Championships and the Olympic Games, where contestants are divided into weight categories. Fittingly enough, judo was first included at the Olympic Games in Tokyo in 1964. Japan won three out of the four gold medals available. Proficiency in judo is signified by the wearing of coloured belts.

DID YOU KNOW?

The greatest judo contestant of modern times was Yashiro Yamashita, who was the Open Olympic Champion in 1984 and won 4 successive World Championship titles. When he retired in 1985, he had not been beaten in 203 successive bouts.

▼ *The judo-gi is strong and allows free movement. The belt knots at the front.*

◄ *A player will try to pin his opponent to the mat after he has thrown him; spread legs ensure good balance and control.*

AIMS OF THE GAME

COMPETITION

● Although judo is very much a contemporary sport, traditional scoring and terminology are always used in contests.

● The mat is 16 m (17 yd) square. In the middle of this, there is a square contest area which measures 10 m (11 yd approx.) square. The contest area is bounded by a 1 m (1 yd) red danger zone which warns players that they are nearing the limit of the mat.

● A contest referee and 2 side judges ensure fair play and decide on the winner. One of the codes of practice of judo is that nobody ever disagrees with the referee or judges. This air of courtesy and respect also exists between opponents.

● At the beginning of a match, the 2 contestants step onto the mat and bow to the referee and to each other. They then grab each other's tunics, usually at the neck and around one arm.

● Bouts usually last for 5 min, but in major championships 7-min rounds are allowed.

● In competitions, contestants wear either a red or a white belt so that they can be distinguished by the referee and the judges. (These are not to be confused with grade belts.)

● It is the aim of each contestant to throw the other to the ground in order to gain points or a submission (an acceptance of an opponent's superior position).

● The scoring system is complicated:
- an ippon (a winning point) is awarded when a contestant throws his opponent perfectly flat onto his back; holds him down with his back to the mat for 30 sec; or achieves a submission. Once an ippon has been achieved, the contest ends.

- a waza-ari is one step down from an ippon and is awarded for a near-perfect throw or if a player is held down for 25 to 29 sec. Two waza-aris equal an ippon.

- a yuko is lower than a waza-ari and is given for a good throw or when a player has been held down for between 20 and 24 sec.

- a koka — the lowest of scores — is awarded whenever a contestant is forced to the ground or held down for 10 to 19 sec.

Any number of yukos and kokas can be scored, but 2 waza-aris mean that the contest is over. One waza-ari is sufficient to beat any number of yukos or kokas. Penalties against a contestant are awarded for foul play (such as bending fingers and attacking the face), passive judo and straying outside the contest area.

SKILLS

● The first skill that judo contestants learn is to fall correctly so that they can be thrown onto their backs without injury. This involves smacking an arm flat on to the mat to break the fall. This common sound can disconcert outsiders to the sport.

● Attacking techniques include throws (over the hips, shoulder and legs), strangleholds and armlocks. Strangleholds are only permitted around the neck, and armlocks can only be applied to the elbow joints. Attackers must always consider the opponent's safety.

● Advanced contestants often use combination throws where they feint one way and go the other, and occasionally they allow sacrifice throws where they permit themselves to be hurled to the ground in order to counter-attack with a strangulhold or armlock.

EQUIPMENT

● A judo-gi and a belt are the only requirements. The judo-gi is a loose-fitting suit of jacket and trousers made from sturdy white cotton or nylon. Because there is a lot of tugging and pulling in judo, the uniform is tougher than those used for similar martial arts. The belt is coloured to denote competence.

● Judo is performed barefoot so no footwear is required.

TECHNICAL TERMS

dan a high grade of proficiency
dojo practice area or school
Hajime! Begin the contest!
judoka judo contestant
kyu a novice grade of proficiency
Sono-mama! Hold! If contestants wander off the contest area, the referee shouts 'Sono-mama!' and hauls them back while they maintain their holds
Sore-made! The contest is over!

FOR THE RECORD

WEIGHT CATEGORIES

MEN	WOMEN
under 60 kg	under 48 kg
under 65 kg	under 52 kg
under 71 kg	under 56 kg
under 78 kg	under 61 kg
under 86 kg	under 66 kg
under 95 kg	under 72 kg
over 95 kg	over 72 kg

In major contests there is also an open class for all-comers.

▶ *Judo throws can be made over the shoulder, over the hips or, as shown here, by using a leg to unbalance an opponent while forcing him downwards onto the mat.*

FOR THE RECORD

JUDO GRADES
Kyu (novice) grades in ascending order
6th —white belt
5th —yellow belt
4th —orange belt
3rd —green belt
2nd—blue belt
1st —brown belt
Dan (degree) grades in ascending order
1st-5th —black belt
6th-8th —red and white belt
9th-11th—red belt
12th —white belt

FAMOUS NAMES

NAME	TITLES
Y. Yamashita (Japan)	World (Open): 1981
	World (over 95kg): 1979, 1981, 1983
	Olympic (Open): 1984
I. Berghmans (Germany)	World (under 72kg): 1989
	Olympic (Open): 1980, 1982, 1984, 1986
	Olympic (under 72kg): 1984

▲ *An arm lock is a common way of immobilizing an assailant and bringing him to the ground.*

▲ *The wrist lock is another attacking technique which leads to a throw or forces a defender into submission.*

AIKIDO

Aikido, which means the 'way of harmony' in Japanese, is the most recent of the formal martial arts to have been devised. It was created by a master of unarmed combat named Morihei Uyeshiba who started life as a weak and sickly child but built up his strength by sheer hard work. When he was 20, Uyeshiba determined to found a way of life that combined health and agility with spiritual well-being. According to his own testament, the notion of a new martial art came to Uyeshiba in a flash of inspiration while he was meditating. This was in 1925, and in 1932 he opened a dojo (school) in Tokyo. He did not name his new art form, aikido, until 1938.

Uyeshiba's new sport, which was largely derived from ju-jitsu, was an instant success and it rapidly gained a huge following, particularly from those that had studied judo. After World War II, all martial arts in Japan were banned until the 1950s. When the constraints were eased, aikido re-emerged as popular as ever.

Aikido is a highly stylized martial art. It also embodies a philosophy which emphasizes the importance of harmony between body and mind. An aikido master is supposed to be like the eye of a hurricane — peaceful within but with swirling forces all around. Indeed, sweeping, circular movements are a characteristic of aikido.

◄ *Aikido is mainly concerned with techniques which adopt circular, flowing movements. This throw has been caused by pressure applied to the wrist.*

When Uyeshiba died in 1969, various masters devised new approaches to aikido — some emphasized the fighting potential of the sport whereas others concentrated on the spiritual side, using the ritual movements as an aid to meditation. Essentially, however, it remains a non-aggressive sport and it is sometimes banded together with tai-chi-ch'uan as a 'soft' martial art.

Some schools of aikido grade pupils and award coloured belts to show proficiency but, as there is no international ruling body covering all styles, gradings are not standardized.

AIMS OF THE GAME

COMPETITION
● Aikido was originally an activity that was only concerned with defence. There were no attacking moves. This made competition difficult! However an aikido master named Tomiki Kenji developed a style which could be used in competition. In Tomiki aikido, one competitor attempts to touch his opponent with a wooden knife while the other defends himself. Every time the defender is touched by the knife, he loses points. The 2 combatants alternate attacking and defending roles. Traditionalists do not use their aikido skills in any form of competition.
● Aikido teaches a philosophy as well as defence skills and techniques. This philosophy stresses the importance of harnessing ki or vital energy. A person with ki is assumed to be strong and powerful.

SKILLS
● The aim of all the formal moves in aikido is to turn an attacker's physical strength against himself. The moves include elaborate throwing and twisting techniques which use wrists, elbows, legs and shoulders. When these moves are practised, they resemble a dance.
● Some of the moves in aikido are designed to apply pressure to vital nerve centres. These moves can be lethal and they are only ever used in self-defence.

EQUIPMENT

● The traditional dress for aikido players is an elaborate suit comprising black baggy trousers, a waistcoat and a white shirt. However, most practitioners wear a simpler martial art suit of thick, white cotton — jacket, trousers and belt.
● Advanced aikido participants use wooden poles in training. These are similar to the bokuto that are used in kendo.

TECHNICAL TERMS

dojo practice hall or school
kata dance-like movements used in training (a term common to most martial arts)
ki vital or cosmic energy; by capturing ki, an aikido participant is supposed to gain inner strength
randori freestyle form of aikido with emphasis on contest
tori attacker
uke defender

KARATE

The basic skills and techniques of karate were developed from the Ancient Chinese art of Shaolin Temple boxing on the Pacific Ocean island of Okinawa during the 16th century. Okinawa was frequently besieged by hostile Japanese armies, and the local inhabitants defended themselves by fighting off the oppressors using their bare hands. The martial art was originally called 'Tang Hand'.

It was not until the 1920s that a master of Tang Hand, Gichin Funakoshi, introduced the fighting system to Japan. He adopted the word 'karate', which means 'empty hand'. Karate proved immensely popular. A number of different styles quickly developed, each putting a slightly differ-

▲ *Ritual exercises (kata) develop physical and mental strength.*

AIMS OF THE GAME

COMPETITION
● Competitions in karate take place on a mat covering 8 m (8½ yd approx.) square and a contest is controlled by a referee, a judge and an arbitrator. Competitors usually wear a red or white sash so that they can be readily identified.
● Points are awarded by the referee for both technique and for blows landing within the scoring areas of the body. Scoring areas include the head and all of the trunk down to the level of the belt.
● Karate competitions are strictly controlled, and for safety's sake many techniques are banned (attacks to eyes, throat, joints etc.). Any contestant who commits a serious foul can be disqualified.
● Contests usually only last for 3 mins of actual fighting time. However, if there is no clear winner, extensions may be allowed.

SKILLS
Punches, throws, holds and kicks are all legitimate in karate. Speed and accuracy are crucial if a blow is not to be parried.
● A punch is usually delivered in a straight line rather than in an arc as in boxing.
● Striking blows, using a chopping action, often employ the open hand.
● Kicks are an important part of karate; the heel delivers the most devastating kick, but the side of the foot is also used. Although they look spectacular when well delivered, kicks can leave a competitor unstable and open to counter-attack.
● Throwing techniques are not as important in karate as they are in some other martial arts. However, some styles do favour throwing skills which are quickly followed up with a punch or kick.
● Blocking is one of the most crucial skills in karate. A block, often with the forearm, parries a blow, either a punch or kick.
● As with many martial arts, karate is not solely a method of fighting, it

ent emphasis on kicking, punching, speed, stance and so on. The four main styles are Chinese, Japanese, Korean and Okinawah.

When the ban on martial arts in Japan was lifted in the 1950s, American servicemen were impressed by karate. A number of schools soon opened in the United States. Film producers soon realized the box office appeal of karate and before long sleuths and secret agents were fending off all-comers with fanciful karate blows in cinemas around the world. Karate's popularity boomed, and the first World Championships were held in 1970.

The ruling body of karate is the World Union of Karate-do Organizations. As in judo and other martial arts, coloured belts are worn to denote ability and experience.

▼ *Karate employs both defensive and attacking techniques. Aggressive moves include punches, kicks and, to a lesser extent, throws. Equally important are the moves to parry blows from the arms and legs, quickly opening up a counter-attack.*

is also a discipline which is intended to strengthen the moral qualities of students as well as the physical ones.

EQUIPMENT

● Very little equipment is needed for karate apart from the loose-fitting, lightweight jacket and trousers which together are called a gi.
● A belt is also essential to tie up the jacket and denote the grade of the contestant.

TECHNICAL TERMS

dojo school or practice area
gi (karate gi) the pyjama-like cotton suit that all karate contestants wear
Hajime! Begin! (a contest)
kata formal exercises, sometimes performed in unison with other karate contestants
Kiai! loud shout that accompanies a karate attack and shows a competitor's spirit
sensei instructor
Yame! Stop!

FOR THE RECORD

KARATE GRADINGS (BELTS)
Junior grades (Kyu) in rising proficiency (subject to some variation in different styles):
white
yellow
green
brown
black (1st Dan)

Senior grades (Dans):
1 to 8 (all wear black belts)

DID YOU KNOW?

Professional wrestling was dropped as a televised sport in Britain in the late 1980s because viewing figures were considered too low. When the sport was re-introduced in 1990 — on satellite television — viewers were treated to the more theatrical American version and it gained a cult following.

▼ *Show business razzmatazz has taken the place of competition in the wild world of American professional wrestling.*

PROFESSIONAL WRESTLING

Hulking great men, bearing tattoos and ferocious masks, are known to have wrestled for money during the Middle Ages. They toured countries as members of itinerant fair groups and challenged all-comers to defeat them for a bag of money. Professional wrestling was a showman sport then and it still is.

Towards the end of the 19th century, this form of wrestling was dubbed 'all-in wrestling'. Huge crowds flocked to see bouts between all-in professionals at the beginning of the century, particularly in the United States. However, it was not until the advent of television that professional wrestling became one of the most popular spectator sports of all.

One of professional wrestling's attractions is its affinity with show business: top performers wear flamboyant clothing and adopt fanciful 'stage names', bouts are usually action-packed, and the wrestlers frequently taunt each other — to the delight of the audience. Some bouts even seem to follow an agreed 'script'.

Professional wrestling has been maligned in the past because bouts were known to have been 'fixed', but it is a sport that has never

been taken terribly seriously and it is usually viewed as entertainment more than anything else. Nevertheless, the skill and speed required of the professional wrestler should not be underestimated.

There is no international governing body of professional wrestling, and individual countries tend to adopt their own rules and regulations.

AIMS OF THE GAME

COMPETITION
● Rings for professional wrestling vary in size from between 14 ft (4.27 m) to 21 ft (6.4 m) square. The 4 posts are well padded and the floor is covered with canvas laid over felt or rubber.
● Bouts usually last for eight 5-min rounds, although they can be longer or shorter. Bouts are judged by a referee who stays in the ring.
● A wrestler can win a bout by forcing his opponent into 2 falls (shoulder blades held to the canvas for 3 sec), 2 submissions (where a wrestler is judged to be 'locked' in a hold), or by a knockout (where a wrestler does not recover during a 10-sec count given by the referee).
● 'Tag team' bouts are also popular. Each wrestler has a partner waiting just outside the ring. This wrestler can replace his partner if he can reach over and 'tag' him in the ring.

SKILLS
● In addition to a sound knowledge of a selection of standard wrestling throws, holds and kicks, strength and agility are essential. Virtually anything goes in professional wrestling although strangles and punches with the fist are forbidden.
● Gaining a psychological advantage over an opponent is crucial to many wrestlers, so goading an opponent into a frenzy is all part of the game.

EQUIPMENT

● Elasticated shorts and lightweight wrestling boots are the bare minimum.
● Most professional wrestlers wear personalized clothing—usually a garish warm-up robe—bearing their legend or name.

FOR THE RECORD

COMMON WEIGHT CATEGORIES

Lightweight	to 70 kg (154 lb)
Welterweight	to 75 kg (165 lb)
Middleweight	to 80 kg (176 lb)
Heavy-middleweight	to 85 kg (187 lb)
Light-heavyweight	to 90 kg (198 lb)
Mid-heavyweight	to 95 kg (209 lb)
Heavyweight	no limit

FAMOUS NAMES

Tosh Togo from Japan became a film star while still being a professional wrestler. He made a big impression in the James Bond film *Goldfinger*, playing the part of the deadly Oddjob.
Brian Glover, an ex-professional wrestler from Yorkshire, is a member of the Royal Shakespeare Company and has appeared in many films as a genial giant, including the award-winning *Kes*.
Billy Two Rivers, who was famed for his war dances and 'tomahawk chops' when he performed in the ring, is a genuine chief of a Canadian Mohawk Indian tribe.

TARGET SPORTS

Most of the common target sports have evolved from hunting and shooting skills but, whereas live animals or enemies were the original targets, inanimate objects are now used in competitions. All the sports included in this section are won by accumulating points; as a general rule, the closer the projectiles land to the middle of the targets, the more points are awarded.

DID YOU KNOW?

The story that tells of Robin Hood splitting one arrow in half with another is pure myth. Unlike the crossbow, the longbow of Robin Hood's time was not accurate; it was only effective in battle if many longbows were used at the same time.

At the Battle of Agincourt (1415), each English archer was said to have had 3 arrows in the air at the same time — one arriving, one in mid-flight and one leaving. Arrows literally rained down on the French army to devastating effect.

ARCHERY

The bow and arrow have been around for at least 10,000 years, and most probably much longer. Bowmen are depicted in ancient Assyrian and Egyptian sculptures and most lost civilizations had armies which included regiments of archers. Archery as a sport did not develop until the 3rd or 4th centuries AD but the bows used in those days were not always very powerful. It was not until the advent of the 6 ft (1.8 m) longbow in medieval Britain that archery as we know it today developed.

Until the middle of the last century, archery contests were regularly held at fairs and local festivals and on country estates in Europe, but there were no standard rules. The first British

► Longbow archers formed the backbone of many armies until the introduction of firearms in the mid-19th century.

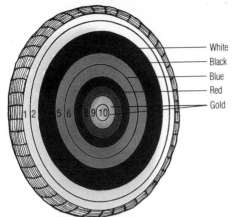

White
Black
Blue
Red
Gold

◀ *Targets are made from reinforced paper or canvas and are mounted on straw bales which are angled slightly backwards. The ten rings denote different score values with the centremost yellow spot (called 'gold') being the most valuable.*

national tournament, held at York in 1844, laid down a set of competition rules.

Archery contests for both men and women were included in the Olympic Games of 1900 but were dropped after the 1920 Games. Thanks to the increasing popularity of the sport worldwide, archery was re-introduced to the Olympics in 1972; the 1988 Olympics had events for both individuals and national teams.

Archery is an amateur sport and its world governing body is the Fédération Internationale de Tir à l'Arc (FITA), formed as recently as 1931, the same year that the first biennial World Championships were held.

AIMS OF THE GAME

COMPETITION
● Under international rules of target archery, competitors shoot a specified number of arrows over 4 different distances at targets marked with concentric circles.
● The number of arrows shot is usually a single FITA Round of 144 arrows, lasting the whole day. For men the targets are set successively at 90, 70, 50 and 30 m (98, 77, 55 and 33 yd) from the shooting line; for women the distances are 70, 60, 50 and 30 m (77, 66, 55 and 33 yd). There are 36 arrows shot at each distance. There is also much competitive archery which takes place under the traditional British rules.

● Archers take it in turns to shoot 3 arrows and then, at the longer distances, shoot another 3. When all have shot their 3 or 6 arrows, the signal is given for all to go to the target to record their scores.

SKILLS
● Archery does not require brute strength. A keen eye and a sense of rhythm are useful while good control of the body and mental self-discipline are essential. The best archers follow a methodical routine.
● Gusts of wind can deflect an arrow's flight or disturb the archer, so archers have to compensate for variations in the wind. This is particularly important when shooting at the longer distances.

EQUIPMENT

• Any form of bow can be used in competitive archery provided that it complies with a number of regulations laid down by FITA. A number of attachments is permitted, including a sight (with certain provisos) and stabilizers, which are the most noticeable attachments on modern bows. These are rods with weights on the end, fixed to the handle section of the bow. They limit movement as the arrow is shot.

• Arrows are usually made from aluminium alloy tubing, although carbon fibre is gaining ground. Arrows must also conform to certain regulations. In competitions all arrows used by an archer must be identical in every way and readily identifiable. Most competition arrows are marked with the initials of the archer.

• Other necessary equipment includes a finger tab, which allows a consistently smooth release of the bowstring for every shot; a bracer or armguard to keep the sleeve out of the path of the bowstring; and a shirt guard to keep clothing out of the path of the bowstring. A wide range of other accessories is in common use.

TECHNICAL TERMS

end the 3 arrows that are shot each time an archer goes to the shooting line. At the longer distances archers shoot 2 ends of 3 arrows before scoring, but only one end of 3 arrows is shot at the shorter distances

Fast! the call which stops all shooting

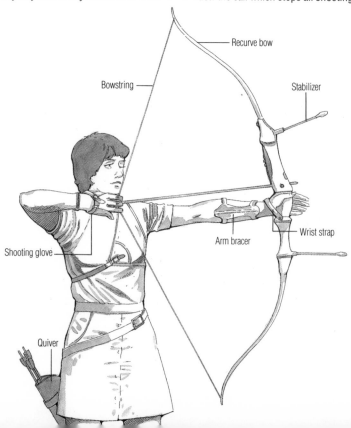

Recurve bow

Bowstring

Stabilizer

Wrist strap

Arm bracer

Shooting glove

Quiver

immediately should a dangerous situation arise

fletchings vanes at the end of an arrow. They were made traditionally from wing feathers of a goose, although today plastic vanes are used throughout the sport

gold the centre of a target face, today always yellow

loosing letting go of the string

nocking placing the bowstring in the nock (notched) end of an arrow. The term is also used to describe placing the fingers on the string before drawing the bow

FOR THE RECORD

Target faces made from reinforced paper are mounted on bosses or buttresses which are angled at 15° to

the vertical. Target faces with a diameter of 122 cm (48 in) are used for the longer distances of the FITA Round. Target faces with a diameter of 80 cm (31 in) are used for the shorter distances. In target archery, both indoor and outdoor, 10 equal scoring zones within 5 equal colour zones are marked on all sizes of target face. The system of scoring under international rules is as follows:

Gold	inner 10 points, outer 9 points
Red	inner 8 points, outer 7 points
Blue	inner 6 points, outer 5 points
Black	inner 4 points, outer 3 points
White	inner 2 points, outer 1 point

Under British rules only the 5 coloured zones are used, each having the odd number values from 9 down to 1.

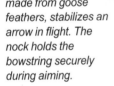

► The fletching, made from goose feathers, stabilizes an arrow in flight. The nock holds the bowstring securely during aiming.

Nock

Fletching

Cresting

Shaft

Target point

◄ Modern bows are very different from the earlier longbows. They are equipped with weighted stabilizers and sights which make it possible to fire arrows consistently straight. Archers are allowed to mark the string with a nose dot or lip dot to indicate exactly how far back the string should be pulled.

▲ The shaft of an arrow may be made of wood, a light metal like aluminium or sometimes of fibreglass. The length and weight depend upon the archer. Arrows used in competition have conical target points rather than bladed heads. Each archer's arrows should be marked so they can be identified.

DID YOU KNOW?

A variation of quoits was initiated by sailors centuries ago while they were on long voyages. Instead of using rings of iron they used coils of rope. 'Deck quoits' is still popular on cruise ships.

QUOITS AND HORSESHOE PITCHING

Both quoits and horseshoe pitching are old games and are thought to have originated from the Ancient Greek pastime of throwing the discus, one of the sports included in the original pentathlon. Roman soldiers modified discus-throwing and took to hurling horseshoes, which were plentiful in army camps. To make events more interesting, the Romans drove stakes into the ground and used them as targets for thrown horseshoes. As a consequence, accurate throwing became more important than simply throwing a long way.

The Romans introduced horseshoe throwing to the British in the 2nd century AD and the British subsequently evolved their own version of the game where iron rings (quoits) were lobbed over stakes.

The game of quoits was enjoyed by all classes of people in England for many centuries and was taken to America by British soldiers who manned colonial garrisons. The Americans were enthusiastic about throwing quoits but eventually reverted to using horseshoes. Today, the game of quoits is only played in rural parts of Britain, while horseshoe throwing (pitching) continues to be a popular game all over the United States. President George Bush is a skilled player. A sport similar to horseshoe pitching is also played in South Africa.

There is no recognized ruling body for quoits but competition rules for horseshoe pitching have been laid down by the National Horseshoe Pitchers Association — an American organization founded in 1920. Both quoits and horseshoe pitching are amateur games, played largely for fun, and little equipment is required.

▼ *A horseshoe is always pitched underarm, with the throwing arm extended throughout the delivery.*

TECHNICAL TERMS

calk the small lip on each end of a horseshoe

leaner a horseshoe that leans against a stake and gains 1 point

pitching box the box that surrounds each stake — horseshoes are thrown from the pitching box

ringer a horseshoe that encircles the stake; worth 3 points unless knocked out of place

AIMS OF THE GAME

Horseshoe Pitching
● Two or 4 people can play; if 4 people play, it is usual for them to form 2 teams of 2.
● A competition shoe must not be more than 7 in (18.4 cm) wide and 7 in long. In addition, it must not weigh more that 2 lb (0.9 kg approx.) and must have a gap no wider than 3 in (8.9 cm) at the open end.
● The 2 targets (stakes) for the horseshoes are spaced 40 ft (12 m approx.) apart for men and 30 ft (9 m approx.) for women. The iron stakes stand 14 in (35.6 cm) high and each stake leans 3 in (7.6 cm) towards the other. The stakes are in the middle of a pitching box 6 ft (1.8 m approx.) square.
● Players score points by getting shoes close to, or around, a stake. Each player throws 2 shoes from one stake to the other, then there is a change of ends. A shoe that completely circles the stake scores 3 points and a shoe that lands within 6 in (15 cm) of the stake gains 1 point. Games are usually won by the person or team to score the best of 51 or 21 points.

● Judging distance and being accurate with a throw are important, but the knack of making a shoe spin in the air so that it lands cleanly on the stake is considered the greatest skill of all.

Quoits
● Rules for quoits vary greatly from area to area and there are no standard 'competition' rules. However, the scoring system is similar to that of horseshoe pitching.
● Quoits are iron rings flat on the bottom and rounded on the top. They weigh around 3 lb (1.4 kg) and can be up to 6 in (15 cm) in diameter; the central hole can be up to 4 in (10 cm) in diameter.
● The pegs (hobs) stand 1 in (2.5 cm) above the ground and are normally spaced about 30 ft (9 m) apart.
● Games are between 2 players or 2 teams of players. A quoit that lands closer to the hob than the opponent's quoit scores 1 point and a quoit that rings a hob scores 2 points.

▼ *Horseshoes and ordinary quoits are made from iron but deck quoits, still used on ocean liners, are made from coiled rope.*

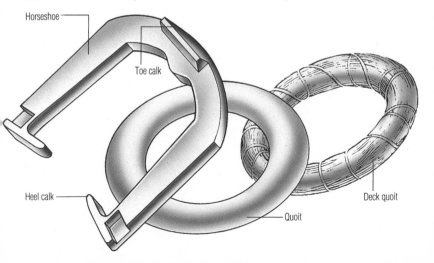

Horseshoe

Toe calk

Heel calk

Deck quoit

Quoit

DARTS

The contemporary game of darts is thought to have derived from a form of archery that involved men throwing broken arrow shafts at targets. The segmented dartboard as we know it today was devised in 1896.

Until the beginning of the 20th century, the rules for darts were haphazard, and varied from area to area. It was not until the National Darts Association was formed in 1924, that the rules were standardized.

The humble English pub is considered the spiritual home of darts, and every day of the week, men, women and, if permitted, children play for nothing more than pleasure. However, the English are by no means the only people to enjoy darts. It is an immensely popular game in Britain and Europe and, since the 1970s, it has become popular in North America and elsewhere.

Darts became a major professional sport in 1978 when the first World Professional Championships were held. An élite few can make large fortunes in professional contests but for most people, darts remains a game of fun.

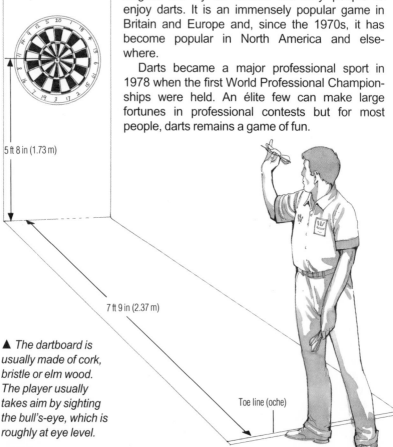

5 ft 8 in (1.73 m)

7 ft 9 in (2.37 m)

Toe line (oche)

▲ *The dartboard is usually made of cork, bristle or elm wood. The player usually takes aim by sighting the bull's-eye, which is roughly at eye level.*

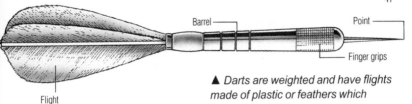

▲ *Darts are weighted and have flights made of plastic or feathers which increase stability.*

Flight

Barrel

Point

Finger grips

AIMS OF THE GAME

COMPETITION
● The segments of the circular board are marked with values on the outer edge and the target area itself is defined by an outer wire. A dart that sticks within a segment acquires that segment's number of points. Two narrow bands — circles within the scoring area — signify a double score (outer band) and a triple score (inner band) of any given segment. In the centre of the board lie 2 bull's-eyes: the innermost circle — about ½ in (1.2 cm) wide — is worth 50 points, the outer one, 25 points.
● The dartboard is hung against a wall so that the centre of the innermost bull's-eye is 5 ft 8 in (1.73 m) off the ground.
● Players throw their darts at the target with their toes touching the back of a wood or aluminium strip along the floor spaced 7 ft 9 in (2.37 m) from the face of the dartboard.
● Scoring:
- each player starts with a total of 501 points and each tries to get that score down to zero with the minimum amount of throws (the maximum score for a dart is 60 — triple 20); players take turns at throwing 3 darts at the board;
- to win, a player must finish exactly on zero and his last dart must land within the double ring or the central bull's-eye;
- usually contests are won by the first player to win 3 games out of 5.

● In fun matches, players usually start with a total of 301 points and they have to both start and finish with a double score.

SKILLS
● Throwing a dart is easy, throwing it with pinpoint accuracy takes practice and demands considerable eye/arm co-ordination.
● Most serious dart players have a head for mathematics — to them, the ability to calculate scores quickly is important.

EQUIPMENT

● Modern darts range in weight from ½ oz (14 g) to 1 oz (28 g). The thickness of a dart is crucial — the thinner it is, the greater the possibility of grouping 3 together for a maximum score (180). Professionals prefer darts made from an amalgam of tungsten and copper.

TECHNICAL TERMS

arrow slang for dart
check-out to finish with a double
double top double 20
leg a game that starts from 501 points; a match is often the best of five legs
oche raised aluminium or wood strip from where players throw darts
wire the segments of a dartboard are outlined by lengths of wire; a wire dart is a dart that strikes a wire and falls (it then becomes an invalid throw)

DID YOU KNOW?

Live birds were used for the pigeon shooting contest in the 1900 Olympics Games which were held in Paris. This is the only time live animals have been killed on purpose during a modern Olympic Games.

SHOOTING

Competitive shooting developed in Switzerland and Germany during the 15th century, only a few years after the first firearms had been introduced to Europe. However, it was not until rifling (the spiral grooving inside the barrel of a gun that spins a bullet) was invented during the second half of the 18th century that single-shot firearms could become consistently accurate.

Men's shooting events were held at the first Olympic Games in 1896, but it was not until the Los Angeles Games of 1984 that women had a chance to shoot for Olympic medals. Although World Championships are held every four years, the Olympics are still considered the most important shooting fixture.

Each of the many different types of gun — pistols, rifles, shotguns and so on — is designed for a different purpose. Consequently there are many sorts of competitive shooting events.

The ruling body of shooting is the Union Internationale de Tir (UIT) which was formed in Zurich in 1907. In addition to UIT, there are national ruling bodies, such as the National Rifle Association of Great Britain founded in 1860, and specialist organizations such as the Clay Bird Shooting Association.

▼ *Competition shooting brings to bear the same skills used in game shooting. This Edwardian print depicts an English pheasant shoot.*

AIMS OF THE GAME

COMPETITION
Only the most commonly practised amateur shooting events are included. These comprise the following:
- smallbore free rifle;
- smallbore rifle, three positions;
- running game target;
- free pistol;
- rapid fire pistol;
- Olympic trap;
- Olympic skeet.

All UIT shooting events (and those orchestrated by most nationally registered organizations) follow a strict code of conduct to minimize risks. The most essential rules are that:
- each competitor be issued with a given number of rounds (ammunition) shortly before the competition;
- no competitor can load a gun before being instructed to do so by a referee;
- once firing has ceased, the gun's breech, loading block or magazine has to be opened for inspection by the referee.

Smallbore free rifle (English match shooting)
● The range is 50 m (55 yd approx.) long and the target has 10 concentric circles. The outside diameter of the outer ring (1 point) measures 154.4 mm (6 in approx.) and the outside diameter of the inner ring (10 points) measures 10.4 mm (½ in approx.).
● The rifle used must be 5.6 mm (.22 in) calibre and must not have any sights that incorporate a lens.
● Sixty shots are fired from the prone (lying) position and the target is replaced after each shot. The time limit for firing 60 shots is either 1 hr 45 min or 2 hr, depending on the nature of the competition. The person with the highest overall score wins.

▼ *In 'three position' events, competitors fire 40 shots lying prone on the ground (1), 40 shots standing (2) and 40 shots kneeling (3). In the standing position, a marksman is not allowed to use a supporting sling but can use a palm rest instead.*

Smallbore rifle, three positions
● The rules for this event are exactly the same as those used in smallbore free rifle (see above) except that 40 shots are fired prone, 40 standing and 40 kneeling.
● The time limit for each batch of 40 shots is 1 hr 15 min for prone, 1 hr 45 min for standing, and 1 hr 30 min for kneeling.

Running game target
This event evolved from the ancient Mediterranean sport of boar hunting — an image of a bolting boar is still used as a target.
● The range is 50 m (55 yd) long and the target moves on a trolley across a gap 10 m (11 yd) wide. The target (the boar) has 10 concentric rings — the outermost ring (1 point) measures 366 mm (13 in approx.) in diameter and the innermost (10 points) measures 60 mm (2⅜ in approx.).

● The rifle is a standard 5.6 mm (.22 in) rifle and sights, including telescopic sights, are permitted.
● The target can be made to move at 2 speeds - 10 m (11 yd) in 5 sec (slow) and 10 m (11 yd) in 2.5 sec (fast). Each competitor fires 30 shots at a slow target and 30 shots at a fast target. After each shot, the score is logged and the person with the highest count after 60 shots is the winner.

Free pistol
● The range is 50 m (55 yd) long and the target is a standard, 10-ring pistol target — the outer diameter of the outer ring (1 point) is 500 mm (19 in approx.), while the outer diameter of the inner ring (10 points) is 50 mm (2 in approx.).
● The 5.6 mm (.22 in) pistol can be of virtually any shape, weight or size but it must not have a lens in the sight and it must not have a wrist support.

▶ The targets in rapid fire pistol competitions follow the approximate outlines of a man and are marked with scoring zones which radiate from the centre. A bullet in the centre zone scores 10 points.

▼ Revolvers or semi-automatic pistols are used in rapid fire events but no wrist or arm supports are allowed.

Target pistol　　　9 mm (0.35 in) ammunition

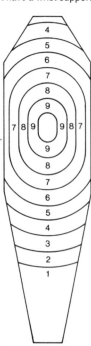

12-bore shotgun

Clay pigeon

Trap

▲ Clay targets are launched into the air by spring-loaded 'traps' and shatter when they are hit. Competitors usually favour 12-bore shotguns (with the barrels arranged 'over and under'), but semi-automatic weapons are allowed.

● A competition comprises 6 rounds, and 10 shots are fired in each round. The total of 60 shots must be fired within 2 hr and the person with the highest score is the winner.

Rapid fire pistol
● The range for this event is just 25 m (27 yd) long but instead of just one target there are 5. Each target is 55 cm (22 in) high and 55 cm (22 in) wide. The 6 scoring zones on each target, scoring 5 to 10 points, are circular in shape, and the central one (10 points) measures 10 cm (4 in) in diameter.

The 5 targets are fitted to frames which can turn them simultaneously through 90°. At the start of a 'shoot out', the targets are edge-on to each marksman but are turned 'face on' for just a short time and it is during this time that the shots are fired.

● The firearm used in rapid fire pistol is a standard 5.6 mm (.22 in) calibre pistol. It cannot be fitted with telescopic sights but semi-automatic pistols or revolvers are permitted so that shots can be discharged rapidly.
● A rapid fire pistol competition is divided into 2 parts, each part comprising 30 shots. These parts are further subdivided into 6 series of 5 shots each — 2 of these series are fired at the targets while they are exposed for 8 sec, 2 more are fired while the targets are exposed for 6 sec, and the last 2 are fired while the targets are exposed for just 4 sec.
● In each of these series, one shot is fired at each target. The time limit for a competition is 2 hr, and the competitor who has accumulated the highest score after 60 shots is the winner of the competition.

▲ A competitor deep in concentration during a shotgun event at the 1986 Commonwealth Games, held in Edinburgh, Scotland. Competition shooting requires great self-control, concentration and general physical conditioning.

▶ Special glasses are useful when shooting. The patch and adapted eyepiece help the competitor to focus accurately when aiming.

Olympic trap

This is one of 2 clay target events (the other being Olympic skeet — see below). Both developed from pigeon shooting which is why they are sometimes referred to as clay pigeon events.

● The range, or field as it is sometimes called, has 5 shooting positions and a resting position. Competitors take it in turns to rest on a rota basis.

There is a trench 15 m (16 yd) in front of the shooting positions from where the clay targets are hurled into the air away from the competitors by spring-loaded catapults called 'traps'. In major competitions, there are 3 traps for every competitor, each one throwing a target in a different direction. The traps can shoot out targets in a number of directions and so the height and angle of each target's trajectory is unpredictable. The catapults are designed to throw the targets a distance of around 75 m (80 yd). The targets are clay saucers which skim through the air.

● Guns must not exceed 12-bore (12-gauge) but can be double-barrelled or semi-automatic. As a rule, over-and-under double-barrel guns are preferred. These have one barrel above the other.

● The aim of each competitor is to break as many targets as possible; firing 2 shots at any one target is permissible.

Normally 200 targets are launched into the air in stages (or rounds) of 25. They are released from the trap on the competitor's cry of 'Pull!' During each round, a competitor fires at 5 targets from each of the 5 shooting positions. Competitions often last 2 or 3 days and the winner is the person who breaks the most targets.

Olympic skeet

● In skeet shooting, competitors fire from 8 different positions (stations). Seven of these stations are on the edge of an arc which has a radius of 21 yd (19.2 m); the eighth station is in the centre of the arc. The targets are released on fixed trajectories from 2 launching points, the 'high house' to the left and the 'low house' to the right. The high house releases targets from 10 ft (3 m approx.) above the ground, the low house from 3 ft (1 m approx.).

● Skeet targets are launched as either 'singles' or 'doubles'. A single target can be catapulted from either the low or the high house; doubles are released simultaneously from both houses.

● 12-bore (12-gauge) shotguns are mostly used, and weapons with expanded muzzles are permissible (a slightly bell-shaped muzzle gives a wider spread of shot so the chances of knocking down a target are greater).

● Groups of competitors, usually 6, move around from station to station shooting in turns. They start at 1 and move onto 8. Each competitor shoots at 200 targets in 8 rounds of 25. A round comprises:

- station 1: single from high house
            double
- station 2: single from high house
            single from low house
            double
- station 3: (as for station 2)
- station 4: single from high house
            single from low house
- station 5: single from high house
            single from low house
            double
- station 6: (as for station 5)
- station 7: double
- station 8: single from high house
            single from low house.

The person to break the most targets wins the contest.

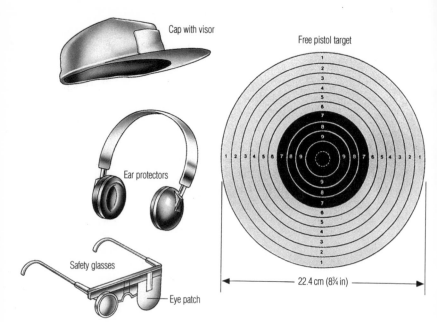

Cap with visor

Ear protectors

Safety glasses

Eye patch

Free pistol target

22.4 cm (8¾ in)

▲ *Visored caps, ear protectors and safety glasses with an eye patch are standard equipment for shooting competitions. The dotted 'bull's-eye' of a free pistol target is only used for tie breaks.*

SKILLS

● All types of competitive shooting are demanding. Not only is it necessary to have a good 'eye', but it is also useful to have a sense of rhythm to be able to anticipate the release of the targets. Perhaps even more important is a cool, steady temperament — some competitions go on for hours, if not days, and can make the fittest of people tired and weary.

In rifle shooting, a good competitor will always try to group shots together, preferably in the middle of the target. Good grouping is a sign of consistency, and consistent marksmen are the ones who win rifle-shooting competitions at the highest level.

EQUIPMENT

Apart from a gun, additional equipment of some kind is usually essential in competitive shooting.

● Ear protectors are often worn by competitors who fire in indoor ranges or use shotguns.

● Some marksmen wear peaked hats while shooting outside to protect their eyes from sunlight, others wear eye patches over the eye that is not being used for aiming. Both are acceptable at most levels of shooting as they do not actually interfere with the shooting as such. Some padded jackets are also acceptable but there are strict regulations on the type of padding used and where it is positioned — in theory, it is possible for padding to help support a gun.

● A telescope or pair of binoculars is important for any rifleman. It enables him to see where he has hit a target so he can make adjustments to his sights.

TECHNICAL TERMS

birds clay targets used in trap and skeet shooting

bull bull's-eye

clays short for clay targets

free conventional term in amateur shooting for a rifle or pistol of 5.6 mm (.22 in) calibre

Pull! a demand in trap and skeet shooting to the operator of the catapult to release a target; in major competitions, traps are voice-activated and computer-operated; any grunt or call from a marksman is sufficient to activate them

round a solitary bullet or a series of 25 shots (in skeet shooting)

trap the machine that launches clay targets into the air

zero a miss (off target)

FAMOUS VENUE

The most famous shooting event in the world is organized by the National Rifle Association of Great Britain and is held annually on the rifle ranges at Bisley, a village in Surrey, just south of London. Each year there are shooting competitions with targets that vary in distance from 1000 m (1100 yd) to 25 m (27 yd). Many of the competitions are confined to military personnel but competitors from all over the world take part.

PERSONALITY PROFILE

Malcolm Cooper

Malcolm Cooper of Great Britain is one of the greatest marksmen of all time. He has won 2 Olympic gold medals and 7 World Championship gold medals in addition to a clutch of European and Commonwealth titles and 12 world records. Cooper's speciality is smallbore rifle shooting. He particularly enjoys 'three position' events, although he is a skilled 'all-rounder'.

He was born in Camberley, England, in 1947 but learned to shoot in New Zealand. He was first selected to shoot for Great Britain in 1970 and has been in the national team ever since.

Cooper is married to another sharpshooter, Sarah, and the couple practise at least 25 hours a week on their private range.

Cooper practises Zen meditation to concentrate his mind, and over the years he has managed to train his eyes so that they can be focused independently.

Cooper's record

1978 2 gold medals at World Championships

1984 gold medal at Olympic Games

1986 3 gold medals at World Championships

1988 gold medal at Olympic Games

1990 2 gold medals at World Championships

CUE SPORTS

The three main cue sports — billiards, snooker and pool — all derive from an outdoor game similar to croquet which was played with a mace, a stick which had a flattened end. Louis XI of France (1461–83) decided that the game should be played indoors and he had a special table built. For 300 years billiards, as the new indoor game was called, flourished, but players were obliged to use the 'wrong end' of the mace to hit balls that were tight up against the side of the table. The cue, invented in the 19th century, allowed for a great variety of shots and the mace fell out of favour.

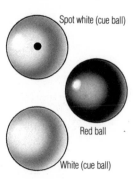

Spot white (cue ball)

Red ball

White (cue ball)

▲ *Billiards players use either the 'plain' white or the 'spot' ball as their cue ball. The red ball is only used as a target ball.*

BILLIARDS

The game of billiards as played by Louis XI and Mary Queen of Scots was very different from the modern game. The 'pockets' were boxes placed at strategic parts of the table, only two balls were used and the top of the table was bare wood. In 1664 the first Duke of Bedford decided to have a table covered with cloth: he chose green baize to resemble grass. A third ball was added to make the game more interesting.

In 1807 a French officer, Captain Mingaud, invented the leather cue tip while serving a prison sentence. The introduction of the cue tip enabled a player to spin a ball — something that was not possible with a wooden tip.

Billiards competitions flourished during the 19th century and the Billiards Association, founded in 1885, helped to establish a standard set of rules. In recent times, billiards has gone through the doldrums because it can appear to be a tedious and monotonous game when compared to snooker. However, it is still played by amateurs and professionals all over the world. One of Britain's most famous snooker champions, Joe Davis, began his career with a string of billiards titles. The main billiards competitions are the biennial World Amateur Championship and the annual World Professional Championship. The ruling body of the amateur game is the International Billiards and Snooker Federation (IBSF) and of the professional game, the World Professional Billiards and Snooker Association (WPBSA).

DID YOU KNOW?

The record for the highest break in billiards belongs to Tom Reece who, in 1907, scored 499,135 (unfinished). The feat took him almost 86 hours at the table over 5 weeks.

AIMS OF THE GAME

COMPETITION

● Three balls are used in billiards — 2 whites and a red; one of the white balls is marked with a black spot. Two people play against each other and try to amass points. One person adopts the 'spot' ball as his cue ball, the other has the 'plain'.

● One player starts the game by cueing away from the 'D' so that his cue ball strikes the red ball which has been placed on a spot at the other end of the table. If he pots a ball, he carries on playing until he either fouls or fails to score. If a foul is committed, any score made during the break is lost. At this stage the second player has a turn at the table and again, he must begin by striking his ball away from the 'D'.

● Scoring in billiards is as follows:
3 points are awarded for:
- potting the red;
- potting the cue ball 'in-off' the red
2 points are awarded for:
- a cannon;
- potting the opponent's ball;
- potting the cue ball in-off the opponent's ball.
(See also illustration opposite.)
Potted balls are returned to the table, so in theory it is possible for a break to last forever. However, most games end when one player reaches an agreed number of points (100, for example). Sometimes players have a specific time period in which to score as many points as possible.

● A team version can be played, with the 2 teams of 2 players taking turns to shoot either the 'plain' or 'spot' ball.

SKILLS

● The cueing techniques used in billiards are virtually identical to those used in snooker (see page 58).

TECHNICAL TERMS

Billiards and snooker (see page 58) share a number of technical terms and phrases. The following, however, are unique to billiards:
cannon when a cue ball hits both the other white ball and the red
in-hand from within the D
in-off when a cue ball goes into a pocket after striking either the other white ball or the red

▼ *Scoring shots in billiards.*
A – red pot (3 points)
B – in-off red (3 points)
C – in-off white (2 points)
D – white pot (2 points)
E – the cannon (2 points)
A player needs a sound knowledge of angles if he or she is to get a run of shots.

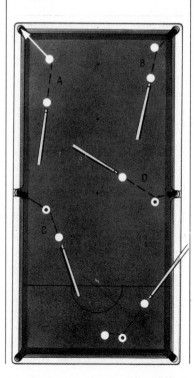

CUE SPORTS

DID YOU KNOW?

In 1990, the WPBSA voted to let anybody play professional snooker in the 1991/92 season provided they could afford to pay entry fees and were over 16. This news meant that Allison Fisher's ambition to become the first lady professional could at last be fulfilled. Ever since she first won the Women's Amateur Championship in 1985, she has been campaigning to compete with men on equal terms.

SNOOKER

Towards the end of the last century, a number of new games were played on billiards tables, including life pool and black pool. In life pool, a number of players each had a cue ball of a different colour. When a player's ball was potted, he lost his 'life' and was out of the game; the winner was the person whose coloured ball remained on the table. Black pool was rather different: there were 15 reds and one black ball on the table. When a player potted a red he had the chance to pot the black, which was more 'valuable'. Both these games were played in various outposts of the British Empire and, in 1875, a certain Neville Chamberlain decided to make things more interesting by combining the two games to form one. Chamberlain was a junior officer at the time, stationed at Jubbulpore in India, and it was he who also gave the new game its name. At the time, 'snooker' was a slang word used to describe a new recruit at the Royal Military Academy at Woolwich. Playing his new game one evening, Chamberlain called his partner a snooker because he had shown his

▼ The cue is supported on the bridging hand and the head is kept low while striking.

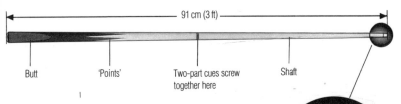

Butt   'Points'   Two-part cues screw   Shaft
together here

91 cm (3 ft)

inexperience by missing an easy shot. The name caught on and the game has been known as snooker ever since.

Snooker was brought to England in due course but did not rival billiards in popularity because it was considered a simple potting game with little skill. In the 1920s, Joe Davis, a champion at both games, proved that this was not the case and snooker gradually became the more popular sport. However, it was not until the advent of colour television that snooker really took off. Today it is one of the most popular of all sports televised in Britain. Extended coverage of major tournaments, such as the annual World Championship, regularly lead the British television ratings. Top snooker players have the same celebrity status as soccer and cricket stars.

The International Billiards and Snooker Federation is the ruling body of amateur snooker, while the World Professional Billiards and Snooker Association (WPBSA) is responsible for the professional game. The world governing body is the Billiards and Snooker Control Council (BSCC).

Leather tip   Brass ferrule

▲ *Cues taper to a leather-covered tip which is rubbed with chalk. A heavy hardwood butt ensures good balance.*

▼ *At the beginning of a frame, the balls are set up on the spots as shown. The first player hits the white ball from anywhere within the D.*

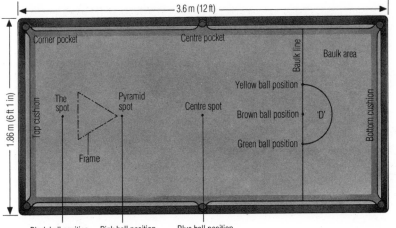

3.6 m (12 ft)

1.86 m (6 ft 1 in)

Corner pocket   Centre pocket   Baulk line   Baulk area

Top cushion

The spot   Pyramid spot   Centre spot

Frame

Yellow ball position

Brown ball position   'D'

Green ball position

Bottom cushion

Black ball position   Pink ball position   Blue ball position

AIMS OF THE GAME

COMPETITION

● A 'frame' of snooker is usually between 2 individuals, although team games are possible: these are usually contested by pairs. At the beginning of a frame, there are 22 balls on the table — 15 reds arranged in a triangle, 6 coloured balls, and a white cue ball. The cue ball is the only one that can be struck with the cue and is used to knock the other balls into position or into pockets. The colours of the balls signify their worth:

red   1 point
yellow 2 points
green   3 points
brown   4 points
blue   5 points
pink   6 points
black   7 points

Penalty points are awarded against a player if he misses a ball, pots the cue ball or strikes the wrong ball. The minimum number of penalty points is 4, but this can rise to 5, 6 or 7 if the blue, pink or black balls are involved.

● To start a frame, one player strikes the cue ball from inside the 'D' so that it hits the triangle of reds. If he pots a red, he must hit a coloured ball (anything other than red). If he pots a coloured ball he goes for another red and so on. If a player fails to pot a ball or commits a foul then his opponent has a turn.

Every red ball that is potted stays out of play but coloured balls are returned to their spots so long as there are red balls on the table. When all the reds have been potted, the player turns to the coloured balls and attempts to pot them in ascending order of value (this time the potted colours stay in the pockets). When the black ball has been potted the frame is over and the player with more points is the winner. Scores are sometimes so close at the end of a frame that it becomes a race to pot the black.

▼ The cue rest is used when it is impossible for a player to reach far enough across the table to form a bridge with a hand. Rests, like cues, can be lengthened by screwing on an extension piece.

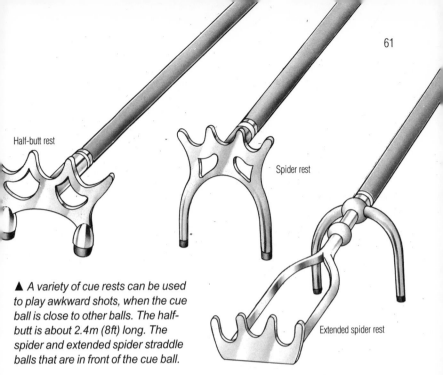

Half-butt rest

Spider rest

Extended spider rest

▲ *A variety of cue rests can be used to play awkward shots, when the cue ball is close to other balls. The half-butt is about 2.4m (8ft) long. The spider and extended spider straddle balls that are in front of the cue ball.*

● Snooker matches consist of a number of frames — the winner being the person who wins the most.

SKILLS

● Snooker requires an agile brain as well as co-ordination between arm and eye. The aim of the game is to accumulate points either by potting balls or by forcing an opponent into making foul shots, for example missing completely or potting a colour out of turn. To do this effectively a good player always aims to do two things while playing the cue ball: first he tries to knock the object ball to where he wants it (often into a pocket) and secondly he attempts to manoeuvre the cue ball into a good position. If a player is attacking, he will try and get the cue ball into a position for another pot; if he is playing defensively, he may try and snooker his opponent, that is, get the cue ball into such a position that his opponent has to commit a foul stroke.

● By making the cue ball spin, a player can control how it strikes an object ball or even a side cushion of the table. At its best, snooker is a game of subtle tactics.

EQUIPMENT

● Snooker cues are traditionally made of wood. Experiments with aluminium have been unsuccessful. The shaft is usually made from polished ash or maple, with a heavier wood such as ebony being used to form the butt, or thick end. The leather tip on the other end of a cue is usually stuck on and can be replaced. Weight and balance are important in a cue — most cues weigh about 0.5 kg (1 lb) and come in two halves that can be screwed together.

● All players prepare the tip of the cue with special chalk before they make a shot. The chalk prevents the tip from glancing off the cue ball.

TECHNICAL TERMS

break a series of scoring shots by one player

cue ball the solitary white ball which must be struck by the cue

cushion the sides of the table made from moulded rubber covered with woollen cloth

D name of the semi-circle marked on a snooker or billiards table to show where the cue ball must be placed before a break

marker a person who keeps score

object ball the ball to be struck by the cue ball

pot to make the cue ball strike another ball so that the latter ends up in a pocket or forces another chosen one in to the pocket

safety shot a non-scoring shot but one that manoeuvres the cue ball into such a position that an opponent finds it difficult to score

screw a backward spin imparted to the cue ball by striking it towards the bottom; it makes the cue ball move backwards down the table after it has struck the object ball or cushion

side side spin that is given to the cue ball by striking it on either side; it has the effect of making the cue ball deviate after it has struck the object ball or cushion

stun a shot which leaves the cue ball stationary immediately after it has hit the object ball, usually achieved by hitting low on the cue ball

FOR THE RECORD

MAJOR PROFESSIONAL COMPETITIONS
World Professional Championship
Masters
United Kingdom Open
Irish Masters
British Open
European Open

TOP RANKED PLAYERS 1989/90 SEASON
 1 Stephen Hendry (Scot)
 2 Steve Davis (Eng)
 3 John Parrott (Eng)
 4 Jimmy White (Eng)
 5 Doug Mountjoy (Wal)
 6 Terry Griffiths (Wal)
 7 Mike Hallett (Eng)
 8 Dean Reynolds (Eng)
 9 Steve James (Eng)
10 Dennis Taylor (NI)

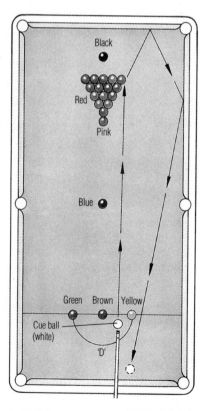

◀ *A typical safety shot at the start of a frame. The cue ball is brought back to 'hug' the bottom cushion and no clear shot is presented to the opponent.*

WORLD CHAMPIONS (1981 – 91)
1981 Steve Davis (Eng)
1982 Alex Higgins (NI)
1983 Steve Davis (Eng)
1984 Steve Davis (Eng)
1985 Dennis Taylor (NI)
1986 Joe Johnson (Eng)
1987 Steve Davis (Eng)
1988 Steve Davis (Eng)
1989 Steve Davis (Eng)
1990 Stephen Hendry (Scot)
1991 John Parrott (Eng)

▲ *Stephen Hendry concentrates as he lines up for a shot. His talent and professionalism took him to the top of the world snooker rankings when he was only 20 years old.*

MOST WORLD TITLES (SINCE 1927)
Joe Davis   15
John Pulman   7
Ray Reardon   6
Steve Davis   6
Fred Davis   3

▲ *In 14:1 continuous pool the object balls are numbered 1 to 15.*

▼ *In 8-ball pool balls are coloured. Black is always centred 2 rows behind the apex ball.*

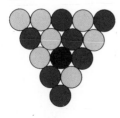

▼ *The American table has 3 spots. At the start of a game or a new break, the apex ball is positioned on the foot spot.*

POOL

The Spaniards introduced a form of billiards to America in the 16th century; 300 years later, English billiards crossed the Atlantic. From these two games, pool evolved. Several variations of the game developed in different parts of the United States and pool is now a generic term for a number of different sports.

During the Depression years, pool in its various forms became hugely popular, played for money in illicit gambling dens and clubs throughout the United States. Legendary heroes arose. Today, pool is probably the most popular derivative of billiards and it is played in pubs and clubs around the globe. This is despite the fact that there is still no unifying set of standard rules. Although there are a number of professional players, particularly in the United States, pool is essentially a game of fun, played for pleasure by old and young of both sexes.

The most prestigious version of the game is 14:1 continuous play, and American championships usually adopt this version of the sport. The most frequently played type of pool, however, is 8-ball — largely because it can be played on coin-operated tables and no equipment, apart from a borrowed cue, is necessary.

The Billiard Congress of America is the main ruling body of the game.

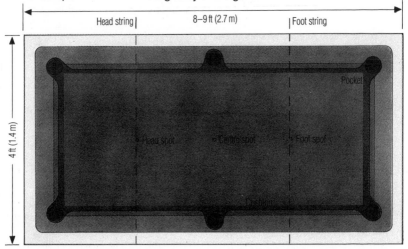

Head string | 8–9 ft (2.7 m) | Foot string

4 ft (1.4 m)

Pocket

Head spot   Centre spot   Foot spot

Cushion

AIMS OF THE GAME

COMPETITION
14:1 continuous play
● The object balls are numbered 1 to 15; those numbered 1 to 8 are allotted a different colour for each; 9 to 15 have stripes of varying colour. The cue ball is white.
● The object is for a player to reach an agreed number of points, usually 150. Each object ball pocketed counts as 1 point.
● At the start, the object balls are positioned in a triangle at one end of the table and the first player cues the white ball from behind a line called the 'head string' at the other end. For a point to be valid, a player must nominate both the ball and the target pocket. A foul (loss of 1 point and a turn) occurs if either the cue ball or an object ball fails to hit a cushion after contact has been made.
● When 14 balls have been pocketed, they are replaced in a triangle with the apex ball missing and play continues until the player either fouls, fails to pocket a ball or reaches the target score.

8-ball pool
● The object of the game is for one player to pocket the balls numbered 1 to 7 while his opponent tries to pocket the 9 to 15 balls. When a player has pocketed all his selected balls, he tries for the 8 ball. The winner is the person who pockets the 8 ball. A player automatically loses if he pockets the 8 ball before pocketing his selected balls.

SKILLS
● Pool is considered a more aggressive game than snooker (see page 58) but techniques and tactics are similar for both sports.

EQUIPMENT

Tables come in 2 recognized sizes: 8 x 4 ft (2.4 x 1.2 m) and 9 x 4 ft (2.7 m x 1.4 m). A slate top ensures the surface is completely flat.

TECHNICAL TERMS

bank side of the table
call to nominate a target ball and pocket
inning a player's turn at the table
run series of scoring shots
scratch to hit the cue ball into a pocket (counts as a foul)
triangle wooden triangle used to arrange the balls at the start
visit another name for a player's turn at the table (8-ball only)

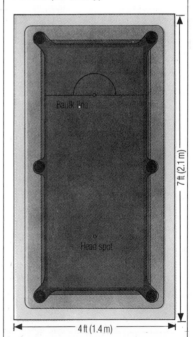

▲ *British tables are smaller than American tables. The first player starts by striking the cue ball from any point within the D.*

WINTER SPORTS

Most of the contemporary winter sports were developed in Europe. Some, such as skating and curling, have ancient origins but others are comparatively new sports. Biathlon, for example, is only about 40 years old. Not surprisingly, the countries which have the strongest traditions in winter sports are those that have snow-covered mountain ranges or cold winter climates.

DID YOU KNOW?

Ice skates were probably first invented as a means of transport. An early form of skate was unearthed among Roman ruins in London. Made of chiselled animal bone and leather, the skates are thought to date back to 50 BC.

FIGURE SKATING

Ice skating is thought to have been developed in Scandinavia, where primitive skates dating back some 2000 years have been found. During mediaeval times, ice skating became a popular pleasure sport in Holland, where the frozen canals proved to be ideal rinks. From Holland the sport spread to England and it was the British who evolved figure skating in preference to speed skating. During the 17th and 18th centuries figure skating became a popular pastime in both Britain and France.

The first skating club was opened in the mid-18th century in Edinburgh. An English club was established in 1830, followed by one opening in Philadelphia in the United States. After the first artificial ice rink was built in London in 1876, figure skating became increasingly popular and the International Skating Union, the ruling body of the sport, was founded in 1892.

The first World Championships were held in Russia in 1896, and figure skating became an Olympic sport in 1924. The Olympics and the annual World Championships are still considered the premier international skating meetings.

A few elite figure skaters turn professional and perform for money. Professional touring extravaganzas, with their clowns and acrobatics, are sometimes described as circuses on ice. However, they provide a chance for the general public to see some of the world's greatest skating talents. Some of the most famous professionals are Germany's Katerina Witt, Britain's singles skaters, John Curry and Robin Cousins and the ice dance duo, Jayne Torvill and Christopher Dean.

▲ *A good ice-dancing routine combines the discipline and technique of pairs skating with the glamour and excitement of choreography.*

AIMS OF THE GAME

COMPETITION

● All figure skating competitions are held on a rink that measures 60 m x 30 m (200 ft x 100 ft approx.). There are 4 main events — singles (men and women), pairs skating and ice dance.

● Marks are awarded by up to 9 judges in international competitions. Each judge awards up to 6 marks after each stage of competition. Each skater's competitive standing is multiplied by an 'x-factor' after every stage, so the skater with the lowest score at the end wins.

Singles — men and women

● Major competitions comprise 2 parts — compulsory figures, and an original programme of 8 required elements and a free skating programme.

● In the compulsory figures, a skater has to trace out on the ice a series of shapes that are based on 2 or 3 linked circles (figures) marked on the ice. Marks out of 6 are awarded, taking into account both the style and the accuracy of the skating.

● In the original programme, each competitor is allowed 2 min to perform 8 specified elements — jumps, spins and step sequences — to non-vocal music of the competitor's choice. No additional movements are allowed and 2 sets of marks are awarded — one set for required elements and the other for artistic impression. The skater's placing at that stage in the programme is multiplied by an x-factor of 0.5 so that the marks represent 33.3% of the total.

▼ A pairs skater needs strength and grace to lift and carry his partner over his head.

● In the free skating section, skaters must perform a well balanced programme of elements (jumps, spins, linking steps, etc) to non-vocal music of their choice. The time limit is 4 min for women and 4½ min for men.
Two sets of marks, from 0 to 6, are awarded — one set for technical merit and the other for artistic impression. Prolonged movements on both feet are penalized and movements that result in a fall are not judged.
The x-factor for free skating is 1.0 and the marks for the section add up to 66.7% of the total.
● The winner of a competition is the person with the lowest total obtained after the 2 sections are combined.

Pairs skating
● The main rule for this is that a pair must comprise a man and a woman — same-sex pairs are forbidden.
● There are just 2 sections in pairs skating — the original programme and the free skating programme.
● In the original programme, each pair has to complete 8 required elements — including partner-assisted jumps, and pair spins — within a time limit of 2 min 15 sec. Music is allowed and at the end of the programme marks are awarded for required elements and artistic impression. Skater's standings are multiplied by an x-factor of 0.5 and represent 33.3% of the total.
● The free skating section lasts 4½ min (seniors) and 4 min (juniors). During this time each pair executes a set number of prescribed movements. At the end, marks are awarded for technical merit and artistic impression. Standings in this section are multiplied by an x-factor of 1.0 and represent 66.7% of the total.
● The winning pair has the lowest total obtained in the 2 parts combined.

Ice dancing
● Ice dancing can appear to be very similar to pairs skating but the essential difference is that it must be dancing; if a couple appear to be going through a pairs routine, they will lose marks. However, many of the movements are similar to those included in pairs skating. Two major differences are that no high lifts are allowed and revolutions are limited in spins.

There are 3 sections to ice dancing:
— compulsory dances;
— an original dance;
— a free dance programme.
Competitors' standings after each of these sections are multiplied by an x-factor so that the lowest number actually wins after the third section.
● In the compulsory dance section, each couple has to perform various rhythms — waltzes, polkas, rhumbas and so on. Judges award one set of marks for each of the dances, taking into account whether or not the skating was in time with the music, as well as the general ability of the skaters. Each dance routine has to follow a given pattern of steps.

The standings after each dance are multiplied by an x-factor of 0.2 each, which means that they represent 20% of the total score for the competition.
● In the original dance, each couple has to perform to a dance rhythm that has been selected several months before, but skaters are allowed to choose their own piece of music.

Two sets of marks are awarded — one for competition and one for presentation and harmony of movement. Each pair's comparative standing for this stage is multiplied by an x-factor of 0.6 to represent 30% of the total score.
● In the free dance section, each couple performs a 5-min dance routine

▲ The axel jump shown here is named after the Norwegian Axel Paulsen. Skaters are penalized for landing on 2 skates.

to music of its choice — several different pieces of music are allowed. Marks are given for ability and artistic merit. Skater's standings in this important stage are equivalent to 50% of the total.
● The winning couple are the ones with the lowest overall placing, after various x-factors have been calculated for each section and the marks combined.

▲ *Figure skates are light and their short blades are only slightly longer than the boot.*

SKILLS

● At the highest level of the sport, all figure skaters must be able to skate backwards, forwards and in curves.

● Spins on the spot are an important feature of all forms of figure skating. The most difficult of all spins is the sitting spin where a skater starts in an upright position and then gradually sinks down to a squatting position often while accelerating.

● There are several different sorts of jump. Height is important in a jump of any kind and so is the cleanness of the take-off and landing. Judges will instantly deduct marks if there is any sign of wobbling.

● In pairs skating and ice dancing lifts are crucial. In these, one partner, usually the man, lifts his opposite number up into the air while still skating. Lifting a person requires strength and agility at the best of times but on ice balance, confidence and consummate skill are essential if a movement is not to end in disaster — or just look clumsy.

● Over and above the skills of skating, come the abilities to move with poise and grace — judges always look for artistic expression.

EQUIPMENT

● Skates for figure skating have blades about 3 mm (⅛ in) wide; most blades have slightly concave bottom edges so that they can grip the ice. The blades are usually slightly longer than the boot to which they are attached and have teeth at the front which enable skaters to perform spins and sudden stops.

● Dress is important to figure skaters because it can be used to draw attention from both judges and spectators. However, it must be dignified and must obviously allow free movement.

TECHNICAL TERMS

axel a one-and-a-half rotation jump, taking off from the leading edge of one skate and landing on the outside edge of the other skate

camel spin a manoeuvre executed in the ballet 'arabesque' position, with one leg extended back

connecting move a flowing movement that links two strenuous moves

counter a figure consisting of 3 circles

crossover a movement where one skate is moved over in front of the other to take the weight of the skater

death spiral a movement in pairs skating and ice dancing when the man acts as a pivot and spins his partner around him

double any jump that has an extra rotation added to it

free foot the non-skating leg, held off the ice during the compulsory competition

loop jump a one-rotation jump, taking off from the back edge of one skate and landing on the same edge

lutz a fast anti-clockwise one-rotation jump, taking off from the back outside edge of one skate while using the toe of the other skate as a pivot; landing is on the outside edge of the opposite skate to that of take-off

mirror skating when a couple in pairs skating or ice dance carry out similar moves while facing each other

rocker a half turn in which the skater turns 180°, eventually facing backwards while still going in the original direction

salchow a one-rotation jump, taking off from the inside edge of one skate and landing on the outside edge of the other skate

shadow skating when a couple carry out identical moves, one behind or parallel with the other

toe jump a jump from the front teeth of a skate's blade

toe rake the teeth on the leading tip of a skate

triple jump a jump that has 2 extra turns added to it.

FOR THE RECORD

ICE SHOWS

Olympic champion figure skaters are often given the chance to pursue lucrative careers in large-scale ice shows. These colourful extravaganzas began in New York City in 1915, when the German ice ballerina Charlotte Oelschlagel led an entire ice ballet troupe from Berlin. Over the course of the next 50 years a number of touring ice shows were formed. 'Ice Follies' played to more than 60 million people between 1936 and 1965. The 'Ice Capades' had 2 US tours constantly on the go in the 1960s. Its rival, 'Holiday on Ice', had six separate full-time productions — one for each continent. Today's ice shows rely less on massive production values and focus instead on the figure skating routines made famous by their star attractions.

▼ *In free-skating sections of a competition, singles skaters interpret music of their choice by carrying out expressive movements including a number of spins and jumps.*

DID YOU KNOW?

Short-course speed skating is an alternative to the more usual long-course version of the sport. Races take place indoors over 4 distances — 500 m (547 yd), 1000 m (1094 yd), 1500 m (1640 yd) and 3000 m (3280 yd). This form of speed skating was included as a demonstration sport at the Winter Olympics in 1988.

SPEED SKATING

Speed skating evolved in Holland as early as the 12th century. This is hardly surprising since the long, straight Dutch canals provide near-perfect venues for fast, precise skating in the winter months. The legacy of speed skating in Holland has proved long-lived and over the years the Dutch have produced several speed skating champions.

Speed skating was taken across the Atlantic Ocean by European emigrants and became a popular sport in the United States and Canada in the 19th century. At the same time, it was adopted by Scandinavian and Baltic countries and, more recently, it has found favour in Japan. There is a simple reason why comparatively few countries produce speed skaters: every speed skating rink covers a considerable area and, with a few exceptions, they are all outdoors. Therefore, they have to be sited in extremely cold places.

▼ *Speed skaters chart an almost zigzag course as they push off on each stride.*

The first speed skating World Championships were held in Amsterdam in 1893 and men's events were introduced in the first Winter Olympics in 1924. (Women's events were not adopted by the Olympics until 1964.)

The ruling body of the sport is the International Skating Union. The headquarters are situated in Switzerland.

▼ *The long blades of a speed skate are flat. This makes it hard to change direction by turning the skate, but it gives the skater more purchase to begin each stride.*

AIMS OF THE GAME

COMPETITION
● A standard speed skating rink is an oval of 400 m (440 yd approx.) and comprises 2 lanes, each up to 5 m (5½ yd) wide.
● In the World Championships there are 4 distances for men (500 m, 1500 m, 5000 m and 10,000 m) and 4 for women (500 m, 1000 m, 1500 m and 3000 m). Competitors have to race in all 4 events. Pairs of skaters race each other round the rink for the various distances and points are awarded according to the time that each skater takes to cross the finish line. After the completion of the 4 races, the person with the lowest number of points (i.e. the lowest aggregate time for the 4 races) is the winner.
● In the Olympic Games, the rules are different. There are 4 distances for women and 5 for men (as above, with the addition of a 1000 m event). Races are still held between 2 people but each distance is taken as a separate event. Medals are awarded to those who finish fastest at each distance, so 9 gold medals are awarded in total.

SKILLS
● A speed skater conserves energy by keeping a low profile and by skating long, rhythmic strides while keeping the hands behind the back. At corners, the right hand (races are always run anticlockwise) is often swung like a

pendulum to maintain rhythm, balance and steady pace.
● Speed skating can look like the least vigorous of sports but it is deceptive. A good skater will start a stride on the outside edge of a skate and roll the blade in so that by the end of the stride only the inside edge of the blade is in contact with the ice. Speeds of up to 50 km/h (30 mph) are often achieved.

EQUIPMENT

● Speed skate blades are unusually long — up to 45 cm (18 in) — and thin. The blades are often no more than 1 mm (1/32 in) wide. This shape of blade helps skaters take long strides. The boots are also light and have flexible ankle supports.
● Lightweight, one-piece body suits are preferred by speed skaters as they cut down wind resistance and can save precious milliseconds. The body suits can be thin because the exercise of skating generates enough heat to keep the body warm.

DID YOU KNOW?

An ice yacht can travel four times faster than the wind propelling it. The fastest speed ever achieved is 230 km/h (143 mph).

ICE YACHTING

Ice yachting, or ice boating as it is sometimes called, is the fastest of all the winter sports. The first ice boats date back 4000 years or more. These were mounted on bone runners and were used by people who lived on the edge of the Arctic Circle to transport equipment.

The first people to take up ice yachting were the Dutch during the 17th century. In turn, they introduced the sport to America. Up until the beginning of the 20th century, ice yachts tended to be made from wood and were steered by a movable blade or rudder at the back. These heavy craft were manned by a crew of up to six people. In 1931, a front rudder was invented, preventing boats from sideslipping. Now nearly all ice yachts have a front rudder.

Modern ice yachts usually comprise a sleek glass fibre hull mounted on a frame that is supported on three steel runners. Two of the runners are rigid and are fixed to outriggers (extensions on either side of the hull), the third can be moved and is used for guiding the yacht. The mast attached to the frame can support either one or two sails.

In the United States, there are two major organizations — the Northwestern Ice Yachting Association (1912) and the Eastern Ice Yachting Association (1937). The premier event is the annual Ice Yacht Challenge Pennant of America which is open to all newcomers. The European Ice Yachting Union was founded in 1928.

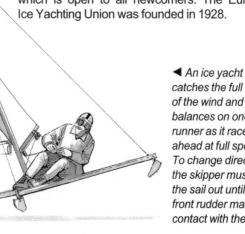

◀ An ice yacht catches the full force of the wind and balances on one runner as it races ahead at full speed. To change direction, the skipper must let the sail out until the front rudder makes contact with the ice.

AIMS OF THE GAME

COMPETITION
● Ice yachts are divided into 5 classes, which are based on the area of the sail or sails:
- Class A: 350 sq ft (32.5 sq m)
- Class B: 200 sq ft (18.6 sq m)
- Class C: 175 sq ft (16.3 sq m)
- Class D: 125 sq ft (11.6 sq m)
- Class E: 75 sq ft (6.97 sq m)
● Races are usually run on a prepared course. Boats typically have to race up and down the course, turning around a marker at each end. The number of laps that have to be completed and the distance between the markers vary from course to course.
● Most boats are manned by just one person but some heavier craft have a crew of 2.

▲ *Warm clothing and quick reflexes are essential as an ice yacht cuts through a bitter wind.*

SKILLS
● Ice yachting is like sailing, except that it is far faster. A skipper has to steer the yacht using pulleys attached to the front rudder and at the same time has to control the sail (or sails) to catch the wind. As ice yachting is such a fast sport, a fair amount of danger is involved.

EQUIPMENT

● Apart from the yacht itself, little essential equipment is necessary. Most ice yachtsmen wear protective goggles, a helmet and warm, wind-proof clothing.

CURLING

The ancient team game of curling originated in Scotland and is sometimes referred to as 'bowls on ice', although granite stones are used instead of wooden balls. The sport spread from Scotland and is now played extensively in North America as well as in Europe.

It is purely an amateur sport played by both sexes and governed by the International Curling Federation (ICF). Each country has its own governing body, but all agree on ICF rules.

The game received a boost in 1988, when it was played as a demonstration sport at the Calgary Winter Olympics. The annual World Championships are well supported.

Tee

◄ 1.83 m ►
(2 yd)

Centre line

42 m (46 yd)

Hog line

Target
('house')

Tee line

Back line

Hack line

◄ 4.26 m (4.7 yd) ►

▲ Curling is played on a level area of ice. Players stand on the hack line and deliver the stones towards the house at the far end of the playing area.

▲ Players are allowed to sweep (soop) away moisture from in front of a team member's stone using a broom in order to make it move faster along the ice. Skilled sooping can also change the direction in which the stone is travelling. The throw does not count if the broom touches the stone.

AIMS OF THE GAME

COMPETITION
● The area of ice used in a game is 42 m (46 yd) long and about 4.26 m (4.7 yd) wide. At each end of the playing area, there is a circular target marked with concentric circles. The outer diameter of each target is 1.83 m (2 yd) and the distance between the centre of the 2 targets is 34.75 m (38 yd).
● Contests are between 2 teams of 4 players. Teams play each other at least once in major competitions. The team with the best score wins the title.
● Taking turns, curlers deliver stones from a metal plate ('hack') at one end of the ice towards the target ('house'). Sixteen stones are played in all (2 from each player); the team that wins in the end is the one with one or more of its stones nearest the centre of the house. All stones nearer than the best opposition stone count. Stones outside the house do not count in the scoring.
● After all the stones have been played from one head (or end), the players play again from the other head. Matches are played over 10 ends.
● Members of a team are allowed to sweep the ice with brooms in front of a moving stone. This melts the ice in front of the stone so that its pace and direction can be changed.

SKILLS
● Curlers use an underarm action to deliver a stone and have a long follow-through. By subtly turning the handle while letting go of the stone, a good curler can make a stone curve in to the right or left ('curling').
● Sweeping is an important part of the game. Furious rubbing with a broom will melt the ice rapidly and enable a stone to move farther down the rink.

EQUIPMENT

● Stones have smooth, rounded edges and resemble flat cheeses. The handles are mounted on top for easier delivery. They weigh about 20 kg (44 lb).
● Shoes must provide grip but must not mark the ice. Some players wear one rubber-soled shoe and one smooth-soled shoe, which enables them to slide on the ice on delivery or in following the stone.

TECHNICAL TERMS

hack the plate from where the stones are delivered
hogline a line on the rink 10 m (11 yd) from a hack which must not be crossed by a player when delivering a stone
house the target
rink ice rink where curling takes place
skip captain
soop to sweep with a broom
strike a stone that knocks an opponent's stone out of the way
tee the centre of a house
throw players 'throw' stones down the rink

▼ *The stone is shaped from granite with a steel band around the girth to prevent damage in collisions. The base is polished to reduce friction and the detachable handle is screwed into the top.*

DID YOU KNOW?

England's former cricket captain, David Gower, is a keen skeleton tobogganer and makes frequent trips to St Moritz during the winter to compete on the Cresta Run.

▼ *A skeleton tobogganer executes a right turn by digging his right toe spikes into the icy surface of the run. The left leg is poised to lessen the effect if the turn is too sharp.*

SKELETON TOBOGGANING

During the winter of 1884, a certain Major Bulpetts decided to build a toboggan run down the Cresta valley near St Moritz in Switzerland. The first riders to use the run sat on toboggans facing forwards, but it was not long before they realized that they could go faster if they lay down on their sleds, which were basic affairs called 'skeletons'. The sport became extremely popular with both the local Swiss and with English holiday-makers.

Although there are one or two other skeleton toboggan tracks, the Cresta Run is by far the most famous, and the St Moritz Tobogganing Club, founded in 1887, is the governing body of the sport. Skeleton tobogganing is extremely dangerous, and speeds approaching 140 km/h (90 mph) have been recorded by racers crossing the finish line on the Cresta Run.

Skeleton toboggan races have been held at two Olympic Games — in 1928 and 1948. On both occasions, the Winter Games were held at St Moritz and the Cresta Run was used as the Olympic track.

Hand grips — Movable seat — Metal runners

AIMS OF THE GAME

COMPETITION
● The St Moritz Tobogganing Club organizes around 50 annual races down the Cresta Run. The season for the Cresta Run lasts from January to the beginning of March.
● Some races start at the head of the 1212 m (¾-mile approx.) course from the starting place known as the 'Top'; other races start from the 'Junction', about a quarter of the way down the run.
● Most races are won by the person achieving the fastest aggregate time for 3 runs, either from the Top or from the Junction.
● When the Olympic Games were held at St Moritz, medals were awarded to those who had the fastest aggregate times on 6 runs, 3 from the Top and 3 from the Junction.

SKILLS
● A skeleton tobogganer lies on a sled and grasps the bows of each runner. Steering a rigid skeleton toboggan is not easy. On straights, the slightest movement of the head is sufficient to make the toboggan move to the left or right; on curves, it is possible to steer either by shifting the body weight or by digging spikes (rakes), attached to the boots, into the ice.

▲ *Steel runners and a heavy framework ensure smooth progress down the ice track. There are no brakes so the rider must control the toboggan's speed.*

● Travelling head-first down an icy track at 140 km/h (90 mph) just a few centimetres off the ground requires more than just a little bit of courage — it demands steel nerves and a great deal of self-belief!

EQUIPMENT

● A skeleton toboggan is comparatively heavy and can weigh as much as 36 kg (80 lb). The 2 steel runners are about 45 cm (18 in) apart and are about 1.2 m (4 ft) long. The 'seat' is made so that it can slide backwards or forwards; on fast stretches, a rider forces the seat forwards; on curves, the seat is slipped backwards so that the body weight can be shifted one way or the other to guard against taking the curve too wide.
● A protective helmet, chin guard and goggles are compulsory. So are specially strengthened gloves which are designed to protect the hands should they get caught under the runners. The boots have spikes or rakes attached to them so that they can be used for steering.

DID YOU KNOW?

Until 1991 bobsleigh competitions had been held exclusively for men since the 19th century. It was only in January 1991 that the British organized the first women's bobsleigh competition.

▼ *The driver and brakesman of a two-man team push the bobsleigh towards the starting line to give it initial momentum. The run itself begins as soon as the bob crosses the line — the clock starts and the team members clamber into the craft.*

BOBSLEIGH RACING

The first bobsleigh was the invention of a group of Englishmen who modified a sleigh while holidaying in St Moritz, Switzerland, in 1890. Their aim was to create a streamlined sled to carry two or four men extremely fast down an improvised track that was nothing more than a snow-covered road leading from St Moritz to the village of Celerina, which lay at the bottom of the valley. The new sport immediately caught on and a special track, complete with banked curves made from ice, was constructed next to the road in 1902.

The first properly organized bobsleigh races were held in 1898 but it was not until the formation of the Fédération Internationale de Bobsleigh et Tobogganing in 1923 that the daredevil sport gained worldwide recognition. A year later, a four-man bobsleigh race was included in the Olympic Games held at Chamonix in France. Two-man bobsleigh racing did not enter the Olympics until 1932.

The most prestigious bobsleigh competition outside the Olympics is the biennial World Championships. The nations with the strongest records in bobsleigh racing are Switzerland, Germany and Italy.

AIMS OF THE GAME

COMPETITION
- There are 2-rider and 4-rider bobsleigh competitions which are run down icy courses that are at least 1500 m (1640 yd) long. A championship course must have at least 15 banked curves.
- At the start of a run, a team is allowed to wait 15 m (16 yd approx.) behind the starting line. When given a signal, the team is then allowed to push its 'bob' down the slope before clambering inside. Timing begins as soon as the front of the bob crosses the starting line.
- Each team takes 4 runs down the course and the one with the lowest aggregate time is the winner.

SKILLS
- Getting a good start is crucial and making a clean getaway requires teamwork; each member of a team must know exactly when to stop pushing and when to climb into the fast-moving bob.
- Steering is also important and is the responsibility of the rider at the front — a badly timed entry into a curve could cost precious time or could lead to disaster.
- During a race teamwork again plays a crucial role, especially in 4-rider races. Around corners, a team has to transfer its weight from one side to the other in perfect harmony.

EQUIPMENT

- Bobsleighs are extremely expensive, high-technology machines made from aluminium and steel. The cockpit is fixed to 4 runners — the rear pair being fixed while the front ones can be steered by means of a rope-and-

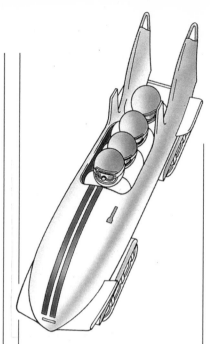

▲ *The man at the front of the four-man bobsleigh steers while the one at the back acts as a brakesman. All four members must lean together into turns and keep their heads in an aerodynamic line.*

pulley system. Two-rider bobs must not exceed 2.70 m (8 ft approx.) in length, 4-rider bobs, 3.80 m (12 ft approx.)
- As speeds of up to 150 km/h (93 mph) can be achieved, all team members are obliged to wear helmets. Most riders also wear goggles and spiked shoes, which enable them to get a good grip on the ice while starting.

TECHNICAL TERMS

ballast weights that can be bolted to sleds to make up the weight allowance
brakeman the rear member of the crew who orchestrates the start and is responsible for using the raked brake in emergencies
driver the front man who steers the sled

DID YOU KNOW?

The fastest recorded speed on a luge track was over 135km/h (84mph). This record is unofficial because it took place outside official international competition.

LUGE TOBOGGANING

Tobogganing of one sort or another dates back to the 16th century, and possibly even earlier. It started as a purely recreational sport in Europe and anything from trays to upturned tables were used as sleds to skid down snowy slopes. During the latter half of the last century, British tourists in Switzerland took tobogganing a step further and devised sled races down snow-covered roads. In 1879, two purpose-made toboggan tracks were constructed at Davos in Switzerland. A couple of years later a competition was held between the villagers of Davos and those of Klosters, a resort further down the mountain.

The first international toboggan racing event was held at Davos in 1883. It had competitors from six nations, including Australia! The sport, which was by now called 'luge tobogganing', had competitors riding feet-first on sleds, and proved so popular that it quickly spread from Switzerland to other Alpine countries. However it was not until 1955 that the first World Championships were held. Lugeing did not become an Olympic sport until 1964.

▼ *The Canadian 2-man team of Gasper and Benoit was the fastest North American pairing at the 1988 Winter Olympics.*

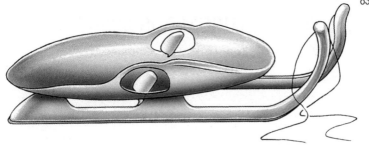

The ruling body of luge tobogganing is the Fédération Internationale de Luge de Course. The most important lugeing contests are those held at the Olympic Games, but it is still a recreational sport and Austrians, in particular, will sled happily down ice-clad roads for nothing more than pleasure.

▲ *The luge toboggan has a rigid frame but the curved runners respond even to light tugs on the reins.*

AIMS OF THE GAME

COMPETITION
● In the Olympics, there are 3 events — singles races for both men and women and doubles races (2 on a sled) for men. Most of the courses are artificially constructed and some double-up as bobsleigh tracks; courses are usually about 1000 m (1090 yd approx.) for men and 700 m (765 yd approx.) for women.
● Winners are those that complete 4 runs down the track in the fastest aggregate time.

SKILLS
● Luge tobogganers lie on their backs and go down a course feet-first. The sled itself can be steered either by shifting bodyweight from one side to the other or by pulling one of the reins. If the left-hand rein is pulled, the end of the left runner bites deeper into the ice and the sled consequently moves to the left. On fast sections of a course, a slight tilting of the head is enough to guide the sled in the required direction.
● Competitors always start sitting on their toboggans and push themselves down the slope using their hands, before adopting the classic flat-on-the-back position. This is often where milliseconds are gained, and serious competitors always concentrate on making a quick getaway.
● Speeds of up to 120 km/h (75 mph) are commonplace on fast runs, so a daredevil mentality is essential!

EQUIPMENT

● Modern luge toboggans usually comprise wooden runners surmounted by a glass fibre seat and can weigh anything up to 24 kg (53 lb approx.). The runners are made of steel and can be polished and waxed before an event. Heating the runners is not allowed in competitions.
● Competitors usually wear tight-fitting clothing that is aerodynamically efficient. Helmets are compulsory and most people also wear sleek visors that cut down wind resistance.
● To make up weight differentials within a competition, tobogganers at major events are allowed to carry lead weights around the waist — heavier people travel faster down icy slopes.

NORDIC SKIING

DID YOU KNOW?

The most famous cross-country ski race in the world is the Vasaloppet, held in Sweden every year. About 12,000 skiers take part and the race covers a distance of 89 km (55 miles approx.).

The oldest known skis date back some 5000 years or more and were found in Sweden. They were about 1 m (3 ft) in length — longer skis were developed in Norway some time later. Those ancient skis were used as simple but practical means of transport, but it is from this use that a whole host of competitive skiing events have evolved.

The first competitive skiing competition was a ski-jumping contest held in Norway in 1840. The first cross-country events were held in 1866. Both these forms of competitive skiing were pioneered by the Norwegians and are collectively called 'Nordic' skiing events. Alpine skiing did not follow until the 1880s.

The ruling body of Nordic skiing is the Fédération Internationale de Ski (FIS), which was formed in 1924, the same year that skiing was included in the first Winter Olympics. Second to the Olympics in importance are the Nordic Skiing World Championships, which are held every four years.

AIMS OF THE GAME

COMPETITION
Nordic skiing encompasses cross-country skiing and ski-jumping.

Cross-country skiing
● In major competitions, there are individual events for both men and women as well as relay races for both. Men race over 15-km (9-mile), 30-km (18-mile) and 50-km (31-mile) courses; women race over 5-km (3-mile), 10-km (6-mile) and 20-km (12-mile) courses. Relay races for men comprise 4 x 10-km (6-mile) courses and for women 4 x 5-km (3-mile) courses.
● In individual competitions, skiers start singly at 30-sec intervals and race against the clock. To ensure that no skier can take a short cut, all courses have a number of control points along their length and competitors have to pass through them all. The skier who completes the course in the fastest time wins.
● Relay races have mass starts; first-leg competitors line up together.

Change-overs between team-mates are usually a tap on the shoulder, but they have to take place within a designated area along the course. The winning team in a relay race is the one whose last skier crosses the finishing line first.

Ski-jumping
● In major championships, there are 2 categories of jump — 70 m (76 yd approx.) and 90 m (98 yd approx.). These lengths have nothing to do with the height of the jump towers (the ramps from which the jumpers launch themselves), but are estimates of the

▼ *Bindings that clip only at the toe enable Nordic skiers to take long strides. The co-ordinated use of leg, chest and arm muscles makes Nordic skiing one of the best aerobic exercises.*

distances that can be jumped from them. The towers themselves usually have 2 starting points — the higher one is used in the 90 m events. Ski-jumping is an exclusively male sport.
● Each skier is allowed 2 jumps and points are awarded for distance achieved and for style.
● The distance is measured from the lip of the take-off ramp to the point where the feet land. Special tables, which take into account the type of jump tower, are used to convert the distance into points.
● Style points are given by 5 judges who take into account control, balance and precision at 3 critical stages — take-off, flight and landing. A 'standing jump' is achieved when a skier takes off and lands with perfect balance. Style points are awarded on a predetermined scale.

● Ski-jumpers are not allowed to use poles to gain impetus down the slope (they would be a hazard anyway).
● The person who gains the most points after 2 jumps wins.

SKILLS
Cross-country skiing
● Cross-country skiing technique involves gliding along on one ski while pushing off with the other. Ski poles play an important role as they can be used to give extra thrust — this is especially important when going uphill.
● Cross-country skiers try to conserve energy by maintaining a steady rhythm — a good skier should be able to average about 16 km/h (10 mph).
● Before a race, competitors are allowed to wax their skis; choosing the right wax for the snow conditions can be a deciding factor in a race.

Ski-jumping

- On take-off from the ramp, a ski-jumper must use his legs as well as the impetus gained from the slope to launch himself high into the air. So as not to lose balance, he has to lean forwards. During the flight, he keeps his arms tight to his sides and his skis close together and parallel.
- Landing, the most dangerous part of a jump, has to be timed to perfection — the knees have to slacken at the exact moment of impact, otherwise disaster will follow.
- Courage is perhaps the most essential quality a ski-jumper needs — without it he will surely fail and fall.

EQUIPMENT

Cross-country skiing
- Cross-country skis are long and narrow with high upturns at the tips to allow them to ride over lumps and bumps in the snow; they usually weigh no more than 2 kg (4½ lb).
- Cross-country skiers wear light-weight shoes which are clipped into the bindings (shoe anchors on the skis) by the toe only. These bindings allow free movement of the heels so that a skier can 'walk' the skis.
- The ski poles used by cross-country racers are long and strong — they are used not just for keeping balance, but also for propulsion. Skiers use their poles in rhythm with their strides.

Ski-jumping
- The skis used for jumping are long and heavy and have grooves on the underside which ensure that they travel in a straight line. The boots, which provide substantial ankle support, are only clipped to the bindings at the toes; this enables a jumper to lean forwards during flight.
- Ski-jumpers usually wear protective helmets and goggles, and the clothing is skin-tight.

TECHNICAL TERMS

critical point a mark on the landing area of a ski-jump that signifies the end of the safe landing area
telemark stance the landing position in ski-jumping where one ski is placed slightly in front of the other (for better balance) while the knees and hips are bent; also a cross-country term describing a turn using that stance
vorlage the lean in ski-jumping where the body arches right over the skis

FAMOUS NAMES

The greatest ski-jumper of modern times is the Finn, Matti Nykanen. The 'Flying Finn' won a gold medal in the 90-m event in the 1982 World Championships. He won his first Olympic gold medal in 1984 in the 90-m event and, largely thanks to Nykanen's contribution, Finland won the team gold medal. Four years later he took both the 70-m and 90-m titles at the Olympic Games in Calgary.

The 1988 Games also saw the one Olympic appearance of Eddie 'The Eagle' Edwards of Great Britain. Edwards briefly became a celebrity with his borrowed equipment and ungainly jumps. Ski-jumping officials are taking steps to prevent others like him from competing — and getting hurt.

▶ *Stefan Spaeni of Switzerland demonstrates the aerodynamic ski-jumping technique in mid-flight. The skis are held parallel with their tips almost touching his nose, his body is straight and his arms are held by his sides to reduce drag.*

DID YOU KNOW?

Freestyle skiing events have become popular since 1980 and were given credibility at the 1988 Winter Olympic Games when they were introduced as demonstration events. There are 3 types of freestyle skiing: acrobatics down bumpy (mogul) slopes; acrobatics off short ski jumps; and 'ballet' skiing, usually performed to music.

ALPINE SKIING

Perhaps surprisingly, Alpine skiing (skiing down mountain slopes as opposed to skiing across flattish terrain) was unheard of until the 1880s. During the latter half of the 19th century, British tourists perennially flocked to Alpine resorts, not to ski, but to soak up healthy sunshine and clean air. It was an English pioneer of the tourist industry, Sir Henry Lunn (and later his son, Arnold), who saw the potential of organizing ski races down mountain slopes.

The first 'downhill' competition was run at Kitzbuhel in Austria in 1905. In 1922, Arnold Lunn devised the first slalom competition — a race that incorporated obstacles down a mountain slope. Today, there are four main Alpine events for both men and women — downhill, slalom, giant slalom and super giant slalom. In addition, there are combination

AIMS OF THE GAME

COMPETITION
Each of the 4 Alpine skiing events — downhill, slalom, giant slalom and super giant slalom — have different courses and different rules. These are explained below.

Downhill
● Courses for downhill racing are designed to test bravery and skill. For men, courses range from between 3000 m (1.8 miles approx.) to 4500 m (2¾ miles approx.) in length; for women, the courses are usually between 1500 m (1 mile approx.) and 2500 m (1½ miles approx.).

All courses follow a sharp descent, which must include a variety of gradients, bumps and jumps.

◀ *The downhill skier adjusts his weight onto the inner edges of his skis to negotiate a curve in the carefully designed course.*

events which include both downhill and the various types of slalom racing.

The international ruling body of amateur Alpine skiing is the Fédération Internationale de Ski (FIS). Some top amateur skiers have turned professional and ski for prize and appearance money. However, professional events are limited (mainly to the United States) and amateur competitions receive the bulk of publicity and corporate sponsorship.

The main amateur competitions are the Olympic Games, the World Championships (held at irregular intervals) and the World Cup races which comprise a series of events held every year in several different countries. Of all the competitions, the World Cup events are probably considered the most prestigious. In the World Cup, trophies are given to winners who accumulate the greatest number of points in each of the four disciplines.

> **DID YOU KNOW?**
>
> Downhill skiers will go to great lengths and expense to experience the ultimate thrill. 'Off-piste' skiing, away from groomed trails, offers excitement, and solitude. Helicopters in the Alps and the Canadian Rockies can be hired to take skiers to remote peaks.

● A series of 'gates', pairs of flags positioned not more than 8 m (9 yd) apart, outline the limits of the course and competitors have to stay within their confines. Officials are positioned at each set of gates to ensure that competitors go through all of them legitimately.

● Competitors are started individually — once the first skier has crossed the finishing line, the second is allowed off the starting block and so on. Competitors always race against the clock. In most competitions, each skier is allowed 2 runs down the course and the winner is the person who achieves the fastest time for the course on either of the 2 runs.

Slalom

● Slalom courses are appreciably shorter than those for downhill races and the vertical drop from start to finish is also less.

● Slalom courses are designed to test the skiers' ability to move quickly through turns and consequently all courses have a number of gates — between 45 and 75 — through which the skiers have to weave their way. On a good course, some gates will be narrow — as little as 3 m (10 ft approx.) apart — and others will be bunched together so that a skier's agility is tried to the limit.

● Competitors are started individually as for downhill races and the winner is the person who achieves the fastest aggregate time for 2 runs.

● 'Parallel slalom' events are occasionally competed in the World Cup series of events. These are organized on a knockout basis. Two competitors race each other down 2 similar courses. After the first race, the skiers swap courses and the winner — the person with the fastest overall time for the 2 races — goes through to the next round to challenge another skier. The overall winner is the person who has the fastest aggregate time for the final 2 races.

● 'Combined' events, which are held at the Olympic Games, combine results from slalom and downhill races. Points are awarded for the 2 types of race and the winner is the person who gains the highest overall score.

Giant slalom
● As the name suggests, this is a type of slalom racing. The courses are longer and faster with a greater vertical drop.
● The number of gates on a giant slalom course can vary greatly and usually depends upon the vertical drop of the course.
● Skiers race against the clock and are allowed 2 runs. The winner is the person with the fastest aggregate time.

Super giant slalom (Super-G)
● The super giant slalom was first raced in 1982. Something of a cross between downhill racing and giant slalom racing, it tests high-speed skiing through twists and turns.
● Racers ski against the clock. The person with the fastest aggregate time for 2 runs down the course wins.

▲ *Franz Heinzer, seen here in the downhill event of the 1991 World Championships at Saalbach, Austria, is one of the brightest hopes of the perennially strong Swiss Alpine team.*

SKILLS
● Downhill racing — the most glamorous and prestigious of the Alpine events — requires steel nerves, an acute sense of balance, and the ability to 'read' a course — that is, to find the fastest way down without committing suicide!
● On fast, straight sections of a course, a downhiller will crouch low to lessen wind resistance; on a curve, he (or she) will lean inwards and dig the ski edges tight into the snow or ice to get enough purchase to make their turn. On bumpy sections, skiers maintain balance by shifting body weight and by using ski poles.
● Slalom skiing requires a calm, precise temperament rather than the 'live-or-die' attitude that downhill skiers adopt. It demands different technical skills from those used in downhill

racing; a good slalom skier will maintain an apparently effortless rhythm while weaving through the gates. Flexibility and smooth movements are what slalom skiing is all about — the most successful slalom skiers appear to be in no great hurry, whereas those who aggressively hurtle down often fail.

● Ingredients for success in the giant slalom and super giant slalom comprise an amalgamation of those needed for downhill and ordinary slalom racing. The faster a race is, the more nerve is required; the more gates there are, the more technical skill comes into play.

EQUIPMENT

● Skis are the most essential piece of equipment. Most modern skis are usually made of reinforced glass fibre and come in many widths, thicknesses and lengths. As a rule, downhill racers prefer heavy skis that are about 2 m

(6 ½ ft) long; slalom skiers usually use shorter skis for easier turning. However, there are no hard and fast rules and serious competitors choose skis according to the conditions — long skis for fast courses, shorter skis for tricky tracks.

● Boots are normally made from rigid plastic and reach half-way up the calves. They are clipped into toe and heel 'bindings' (fastenings) on the skis. Bindings release if a skier falls.

▲ Goggles are an essential piece of equipment; most types are tinted to reduce the dazzling glare that can be reflected from snow.

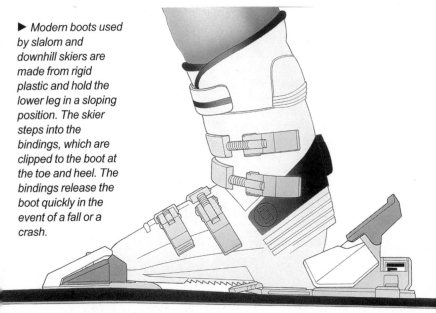

▶ Modern boots used by slalom and downhill skiers are made from rigid plastic and hold the lower leg in a sloping position. The skier steps into the bindings, which are clipped to the boot at the toe and heel. The bindings release the boot quickly in the event of a fall or a crash.

● Ski poles are also made from reinforced plastic. Downhill poles are often curved so that they can be swept cleanly behind the body; slalom ski poles are usually straighter so that they can provide more direct support.

● Downhill racers prefer tight-fitting clothing that offers little wind-resistance; slalom skiers wear looser-fitting gear that allows freedom of movement. Downhill racers are obliged to wear helmets, and goggles are usually worn by all Alpine skiers to protect the eyes from flying fragments of snow and ice.

TECHNICAL TERMS

mogul hard mound of snow on a ski slope
piste prepared track of snow, often compacted by special machines
schuss a fast stretch of course

FAMOUS VENUES

World Cup events in all 4 disciplines are held in the following countries:
Argentina
Austria
Bulgaria
Canada
Czechoslovakia
France
Germany
Italy
Japan
Norway
Poland
Spain
Sweden
Switzerland
United States
Yugoslavia

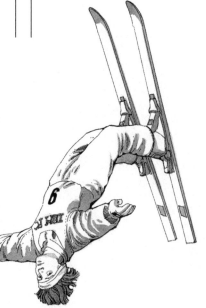

▼ Freestyle skiing, in which artistic and acrobatic skills are tested, is a recent innovation. Aerial skiing, below, is the most dramatic of freestyle skiing. In this event skiers jump off a platform and perform flips and spins in mid-air. The other freestyle forms are called mogul and ballet.

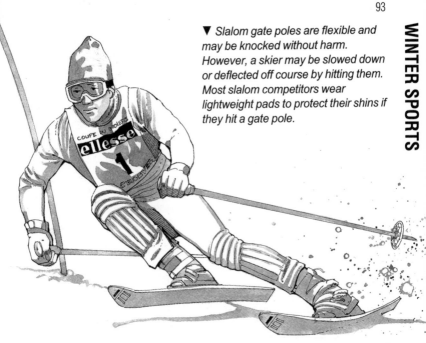

▼ *Slalom gate poles are flexible and may be knocked without harm. However, a skier may be slowed down or deflected off course by hitting them. Most slalom competitors wear lightweight pads to protect their shins if they hit a gate pole.*

FAMOUS NAMES

Jean-Claude Killy (France)
Killy is considered to have been the most accomplished all-round skier of modern times. After becoming a folk legend in France, he turned professional and became a leading figure in organizing the 1992 Winter Olympics in his home town of Albertville in France. At his peak, he won:
- 3 gold medals at the 1968 Olympic Games (downhill, slalom, giant slalom);
- 2 overall titles in the World Cup 1967-68);
- 6 titles in the World Championships.

Ingemar Stenmark (Sweden)
Stenmark is undoubtedly the best slalom skier of all time. An apparently shy man, he showed his mettle on the piste. He dominated the slalom world at the same time as his compatriot Bjorn Borg ruled tennis. His achievements are:
- 2 gold medals at the 1980 Olympic Games;
- 3 overall titles in the World Cup (1976/77/78);
- 3 titles in the World Championships.

Annemarie Moser-Proell (Austria)
It is extremely unlikely that any person — male or female — will ever surpass Moser-Proell's record:
- gold medal at the 1980 Olympic Games (downhill);
- 6 overall titles in the World Cup (1971/72/73//74/75/79);
- 4 titles in the World Championships.

Pirmin Zurbriggen (Switzerland)
The modest hotelier was a dominant downhill and combined skier in the 1980s. He won:
- a gold medal at the 1988 Olympic Games;
- 4 overall titles in the World Cup (1984/87/88/90).

BIATHLON

Biathlon combines cross-country skiing with smallbore rifle shooting. It is a comparatively new sport and only gained Olympic status in 1960. It is essentially a military sport which was devised by northern European nations. Not surprisingly, most of its leading exponents are army personnel. The countries with the best records in biathlon are the USSR, Germany and Finland.

Biathlon's ruling body is the Union Internationale de Pentathlon Moderne et Biathlon. Annual World Championships are held in addition to events at the Olympic Games.

AIMS OF THE GAME

COMPETITION
There are 4 main events. For men these comprise the 20 km (12½ mile approx.) individual race, the 10 km (6 mile approx.) sprint race, the 4 x 7.5 km (4½ mile approx.) relay and the 20 km (12 mile) team race. For women (in the World Championships only) there are the 10 km (6 mile approx.) individual race, the 5 km (3 mile approx.) sprint, the 3 x 5 km relay and the 15 km (9 mile approx.) team race. Competitors carry their rifles and ammunition when skiing.

Individual events
● In major events, competitors are started at 1-min intervals.
● During a race, over a cross-country course (see page 54), each competitor has to stop 4 times at a 50 m (54 yd approx.) rifle range to fire 5 shots at 5 solid targets. A penalty point of 1 min is imposed for each target missed. At 2 of the ranges, shots are fired from a prone position; at the other 2 they are fired while standing.
● The winner is the person with the fastest time after penalty points have been added.

Sprint events
● As with the longer events, competitors are started individually at set intervals. The course is also a cross-country one.
● There are only 2 shooting sessions in sprint events — one prone, the other standing. If a competitor fails to hit a target, he or she must ski round a penalty loop about 150 m (164 yd) long.
● The winner is the person who finishes in the fastest time.

Relay races
● Relay races have massed starts with the competitors on the first leg being started together by a gun.
● Each competitor has to shoot twice, once prone and once standing. Competitors fire 8 shots at each set of 5 targets and for each one missed, he or she has to ski a penalty loop as in the sprint events. Penalty points are added to a competitor's time if all 8 shots are not fired.
● Change-overs from one skier to another have to take place within a specially designated area. A tap on the shoulder is sufficient contact between team-mates.
● The team with the fastest overall time is the winner.

▲ The rifle must not be automatic or semi-automatic and its magazine should not be capable of holding more than five rounds. Other regulations restrict the type of sights that can be used – telescopic sights are not allowed.

Team races
● Teams of 4 are started at 2-min intervals and are obliged to ski together. Each member fires 5 shots once, while the other 3 team-mates wait in a pen. The penalty for a miss involves the whole team skiing around a 300 m (330 yd) penalty loop.
● The team with the fastest overall time wins.

SKILLS
● Biathlon is a test of stamina, skiing skills and tactical ability. A competitor must go flat out while skiing, but then has to change the pace completely, in order to be calm and steady when shooting.

EQUIPMENT

● There are few restrictions on clothing and most competitors prefer loose-fitting gear that facilitates easy movement while both skiing and shooting. Some use cross-country racing suits, which are close-fitting but flexible.
● The rifles used are restricted to 5.6 mm (.22 in) calibre. Automatic or semi-automatic weapons are forbidden from all events.

▲ A competitor shooting prone has to support the rifle with his or her hands – resting it on the ground is not allowed.

▲ Competitors can take off their skis when shooting but this can cost valuable time. When firing in the standing position, they stand at right angles to the target. Ski poles are always kept to hand.

WATER SPORTS

Most of the well-known water sports can be enjoyed either as pastimes or as serious competitive events. All of them — apart from swimming — require some equipment but it is often possible to hire or borrow it. A few, most notably powerboating, require such an outlay that they are beyond the means of the average person.

SWIMMING

Swimming has been appreciated for its thera-peutic effects for several thousand years. The Ancient Egyptians, Greeks, Etruscans and Romans included swimming in military training. The Romans enjoyed it so much that they built large-scale swimming pools, some of which were heated. Competitive swimming is reputed to have started in Japan about 2000 years ago but it did not catch on in Europe until the middle of the 19th century.

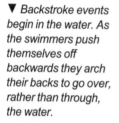

▼ *Backstroke events begin in the water. As the swimmers push themselves off backwards they arch their backs to go over, rather than through, the water.*

There are four recognized swimming strokes in competitions. Breaststroke is the slowest stroke and

over the centuries front crawl and back crawl (now known as backstroke) were developed. The 'youngest' stroke, butterfly, was not recognized as an official stroke until as recently as 1952. Medley events, which can be swum either individually or as team races, combine all four strokes. In 'freestyle' events, competitors are theoretically permitted to chose any stroke they wish but most chose front crawl as it is the fastest.

Swimming is an amateur sport enjoyed by women and men alike. Competition events range from 50 m to 1500 m in length but specialists tackle ultra-long distances such as the English Channel. The world governing body is the Fédération Internationale de Natation Amateur (FINA), which was founded in 1908. FINA introduced competition rules and the first world record list. The first modern Olympic Games, held in Athens in 1896, hosted a few swimming events and ever since the sport has been a major feature. Second in importance to the Olympics are the four-yearly World Championships, which were first held in 1973.

DID YOU KNOW?

Johnny Weissmuller of the United States won 5 Olympic gold medals in 1924 and 1928 and went on to gain international fame as an actor playing Tarzan.

AIMS OF THE GAME

COMPETITION
In major competitions, a number of regulations, for competitors and organizers alike, are enforced.
● A championship pool must be exactly 50 m (54.7 yd approx.) long and at least 21 m (23 yd approx.) wide.
● The pool must be divided into 8 lanes which have to be marked on the surface with strings of perforated 'anti-turbulence' floats, and with lines on the bottom of the pool to show the middle of each lane.
● Competitors have to wear swimsuits that conform to FINA rules. No swimming aids are allowed. Bathing caps may be worn.
● The fastest swimmers — decided either by preliminary heats or on previous times — get the centremost lanes; the slowest swimmers are relegated to the 2 outside lanes which are more turbulent during a race. Top events use a 10-lane pool, with the 2 outermost lanes left empty.
● In breaststroke, freestyle (front crawl) and butterfly races, all competitors start by diving into the water off blocks; in backstroke, competitors start in the water. All races are started by just 2 commands — 'take your marks' and 'go' ('go' is usually signalled by a starting gun).
● The winner of a race is the person who finishes first without breaking any of the rules governing the stroke. This may sound obvious but gold medals have been lost by competitors who have failed to turn correctly or who have abused the rules in some way.
● In addition, there are regulations to determine the temperature of the water (24°C/75°F), starting and timing equipment, and the depth of the water.

Breaststroke

More rules govern breaststroke than any of the other 3 strokes. This is because people have found loopholes in the regulations which have enabled them to swim faster unfairly.

● The swimmer must keep his or her shoulders parallel to the surface of the water and must swim 'on the breast' at all times (a loophole in this law was found, and some competitors used to swim side-stroke, a variation of breaststroke). The only time a swimmer is allowed to breach this rule is at the turn when a twisting movement is permitted.

● Both arms must be worked together, from the front to the back, underwater, and the legs must also work simultaneously beneath the surface, either in a 'wedge-kick' or in the more sophisticated 'whip-kick'.

● When turning, and again at the end of a race, a swimmer must touch the wall with both hands. (Great Britain's Olympic champion, Adrian Moorehouse, was once denied a medal in a major championship because he failed to touch the wall of the pool with both hands.)

● Apart from at the start of the race and during turns, part of the head must break the water surface on each stroke. (Thirty years ago, breaststrokers found that swimming under the surface was swifter than swimming on top!)

Freestyle (front crawl)

This is the fastest, and most familiar, of all strokes.

● Unlike breaststroke where much of the power comes from the leg kick, freestyle relies more heavily on the arms. The arms are used alternately in an overarm motion and are drawn through the water under the body while the legs are kicked 2, 4 or 6 times for each stroke.

● When turning or finishing, a swimmer can touch the wall with any part of the body; in turns this is most often the legs.

Backstroke

● Backstroke is unusual in that it is the only stroke where competitors actually start the race in the water. The one essential rule is that competitors have to swim on their backs at all times, except when they are turning.

● During a turn, a backstroke swimmer is allowed to touch the wall with any part of the body before pushing off.

Butterfly

This is the hardest stroke of all to master but it is second only to freestyle in speed despite being a variation of breaststroke. The butterfly stroke can look smooth and graceful if performed properly.

● The arms are moved together in an overarm motion — no alternate movements are allowed. The feet and legs are usually worked in an up-and-down 'dolphin kick' with the knees kept close together, but a 'breaststroke kick' is permitted under the regulations.

● At a turn, and when finishing, both hands must touch the wall.

Medley races

● In an individual medley race, each competitor has to swim 1 or 2 lengths using each of the 4 strokes. The usual order is butterfly, backstroke, breaststroke, freestyle.

● In relay medleys, 4 individuals from a team each use one of the four different strokes. The traditional order is backstroke, breaststroke, butterfly and freestyle.

SKILLS

● For all but backstroke specialists, the racing dive is crucial, especially in short sprint races where split seconds

▲ *The forward drive in breaststroke comes from both legs and arms. The legs power the shoulders out of the water; the arms are pulled back in the water in a sweeping motion.*

count for a great deal. A good racing dive is shallow, fast and clean, although some breaststrokers dive deeper to take advantage of the fact that they are entitled to underwater actions on the first stroke.

In backstroke, where competitors start in the water, a good swimmer will use his or her legs to launch off the wall into an arched backwards dive.

● Turns can also decide who wins a race. The 'flip' or 'tumble turn' is used in freestyle and sometimes in backstroke. With this, a swimmer somersaults just before reaching the end of the pool and, once he or she has turned, pushes off the wall with the legs. With breaststroke and butterfly, both hands have to touch the wall, so the turning is slower.

▼ *Freestyle (front crawl) swimming synchronizes the beats of the kick to the number of arm strokes. Sprinters use 6 beats per stroke; over longer distances swimmers kick 2 or 4 times per stroke.*

● Rhythm is important to all kinds of swimming. For example in breaststroke arms and legs have to be co-ordinated. A breathing rhythm is also important, particularly in freestyle and butterfly, where the head is kept partially submerged for several strokes. Breathing has to be co-ordinated with what the arms are doing.

● Swimming itself is excellent exercise, but many competitors use other techniques, such as weight training, to build strength. They take care not to gain bulk at the expense of suppleness — essential to all strokes.

EQUIPMENT

● In competition, swimsuits have to be 'modest', as judged by a referee. They hug the body tightly so that they do not catch any water and increase drag.

● Goggles are frequently worn by competitors for two reasons. First, they protect the eyes and second, they enable people to see underwater — important when coming up to a turn or when assessing how other swimmers are progressing in the race.

● Swimming hats are often worn by men as well as women. They dramatically reduce water resistance created even by short hair.

FOR THE RECORD

SYNCHRONIZED SWIMMING
Synchronized swimming was adopted as an Olympic sport in 1984. It is a predominantly female sport and has been described as 'ballet in water'. Events are held for individuals, duets and teams.

Competitions usually comprise 2 sections. In the first section, competitors have to perform 6 pre-determined figures which are assessed by a panel of judges. The second section, the routine section, is performed to music and has to be completed within a given period of time. In this section judges look for artistic interpretation as well as sheer skill. At the end of a competition, points for both figures and routines are added together and the winners are those with the highest total once penalty points (deducted for such things as exceeding time limits) have been taken into account.

Although synchronized swimming has been derided by the popular press, it is an extremely skilful sport which requires self-control, a musical ear, and a total mastery of swimming techniques. Leading nations are the United States, Canada and Japan.

FAMOUS NAMES

Matt Biondi (US) 5 Olympic gold medals (all in 1988)

Gertrude Ederle (US) the first woman to swim the English Channel (1926); she also broke the men's record.

Dawn Fraser (AUS) 4 gold medals over 3 Olympic Games (1956, 1960, 1964)

Michael Gross (FRG) 3 Olympic gold medals over 3 different events (1984, 1988)

Roland Matthes (GDR) 7 Olympic medals, including 4 gold, in 1968 and 1972

Kristin Otto (GDR) 6 Olympic gold medals (all in 1988)

Don Schollander (US) 4 Olympic gold medals in 1964, and a gold medal and a silver medal in 1968

Mark Spitz (US) 9 Olympic gold medals (2 in 1968, 7 in 1972); attempted a comeback in 1991

Matthew Webb (GB) the first person to swim the English Channel (1875)

Johnny Weissmuller (US) 5 Olympic gold medals and 67 world records between 1920 and 1928

David Wilkie (GB) smashed the 200 m breaststroke world record to take the Olympic gold in 1976.

▲ *In backstroke the arms are worked alternately backwards over the shoulders and the legs kicked up and down as in freestyle. The head is kept back low in the water, so that the body stays level.*

FOR THE RECORD

OLYMPIC SWIMMING EVENTS
50 m (all 4 strokes)
100 m freestyle
200 m freestyle
400 m freestyle
800 m freestyle (women only)
1500 m freestyle (men only)
100 m backstroke
200 m backstroke
100 m breaststroke
200 m breaststroke
100 m butterfly
200 m butterfly
200 m individual medley
400 m individual medley
4x100 m freestyle relay
4x200 m freestyle relay (men only)
4x100 m medley relay

▼ *Butterfly is the most difficult stroke — and also the most tiring. The arms are moved together over head and the legs are worked in a rhythmical 'dolphin kick'.*

DID YOU KNOW?

A seaside resort near Acapulco in Mexico is famous for its fearless divers who regularly plunge off rocky cliffs into surf more than 30 m (100 ft) below to entertain tourists.

DIVING

Diving is as old as swimming but it did not become an organized or recognized sport until the end of the 19th century. The first Olympic event, for men only, was held in 1904 at the St Louis Games. By all accounts rules were somewhat haphazard in those days and the German team complained bitterly that George Sheldon, an American, was awarded the gold medal. The Americans reckoned that it was crucially important how a diver entered the water; the Germans on the other hand thought that the difficulty of a dive was more relevant, even if it meant that a diver ended up doing a bellyflop on the water. The rules and marking systems have been clarified since then, and there are now two categories of diving — springboard and highboard.

The ruling body of diving is the same as for swimming and water polo — the Fédération Internationale de Natation Amateur (FINA). The most coveted prizes for both men and women are awarded at the Olympic Games, but medals given at the World Championships, which are run every four years, are also prestigious.

AIMS OF THE GAME

COMPETITION
● In major competitions, only 3-m and 10-m boards are used. The 3-m board is flexible and is 3-m (10 ft approx.) above the level of the water. The rigid 10-m board stands 10 m (11 yd approx.) above the water.
● Many different dives are permitted by FINA and each one has a tariff value. For example a difficult dive might have a tariff of 8 and an easier one a tariff of 3.5. After points from 0 to 10 have been awarded for a dive by each of the judges (usually 7), the highest and lowest marks are discarded and the rest are added together. This total is then multiplied by the tariff figure to give a final mark.

● Events are organized as follows:
- men's springboard — 5 dives which do not exceed a total tariff value of more than 9.5 followed by 6 dives which do not have a tariff limit.
- men's highboard — 4 dives which do not exceed a total tariff value of 7.5 and 6 dives with unlimited tariff values.
- women's springboard — 5 dives which do not exceed a total tariff value of 9.5 followed by 5 dives which have unlimited tariffs.
- women's highboard — 4 dives with tariffs that do not exceed a total of 7.5 and 4 dives with unlimited tariff values.
● The winner of a competition is the person with the highest tally after all the dives have been completed. Divers are free to compete in both highboard and springboard sections.

▲ *The pike position is used in dives off springboards and highboards. Legs must be kept together and extended if the diver is to earn full marks.*

SKILLS

● In both types of diving, judges assess all stages — the start, run-up, flight and entry into the water. This means that a diver has to be in control throughout and must remain balanced at all stages.

● In many respects, many of the movements in diving are similar to those of gymnastics — tucks, pikes, somersaults and so on — but they have to be carried out at lightning speed before the diver enters the water with a smooth entry.

● Some of the most dangerous dives are reverses, where the diver leaps backwards from the board and begins the movements facing the board. Reverses increase the overall tariff value of a set of movements.

PERSONALITY PROFILE

Greg Louganis

Probably the greatest of all modern divers is the American Greg Louganis who won 5 World Championship competitions and 4 Olympic gold medals. Born in California in 1960, Louganis had a traumatic childhood: he was given up by his parents when he was a baby and later adopted. After he learned that he was dyslexic, he left school early and took to drugs and alcohol. When he was 16, he was discovered by an ex-Olympic Champion, Samuel Lee, who started to coach him in diving. That year he came 16th in springboard, and second in highboard at the 1976 Olympic Games in Montreal. He won his first 2 Olympic gold medals at the 1984 Los Angeles Games and successfully defended both the highboard and springboard titles 4 years later. In the springboard event in Seoul, Louganis cut his head open on the board while performing a reverse dive. He went on to take the gold medal with his head still bandaged. He retired from diving in 1988 to pursue a career in acting.

DID YOU KNOW?

Rafting is becoming an increasingly popular pastime. In this sport, 10 or so people, armed with paddles and protected by helmets and life jackets, work as a team to steer an inflatable raft through the rapids and gorges of a fast-flowing river.

CANOEING

The first canoes date back to prehistoric times and were made from hollowed-out tree trunks. Modern competition canoes are very different from dugouts, however, and are divided into two classes — kayaks and open canoes.

Traditional kayaks were, and still are, made by Eskimos from seal skins strapped and greased over bone frames. Competition kayaks, although moulded from glass fibre, still imitate the arrow-shaped profile of the originals. The tops of competition kayaks are completely covered apart from the holes in which one, two, three or four canoeists sit and paddle, depending on the size of the canoe.

Open canoes are derived from the light birch-bark boats that were used by North American Indians and, unlike kayaks, they are open. The largest ones are designed to be paddled by eight people.

Canoeing has long been a popular amateur sport in North America but only became known in Europe in the latter half of the 19th century. The first Olympic canoe races were held in 1936 and the ruling body of the sport is the International Canoe Federation, formed in 1924.

▼ *A 'spray deck' sealed to the kayak opening keeps water out of the craft.*

AIMS OF THE GAME

COMPETITION
Separate events are held for both kayak and open (formerly Canadian) canoe classes. In the Olympic Games, races are usually held on flat water (such as a lake) over distances ranging from 500 m (550 yds approx.) to 10,000 m (6¼ miles approx.). In other championships, slalom, wildwater and marathon events are held.

A kayak with 4 paddlers is referred to as a K4, an open canoe with 2 paddlers is called a C2. Individual and team races are held for both men and women.
● In flat water races competitors stay in lanes. Heats lead to a final.
● Slalom races are usually about 800 m (880 yd approx.) long and are held on rivers. Competitors start at intervals and negotiate up to 30 slalom gates. Penalty time points, from 10 to 50 sec, are incurred for touching, or failing to go through, a gate. The winner is the person with the fastest time after penalty points have been added.
● Wildwater races are similar to slalom races except that there are no gates along a turbulent stretch of river.
● Marathon races — no shorter than 15 km (9 miles approx.) for women and 20 km (12½ miles approx.) for men — have a massed start and the winner is the one first past the finishing line.

▲ *Powerful arms and a good sense of balance are essential when paddling a Canadian canoe. A kneeling pad may be used.*

SKILLS
● Different paddling techniques are required for kayak and open canoe racing. Kayak canoeists sit down and use double-bladed paddles whereas single-bladed paddles wielded from a kneeling position are used in open canoes.
● All types of canoeing demand strength, particularly in the upper body and arms. Serious competitors are among the fittest of all athletes.

EQUIPMENT

● Little special equipment is required for sprint racing but a safety helmet and a life-jacket have to be worn by competitors in slalom and wildwater races.

TECHNICAL TERMS

deck the top of a kayak
Eskimo roll a technique used to right a capsized kayak
spray deck a waterproof garment that seals a canoeist into a kayak so that water cannot enter the boat
Telemark turn a swift turn in which the paddle is used as a pivot

ROWING

▼ *Rowing can be either a fiercely contested sport or a pleasurable pastime. This print from the 19th century shows scullers entertaining fashionable lady friends.*

Rowing of one kind or another is almost as old as the first boat, but it did not become a competitive sport until the 18th century. Although continental Europeans were the first to adopt rowing as a sport, Americans were quick to follow and at the start of the 19th century, rowing was a popular pastime at schools and colleges on both sides of the Atlantic. The sport developed as a competition for gentlemen.

DID YOU KNOW?

The most famous rowing race in the world — the annual Oxford and Cambridge Boat Race — is one of the world's few races rowed on tidal water. Two crews from the universities race each other along the Thames River from Putney to Mortlake over a course that is 4 miles, 374 yards (6.78 km) long and includes several bends in the river. The race was first rowed in 1829.

The early racing boats were crude in comparison to the sleekly designed boats used today. Until the mid-19th century racing boats were comparatively broad (and therefore slow) and oarsmen sat on stationary seats. However, the introduction of rowlocks supported on outriggers meant that the boats could be made slimmer, and sliding seats enabled rowers to maintain a powerful rhythm without unduly straining their backs. Top-class contemporary racing boats cost more than the average house to design and produce, and can take many months, if not years, to make. When it comes to designing boats, engineers try to make them as light and as water-dynamic as possible, sometimes at the cost of being realistic — several 'super boats' have capsized before reaching the finish line!

Although rowing is nominally an amateur sport enjoyed by both women and men, like athletics it has faced the threat of drug abuse in recent years. Strict regulations ensure that no rower gets an artificial advantage in strength or stamina. The international ruling body is the Fédération Internationale des Sociétés d'Aviron (FISA) which was founded in 1892 and whose headquarters are in Switzerland.

▲ *A quadruple sculling team straining at the oars during the 1991 Henley Royal Regatta on the Thames. The Regatta was first held in 1839.*

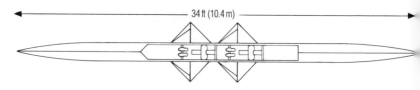

← 34 ft (10.4 m) →

AIMS OF THE GAME

COMPETITION
- There are 2 forms of rowing —
rowing proper and sculling. In rowing,
each woman or man uses a single,
double-handed oar whereas in sculling,
a rower uses 2 oars — one held in each
hand.
- Both rowing and sculling events can
be held on different types of water. In
the Olympics — the premier
international competition — and
several other major events, races are
over flat (non-flowing) water. For many
such competitions, shallow artificial
lakes are built. However, important and
prestigious events are also held on
flowing rivers: these can be either one-
versus-one or contests known as 'head'
races (see below).
- There are many different categories
for rowing and sculling. Some rowing
categories allow for the provision of a
cox to set the pace. The most important
categories are:
- single sculls;
- double sculls;
- quadruple sculls;
- coxless pair (rowing);
- coxed pair (rowing);
- coxless four (rowing);
- coxed four (rowing);
- and coxed eight (rowing).

Flat water races
- For women, the standard length for
a flat water race is 1000 m (1100 yd
approx.); for men, 2000m (2200 yd
approx.).

▲ *An overhead view shows the
streamlined design of this double
scull.*

- Courses have to be dead straight
and crews have to stay in their
designated lanes (there are usually 6)
for the duration of each race. In major
competitions where there are many
teams competing for a prize,
eliminating heats are run before the
final. The first person, or crew, past the
finish line wins.

River races
- Most of the rivers that host rowing
races only have room for 2 or 3 boats
abreast, so competitions are won
through a series of heats: the winner of
a final is the overall winner of an event.
This type of racing is commonly called
'regatta' racing and festivities along the
river banks accompany the rowing.
- 'Head' races along a river follow a
unique format. Crews — only 'eights'
usually take part in a head race — are
unleashed from a starting point at
regular intervals about 10 or 20 sec
apart. The winning crew is the one that
finishes in the fastest time, but a major
part of the entertainment is what
happens during the race — bumps
between boats and similar mishaps are
cheered by spectators along the banks.
The victorious team is awarded the title
'Head of the River'. Although head
rowing sounds as if it is an exclusively
British pastime, it is in fact enjoyed in
many other countries such as Australia,
the United States and Germany.

SKILLS

● Rowing is one of the most physically demanding of all sports. The arm and chest muscles are the most used, but without powerful leg and stomach muscles as well an aspiring rower will not get far. In addition, any rower of any category must have enough stamina to survive a course while going flat out.

● A sound sense of rhythm is crucial for solitary scullers and crews alike. An imaginary metronome — 'in-out, in-out' — must tick within an oarsman or he (or she) will rapidly lose pace. With a crew, all members have to tick with the same rhythm — those crews with the most powerful, systematic timing are usually winners. In coxed boats, it is down to the cox, a lightweight person, to dictate the pace and rhythm of the crew as well as to steer the boat. Coxes are often underrated — a good cox will know how fast to let his (or her) crew start a race, when to let it relax in the middle, and when to put on a burst of speed towards the end. If a cox mismanages a crew, the strongest member will outrow the weakest and disrupt the rhythm.

EQUIPMENT

Rowing requires little equipment beyond a boat and an oar or scull; these are usually provided by a club or team as both are beyond the means of the average person. The only additional essentials are a pair of rowing shoes (established members of a crew have their shoes screwed to the footplate within a boat as a sign of permanence) and possibly a pair of shorts with a padded seat.

TECHNICAL TERMS

bow the front of a boat; alternatively the title given to the person who rows at the front of a crew
feathering a skill which involves turning the blade of an oar parallel to the water so that it does not catch the wind on the backstroke
stroke the name given to the person who rows at the back of a crew, often the strongest rower

▼ *The rigger extension and sliding seats of modern rowing boats increase the power of each stroke.*

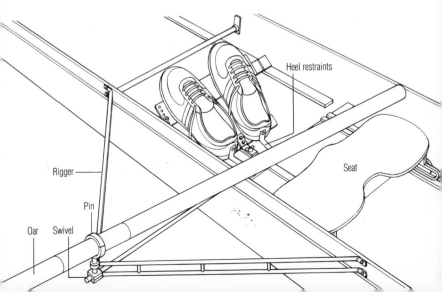

Heel restraints

Rigger

Pin

Oar   Swivel

Seat

DID YOU KNOW?

The **America's Cup** is the most famous of all yachting trophies. It was first awarded in 1851 to the schooner *America* for winning a race around the Isle of Wight. The owner of the boat donated the silver cup to the New York Yacht Club in 1857 and he offered it later as a challenge prize to be won every 3 years (the number of years is now variable). Until 1983, when *Australia II* won the challenge, the cup had always been won by an American boat. In 1987, *Stars and Stripes* regained the America's Cup for the United States and retained it in 1988.

The **Whitbread Round the World Race** is held every 4 years and is open to several classes of boat. The race consists of 4 stages, which take about 6 months to complete.

SAILING

People have been sailing boats for many thousands of years and there is no known date for when the first sail was rigged up on a boat to harness wind power. In many parts of the world sailing boats are still used much as they were centuries ago — for fishing, for pleasure and as an efficient means of travelling. Competitive sailing as it is today did not come into being until the beginning of the 19th century. Small sailing boats were then referred to as yachts; the term derives from a Dutch word meaning a 'fast pirate ship'. Nowadays the word 'yacht' can be confusing. The turbine-driven Royal Yacht *Britannia* is an ocean liner that carries a crew of dozens; at the other extreme, one-person dinghies are also described as yachts. For the purposes of this book, the word 'yacht' is used to describe sailing boats only.

One of the first sailing clubs to be formed was the Royal Yacht Squadron (RYS). In 1812 it established its headquarters on the Isle of Wight, England. The RYS organized races for large sailing ships — schooners. One of these races evolved into the America's Cup. It was not until the Yacht Racing Association was formed in England some 50 years later that smaller craft had a chance to compete against each other in formal competition.

Today, there are literally hundreds of types of yacht, and races can be over just a few kilometres or right the way round the globe. However, for national teams and for individuals representing their countries, the events in the Olympics remain the most prestigious of all competitions. Other important races include the Singlehanded Transatlantic Race, the Admiral's Cup, the America's Cup and the Round the World Race. The ruling body for the sport is the International Yacht Racing Union, but some major competitions have rules and regulations laid down by independent organizations.

Yachting competitions are open to women at all levels. A British all-women crew finished strongly in the 1990 Whitbread Round the World Race, defying male sceptics.

▲ *Yachts use a balloon-shaped sail called a spinnaker when sailing with the wind. It is quickly lowered when the yacht changes direction.*

AIMS OF THE GAME

COMPETITION
● For the purposes of most competitions, boats are separated into 3 categories:
- the 'one-design' category, where all the craft are identical;
- the 'development' category, where modifications to the sail, hull and keel are permitted to encourage faster boats;
- the 'formula' category where boats are built to the so-called International Off-shore Rule. In this category certain measurements, such as the size of the sails and the length of a boat, are converted through a formula to provide a 'rating'. When boats of different ratings compete against each other, a handicap system is used so that all boats compete on equal terms.

Within each of these categories there are many boat 'classes', each named after a different size and shape of boat. For example, a Finn class boat is a small single-hulled yacht manned by just one person, a Tornado class boat is a large catamaran manned by a crew of 2.

▼ An Olympic 'triangle' course is marked by buoys. It tests a crew's ability to sail with the wind behind, in front or to the side.

● Courses for yacht racing vary enormously and there is no standard design. Some races can be round an island (such as the Isle of Wight) or across the Atlantic, but the 'Olympic course' is the one most commonly used because it provides a thorough test of seamanship. An Olympic course comprises a triangle marked out by buoys. The distances between the buoys can vary according to the design committee's preference and the number of times competitors have to round the buoys may also vary. In general, competitors have to complete one triangle followed by one and a half laps round just 2 buoys (see diagram below).
● Competitions on an Olympic course are only held between similar classes of boat, so a Finn will not race against a Tornado. Each competition usually consists of several races round the course. The winner of each race is awarded 0 points, second place is given 3 points and third place 5.7 points. The ultimate winner for a class is the boat and crew that have amassed the fewest number of points over the statutory number of races.

SKILLS
● In boats where there is more than one crew member, there is always a skipper and it is up to him or her to

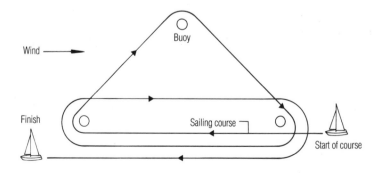

make the decisions and plan the tactics. Every other crew member's specific tasks are carried out on a signal from the skipper. The most successful crews are often those that have worked together for some time and know each other well.

● Sailing requires immense skill, especially when tacking — sailing into the wind on a zig-zag course. Timing exactly when to change course can be crucial and a skipper must be a fair judge of both the wind and water conditions — adjusting the sails to catch the wind efficiently and reacting quickly is no mean task.

EQUIPMENT

● To protect themselves from wind, water and spray, most sailors wear waterproof clothing. Oilskins (made from welded plastic these days) are usually preferred. In cold weather, some sailors wear wetsuits, which afford insulated protection even if the boat capsizes.

● Life-jackets are essential for novices or weak swimmers.

● Sailing boots have slightly ribbed soles to grip the deck. They should be light, flexible and waterproof.

● Off-shore sailors often attach themselves to the boat with a safety harness in bad weather — this prevents a person from being lost overboard.

TECHNICAL TERMS

beat a stretch of course that forces a crew to sail into the wind
helmsman the person who steers the boat by operating the tiller or wheel
knot one nautical mile per hour — equivalent to 1.85 km/h (1.15 mph approx.)
luff to head into the wind

▲ *A crew member can balance a boat while suspended from a cable. This is called 'hiking out' or 'flying the trapeze'.*

port the left side of a boat; a port tack is used when the wind blows from the left
run a stretch of course where a boat sails with the wind behind
skipper the person in charge of a boat
starboard the right side of a boat
tack a zig-zag manoeuvre that makes a boat sail forwards against the wind

FOR THE RECORD

1988 OLYMPIC CLASSES

Class	Crew
Soling	3
Star	2
FD	2
Finn	1
Tornado	2
Division II	1
M/470	2
W/470	2

SAILBOARDING

DID YOU KNOW?

Doubles sailboards are becoming increasingly fashionable. With these, two independently operated sails are mounted one behind the other. Sailing such a board is not easy as the sails have to be manoeuvred in perfect harmony — the slightest error in teamwork can lead to a capsize — but high speeds can be achieved.

During the 1970s a new water sport came into being. In the United States it was called either board sailing or windgliding; in Britain it was dubbed surfboarding. The most globally accepted term for the sport today is sailboarding.

Sailboarding arose as a result of surfers and yachtsmen meeting together. It seemed an obvious step to amalgamate the two disciplines to form a new pastime: hoist a sail on a surfboard and you have the best of both worlds — the joys of riding the surf while at the same time manipulating the wind.

The new sport proved so popular, and people became so proficient at manoeuvring sailboards, that it was given Olympic status at the 1984 Olympic Games in Los Angeles. It is called board sailing in the Olympics.

Women and men enjoy sailboarding at every level, on calm water as well as out at sea. The two essential ingredients for sailboarding are water and wind — heavy surf provides an extra excitement for the experienced.

Most, but not all, sailboarding competitions are governed by the International Yacht Racing Union. The most prestigious events, other than those of the Olympic Games, ' are the annual World Championships.

AIMS OF THE GAME

COMPETITION
● Although there are different designs, a sailboard is in effect a surfboard to which a mast and sail are attached. The aim is to stand on the board and move forwards, using the sail to catch the wind and the board to catch the surf (or local water currents).

● Many different types of competition are held for sailboarding. At the 1984 Olympics, the sailboarding event was triangle racing. This is an event in which competitors race against each other over a triangular course that is marked out by buoys.

● There are several other kinds of competitive events. Competitions are often held out in oceans, as at the Los Angeles Olympics.

- In slalom competitions, competitors have to round a number of buoys (usually 6) in a specific order. Events are held normally on a knockout basis, so the fastest person in one round goes on to the next until an ultimate champion is found.

- In freestyle competitions, competitors perform tricks either on or with their boards. Points are awarded by judges according to the difficulty of the tricks and the proficiency with which they are executed.

- Marathon racing is very different from all of the above. In this event, which can last for many weeks, competitors race over long distances (sometimes several thousand km) on open water and have to master assorted weather conditions. Races are usually divided into stages (daily legs). One recent competition went from Barcelona to Venice, with each stage beginning from and ending at a Mediterranean holiday resort.

SKILLS
● Being able to harness 2 of nature's elements — the wind and the waves — while still keeping aloft on a narrow surfboard demands skill from every quarter. A sense of balance is essential, as are the navigating skills associated with sailing.
● All-round fitness is important for a sailboarder, who must have strong arms, sharp eyes and an ability to swim.

EQUIPMENT

● Little is required apart from a sailboard, which can be expensive, although it is often possible to hire one. Sailboards are about 3.5 m (11½ ft approx.) long and 60 cm (2 ft approx.) wide at the broadest point. Boards have a stabilizing fin on the underside and on top there are plastic foot loops to hold the sailboarder steady. The sail covers an area of 6 sq m (7 sq yd approx.) and is mounted on a mast that can swivel so that the sailboarder can manoeuvre it to any angle. The sail is controlled by an oval-shaped boom that is fixed to the mast and completely loops around the sail.
● In cool waters, sailboarders always wear wetsuits, but their feet are usually kept bare for a good grip.

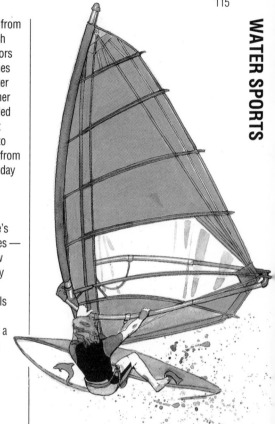

▲ *Sailboarders manipulate the sail by moving a 'wishbone' which is attached to the mast. Feet can be slotted into loops on the board to secure stable footholds.*

FOR THE RECORD

The record for the highest speed achieved under sail was set by the French sailboarder Pascal Maka in February 1990. The speed he reached was 42.91 knots (79.5 km/h).

Baron Arnaud de Rosnay of France sailboarded across the English Channel in the fastest time — 1 hr 4 min 33 sec in 1982. The average speed for the journey was 16.9 knots (31.3 km/h).

DID YOU KNOW?

The match between Hungary and the USSR in the 1956 Olympics was one of the bitterest in sporting history. Soviet troops had invaded Hungary one month before, and the match turned into a near-brawl, with one Hungarian forced to retire with a gashed face. Hungary won the match 4–0 and went on to take the gold medal.

WATER POLO

Water polo developed in England during the middle of the 19th century and was recognized as a sport by the Amateur Swimming Association in 1885. Its popularity as a fast, invigorating game rapidly spread to other countries. It was included in the Olympic Games for the first time in 1900.

The most important international competition remains the Olympic Games, although World Championships are held every four years in addition to the World Cup which is held biennially. Until the mid-1920s, Great Britain remained the most dominant nation at water polo, but Yugoslavia, the USSR, the United States, Italy and Hungary are now the most powerful countries. Great Britain did not even qualify to compete at the 1988 Seoul Olympics. The ruling body is the Fédération Internationale de Natation Amateur (FINA), the same organization that governs swimming and diving.

AIMS OF THE GAME

COMPETITION
- The game is played between two 7-a-side teams in a swimming pool.
- In major competitions, the pool must be 30 m (33 yd approx.) long and 20 m (22 yd) wide. The pool must also be at least 1.8 m (6 ft) deep because only the 2 goalkeepers are permitted to touch the bottom during play. At each end of the pool, there is a goal measuring 3 m (10 ft approx.) across and 0.9 m (3 ft approx.) tall. The object is to score goals with the inflated ball which is about 22 cm (9 in approx.) in diameter.
- Water polo strategy and tactics resemble those of soccer.
- Across the bottom of the pool and up the sides, there are several lines:
- the goal lines which are 30 cm (12 in approx.) from the ends;
- the 2-m and 4-m lines, spaced accordingly from the ends of the pool;

- the half-distance line where play begins.
- For fouls, such as dunking or holding an opponent, committed within the area between the goal and the 2-m line, free throws are taken from the edge of the pool at the 2-m mark. The 4-m lines mark the edges of the goalkeepers' areas.
- If the ball goes out of play off a defending player, a corner throw is taken from the edge of the pool by the attacking side; if the ball goes off an attacker, the defending goalkeeper is given a goal throw.
- A match is divided into 4 quarters, each of which lasts 7 mins. During intervals, teams are allowed to substitute players — 4 substitutes are allowed per team.
- Matches are ruled by 2 referees and several other officials. The latter look out for fouls and award goals. The team with more goals is the winner.

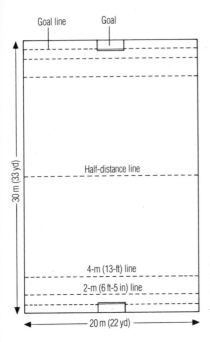

Goal line   Goal

Half-distance line

30 m (33 yd)

4-m (13-ft) line

2-m (6 ft-5 in) line

20 m (22 yd)

▼ *A water polo player takes aim to shoot. As defenders will try to block the shot with upraised arms, he must use his legs to power himself out of the water to get the shot high enough.*

▲ *The minimum depth of the pool for major matches is 1.8 m (6 ft) so that players cannot walk on the bottom.*

SKILLS

● Water polo is a fast-moving game that demands all-round swimming ability. Players other than goalkeepers must go for tiring periods without touching the bottom of the pool. Dribbling involves swimming with the ball kept under control at the chest. Players, with the exception of goalkeepers, are only allowed to use one hand at a time when passing the ball or shooting.

● Defenders use a blocking technique to impede a pass or a shot at goal. To do this effectively timing is crucial: they have to leap out of the water in front of the attacker at the moment that the ball is released. The idea is to block the ball with either the body or the arms.

EQUIPMENT

● Swimming trunks or bathing suits and a cap with ear protectors are the only essential pieces of equipment. Players wear blue or white caps to aid identification of each team. Goggles are not allowed because they could cause injury.

TECHNICAL TERMS

field goal a goal scored during normal play rather than as a result of a penalty throw

penalty throw a throw awarded for a major foul and taken from the 4-m line marking the edge of the goalkeeper's area in front of the goal

personal fault a penalty awarded against a player for a major foul; normally the penalty is 45 sec out of the pool but a player who commits 3 such fouls is banned for the rest of the game

DID YOU KNOW?

Offshore powerboats frequently achieve speeds of over 190 km/h (120 mph), even in rough seas. To protect the crew, many boat owners use jet fighter canopies to cover the cockpits of the driver and throttleman.

▼ *A powerful offshore boat leaps out after cresting a wave. Too much throttle can turn the leap into a dangerous flip.*

POWERBOAT RACING

The glamorous and dangerous sport of powerboat racing has a surprisingly long history. The first petrol-driven engines were fitted to boats in the late 1800s, and by 1900 motor boat races were common. Powerboat racing has been included in the Olympics once — at the 1908 Games held in London.

Today, there are two broad categories of powerboat racing — inshore and offshore. Several classes of boat exist within these groups, and races are organized between craft of similar shape and power. Of the two categories, offshore racing gains the most publicity because the speeds are greater as well as the dangers — many people have died while racing offshore. Stefano Casiraghi, husband of Princess Caroline of Monaco, died in a powerboat accident in 1990.

The ruling body of the sport is the Union Internationale Motonautique.

AIMS OF THE GAME

COMPETITION
Offshore racing
The 2 main categories for offshore powerboating are simply called Class I and Class II — the difference is in the engine size. In offshore racing, boats can be either monohulls or catamarans — monohulls are favoured in rough seas but catamarans are usually faster in calm water.

● Offshore powerboats require a crew of at least 2 — one navigates and steers (or these tasks can be taken by different crew members if there are more than 2), the other operates the throttle.

● Courses vary greatly in length and design — some are straight lines and others follow a circuit marked out by buoys. All take place on the open sea.

Inshore racing
The most common categories for inshore racing — usually held on lakes — are Formula One and Formula Two. Inshore boats are far smaller than their offshore counterparts and, as they lie low in the water, they can turn right-angled corners extremely swiftly.

● Inshore powerboats are driven by just one person.

● Usually, a number of buoys marks out the course which has to be negotiated over a number of laps.

▲ *Inshore powerboats are piloted by one person. The compact design enables them to make tight turns.*

SKILLS
● In offshore racing, the driver/navigator has the easiest job — simply to guide the boat round the course. Throttling the boat, on the other hand, usually requires greater technique. Offshore powerboats leap off waves high into the air. If the engine is going full power when the boat lands on the water, the propellers can, and often do, disintegrate. The skill of the throttle operator — the 'throttleman' — is to turn off the power on take-off and to turn it back on again a split second after the boat re-enters the water.

● Inshore racing is similar to driving a racing car, requiring the ability to steer accurately at speed while still maintaining power. The driver must be navigator and throttleman.

EQUIPMENT

● Powerboat racing of any kind is a high-technology, high-speed sport. Because of the dangers involved, safety is paramount and all competitors wear helmets and life-jackets.

● In offshore racing, the driver and throttleman sit in separate cockpits and usually communicate with each other via a radio link.

DID YOU KNOW?

Many skiers in the jumps section use a technique called a 'double wake cut' to gain speed as they approach the jump. They cut across the wake of the boat and then turn sharply — like a whip cracking — to double back across the wake again.

WATER SKIING

Water skiing is a comparatively young sport because, until the advent of the speedboat, there was no means of towing a skier at sufficient speed for him or her to stay above water. It developed in the United States during the 1920s and has since become a popular holiday recreation as well as a competitive sport. Water skiing has remained an essentially amateur sport, although an increasing number of skiers are turning professional. Some professional display teams go on tour performing stunts.

Competitive water skiing can be divided into three broad categories: tournament, racing and barefoot. The ruling body of the sport is the International Water Ski Federation, which was formed in 1946. The premier competitions for all categories of water skiing are the biennial World Championships and the annual European Championships.

AIMS OF THE GAME

COMPETITION
Tournament events
● In tournament events — which are held for both men and women — each water skier has to compete in 3 different events: slaloms, tricks and jumps.
● In the slalom, a zig-zag course is marked out on the water by 6 coloured buoys. The skier is towed by a boat that maintains a constant 58 km/h (36 mph) for men and 55 km/h (34 mph) for women along a straight line down the centre of the course. The aim of the skier is to round all the coloured buoys alternately without falling. If a skier completes the course satisfactorily, the tow rope is shortened by a specified length and the slalom course is tackled again. This procedure continues until the skier falls. Points are calculated on the number of buoys that have been successfully negotiated.

▼ *Mono-skis are used in slalom events as they have less drag and are easier to manoeuvre round buoys; in jumping events, two skis are preferred.*

- In the tricks section, each skier carries out a programme of tricks which range in value from 20 to 450 points according to their difficulty. If a trick is not executed satisfactorily, no points are awarded. In most competitions, skiers perform up to 30 tricks in each of the two 20-sec runs.
- In the jumps section, the boat travels straight past a ramp in the water at around 100 km/h (60 mph approx.). As the skier approaches, he or she cuts across the wake of the boat and takes off up the ramp. Each skier is allowed 3 attempts and points are awarded for his longest jump only.
- Points from the 3 disciplines are added together to decide the winner.

Ski racing
- In ski racing a number of challengers compete over a 90-km (50-mile) course set over a number of laps near the sea-front. Boats reach speeds of up to 150 km/h (80 mph).
- Sprint racing takes place on inland waterways. Evenly matched boats, race for a set period of time, usually 20 mins.

Barefoot skiing
'Barefooting' is where skiers race barefoot; high speeds are needed to keep skiers upright. There are 3 categories. In the slalom section, skiers cross the wake of the boat as often as possible in two 15-sec passes. In the tricks section, barefooters perform as many tricks as possible in two 15-sec passes. In the jumps section, skiers negotiate ramps in the same style as in tournament events.

SKILLS
- Water skiers tend to have strong arms and thighs. For points events, agility, co-ordination and an acute sense of balance are essential.
- A good understanding between ski racer and driver is essential.

EQUIPMENT

- For slalom competitions, a mono-ski is always used. This has separate bindings, one behind the other, for the 2 feet. Mono-skis are also used for tricks, but these tend to be short and wide to allow swift movement. Jumping skis tend to be long and wide.

▼ *A typical slalom course. The towboat travels at a constant speed down the centre and the skier tries to round all the buoys without falling. The towrope is shortened after each successful passage.*

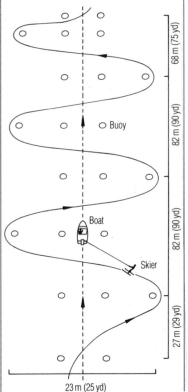

68 m (75 yd)

82 m (90 yd)

Buoy

82 m (90 yd)

Boat

Skier

27 m (29 yd)

23 m (25 yd)

DID YOU KNOW?

The longest surf rides are not always to be found out at sea. It is possible for surfers to ride the bore (a tidal wave) that rushes up the River Severn in England for a kilometre or more.

SURFING

Surfing was devised by Polynesian islanders centuries ago. The Hawaiian Islands of the Pacific are still considered to be the spiritual home of surfing. The original boards were little more than wooden planks which the islanders paddled out to sea. When a large wave came up behind them, they used the energy of the wave to drive them, and their boards, to the shore. They, like millions to follow, discovered that harnessing a wave's energy by 'riding' it on a board can be thrilling, dangerous, occasionally disappointing, but ultimately exhilarating.

During the 1960s, surfing developed into a hugely popular amateur sport in California. It became so glamorous that a rock group, the Beach Boys, wrote a hit song about it — *Surfin' USA*. The rediscovered sport rapidly gained a vast cult following all over the world. Today dedicated surfers can be found on virtually any beach where large waves break, at any time of year. The countries that have the most sought-after surf are the United States, South Africa and Australia, but ideal waves can also be found in countries where the sun does not shine all the time — such as France, New Zealand and Great Britain.

▼ *Martin Potter from Great Britain demonstrates how a surfer can ride the waves with an air of ease and sure-footed balance.*

Although surfing is largely an amateur sport, enjoyed by both men and women, a few experts have turned professional. There are many national and international competitions. The most prestigious are the biennial World Amateur Championships and the annual World Professional Circuit. The world ruling body is the International Surfing Federation, which has its headquarters in Torquay, Australia.

AIMS OF THE GAME

COMPETITION
● In most competitions, heats are held on a knockout basis — the winner of a heat goes through to the next round and so on until just 2 surfers are left in the competition.
● Heats usually comprise 4 or 6 competitors who are assessed from the shore by a panel of judges. Each judge awards marks out of 20, taking into account the length of the ride, the skill of the surfer in manipulating the wave, and any tricks he or she might perform while surfing. In order to be judged, a surfer must stand up on the board; kneeling does not count.
● In each heat, any one surfer may have a number of rides, the best 3 or 5 counting towards the final score.

SKILLS
● Once a surfer has paddled his board out to beyond where the waves start to break, he waits for a swell that signifies a large wave. Paddling furiously to catch the wave, he will stand up on his board only when it has started to carry him with its power.
● After the wave has started to roll, the surfer rides in front of it. By transferring his weight up and down the board, he can control its impetus: stepping forwards makes the board go downwards and faster; leaning back makes it rise up the wave.

● Balance and a sure knowledge of what the wave is going to do are imperative to a surfer. Some waves can break or fade suddenly, ruining a good ride or even endangering the surfer by tossing his board dangerously or dashing him onto a rocky shore.

EQUIPMENT

● Modern surfboards are fish-shaped and are made from a hand-modelled polyurethane foam core covered with glass fibre. They range in length from 2 m (6½ ft approx.) to 2.3 m (7½ ft approx.). Longer boards tend to be harder to manoeuvre but they are more graceful and provide the longest runs. Most boards have 3 'dolphin' fins underneath, which aid stability.
● Surfboards are usually waxed on the topside so that the rider does not slip off the board.
● In cold waters — to be found off California as well as off Britain — surfers wear wet suits.

TECHNICAL TERMS

dumper a wave that breaks suddenly, and 'dumps' the surfer on to the shore
ride when a surfer is carried in by a wave
tube the funnel created by huge waves as they break; 'riding a tube', or ducking into the funnel, is considered one of the ultimate surfing experiences

COURT GAMES

In court sports a ball is played by the hand or with a racket and is not allowed to be kicked. Some court games are played much as they were centuries ago; others have evolved over the years.

BASKETBALL

Arguments rage over which was the first court game. The honour almost certainly goes to basketball, which was played in a primitive form by Olmecs and after them Aztecs in Central America as early as 3000 years ago. The modern game is merely 100 years old.

▼ *A basketball court has a hard surface — most indoor courts are made of wood. The baskets at each end are mounted on backboards. The small size of a basketball court ensures that the game is fast-paced and high-scoring.*

In 1891, a Canadian preacher, James Naismith, was teaching at a YMCA College in Springfield, Massachusetts, when he decided to give the ancient game a new trial. He rigged up old peach baskets at each end of a balcony and invited students to 'net the ball'. He saw it as an interesting way to keep fit during the winter. Since then, basketball, as it became known, has risen to become one of the most popular of all team games in the United States, and it also has a large following in the rest of the world.

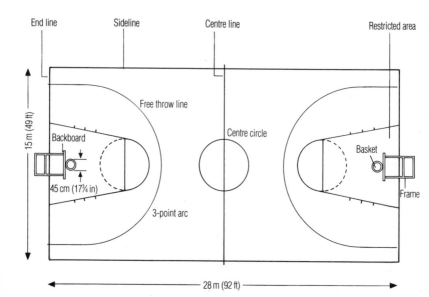

End line · Sideline · Centre line · Restricted area

15 m (49 ft)

Free throw line

Centre circle

Backboard

Basket

45 cm (17¾ in)

Frame

3-point arc

28 m (92 ft)

Although basketball is sometimes assumed to be a man's sport it is also played by women to the highest international level, making it one of the world's most popular sports. The game is usually played according to rules laid down by the international governing body — the Fédération Internationale de Basketball Amateur (FIBA). Professional basketball — with slightly changed rules — is played by top teams in the United States. The professional game rivals baseball, football and ice hockey in popularity. The National Basketball Association (NBA) governs the professional game in the United States. The National Collegiate Athletic Association (NCAA) also organizes prestigious, amateur matches to establish champion university teams.

For national teams, the most important competitions are the Olympic Games (men and women) and the four-yearly World Championships (also for men and women). Major club competitions include the European Cup, the McDonald's Open (where top European clubs meet NBA teams) and the South American Cup. For professional teams in the United States winning the annual NBA Championship is the ultimate goal.

DID YOU KNOW?

A scoring average of 25 points per game is enough to ensure NBA players of multi-million-dollar contracts. But the great centre, Wilt Chamberlain, achieved double that amount (50.4 points average) in the 1962 season, including one game in which he scored 100 points.

AIMS OF THE GAME

COMPETITION
Although there are some slightly different versions of basketball — international, NBA and NCAA — the essential objectives are the same. For convenience the essential rules for the international game are explained first; major differences are given later.

International basketball
● The game is played between 2 teams of 5 players on each side (up to 5 substitutes are usually allowed per side and 7 in some tournaments). The object of the game is for a side to score points by shooting the ball into a high ring and net at the end of the court. Although it might not seem like it at first, basketball is theoretically a non-contact sport — players are only allowed to 'play the ball', not each other.
● The court measures 28 m (92 ft) long and 15 m (49 ft) wide. At each end of the court there is a 45 cm (17¾ in) diameter 'basket', mounted on a vertical backboard. The top of the ring of the basket must be fixed horizontally, 3.05 m (10 ft) above the floor. The court itself is marked with:
- side and end lines;
- a centre circle;
- free throw lines;
- restricted areas near each basket;
- a 3-point arc.
● At the start of a game, the referee throws the ball up into the air at the centre circle for a 'jump ball'. Opposing

'centres' — usually the tallest players — try to gain possession of the ball by tapping it to a team-mate. They try to move the ball towards the opponents' basket, and shoot and score.

● One of the essential rules of basketball is that a player has to 'dribble' (bounce) the ball on the floor, or pass it, or aim to shoot it into the opposition basket. A player cannot move more than one pace while holding the ball, but can dribble the ball around the court. Any breach of these rules is a violation, and the other team is given possession.

● Points are scored by shooting the ball through the opposition basket — 2 points if the ball is in normal play and 3 points if shot from long range. However, penalty throws are awarded for fouls, and these, taken from the 'free throw' lines in front of the baskets, account for 1 point each.

● Certain rules keep the pace of a game exciting. For example, a team has to manoeuvre the ball out of its own half within 10 secs and must shoot for a basket within 30 secs. A game usually comprises two 20-min halves. The winning team is the one with the higher number of points.

NBA basketball

Among the major differences between the 2 NBA codes and the standard FIBA rules are:
- NBA games comprise four 12-min periods;
- NBA teams have to shoot at the basket within 24 secs after gaining possession of the ball — failure to do so means losing possession.

SKILLS

● Basketball is one of the fastest of all team court games. It is usually considered a tall person's sport because the baskets stand so high off the ground. Many of the best players are giants, but people of average height also play effectively.

● The essential skill in basketball is shooting the ball into the basket. Most good shooters combine grace, balance and power, as they avoid defenders and judge the flight of the shot. There are several kinds of shots. One is the 'lay up' where a player dribbles right up to underneath the basket and then leaps up to drop it in. The most spectacular shot of all is the 'dunk', in which a player near the basket leaps up and forces the ball down into the basket from above. This shot needs a tall player who leaps well.

● Although any of the 5 players in a team can shoot the ball at the basket, each person has a specific role to play. There are usually 2 'forwards' who often work to the sides of the basket, so they must be able to shoot accurately from acute angles and 'rebound' missed shots that bounce off the backboard or basket at both ends of the court.

'Centres' patrol the area of the court under the baskets in both defence and attack. Centres are often the tallest players on the court and they frequently play with their backs towards the opponents' basket when on the attack. This is so that they can receive passes from team-mates, swivel round quickly and shoot for the basket. When playing in defence, a centre is often the last defender between an attacker and the basket. A good centre will use his height to harry attackers and to block shots. Another key task for a centre is 'rebounding'.

The 2 'guards' play most of the time in the middle of the court. They are usually smaller players whose job is to pass the ball down to their forwards.

▶ *Defenders must be skilled in 'blocking' passes or shots. Body contact is not allowed so anticipation plays an important role.*

However, good guards are always on the lookout for fast breaks that will allow them to sprint with the ball up the court before the opposition defence is ready. Another common tactic played by guards is to shoot from long range or use their skill and speed to get nearer the basket where they can take an easier shot.

● Quick and accurate passing, over long and short distances, is often the decisive factor between 2 teams. Passes can be made in a straightforward fashion through the air but more subtle passes, that confuse defenders, include bouncing the ball to a team-mate.

● Tactics play an important part in basketball. If a team is good at passing the ball around, it may favour a 'pattern' game in which team members space themselves out over the court and try to move the ball to players who are in good shooting positions. A more exciting type of game relies on fast breaks as described above.

In defence, teams usually adopt one of 2 strategies. In a 'zone' defence, players defend a specific area of the court; in a 'man-to-man' defence, each player shadows an opponent. In either case, the defenders try to keep the ball away from the basket and to pressurize anybody who attempts to shoot the ball into the basket.

EQUIPMENT

● A basketball is usually orange in colour and weighs between 600 and 650 g (21 and 23 oz). The circumference of the ball is between 75 and 78 cm (30 in approx.)
● Very little special clothing is required. Basketball shoes usually provide some ankle support. Their dimpled rubber soles provide the traction needed for start-stop play. Knee and elbow pads must be soft so they cannot cause injury to other players.

▼ *The annual NBA All-Star Game sets the best players from its 2 conferences against each other. The game marks the midway point of a gruelling 8-month season.*

TECHNICAL TERMS

assist a pass to a team-mate that results in a score

basket informal for a successful shot

double-team when a key attacker is shadowed by 2 defenders

field goal a shot that scores 2 points in normal play

free throw a shot awarded as a result of a foul; taken from a free throw line by the fouled player, it is worth 1 point.

held ball when 2 members of opposing teams are both holding the ball

jump ball when the referee starts play by throwing the ball up in the air between two opposing players

out of bounds on the boundary lines and off the edge of the court

personal foul a foul involving physical contact; if a player commits 5 such fouls he is sent off (6 in the NBA)

slam dunk another name for a dunk

stalling slowing down the pace of a game and trying to keep possession of the ball

technical foul a foul involving unsportsmanlike conduct

three points a basket scored from long range and worth 3 points

time out a limited number of times when a team asks for the clock to be stopped so that tactics can be discussed

travelling running with the ball without dribbling it (a violation)

turn-over when the ball passes to the defending team, before the offensive team have attempted a basket

FOR THE RECORD

LEADING NATIONS
The United States has by far the best record in Olympic basketball but the USSR and Yugoslavia also have outstanding teams.

FOR THE RECORD

NBA TEAMS
The NBA is divided into 2 'conferences' — Eastern and Western. The best teams in each conference contest 'play-offs' each year.

Eastern Conference — Atlantic Division

Boston Celtics
New York Knicks
Miami Heat
Philadelphia 76ers
Washington Bullets
New Jersey Nets

Eastern Conference — Central Division

Atlanta Hawks
Milwaukee Bucks
Detroit Pistons
Indiana Pacers
Chicago Bulls
Cleveland Cavaliers
Charlotte Hornets

Western Conference — Midwest Division

Dallas Mavericks
San Antonio Spurs
Houston Rockets
Minnesota Timberwolves
Utah Jazz
Denver Nuggets
Orlando Magic

Western Conference — Pacific Division

Portland Trail Blazers
Phoenix Suns
Seattle Supersonics
Golden State Warriors
Los Angeles Clippers
Los Angeles Lakers
Sacramento Kings

DID YOU KNOW?

The Royal Tennis Court at Hampton Court Palace near London is the most famous real court in the world, largely because Henry VIII arranged for its building in 1530 and played on the court himself. Matches are still played on the court to this day.

The court at Lord's Cricket Ground does not date back as far as Henry VIII's time but it is probably the most used real tennis court in the world. Its use is governed by the Marylebone Cricket Club (MCC).

REAL TENNIS

One of the oldest of all court games, real tennis is also known by a host of other names including *jeu de paume* (in France), court tennis, royal tennis, or just tennis. The game is thought to have been devised by French monks in the 11th century. In the Middle Ages it was played by the nobility and even by royalty (hence the tags of royal tennis and court tennis). Among the most famous of players was Henry VIII of England.

The heyday of real tennis was during the 17th and 18th centuries, but in reality it was played only by a few, just as it is now. However, from this noble game evolved many more popular court sports, such as lawn tennis. Real tennis lovers have long maintained that their sport is the greatest of all court games, but they have been the lucky ones who have had the chance to play. Real tennis remains exclusive — most courts are in England but there are a few in the United States, Australia and France. The number of people playing the game remained somewhat static until the 1970s, when the lawn tennis boom led to renewed curiosity about older racket sports.

The premier governing body of the game is the Tennis and Rackets Association, which was formed as recently as 1907. The major trophy to be won in international real tennis competition is the World Championship.

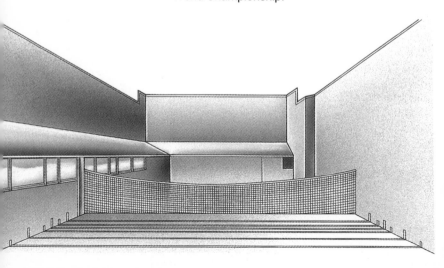

AIMS OF THE GAME

COMPETITION
● Games can be between individuals or pairs; both men and women play and frequently 'pair-up' to form mixed doubles teams. The object of the game is to win points by hitting a ball over a net into an opposing court. But that is where the simplicity ends — of all games, including cricket and baseball, none is more complicated than real tennis.
● No two real tennis courts are identical. They are, however, all enclosed by 4 walls and must have:
- a net that hangs across the centre of the court;
- a 'penthouse' down one side of the court — a sloping roof, off which the ball has to be served at the start of each point;
- a 'grille penthouse' — a sloping roof at one end of the court;
- a 'dedans' at the opposite end to the grille penthouse — an open area usually covered by mesh — and above it lies a 'dedans penthouse' (another sloping roof).
● Once a player has served (service only takes place from one end of the court), an opponent tries to return the ball over the net. The ball is only allowed to bounce once but may be struck off one of the penthouse roofs or the enclosing walls. As in lawn tennis the ball may be struck on the 'volley', or before its first bounce. Points are won when an opponent is unable to return the ball or hits it into the net.
● Points, games and sets are scored along the lines of lawn tennis. Matches are the best of 3 or 5 sets.

◄ *Each real tennis court has some unique hazards, but floor markings are standard for all courts.*

SKILLS
● Real tennis rules and courts take a great deal of understanding but once mastered they can invite a truly stimulating game. Real tennis is often likened to chess played with balls. Hard hitting counts for little; subtlety is paramount — hitting the relatively heavy ball into corners, and bouncing it off sloping roofs and into inaccessible crannies are the essential tactics.

EQUIPMENT

● Real tennis rackets are shorter and stubbier than those used in lawn tennis and they are not so tightly strung. The rackets are made of wood.
● The balls are similar in size to lawn tennis balls but they are hard because they are made of cork bound with horsehair.

▼ *Real tennis rackets have a smaller head than those used for lawn tennis. The loose stringing gives more subtlety to shots. Some players grip the racket well down the shaft for greater control.*

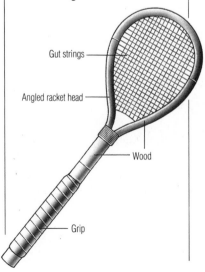

Gut strings

Angled racket head

Wood

Grip

PELOTA

DID YOU KNOW?

A pelota ball can be hurled at speeds of up to 300 km/h (186 mph), double that of a top-class tennis serve of 145 km/h (90 mph).

Without doubt pelota is the fastest of all court games. It has a long history and several different versions are played today. The game is a derivative of one of the many handball games that were played throughout Europe during the Middle Ages. In some cases, rackets were introduced into these games so that the ball could be hit harder and would not cause damage to the hands.

During the middle of the 19th century, the Basques, in the Pyrenees between France and Spain, began to strap a basket to their throwing arm to propel the ball with greater force — up to 250 km/h (150 mph). The baskets were an obvious choice for the Basques as they were farmers, and fruit baskets abounded.

From the tiny, isolated Basque region, the game of pelota (which means 'ball') spread south into Spain and north into France. From these two countries, it spread to Latin America, Mexico and the United States.

Pelota has avid followers in the areas where it is played. Pelota tournaments played in the Basque country today are frequently accompanied by fiestas, and champions become local heroes. It is still also played in France. In Florida, where many inhabitants are of Latin American

AIMS OF THE GAME

COMPETITION
● Pelota is usually played as doubles. Players hurl the ball, with a basket attached to an arm, against a front wall. To return the ball successfully, and thereby start a rally, an opponent has to scoop it up and fire it at the front wall before it bounces twice.
● There are many different types of pelota. The size, character and shape of the courts vary greatly from region to region and from country to country. Some French courts are open to the elements and are little more than a high wall on a concrete playing area. In the

United States and such Latin American countries as Argentina, the courts are enclosed by at least 3 and possibly 4 walls. There are also 'long' courts and 'short' courts. Scoring differs according to local rules, so there are no definitive international laws. The essential rules are similar to those of squash — one person serves and an opponent tries to return the ball off the front wall so that it lands within bounds.

SKILLS
● As pelota is the fastest of all court games, quick reactions are crucial. A keen eye enables a player to catch the ball in his basket before leaning back

extraction, the game flourishes. Pelota's popularity has spread to other parts of the United States, where it is more commonly called 'jai alai'. It has become a popular betting sport in some parts of the eastern United States.

There are several ruling bodies which organize local and international tournaments.

▲ *A pelota player arches his back as he scoops the ball into the chistera. He puts all his weight into the powerful whip-like release.*

and flinging it against the front wall.
● When returning the ball, a player tends to catch it before swinging it out of his or her basket; the ball is rarely hit or struck, as in tennis or squash.

EQUIPMENT

● The ball used in most forms of pelota is similar to a baseball in size, but it has a higher bounce — which is one reason why the game is so fast. A ball weighs around 130 g (4½ oz).
● The baskets used for hurling the ball are made of wicker and are surprisingly light. They are often custom-made and there are no standard sizes or shapes — some players prefer long baskets, others shorter ones. All baskets have a scoop shape — an ideal design for capturing as well as hurling the ball.

TECHNICAL TERMS

cancha a walled court
chistera a player's basket
fronton a 2- or 3-walled court
jai alai (pronounced 'hi-li') the name of the game in Latin America and the United States; the literal meaning is 'merry festival'
trinquet a traditional Basque court

RACKETS

DID YOU KNOW?

On one occasion only, rackets has been included in the Olympic Games — those held in London in 1908. To nobody's great surprise, all medals awarded, for both singles and doubles, went to Englishmen.

Rackets has a curious history in that it was developed inside a prison during the mid-18th century. Whether out of boredom or out of a need for physical exercise, the inmates of Fleet Prison in London adapted one of the many types of handball that were played at the time in the courtyards at the jail. Instead of using their hands they used rackets to hit the ball. In 1820, a prisoner named Robert Mackay claimed the title of World Champion. Gradually, the game became known outside the confines of the prison and one of the first purpose-made courts to be built was at the élite Harrow School. This court had no roof, which limited its use. The first covered courts were not erected until the mid-19th century. From Harrow, the game spread to other public schools and became better known, although its popularity has never rivalled that of squash rackets.

Rackets is mainly played in England, but courts exist in other countries, including the United States and Canada. Comparatively few exist because they are extremely large and therefore expensive to construct.

Rackets is played by both amateurs and professionals, most of whom also play squash. It is more popular with men than women, although some women do play. The sport is known as either 'racquet' or 'racquets' in the United States. The ruling body is the Tennis and Rackets Association and the main tournaments are the British Open and the World Championships.

▼ *The markings on a rackets court show the sport's similarities to squash and other indoor racket sports. The major difference is in the size – rackets courts are half as large again as their squash counterparts.*

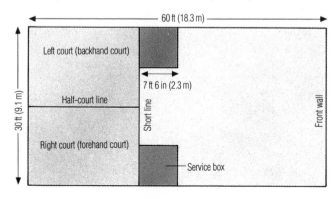

AIMS OF THE GAME

COMPETITION
● Rackets can be played as singles or doubles. In many respects the objectives are similar to those of squash. Players aim to hit the ball against the front wall with their rackets. For a return to be good, the ball must be struck before it bounces twice.
● The court is enclosed by high walls and is 60 ft (18.3 m) long by 30 ft (9.1 m) wide. The markings on the floor of the court are as shown in the diagram. Markings on the front wall include a horizontal service line 9 ft (2.75 m) above the ground and a horizontal board 27 in (68.5 cm) above the ground.
● The server has to stand in a service box and hit the ball off the front wall above the service line, so that it rebounds into the opposing service court. Thereafter, a rally can follow; if the server wins he gains a point; if the receiver wins the rally, he wins the right to serve. Only the server can win points.
● The first person (or partnership in doubles) to reach 15 points is the winner of a game. Matches are usually the best of 5 or 7 games.

SKILLS
● A rackets ball has a high bounce and one of the main skills of the game is to judge the pace of the ball: it is easy to misjudge a bounce or rebound and thereby mishit a return.
● Tactics are very important in rackets. As the court is so large, subtlety in placing the ball is more crucial than just striking it hard. Drop-shots, like those used in squash, are particularly effective, but difficult to execute because of the ball's naturally high bounce.

▼ *The server uses a flick of his wrist to put spin on the ball. It is struck in a high looping arc against the front wall.*

● When the ball hits a wall it makes a characteristic cracking noise. This is a satisfying sound for most players, as it usually indicates a well hit shot.

EQUIPMENT

● The racket is similar to a squash racket but the handle is longer — a typical racket would measure about 30 in (75 cm) long and weigh 9 oz (255 g).
● The hard, white ball has a diameter of 1 in (25 mm) and a weight of 1 oz (28 g).
● Traditionally, white clothes are worn.

TECHNICAL TERMS

bully a rally
hand-in the server
hand-out the receiver

← 18.4 cm (7¼ in) →

21.5 cm (8½ in)

68.5 cm (27 in)

SQUASH RACKETS

The game of squash rackets (usually referred to as squash) is a derivative of rackets (see page 134). In the early 19th century, boys at Harrow School practised knocking a ball about in a courtyard while waiting to gain access to a rackets court. A rackets ball is hard, but they decided to practise with a soft or 'squash' ball. The game became so popular at the school that special 'squash' courts were built.

Initially, squash was slow to catch on with the public but by the turn of the century it was being played in the United States, Canada and South Africa as well as in Britain. The Squash Rackets Association was formed in 1928 and the game took on a new lease of life. It was played by British Army officers and civilians who, when posted abroad, introduced the game to India, Pakistan, Australia and Egypt.

During the 1960s, more and more people took up squash as a means of getting fit: it is one of the fastest and most energetic of all sports.

▲ *Squash rackets have maintained their shape since the 19th century but modern frames are rarely made of wood.*

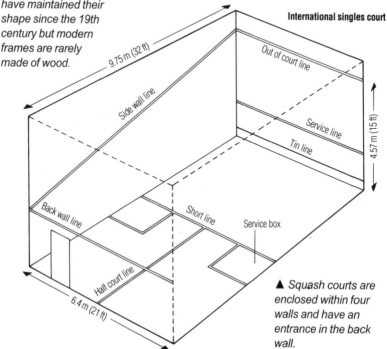

International singles court

9.75 m (32 ft)

Out of court line

Side wall line

Service line

Tin line

4.57 m (15 ft)

Back wall line

Short line

Service box

Half court line

6.4 m (21 ft)

▲ *Squash courts are enclosed within four walls and have an entrance in the back wall.*

Consequently, more courts were built and it no longer remained a game for the select few who could afford to play on private courts. Squash has never been a great spectator sport because the four walls that enclose the court tend to exclude viewers: before the advent of glass walls, spectators had to watch from balconies. Even today it is only occasionally televised because the fast-moving ball is hard to see on the television screen.

Squash is played by amateurs and professionals of both sexes. Many international tournaments are held, the most important being the annual World Championships for both men and women. The major ruling body of the sport is the International Squash Rackets Federation (ISRF), which was formed in 1967. In North America, a variation of the game is played according to rules laid down by the United States Squash Racquets Association (USSRA). University and club-level competitions — as well as some professional tournaments — reflect the growing popularity of the sport there.

▼ *Backhand shots played up against a side wall are difficult to execute because there is little room to swing a racket fully. Often a delicate 'drop shot' is played from such a position, so an opponent has to be vigilant if he or she is to retrieve it successfully.*

AIMS OF THE GAME

The outlines given immediately below are for the ISRF version of the game. Major differences in rules for the USSRA game follow.

COMPETITION
- Squash is normally played between 2 individuals. (It is theoretically possible to play doubles but few people do so.) The object of the game is for a player to hit the ball against the front wall, using a racket. Points are scored when a player is unable to retrieve a shot or when it is hit 'out', that is, out of the playing area.
- The court, including the walls and the floor, is marked by red lines as shown in the diagram.
- On winning the toss of a coin, one player elects to serve from one of the two 'service boxes'. The ball must hit the front wall above the service line and below the out of court line; it must also rebound and land behind the 'short line' on the floor and beneath the side and back wall lines. If the ball is returned successfully — it can only bounce once and must hit the front wall above the 'tin line' and below the out of court line — a rally follows. If the server wins the rally, he or she gains a point; if the opponent wins, he or she gets to serve. Only the server can win a point.
- The first person to win 9 points wins the game; a match usually comprises the best of 5 games.

Note: A few major competitions have adopted experimental rules to make the game more interesting for spectators. These include:
- a lowered 'tin line' to 17 in (43 cm approx.);
- the chance for either player to score points, regardless of who is serving;
- games that comprise 15 points.

Major USSRA variations
- There are two standard courts, one designed for singles play and the other for doubles. The singles court is 30 in (75 cm) narrower than that used for ISRF matches and is only 18 ft 6 in (5.64 m) wide.
- The ball is harder and the markings on the walls and floor are slightly different.

SKILLS
- Squash demands fitness — an unfit player will soon feel the pain! But tactics and delicate strokeplay also play important roles.
- The main tactic of any player is to place shots so that the ball is extremely difficult to return. The most difficult shots to return are those in which the ball goes into the corners of the court, where it is difficult for anybody to wield a racket. Sometimes pace and hard hitting are important but subtle lobs can be just as successful.
- To counter shots played into corners, players develop techniques that enable them to hit the ball hard from the most confined of spaces. This demands strength and flexibility in the wrists.
- After striking the ball, players try to return to the centre of the court — the 'T' — from where they will be able to dominate the rally.

EQUIPMENT

- A squash ball is made of hollow rubber and measures about 4 cm (1½ in) in diameter. They are graded according to their 'speed'. Fast balls, which do not encourage much running around the court, are marked with a red or blue dot; slow balls, used by experienced players, are marked with a yellow dot.

- Rackets come in a number of shapes these days. Their overall dimensions must not exceed 27 in (68.5 cm) in length or 8.36 in (21.2 cm) across the head. Rackets can be made of wood, metal or composite fibres.
- Shoes worn on a squash court must not have black or coloured soles that could leave marks on the wooden floor.

TECHNICAL TERMS

boast a shot, usually a defensive one, that is hit off a side wall onto the front wall

drop shot a delicate shot that hits the front wall just above the 'tin' and drops onto the floor; a good drop shot is difficult to return

rail a shot that hugs the side wall after bouncing off the front wall; difficult to return without damaging the racket

tin the strip of metal that runs along the bottom of the front wall and is topped by an angled strip of wood; it is sometimes called the 'tell-tale' for the simple reason that if the ball hits it, it makes a characteristic noise.

PERSONALITY PROFILES

THE TWO KHANS
Two Pakistanis, who share a name but differ in every other respect, have dominated squash for the last decade.

Jahangir Khan, born in Peshawar in 1963, is the greatest player of recent times. As a child he was weak and feeble but, following in his elder brother's footsteps, he took up squash and became a supreme athlete.

Tragically, his brother Torsam died while playing squash in Australia but Jahangir went on to win a unique total of 7 World Championships (1981–1986 and 1988). Due to a persistent injury, he retired from competitive international squash in 1990.

Jansher Khan pictured above, an effervescent prodigy has taken over the mantle laid down by his namesake. The 2 players temperaments and styles are completely opposed. Jansher has won 3 World Championships — 1987, 1989 and 1990.

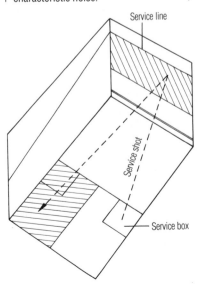

Service line

Service shot

Service box

◄ *The course of the ball in a serve. The ball has to be struck from a service box against the front wall, above the tin and below the out-of-court lines, so that it rebounds into the opponent's section of the court (the shaded area).*

DID YOU KNOW?

The longest-ever singles match in Wimbledon history took place in 1969, before tie-breaks were introduced. Pancho Gonzales outlasted fellow American Charlie Pasarel in five sets: 22–24, 1–6, 16–14, 6–3, 11–9.

TENNIS

Lawn tennis, or tennis as it is now called internationally, is one of the most popular of all court games, both to play and to watch. It developed out of the ancient game of real tennis (see page 130), which fell into a sorry decline at the beginning of the last century because there were so few courts and only a few could understand the game. There are many tales and stories told of who actually 'invented' the modern game. The most widely recognized 'inventor' was a certain Major Walter Clopton Wingfield, who introduced his new game (which he called Sphairistike) to friends at a Christmas party in 1873. Major Wingfield was so entranced by his own game that he bothered to patent it. A year later, the All England Croquet Club took responsibility for the game and the Marylebone Cricket Club rewrote Wingfield's rules.

Since those founding days, tennis has risen in stature to become an international sport. It was originally called lawn tennis because it was played on lawns but now it is played on many different surfaces, both indoors and out — wood, clay, grass, concrete and even asphalt.

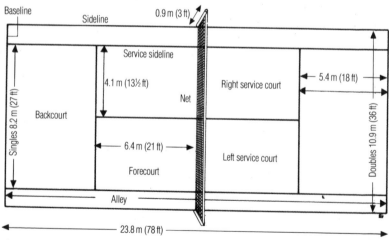

▲ The markings on a tennis court are the same regardless of its surface. Lines are painted on hard courts, but chalk lines mark grass courts. In doubles matches, the playing area is enlarged by including the spaces in both alleys. Serves in doubles games must still land into the service courts.

Tennis is enjoyed by young and old, men and women, at all levels, in recreation halls, parks and even on beaches. Tennis professionals play in many hundreds of tournaments around the world. They can earn phenomenal amounts of money and leading stars are some of the best known personalities in the world. There are several organizations that rule tennis. The International Tennis Federation (ITF) is one of the most important and is the governing body for the world game, but professional set-ups, such as the Association of Tennis Professionals (ATP) and the Women's Tennis Association (WTA) wield great power. They have on occasion threatened to upset the traditional approach to the game with an aim towards gaining greater prize money and more publicity for their members. Top players are constantly tempted to play in lucrative 'exhibition' matches around the world. These are not recognized by any of the tennis organizations, but they can offer players up to $250,000 for a day's work.

Tennis was reinstated as a recognized sport at the 1988 Olympic Games in Seoul. Many of those that took part were professionals. Winners were given medals and not cheques.

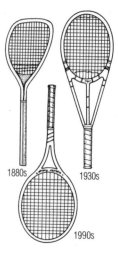

▲ *The oval shape of the racket head had become standard by the 1930s. Modern rackets have larger heads and their frames are made of fibreglass or graphite rather than wood.*

AIMS OF THE GAME

COMPETITION

● Tennis can be played as singles, doubles or mixed doubles. The essential object of the game is for a player to hit the ball with a racket, over a net, and into the opponent's half of the court so that it cannot be returned successfully.

● Tennis courts are marked out as shown in the diagram. The 2 alleys between the tram lines are only used in doubles matches.

The net across the middle of the court is suspended from 2 side posts which stand 3 ft 6 in (106 cm approx.) high; the net sags slightly but its top has to hang exactly 3 ft (91.4 cm) from the ground at the centre.

● After winning the toss of a coin or the twist of a racket ('rough or smooth'), a player or partnership chooses either to serve or to select which end of the court to start. From the right-hand side of the centre mark on the baseline, the server has to hit the ball over the net and into the diagonally opposite service court. If it bounces in the service court, the opponent attempts to return the ball over the net before the second bounce. The first person (or pair) who hits the ball out of play or into the net, or who fails to retrieve the ball before it has bounced twice, loses a point. Two serves are allowed in tennis; if the first lands out of play, a second serve is permissible.

After each point, the server has to serve into the other service court.

● Point scoring in tennis is peculiar. According to legend the scoring follows the quarters of the clock: 15 = 1 point, 30 = 2 points; 40 (originally 45) = 3 points and 60 = 'game'. A score of 0 points is called 'love'. If players reach 40-all ('deuce'), one person or pair must gain 2 points in succession to win the 'game'. The first person or pair to win 6 games by a margin of 2 games wins the 'set'. If scores are level at 6 games each, a 'tie-break' is often played. In this the first person or pair to reach 7 points with a 2-point lead wins the set. For men, matches are the best of 5 (or sometimes 3) sets; for women and mixed doubles, matches are nearly always the best of 3.

● Line judges and umpires play an ever-increasing role in professional tennis because of the number of disputes over whether a ball bounced in or out of court. In major tournaments, several line judges keep their eyes on specific lines (the baseline, for example) to judge whether a ball was in; the umpire sits in an elevated chair at the side of the court and has the right to overrule line judges. The ultimate arbiter is the referee, rarely called upon, who has the right to give an absolute decision.

SKILLS

● Broadly speaking, tennis players can be divided into 2 categories — those that favour playing at the back of the court ('baseliners') and those that favour hitting decisive shots near the net ('volleyers'). Baseliners can usually strike the ball with both speed and accuracy but they prefer to remain back because they like to have the time to place the ball exactly where they want. Baseliners try to maintain a rhythm and are prepared to endure matches for as long as it takes. Volleyers, on the other hand, tend to be more adventurous. They take risks by trying to take the ball on the 'volley', before it bounces, and consequently take their opponents by surprise. Volleyers run up to the net after they have served or struck a good return and have to have lightning-quick reactions as well as a degree of control. Good volleyers usually have devastatingly fast serves which result in weak returns that can be 'put away' with ease.

▼ *The server keeps both feet behind the service line and tosses the ball high into the air …*

• Serving is important in tennis and most experts are able to serve in different ways, either by spinning the ball so that it jumps up, down or sideways when it lands, or by varying the pace — a slow serve can be extremely deceptive.

• As with serving, hitting the ball in normal play can be subtle. Some players prefer to 'slice' the ball, causing it to bounce slowly, others hit the ball with topspin to make it 'kick' and bounce high.

EQUIPMENT

• Tennis balls are now usually yellow or orange, although white ones are still permissible. They must weigh between 2 and 2$\frac{1}{16}$ oz (56.7 and 58.5 g) and have a diameter of no more than 2$\frac{5}{8}$ in (6.66 cm). The weights and measures are considered highly important in top tournaments and balls are usually kept in refrigerators before matches to ensure consistency.

• Rackets must not be more that 32 in (81 cm approx.) long and the head must not be more than 12$\frac{1}{2}$ in (31.75 cm) wide. However, the exact shape of the racket head and the tension of the stringing are a matter of personal preference.

• Traditional tennis clothing is white, but professionals are increasingly adorned with multi-coloured logos and designer clothing.

TECHNICAL TERMS

ace a serve that is so good that the opponent cannot even reach it
approach shot a shot to the back of the opposing court that allows the hitter to run up to the net ready to volley
break point point when the receiver of service has the chance to win thereby 'breaking' the opponent's service
double-handed some players hold the racket with both hands, usually when playing a backhand, to gain extra control and power

▼ ... to get the full power of the overarm serving motion just as the ball begins to drop.

down the line a shot that is hit parallel to one of the sidelines

drop shot a gently hit shot that makes the ball just drop over the net

fault a foul while serving — either because the ball has been hit out of play or because the server has touched or stepped forward of the baseline while serving (foot fault). A second service is allowed but if another fault occurs the server loses the point.

ground stroke a shot hit after the ball has bounced; the opposite of a volley

half-volley a ball that is hit just as it bounces

lob a high shot that loops over the opponent's head into the back of the court

net cord literally, the white band that runs along the top of the net; 'net' is an umpire's 'call' which indicates that a serve touched the top of the net (if the ball goes over the net and into the receiver's court, another serve is allowed)

passing shot a hard shot that passes a volleyer who is approaching, or standing by the net

smash an overhead shot, hit hard and ferociously down into the court, often while standing at the net

tramlines the parallel sidelines along the court; the outer lines are used only in doubles matches

volley when a ball is hit before it bounces

FOR THE RECORD

PLAYING SURFACES

Three main surfaces are used on outdoor courts — cement, clay and grass. The first 2 are often termed 'slow' courts because the ball bounces relatively high and evenly. Grass courts are called 'fast' because the ball can skid low and unpredictably. As a general rule, baseline players prefer playing on slow courts whereas volleyers like grass courts.

Grass courts are becoming increasingly rare these days because they demand a great deal of upkeep. The only major tournament still played on grass courts is the All England Championships at Wimbledon.

FOR THE RECORD

THE GRAND SLAM EVENTS

The 4 most prestigious annual international tournaments are collectively called the Grand Slam events. The oldest (first played in 1877) and most important of the 4 is the All England Championships held at Wimbledon. The other tournaments are the US Championships (1881), the French Championships (1891) and the Australian Championships (1905). All 4 hold events for men's singles and doubles, women's singles and doubles, and mixed doubles.

FOR THE RECORD

OTHER MAJOR TOURNAMENTS AND EVENTS

- The Davis Cup (men) is contested annually between national teams.
- The Federation Cup is an annual competition for national teams made up of women players only.
- Men's Grand Prix Masters — throughout the season, certain tournaments carry 'ranking points'. At the end of the year, the 16 players with the most points compete for the title of Masters Champion. A similar set-up is also used for a men's doubles title.
- Women's International Series — an annnual women's championship along similar lines to the Grand Prix Masters for men.

▲ *Boris Becker during the 1990 Australian Open. He is poised for a perfect backhand drive, with his shoulder to the net and racket back, ready to swing forward and strike the ball. He was the youngest-ever male champion when he won Wimbledon in 1985 at the age of 17yr 227 days.*

DID YOU KNOW?

In Britain and other parts of the world, racketball is often played in squash courts. However, as the markings in a squash court are different, the rules have to be adjusted slightly.

RACKETBALL

Racketball (spelt racquetball in the United States) is a comparatively modern game. It developed from the older game of paddleball which involved players hitting a ball with a wooden paddle. Soon after World War II, American paddleball players reckoned that they would be able to hit the ball with more control if they used strung rackets instead. The new game was given its official name of racketball in the late 1960s.

Since the 1960s, racketball has become a hugely popular sport in the United States where there are now more than 10 million players. It is also played in other parts of the world, including Britain. Racketball is a fast, energetic game. The short-handled rackets and large court guarantee exercise.

The ruling body of the sport is the International Racquetball Federation (IRF) and the premier competitions are the biennial World Championships, for both men and women.

▶ *The playing area in racketball extends to all four walls of the court and the ceiling when returning a serve or during a rally.*

Four-wall court

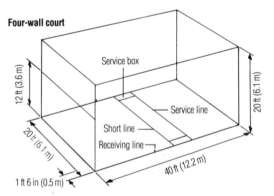

AIMS OF THE GAME

COMPETITION
● Racketball is usually played between 2 people, although doubles can be played. The object of the game is to strike the ball with a short racket against a front wall so that when it bounces back, an opponent is unable to return it successfully.

● Courts are usually enclosed by 4 walls but a variation can be played on a 'one-wall court'. A standard court is 40 ft (12.2 m approx.) long and 20 ft (6.1 m approx.) wide. The front and side walls should be 20 ft (6.1 m) high and the back wall at least 12 ft (3.6 m approx.) high. Floor markings include:
- a 'short' line 20 ft (6.1 m) from the front wall;

- a 'service' line 15 ft (4.6 m approx.) from the front wall;
- 2 'service boxes' marked by lines 1 ft 6 in (0.5 m approx.) from the side walls;
- and 2 'receiving' lines marked on the side walls, 5 ft (1.5 m approx.) from the short line.

● Who serves first is decided by the toss of a coin. The server has to stand with both feet in the area defined by the short and service lines (the 'service zone') and has to bounce the ball once on the ground before hitting it. For a service to be good, it has to hit the front wall before rebounding back behind the service line. In doubles, the server's partner has to stand in a service box until the service has crossed the short line on the rebound. The receiver must stand behind the receiving lines until the ball has bounced.

● For a return of service to be good, a receiver must hit the ball against the front wall before it bounces twice. The ball may touch a side wall or the back wall. Rallies are won as in squash — by forcing the opponent to let the ball bounce twice or to hit the ball outside the playing area.

● Only the server, or serving side, can score a point; if they lose a rally, service transfers to the other person or team.

● Matches usually consist of 2 games. A tie-breaker is used if the match is one game all. A game is won by the first person or side to reach 21 points and a tie-breaker is won by the first person or side to reach 11 points.

SKILLS

● Racketball is a fast game, so a keen eye is essential. As with other court sports such as squash, winning shots are often those that are struck into awkward corners, making it hard for the opponent to hit the ball.

EQUIPMENT

● The head of a racket must not exceed 13⅓ in (34.3 cm) in length and 9 in (22.9 cm) in width. The handle can be up to 7 in (17.8 cm) long and it must have a looped thong attached to it; the thong has to be worn around the wrist during play.

● The ball is 2¼ in (5.7 cm) in diameter and weighs around 1½ oz (42.5 g). The ball is pressurized and extremely bouncy.

▼ *Racketball is a fast game demanding quick thinking to anticipate the opponent's next move and the ball's direction. Rallies occur frequently as the ball is bouncy and this helps to keep it in play for long periods of time.*

DID YOU KNOW?

A third type of fives — named after yet another public school, Winchester College, is something of a cross between the Eton and Rugby versions. It is played in an enclosed court, but the left-hand wall has a kink in it which provides a hazard. Winchester fives is played by far fewer people than the other 2 games.

FIVES

Fives is a uniquely English game, rarely, if ever, played elsewhere. There are two popular versions, both of which gained their names from the English public schools where they were first played. Eton fives was practised first under rudimentary rules at the beginning of the 19th century. Boys at the college played a type of handball against the chapel wall, but in 1840 special courts were built. These unusual courts copied features of the chapel — each one incorporated a buttress identical to the one on the chapel wall, and steps. The game spread from Eton to other public schools around the country and its popularity began to grow.

Around 1850, Rugby School developed its own form of fives. This version of the game differs slightly from Eton fives. The court is enclosed and there are no buttresses or steps. It is essentially a simpler game than Eton fives and easier to understand and play.

Both types of fives are still popular at certain public schools, but neither has gained a substantial following. Both are strictly amateur games and are exclusively played by men. Competitions are mainly confined to inter-school affairs, although a small number of club championships are played.

◀ *A rugby fives player stands to lose the point if he waits and watches what he thinks is his winning shot.*

A good player watches his opponent strike the ball, in order to have a better view of his shot and the path it is likely to take.

AIMS OF THE GAME

COMPETITION

Eton fives

● Eton fives is a doubles game played in a court that is surrounded on 3 sides by walls but open at the back. The court measures 14 ft (4.25 m approx.) wide and 25 ft 3 in (7.7 m approx.) long. There is a shallow step 10 ft (3 m approx.) from the front wall, and on the left side there is a buttress which has a sloping coving on top.

● The object of the game is for players to hit a hard, white ball with their hands against the front wall. The ball can hit the side walls and the buttress but it must be hit before it bounces twice. The ball is played alternately by members of opposing teams and a rally is won when a player strikes the ball against the front wall and an opponent cannot return it.

● A game is played up to 15 points, and a match usually comprises the best of 3 games. Only the pair serving can score points; if a rally is lost, service goes to the opposition.

Rugby fives

● Rugby fives can be played as singles or doubles. The rectangular court, which is 28 ft (8.5 m approx.) long and 18 ft (5.5 m approx.) wide, is enclosed by 4 walls. Across the front wall, there is a wooden board 2 ft 6 in (76 cm approx.) above the ground.

● As in Eton fives, the object of the game is to score points by hitting the ball against the front wall above the wooden board in such a way that an opponent is unable to return it. The side walls can be used but the ball must not be allowed to bounce more than once.

● Games are played to 15 points and only the server or serving team can score. Matches are best of 3 games.

SKILLS

● In Eton fives, the various obstacles around the court make it difficult to predict where and how the ball is going to bounce. For this reason, an agile mind must complement a fit body. One of the tactics is to try and make the ball hit one of the obstructions so that an opponent will be confused or caught out of position. It is a subtle game, not easily mastered.

● Rugby fives is a faster game and requires great fitness and agility as players have to reach down, up or sideways to reach the ball with their hands. Either hand can be used to hit the ball, but with most people the left hand is weaker. For this reason, skilled players try to force opponents into using their left hands — backhands are virtually impossible in fives.

EQUIPMENT

● Special gloves are essential when playing fives. Fives gloves have thickly padded palms to reduce the likelihood of injury. Nevertheless, bruising is common, and fingers can be sprained when players try to return a shot that hugs one of the walls.

▼ *The leather gloves have padded palms which protect the hands from getting bruised by the hard ball.*

DID YOU KNOW?

A smash shot can make the shuttlecock leave the racket at a speed of over 160 km/h (100 mph). But even a shuttlecock hit that hard will lose speed dramatically.

BADMINTON

The game of badminton takes its name from Badminton House, the Gloucestershire seat of the Dukes of Beaufort, where the children's racket game of shuttlecock was played by guests during the late 19th century. The rules of shuttlecock were slightly modified by the guests, and the new game became popular with army officers. In the 1870s, badminton was played by the British army in India, where the first standardized rules were drawn up. At the same time, the game developed a growing following in England and the Badminton Association of England was formed in 1893.

Badminton is a fast and skilful indoor game that can be played by men and women of virtually any age. It is one of the fastest growing of all sports, particularly in the Far East and in continental Europe.

The international ruling body is the International Badminton Federation, which was founded in 1934. The most important championships are the biennial World Championships, the annual All England Championships and the Commonwealth Games.

▼ *Teamwork is essential in doubles; one player makes a forehand drive while her partner keeps her racket poised to anticipate their opponents' return.*

AIMS OF THE GAME

COMPETITION

● Badminton can be played as singles or as doubles, including mixed doubles which is played to the highest international standards. The object of the game is for players to use a racket to hit a 'shuttlecock' over a net suspended across a court.

● Courts are usually marked out for both singles and doubles play, just as a tennis court is. A full-size court measures 44 ft (13.4 m approx.) long and 20 ft (6.1 m) wide. Markings on the court include:
- back boundary lines (the 'long service' lines for singles);
- long service lines for doubles;
- sidelines for both doubles and singles;
- centre lines;
- 'short service' lines.

The area for singles play is narrower (inside the singles sidelines) than that used for doubles, but the service courts are longer: in singles, a player can serve from right at the back of the court on the boundary line.

● The net that divides the court stands 5 ft (1.5 m approx) high in the centre and 5 ft 1 in (1.55 m approx.) high at the sides.

● After winning the toss of a coin, a person or team elects either to serve or to choose in which end of the court to start. In singles, the server hits the shuttlecock from one service court, over the net, and into the diagonally opposite service court. When the score is even, the server always serves from the right-hand service court.

● The receiver of the serve tries to return the shuttlecock and a rally continues until one player either fails to make a return, or hits the shuttlecock out of court or into the net. If the server wins the rally, he gains one point and serves again from the other service court. If the server fails to win, then his opponent takes over the service. Points can only be scored by the server.

● In doubles, the serving routine is more complicated. Before a match, each couple must decide which of them is to serve first.
- The 'first server' continues to serve from alternate service courts until a rally is lost. Then the right to serve moves to the opposition.
- When the opposition's 'first server' loses a point, service is handed over to his partner. And when a further point is lost, service is handed back to the 'second server' of the first pair to serve. Thereafter, both servers on each team have to serve before the shuttlecock is handed over to the opposition.

● In doubles competitions and in men's singles, the winner is the first person or side to reach 15 points; in women's singles 11 points.

● A system of 'setting' is used in badminton. With this system, extra points can be played if the score is tied late in a game. In a 15-point game, 5 extra points can be played if the score is 13-all, or 3 at 14-all. In an 11-point game, 3 extra points can be played at 9-all or 2 at 10-all.

● The first person or side to win 2 games out of 3 wins the match.

● The most important basic rules of badminton (for both doubles and singles are that:
- when serving, a player must serve underarm with both feet inside the service area;
- the server must hit the shuttlecock into the diagonally opposite service area for the serve to be valid;
- the shuttlecock must not be allowed to touch the ground;
- players must not reach over the net to hit the shuttlecock.

SKILLS

- Badminton demands all-round agility. Good players are able to reach high up to retrieve overhead lobs as well as stoop low down to catch drop shots and smashes.
- Badminton is both an energetic and a subtle game — tactics and techniques play a great part. A variety of shots is essential — from powerful smashes and well-timed lobs to delicate taps that just manage to loop the shuttlecock over the net. A shuttlecock has a deceptive flight, slowing suddenly from high speed. Guile and deception play a part in badminton: one of the many skills is feigning hard shots while playing soft ones.
- In doubles play, co-operation between partners is crucial; if one partner is forced out to one side, the other must cover the vacant area of the court. In mixed doubles, it is usual for the woman to stay close to the net while her partner scurries around at the back chasing deep shots.

▼ *Badminton is usually played indoors on a court with a wooden or a synthetic non-slip surface.*

▲ *The tightly strung racket is usually made of steel or carbon fibre. It is light enough to be swung with a flick of the wrist. The shuttlecock has a cork head to which are attached up to 16 feathers that govern its flight.*

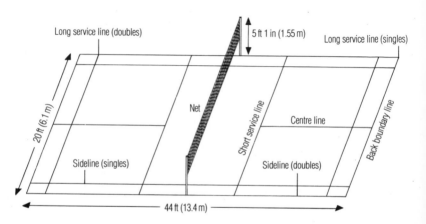

Long service line (doubles)

5 ft 1 in (1.55 m)

Long service line (singles)

Net

Short service line

Centre line

Back boundary line

20 ft (6.1 m)

Sideline (singles)

Sideline (doubles)

44 ft (13.4 m)

▶ *The shuttlecock is served underarm. It cannot be struck directly from the hand but must first be dropped and then struck beneath the line of the server's waist. Most players prefer to use a high, lofted serve.*

EQUIPMENT

● The shuttlecock itself weighs between 4.74 g (⅙ oz) and 5.5 g (⅕ oz); it comprises a hemispherical cork base to which are fastened 16 goose feathers. As the lifespan of feather shuttlecocks is short, synthetic-feather shuttlecocks are often used in informal games.

● Badminton rackets are very light — about 100 g (3½ oz) — and are usually made from steel or carbon fibre.
Strict rules govern the size of racket heads, which are usually about the size of squash racket heads and always extremely tightly strung.

● White clothing is usually worn and white-soled shoes are recommended, so as not to mark the floor of the court.

TECHNICAL TERMS

drive an attacking shot played from the middle of the court
drop-shot a stroke that makes the shuttlecock only just clear the net and 'drop'. Drop shots are often disguised as much harder shots
lob a lofted shot that is hit over the heads of defenders. It can be either defensive or offensive
round the head a forehand shot, played as an alternative to a backhand, over the top of the head
smash a decisive, hard-hitting stroke delivered from overhead, often hit while jumping
tape the white tape running along the top of the net

FOR THE RECORD

LEADING NATIONS
China
Denmark
England
Indonesia
Japan
Korea
Malaysia
Sweden

▼ *The netball hoop is the same height off the ground as a basketball hoop. Unlike basketball, there is no backboard, so shooting is more difficult.*

15 in (38 cm)

10 ft (3.05 m)

NETBALL

Netball is one of the few sports that is only played by women. Fast, skilful and exciting to watch, it is a derivative of the predominantly male sport of basketball. The game originated in the United States towards the end of the 19th century but waned in popularity as opportunities grew for women to play basketball. If Americans no longer enjoy it (perhaps because of basketball's large following), many other people do, most notably Australians, New Zealanders and English women. It is also played in South Africa, India and the Far East with great enthusiasm. One of the reasons for its popularity in Commonwealth countries is that it was adopted by English-speaking girls' schools around the globe as a recreational sport at the time of the British Empire.

The ruling body of netball is the International Federation of Netball Associations. The most important international competition is the four-yearly World Championships, which have long been dominated by the Australians and New Zealanders.

Key to diagram
GS Goal shooter
GA Goal attack
WA Wing attack
C   Centre
WD Wing defence
GD Goal defence
GK Goalkeeper

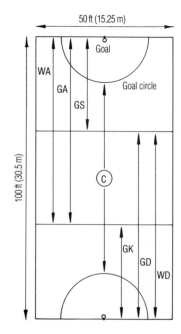

50 ft (15.25 m)

100 ft (30.5 m)

Goal

WA

GA

Goal circle

GS

C

GK

GD

WD

AIMS OF THE GAME

COMPETITION
● A game of netball is played between 2 teams of 7 players each on a hard court, usually indoors. The object is for teams to score 'goals' by slotting the ball into rings at each end of the court.

● The court measures 100 by 50 ft (30.5 by 15.25 m) and is divided into 3 equal areas. The goals, placed centrally at each end of the court, comprise 15 in (38 cm) hoops mounted on 10 ft (3.05 m) posts. There are no backboards behind the goals, as there are in basketball.

● Each player wears a 'bib' which bears letters that denote her position on the court. Standard positions are:
- goal shooter (GS)
- goal attack (GA)
- wing attack (WA)
- centre (C)
- wing defence (WD)
- goal defence (GD)
- goalkeeper (GK)

Each player is only allowed to move within a limited area of the court (see diagram) with the exception of the centre who can go anywhere except in the 2 'goal circles'.

● After a game has started, players are not allowed to hold the ball for more than 3 sec. Nor are they allowed to dribble it (as in basketball) but have to pass before taking 2 steps. The only players who are allowed to score goals are the GS and GA, and they have to shoot from within the 'goal circle'. Games last for 1 hr and are usually divided into 4 quarters. The team with more goals is the winner.

SKILLS
● Netball is a non-contact sport so skill in passing and making openings is more important than aggression. Most players are confined by both space and time when manoeuvring the ball about the court, so play is extremely fast and energetic.

● Shooting must be more accurate than in basketball, as there are no backboards.

● Each player has a specific role and a preference for either handling ability, defending or shooting. Tall players tend to be shooters or defenders but the most crucial role is usually played by the centre: as she is the only person who is permitted to patrol most of the court, she must have all-round skills and be able to act as 'playmaker'.

EQUIPMENT

● The ball should weigh 14–16 oz (400–450 g) and measure about 27–28 in (69–71 cm) in circumference. For informal games a soccer ball can be used.

● The only essential attire beyond skirt, top and rubber-soled shoes is the bib which is worn over a shirt.

TECHNICAL TERMS

bib a short apron, worn over the top of a shirt that has a player's position marked on both back and front
circle the semi-circle around the goal at each end of the court, otherwise called the 'goal circle'
offside when a player steps out of her designated area

◀ *All the members of the netball team have to stay within specific areas of the court. A player who oversteps her designated area is deemed offside. This diagram shows the seven standard positions of a team defending the goal at the bottom and attacking the goal at the top.*

Players' rotation

Serving zone

Server

▲ *When there is a change of serve, all the players in a team rotate one position round the court. The 'serving zone' is behind the baseline.*

VOLLEYBALL

Volleyball is one of the few games that have genuinely been invented from scratch. The honour of invention goes to an American, William G. Morgan, who was a physical training instructor at the YMCA in Holyoke, Massachusetts in the late 19th century. The game was taken to the Far East by American missionaries at the beginning of this century and American servicemen introduced it to Europe during World War I. Since then, volleyball has grown to become one of the most widely played and popular of all ball games.

Volleyball is an amateur sport enjoyed by both men and women and it is played in thousands of schools as it provides good all-round exercise.

The ruling body of the sport is the Fédération Internationale de Volleyball (FIVB), which was established in 1947. The first World Championships were held in 1949 and currently take place every four years. Volleyball became an established Olympic sport in 1964.

▶ *Players at the net try to spike the ball or smash it down. The opposing team leap up to return the ball before it touches the ground.*

AIMS OF THE GAME

COMPETITION

● Volleyball is a team game with 6 players on each side. The object of the game is for a team to score points by hitting the ball over a net into the opposition's half of the court in such a way that the opposing team cannot return it or cannot prevent it bouncing on the ground.

● The court, which can be either outside or indoors, measures 18 m (19.7 yd approx.) long and 9 m (9.8 yd approx.) wide. The top of the net suspended across the middle of the court should be 2.43 m (2.66 yd) above the ground for men's games and 2.24 m (2.45 yd) for women's. Each half of the court is further divided into 2 zones — the 'attack zone' which is near the net and the 'back court'.

● At the start of a game, each player adopts a position on the court. The server on one team stands behind the baseline within the so-called 'serving zone', which is marked on the right hand side by 2 parallel lines 3 m (3 yd approx.) wide. The server hits the ball over the net with a hand. The team receiving serve then tries to return the ball, with open hands, back over the net. A maximum of 2 'passes' to teammates is permitted. On the third contact the ball must be directed over the net. The ball has to be hit, not caught and thrown over the net. Points are won when a receiving team is unable to return the ball over the net, hits it out of the court or allows it to touch the ground.

● Points can only be won by the serving side. If the serving side loses a rally, the serve moves to the opposition. When the right to serve reverts to the first team, all the members of that team rotate one position in a clockwise direction round the court, so a different person serves. In volleyball, all members of a team serve.

● Matches comprise the best of 5 sets. A set is won by the first side to reach 15 points unless the teams are tied at 14-all, in which case, the game carries on until one team gains a 2-point advantage.

● A variation known as 'beach volleyball' is popular in California. Two-man teams play outdoors, sometimes for cash prizes.

SKILLS

● Volleyball is a skilful team game. The essential art is for the team member who receives the ball from over the net to play it up in the air towards another member. The second person then tries to set the ball up with a delicate lob to a third person who runs, jumps and smashes the ball back into the other half of the court.

● One of the crucial skills in defending is the 'block'. With this tactic, a defender leaps up to block a fierce shot from an attacker immediately after it has crossed the net.

EQUIPMENT

● The ball weighs around 270 g (9½ oz) and has a circumference of about 66 cm (26 in). It is usually white and is faced with thin leather.

● No special equipment is required, although in important competitions, numbered shirts are worn.

TECHNICAL TERMS

dig a pass made using the forearm
side out when a team loses the right to serve
spike a decisive smash shot over the net

▲ *The modern table tennis bat (right) has evolved from a long-handled 'racket'. The surface of current bats is usually covered with rubber which allows a player to give spin to the ball.*

TABLE TENNIS

Table tennis, or ping-pong as it was originally called, was invented by the English as an after-dinner game at the end of the 19th century It was popular for a time but lost favour after the turn of the 20th century. During the 1920s, ping-pong was renamed table tennis and a standard set of rules was drawn up. Since then the game has been taken to all parts of the world and it is now the second most popular indoor sport. More than 100 countries are members of the ITTF (see below). The Chinese and Swedes are particularly good at table tennis.

Table tennis is an amateur sport enjoyed by men and women of all ages. Essentially a straightforward and simple game, it can never-theless be immensely fast and subtle. It calls for lightning reflexes and good mobility.

The world governing body for the sport is the International Table Tennis Federation (ITTF). There are a number of important competitions including the biennial World Championships (for men's and women's singles and doubles), the Swathling Cup (a men's team competition) and the Corbillon Cup (a team competition for women). Table tennis was played at the Olympic Games for the first time in Seoul in 1988, with the host nation, South Korea, and China sharing the honours.

▼ *The playing area for table tennis extends beyond the table to 5 ft (1.5 m) on either side and 8 ft (2.5 m) at the ends.*

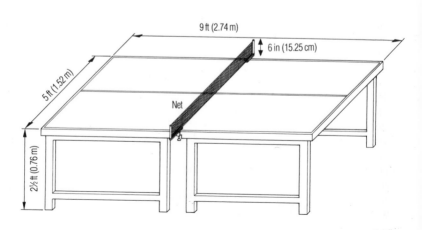

AIMS OF THE GAME

COMPETITION
● Table tennis is played indoors as either singles or doubles. Each player uses a small 'bat'or 'paddle' to hit a light ball over a net stretched over a table. Points are won when a player makes a shot that an opponent is unable to return successfully.
● The table is 9 ft (2.74 m) long, 5 ft (1.52 m) wide and stands 2½ ft (0.76 m) off the ground. The top of the table must be smooth and is usually coloured green with white bands along the edges and a white stripe down the centre. For major competitions the area around the table appears disproportionately large (to give players more room) and can measure 40 ft (12 m) by 20 ft (6 m). The net across the middle of the table is stretched taut so that the top is 6 in (15.25 cm) off the table.
● In singles, one player serves and the other returns. For a serve to be good, the server must strike the ball cleanly so that it bounces once on his side of the table, goes over the net, and lands on the opponent's side. The receiver has to hit the ball after it has bounced only once, directly over the net so that it lands on the server's side. During a rally each player attempts to hit the ball directly over the net. No volleys are allowed and a point is won when a player makes a shot that cannot be returned.
   In doubles, the server has to make the ball bounce diagonally over the net on to the opposite quarter of the table. Thereafter partners have to take it in turns to play the ball.
● Players take it in turns to serve the ball 5 times each unless the score reaches 20-all, when they serve alternately. Both server and returner can score points.

● Matches are usually the best of 3 or 5 games. A game is played to 21 points unless the score reaches 20-all in which case play continues until one player goes 2 points ahead.

SKILLS
● There is a lot more to table tennis than just tapping the ball over the net. When attacking, players often spin the ball by slicing it; when the ball bounces, it veers off at an angle. Another attacking shot is the smash — a hard hit that forces an opponent backwards.
● Some of the most spectacular shots are played in defence from well behind the table. To loop the ball on to the table while standing back takes phenomenal control.
● Played at its best, table tennis is fast: quick reflexes and eye–hand co-ordination are essential.

EQUIPMENT

● The white ball is hollow and made from light plastic or celluloid: it weighs around 0.09 oz (2.5 g) and has a diameter of about 1½ in (38 mm).
● Table tennis bats can be of any size or weight but must be made of wood. Each side of the bat is covered with a pimpled rubber surface or a 'sandwich' — a layer of sponge faced with pimpled rubber.

TECHNICAL TERMS

chop a sliced, downwards stroke that gives the ball backspin
penhold grip a way of holding the bat, much favoured by Oriental players — the handle is gripped as if holding a pen
Western grip the traditional way of holding the bat — as if shaking hands with it

MOTOR SPORTS

The first cars were built in 1885. Nine years later the first car competition was organized — a 135-km (80-mile) reliability run from Paris to Rouen and back. The first race was held a year later — from Paris to Bordeaux and the return journey. Since then many motor sports have evolved, from motorcycle racing to rally driving. Most motor sports that involve cars are governed by the Fédération Internationale de l'Automobile (FIA). The ruling body of motorcycling is the Fédération Internationale Motorcycliste (FIM).

▼ *Races are started from a 'grid' on the track. The driver with the fastest time in practice runs starts from the 'pole position' (1).*

1	2
3	4
5	6
7	8
9	10
11	12
13	14
15	16
17	18
19	20
21	22
23	24
25	26

GRAND PRIX RACING

At the turn of the century, most motor races were town-to-town affairs, but by 1903 special race tracks had been built. The first Grand Prix race, in 1906, was held on a road track at Le Mans in France. The winning car, a Renault, finished with an average speed of 101 km/h (63 mph). The race was called a 'Grand Prix' because it was considered to be the ultimate prize in motor sport. Indeed, it was the only annual Grand Prix race to be held until the 1920s. In 1921, Italy introduced its own version of a one-day 'Grand Prix' race and gradually more and more nations followed suit.

In 1950, the World Drivers' Championship was introduced by the world governing body of motor sport, the Fédération Internationale de l'Automobile, and Grand Prix racing as it is known today came into being. Grand Prix racing is governed by the Fédération Internationale du Sport Automobile (FISA), affiliated to FIA.

Modern Grand Prix motor racing is open only to drivers of Formula 1 cars — a category which includes the fastest and most expensive of all cars. (Other categories of car are raced in separate championship events, but these are not to be confused with the Grand Prix races.) It is an exciting and dangerous sport. Only the very best drivers ever get to sit in a Formula 1 car and, before they do, they have to prove their worth by driving successfully in less precious and powerful machines. In theory, Grand Prix racing is open to either sex, but in practice, men have always dominated the sport.

AIMS OF THE GAME

COMPETITION
● The simple object of Grand Prix racing is for drivers to win races. The World Championship series comprises 16 races per year which are held in a number of different countries around the world.
● Racing circuits vary enormously — from about 3.2 km (2 miles) up to 8 km (5 miles). A few races are driven over ordinary roads that are specially prepared and cordoned off before the race. The Monaco Grand Prix has a circuit of this kind, and drivers have to negotiate the sharp bends and narrow streets of Monte Carlo. The majority of circuits are, however, built for motor racing. Most of these tracks comprise fast 'straights' and tight curves to test the ability of the drivers to the utmost. In Grand Prix races, drivers have to complete a certain number of laps of the circuit — as few as 30 for long circuits or as many as 80 for short ones. The average speed on the fastest tracks can be as high as 240 km/h (150 mph).

● All Grand Prix races are started from a 'grid' — a series of marks on the track behind the starting line. There is usually only room for 2 cars abreast, so the fastest cars start at the front of the grid and the slower ones towards the back. Each driver's position is based on a series of timed trials before the race.
● Drivers have their engines running before the start. 'Get ready' is signalled by a series of red flashing lights. When the lights turn to green, the drivers are allowed to accelerate ahead.
● Formula 1 cars have 3.5-litre engines; strict rules govern the size of tyres, aerofoils and fuel tanks.
● The World Championship is decided on a points system, which is currently under review by FISA. The winner of each race gets a certain number of points; second place earns slightly fewer, and so on. At the end of the season, the person with the most points wins the championship.

▼ *Pole position at the start of a race gives a driver a psychological and tactical edge over his rivals.*

SKILLS

- Drivers race for teams which are usually owned and organized by a sponsor or a car manufacturer. Ford, Honda and Yamaha, for example, work with specialist constructors such as Lotus, Lola, McLaren or Williams. Each team comprises 2 drivers, their cars (including spare cars), managers, designers, time-keepers, sponsors and highly trained mechanics. Although the drivers actually do the racing, the back-up squads and the design of a car can often make the difference between victory or defeat.

- Driving a Formula 1 car demands formidable skill and courage. Most cars can move at over 320 km/h (200 mph) so drivers have to be able to make lightning-quick reactions in hot, noisy and cramped conditions. There is no denying that Grand Prix racing is a dangerous sport and it is definitely not for the faint-hearted.

▼ *Formula One racing cars must be able to 'hug' the track if they are to corner at speeds of 250km/h (150mph). Wing-like aerofoils by the rear wheels use air pressure to hold the car on the circuit.*

- Managers and drivers have to make calculated decisions when it comes to choosing the type of tyres to be used. A whole range of tyres is available — from those with a heavy tread (for slippery conditions) to those with no tread at all. The type picked is chosen according to weather conditions. A bad decision can prove costly.

- When a driver makes a 'pit stop' in the middle of a race to change tyres, for example, he relies on the skills of the mechanics. Speed is everything — 4 new tyres and a full tank of fuel can take as little as 14 secs!

EQUIPMENT

- Drivers wear fire-proof clothing under their fire-proof overalls, boots, fire-proof balaclavas and helmets. The latter include special safety devices, such as an air supply that is automatically released in an accident. Drivers are held into their seats by safety straps which can be released quickly in an emergency.

- The cars themselves are subject to constantly changing FISA rules, which regulate power and dictate safety features.

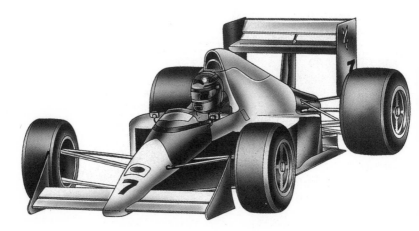

PERSONALITY PROFILE

Ayrton Senna

Born in Brazil in 1960, Ayrton Senna has won 2 World Championships — in 1988 and 1990. He came up through the ranks and proved his ability in Formula Ford and Formula 3. He is renowned for his ruthless approach to motor racing, and some despise his 'win-at-any-cost' tactics. However, few would deny that he is one of the greatest of modern drivers and his calm, calculating style and his courage have brought him handsome rewards.

TECHNICAL TERMS

aerofoil a winglike structure above the rear wheels, to help the car maintain road contact

aquaplane to ride on a film of water on a wet surface; decreases steering and braking capabilities

shunt an accident; drivers are reluctant to use the word 'crash'

slicks tyres that have no tread on them — this enables them to keep excellent grip on dry surfaces but they are lethal if used in wet weather

turbo a turbine to force air into the engine for increased power

FOR THE RECORD

Nearly all Grand Prix drivers graduate to the top via one, or possibly more, of the so-called minor classes of motor racing. There are numerous categories but the most important are as follows:

- Formula 3000: A category using cars that are fundamentally the same as the old Formula 1 design. The cars in this class have 3-litre engines and are only marginally slower than Formula 1 cars.

- Formula 3: Many argue that this category demands the best from the drivers. All cars have 2-litre engines but relatively narrow tyres are used and strict rules govern the power output of the engines.

- Formula Ford: In this class, all cars must have either a Ford 1600 cc or Ford 2000 cc engine. Separate races are held for the two engine sizes. As the engines are virtually identical in each car, a driver's ability quickly becomes apparent. Similar categories include Formula Renault, Formula Vauxhall and Formula Lotus.

FOR THE RECORD

RECENT WORLD CHAMPIONS

1981	Nelson Piquet	(Bra)
1982	Keke Rosberg	(Fin)
1983	Nelson Piquet	(Bra)
1984	Niki Lauda	(Austria)
1985	Alain Prost	(Fra)
1986	Alain Prost	(Fra)
1987	Nelson Piquet	(Bra)
1988	Ayrton Senna	(Bra)
1989	Alain Prost	(Fra)
1990	Ayrton Senna	(Bra)

CART RACING

Cars of all kinds have been developed independently on both sides of the Atlantic for 70 years or more, and single-seat racing cars are no exception. Not surprisingly different types of racing have also evolved. In Europe, Grand Prix racing is considered the most important, but in the United States this honour goes to Championship Auto Racing Teams, or CART racing. Races involve high-speed Indy cars, which take their name from the most important race in the CART calendar — the Indianapolis 500.

CART racing was organized as an official sport in 1978. Since then it has established its own championship — the Indy Car World Series — which is exclusively run in the United States but which attracts drivers from around the world.

Because it is so popular in the United States, the rewards in CART racing can be very high. Drivers and teams can reap huge rewards if they win races, especially if they are successful in the Indianapolis 500, which can be viewed on television worldwide.

▼ *During the few seconds of a pit stop the car can be refuelled and fitted with new tyres by expert mechanics. It also gives the driver a chance to discuss tactics with team managers.*

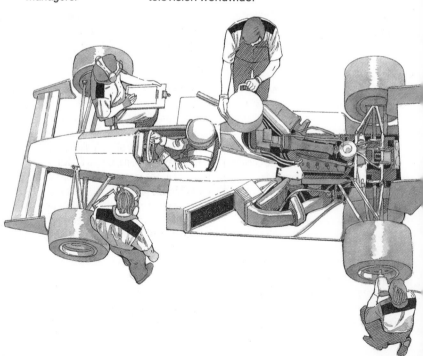

AIMS OF THE GAME

COMPETITION

● Indy cars are single-seaters and outwardly appear very similar to those automobiles used in Formula 1 racing. However, there are fewer restrictions on design and engine size, so the racing cars develop more power and are faster.

● The object of racing in CART events is to win or score well in individual races, with an eye on success in the overall season. Points are awarded according to finishing positions in each race. The person who accumulates the most points at the end of the season wins the Indy Car World Series, which usually includes at least 16 races.

● Two types of race track are used in CART racing — oval circuits and road circuits. The oval circuits are comparatively plain in outline — the Indianapolis 500 circuit is a good example — and comprise little more than 2 straights which are joined together by two long bends. The races on 'ovals' are extremely fast and there is plenty of room for overtaking — something that is not always easy to achieve on bendy Grand Prix circuits. CART road circuits are more like Grand Prix tracks but they, too, have comparatively few bends, and therefore allow for higher speeds than the circuits used in the Formula 1 Grand Prix Championships.

● Unlike the starting procedure used in Grand Prix races, CART events are started with the cars on the move. This type of start is known as a 'rolling start'. Pit stops for engine adjustments, changes of tyres and to take on fuel are permitted. The winner of the race is the person who finishes first after driving his car round a circuit for a given number of laps.

SKILLS

● Because the circuits in CART racing are so fast with comparatively few corners, drivers only occasionally let up on the throttle and virtually run their cars flat out all the time. This demands great concentration, particularly as engines and equipment are constantly pushed to straining point. As the lap speeds are so high — anything up to 354 km/h (220 mph) — the risks are huge and the slightest error can prove fatal. High speed and high risk factors are what make the sport attractive to American spectators and television viewers worldwide.

● As with Grand Prix racing, the back-up team plays an important role — managers, designers and mechanics must all work together in race preparation and pit stops.

EQUIPMENT

● Safety equipment is compulsory. Drivers are obliged to wear fire-proof clothing as well as helmets and safety harnesses.

FOR THE RECORD

One of the most famous motor races in the world, the Indianapolis 500, is held every year in May at the Indianapolis Raceway in Indiana, United States of America. The race is over 200 laps of the 2.5 mile (4 km) circuit. The race was first run in 1911 and by 1925 the winners were clocking up average speeds of 160 km/h (100 mph) or more. Today average speeds reach 282.3 km/h (176.46 mph). Only 4 non-Americans have won the race since 1950: Jim Clark (UK) in 1965, Graham Hill (UK) in 1966, Emerson Fittipaldi (Bra) in 1989 and Arie Luyendyk (Neth) in 1990.

DID YOU KNOW?

The most successful Le Mans 24 Hour driver was Jacky Ickx of Belgium who won the race 6 times from 1969 to 1982. Ickx was also a Grand Prix driver but achieved greater success in sports car racing.

SPORTS CAR RACING

The bald definition of a sports car in racing terms is a racing car that has two seats. Ordinary production sports cars are successfully raced at club meetings, but the most prestigious events are contests between prototype cars that would never be allowed to be driven on ordinary roads. Instead they are raced on special circuits around the world; some of these circuits are also used for Grand Prix and other races.

As with so many of the motor sports, different versions of sports car racing have evolved on either side of the Atlantic. The International Motor Sports Association (IMSA) organizes a series of events which make up a Grand Touring (GT) Championship in the United States. The rival European competition is the World Sports Car Championship, which is decided after a number of races, including the most famous motor race in the world — the Le Mans 24-hour. However, many American drivers and racing teams take part in the World Championship series, and many European drivers and cars are involved with IMSA racing. Some drivers even take part in both.

Sports car racing is sometimes considered a poor relation to Grand Prix and CART racing and, as a rule, it does not receive as much attention. However, manufacturers spend large amounts of money in promoting their machines, and the maker of the winning car at Le Mans can expect its production car sales to soar.

AIMS OF THE GAME

COMPETITION
● Although there are a few differences in the rules between IMSA and World Sports Car Championship racing, the basic object of the sport is the same for both. Cars are driven for a specific period of time round a circuit — 6 hr, 12 hr or 24 hr, for example — and at the end of that time, the car that has covered the greatest distance is the winner. Alternatively, some races cover a given length — 1000 km (621 miles) for instance — and the car that finishes this distance first is the winner.
● The cars have 2 seats and are usually powered by 3.5 litre engines. They are heavier and wider than single-seat racing cars, but nevertheless they can achieve speeds well over 320 km/h (200 mph).
● In sports car racing, each car is driven by 2, or even 3, people who take it in turn to drive: it would be impossible — and dangerous — for a solitary driver to complete the longest races. It is for this reason that the winning sports car usually gets more publicity than its team of drivers.
● At the end of a race, cars and their drivers are awarded points according to the position in which they finished. At the end of the season the car and drivers with the highest number of points win the appropriate championship. Drivers can expect substantial pay bonuses for victories in races or the championship.

◄ The low-slung design of a sports car improves its wind resistance and fuel economy. The engine is behind the drivers' cockpit. The rear wing and wide tyres improve handling by 'anchoring' the car to the road surface.

SKILLS
● Sports car driving requires great stamina as concentration has to be maintained for considerable lengths of time. In the longest races, the drivers only snatch a couple of hours' sleep before they have to take the wheel again. This can obviously be extremely tiring and can test the nerves to the full. In addition, drivers have to be able to drive flat out at night, sometimes in the rain. This demands acute awareness — the slightest error could lead to complete disaster.
● As with most other types of motor racing, the back-up team to a car plays a very important role in keeping the car on the road and out of the pits. The pit crews take more time than their Grand Prix counterparts: spotting a potential problem may save the car 12 hr later.

EQUIPMENT

● Standard safety equipment is employed by both drivers and car manufacturers. As fire is the most feared hazard, protective clothing is essential.

FOR THE RECORD

The 24-hr race at Le Mans in France provides the ultimate test for drivers and cars. The first race was run in May 1923 and the current circuit measures 13.64 km (8.48 miles). There have been several major tragedies at Le Mans. The most horrific was in 1955 when a car ran into the crowd and 82 people were killed. The race always used to start with drivers running across the track to their waiting cars on the drop of a flag, but nowadays the cars start from a grid. Average speeds may reach 204km/h (127 mph).

DID YOU KNOW?

Actor Steve McQueen was famous for his driving exploits. He once drove at Le Mans. What is not so well known is that Paul Newman is also a car fanatic and was highly successful at driving in NASCAR events.

SALOON CAR RACING

The sport of racing saloon cars really only developed after World War II, but in the United States it has risen to become probably the most watched motor sport. The sport goes by the name of stock car racing in the United States. It is also popular, to a lesser degree, in other parts of the world such as Australia, Britain and Japan.

Many different types of car can be raced in the various categories of saloon car racing — from the humble Mini Minor to giant Buicks and Chevrolets. In the United States, saloon car racing is dominated by NASCAR events. NASCAR (the National Association for Stock Car Auto Racing) was founded in 1947 by Bill France, who organized his first race meeting on the hard-packed sand of Daytona Beach, Florida. Today, Daytona hosts one of the most glamorous of all motor racing events, the Daytona 500, run on a standard paved track. Many successful NASCAR drivers are millionaires and the prizes are huge. The rest of saloon car racing is more modest, but some adventurous car manufacturers are prepared to promote their vehicles in races, to show that they are reliable as well as speedy.

AIMS OF THE GAME

COMPETITION
● There are literally hundreds of different categories for saloon car racing. The most important are listed below. Most races take place on ordinary motor racing circuits. The car and driver to cross the line first after completing a given number of laps is the winner.

'One-make' racing
In this category all the cars in a race are made by the same manufacturer. This ensures that it is driving skills that tell. This form of racing is particularly popular in Britain.

Group A racing
With this class, all cars have to be basically standard production models, but a certain amount of tinkering and tuning is allowed and racing tyres are permitted. Manufacturers are particularly interested in this category as rival models are frequently raced against each other; it is in their interests to show that their cars are better than those of their competitors. Many standard features common to ordinary saloon cars were first tested on the Group A racing circuit. This form of racing is popular in Britain, Japan, Australia and continental Europe. Car manufacturers provide most of the sponsorship.

Production saloon racing

As the title suggests, all the cars that take part in this category must be ordinary road-going cars, although special safety features like rollbars and safety windscreens must be fitted. In Britain, races of this kind take place almost every weekend and they prove sure testing grounds for ambitious drivers.

NASCAR

There is no racing like NASCAR. The cars are nominally production saloons but their huge 5-litre engines can be modified and most cars can travel well over 320 km/h (200 mph). In NASCAR, entertainment is all-important and so if one make of car is seen to gain an outrageous advantage, new rules are introduced to make things more equal. The cars race dangerously close together — which adds to the excitement — and accidents are quite commonplace. However, all cars have to conform to safety regulations and the chassis and bodies are specially strengthened.

Most of the circuits are oval in shape and some have banked corners which are a safety feature as much as a gimmick to please spectators. There are usually about 30 NASCAR races in a year but the highlight is undoubtedly the Daytona 500.

▲ *In NASCAR events, a common tactic is to slot the car into the slipstream of one in front while waiting for an opportune moment to overtake. This saves fuel. Cars race perilously close together but severe driver injuries are rare.*

SKILLS

● All drivers, even in the more modest races, have to be aware of racing etiquette. They must be able to recognize signals from pits or from race marshals. These are usually given by waving coloured flags — yellow for danger, red for oil on the track, and so on.
● All cars have a back-up team of some description, but nowhere is a team of mechanics more valuable than in NASCAR. Because the prizes are so large in NASCAR, top teams have some of the most highly trained and efficient mechanics in motor racing.

EQUIPMENT

● Safety equipment is compulsory in all forms of saloon car racing and the faster the cars can travel, the more stringent the rules are. All cars must be fitted with rollbars, and safety seats with harnesses at the very least. It is usual for drivers to wear fireproof clothing in addition to helmets.

DID YOU KNOW?

One of the world's most famous — and dangerous — rallies is the Paris–Dakar. The stages cover some of the roughest terrain in Africa. Former UK prime minister Margaret Thatcher's son, Mark, took part in 1982, but went missing in the Sahara. He and his French co-driver were rescued when they were spotted by a rescue plane after 2 days in the desert.

▼ *'Special stages' are held on all kinds of terrain, from mud- or snow-covered tracks to desert wilderness. A good partnership between driver and co-driver can make the most of a special stage.*

RALLYING

Rallying is almost as old as motor racing, with the first long-distance rally being held in 1907. Despite the dramatic developments in car technology, the principle of rallying has remained constant. Drivers take their cars over a prescribed route across country, competing against the clock. There was a time when drivers used to enter both rally and Grand Prix events. Britain's Stirling Moss was a success in rallying (he came second in the Monte Carlo Rally in 1952), sports car racing (he came second at Le Mans in 1956) as well as Grand Prix racing, for which he is best known (he won 36 Grand Prix races). Today, however, the specialist demands of racing mean that drivers rarely compete in both rally and track events.

Major international rallying events are held in such diverse places as the Arctic and the Sahara. Because one of the aims of rallying is to test cars as well as drivers, motor manufacturers invest huge amounts of money in cars that take part in the most famous rallies — success in an important rally will almost certainly boost sales. Amateur drivers and teams enter many events. Women, too, can take part — some women drivers have been extremely successful, most notably Pat Moss, Stirling's sister. The most successful of all rallying nations is Finland, which has produced more drivers to clinch the prestigious World Rally Championship than any other country.

AIMS OF THE GAME

COMPETITION

● Like all motor sports, rallying can be taken at many different levels. At the bottom end of the scale, there is club rallying in which enthusiastic amateurs compete for the fun of it. At the top end lies international rallying which is a glamorous, potentially lucrative and highly prestigious sport.

Rally drivers always compete against the clock — events are not head-to-head races as such. The essential aim is to complete a course in the shortest possible time. Some rallies last for just a few hours, but the most important ones last for several days or even weeks.

● Courses are organized in 'stages' (separate legs), with the cars being started separately at regular intervals at the beginning of each one. Some stages are over ordinary public roads and the cars have to comply with local laws and regulations: for example, cars have to keep within speed limits if they are not to be disqualified. Other stages can comprise dirt roads, mountain tracks, barren desert or even snow fields. It is in these 'special stages' that rallies are usually won and lost, and they provide the toughest of

all tests for both driver and car. The character of a rally is largely dependent on how many special stages there are. Some of the most gruelling, week-long rallies held in remote parts of the world consist of little else; other rallies, most notably those held in Europe, have comparatively few special stages.

● In road stages, drivers have to finish the sections within a given time. If they fail to meet the deadline, they incur time penalties. In special stages, the rules are slightly different. As competitors do not have to stay within speed limits, they can drive flat out in a race against time.

● The cars used in rallying are based very loosely on standard production models but the engines are highly tuned and the suspension is strengthened. Extra equipment such as banks of fog lights are permitted and a whole range of tyres can be used. Each car has a driver and a co-driver. The co-driver is in fact a navigator and it is his or her responsibility to instruct the driver where to go and what sort of road and terrain to expect.

● At the end of a rally, the winning team is the one that has completed all the special stages in the quickest overall time after time penalties on road stages have been taken into account.

SKILLS

● Driver and co-driver must work closely as a team. Both must possess stamina, especially during the longer rallies, and both must have quick reactions.

● In a good rally, a driver's ability should be tested to the limit. He should be able to drive fast over treacherous terrain where the slightest mistake could prove fatal; but he must also be able to drive safely within speed limits. Judgement is at the heart of rally driving — an over-enthusiastic slide into a corner could cost precious seconds on a special stage but, if it is timed correctly, a controlled slide could be the quickest way round.

● The co-driver's job is to instruct the driver at every point in a rally. On some rallies, co-drivers are allowed to scout out the course first and they will make detailed notes for each corner and every stretch. Co-drivers use their own type of shorthand. A notebook might contain an entry that reads: '46 - S = fast right, slow left - 3-2-3 - slip, no slip (ravine).' This would mean: point 46 is a double-bend, the first corner is to the right and can be taken fast in third gear in a slide, the second part is tighter and has to be taken in second gear as there is no room for a skid and a ravine is on the far side. On long rallies, a co-driver has only a map with marked co-ordinates on it to tell the driver where to go.

● In the most prestigious rallies, cars have back-up teams which help with repairs and usually carry a huge selection of tyres which can be changed according to road and weather conditions.

◀ *Dust flies during one of the remote desert stages of the 1990 Paris–Dakar Rally.*

EQUIPMENT

● Safety equipment is paramount in rallying, and drivers and co-drivers are obliged to wear helmets and safety harnesses as well as some fire-proof clothing. Drivers and co-drivers talk to each other via radios which are fitted to the helmets: without the radios, they would not be able to hear each other because the engines are so loud.

FOR THE RECORD

THE MAJOR RALLIES

The most famous rally in the world is the Monte Carlo Rally, which is unusual in that there are several starting points dotted around various parts of Europe. From these starting points, competitors head for Monte Carlo and once there, they embark on a series of special stages which are held in the Alps. All the stages are on cordoned-off public roads: mountain roads are usually covered with ice and snow. The final special stages are held at night.

The Safari Rally is held every year in East Africa. Unlike most, it does not have any special stages: it is in a sense one long special stage and competitors drive over unmade roads which are often little more than mud lakes as the rally takes place in the rainy season.

At the other extreme is the 1000 Lakes Rally, which is held in Finland. The course frequently takes in frozen lakes, forest tracks and dirt roads.

The Lombard RAC Rally is the premier event held in England and Wales. Co-drivers cannot scout the course before the event, so navigation and driving skills are fully tested. Special stages usually include a selection of forest tracks and dirt roads, but the British weather is often the most unpredictable factor.

DID YOU KNOW?

The world land speed record is held by Britain's Richard Noble who, in 1983, drove his car, *Thrust 2*, at a speed of 1019.44 km/h (633.47 mph) in the Black Rock Desert in the United States. *Thrust 2* was powered by a Lightning jet engine and had no tyres — it rode on aluminium wheels.

MISCELLANEOUS MOTOR SPORTS

New motor sports of various types are evolving all the time. For example, with the current proliferation of four-wheel drive cars that can be driven on both roads and over rugged terrain, numerous clubs and organizations run rallies which are exclusive to four-wheel drive cars. However, a number of motor sports have been seriously contested for many years. These include autocross, hill climbing, ice racing, rallycross and truck racing. In addition, there is land speed record breaking.

All of these sports are organized according to defined rules and some are more popular in some countries than in others.

AUTOCROSS

Autocross is particularly popular in Britain but is also contested in other countries. Tracks are grass circuits that average about 800 m (880 yd approx.) long. Competitors race against the clock but there are usually several cars in each run. Runs comprise three or four laps of the circuit. Each car is timed to hundredths of a second. There are often a number of different classes which are determined by the capacity of the cars' engines. Very little prize money is awarded to winners and the sport is largely enjoyed by amateur drivers.

Grass racing is similar to autocross except that the emphasis is on drivers racing against each other, not against the clock.

HILL CLIMBING

Courses for hill-climbing events are not circuits — the start is at the bottom of a hill and the finish is at the top. The track is usually a winding road or lane with steep gradients and sharp bends. Competitors are started individually and timed; each competitor has two or three runs. Separate events are held for vintage cars, saloon cars and single-seat racing cars. Hill climbing is a popular sport in Britain and many other places, including Hong Kong and Gibraltar.

DID YOU KNOW?

Truck racing was practically unheard-of in Britain until the late 1980s, when a sports channel on satellite television began broadcasting races from the United States. This media exposure helped the sport establish a foothold in Britain almost overnight.

ICE RACING

This form of racing is popular in the Scandinavian countries, especially Finland, where it is considered useful training for rally driving. The cars are driven on circuits or straights, often on frozen rivers, and they race against the clock. The tyres on the cars are covered with steel studs to aid traction.

RALLYCROSS

Rallycross was devised to be a spectacular television sport in the 1960s. For top drivers it can be lucrative, as sponsorship and prize money are substantial. It is a popular sport all over Europe. Circuits comprise a mixture of surfaces — asphalt, mud, grass and shale — so a driver's skill in controlling the car is tested to the full. Events are usually held on a knockout basis, and winners of heats go through to a final. Competitions are held for cars of different sizes and capacities.

▼ *Reinforced saloon cars with modified engines compete in autocross and rallycross competitions. Their interiors are often empty except for a strengthened driver's seat.*

TRUCK RACING

This is a comparatively new sport but it attracts huge crowds in Britain, Europe and Australia. The drivers are professionals (racing drivers, not truck drivers), and events are held on standard race tracks. Each race comprises a certain number of laps. The trucks themselves are designed to tow trailers. Racing trucks do not tow trailers, but they produce a phenomenal amount of noise, smoke and spectacle.

Perhaps the best known truck racer is Barry Sheene, Britain's former 500 cc motorcycle world champion.

DID YOU KNOW?

Not all drag racing takes place between supercharged dragsters resembling rockets on wheels. There are 8 competition categories, including 2 for normal production cars in which only the clutches and tyres are modified.

DRAG RACING

The spectacular, noisy and swift sport of drag racing started in the United States. It developed from hot rod racing, which became especially popular in certain parts of the United States, particularly California, after World War II. In hot rod racing — which still continues — ordinary cars fitted with extraordinary engines, raced round oval tracks at great speed. When not racing their vehicles, drivers used to storm down straight roads (drags) to show off the speed of their cars. It was not long before special tracks were constructed and official drag racing came into being. The sport spread eastwards within the United States, but is concentrated still in California.

From the United States, drag racing has spread to various parts of the world and it is now extremely popular in Britain. At first, disused airstrips were converted for the sport, but now there are special drag-racing facilities.

Women take part in some events, and Shirley Muldawney has been World Champion. It is definitely not a sport for the faint-hearted — speeds approaching 482 km/h (300 mph) have been recorded from a standing start along a 400-metre (440-yard) track!

▼ An aerofoil fitted by the front wheels of dragsters directs some of the airflow down onto the wheels. Otherwise the extreme acceleration would pull the front wheels off the ground in what is known as a 'wheelie'.

AIMS OF THE GAME

COMPETITION

● There are many different classes in drag racing. Although some events are reserved for comparatively tame, standard production cars, most competitions are between custom-built 'dragsters' — racing machines that would make most traffic police blanch. The object of drag racing is to race down a straight track in the quickest possible time from a stationary start. As there is only room for 2 cars on the track, competitions in each class are usually held on a knockout basis, with the winner in one race going through to the next heat and an eventual final between 2 cars.

● The tracks must be totally straight and absolutely smooth. They are usually 400 m (440 yd) long. Down the centre runs a white line which divides the two racing lanes; if a car crosses the line during a race, it is automatically disqualified.

● Cars start from a line with their engines running. The signal to go is given by a set of lights which change from red to amber to green. If a driver starts moving before the lights change to green, his car is eliminated.

● Dragsters vary enormously in size and shape. The purpose-built machines usually have engines mounted at the back behind the driver. Engine sizes differ according to the class of car and some can be turbocharged (extra air pumped into the engine). Many categories of car are allowed to be fitted with aerofoils (wing-like appendages for better control) and it is compulsory for some to carry parachutes to aid braking at the end of a race. One characteristic of dragsters is the size of the rear wheels which can be vast, to gain traction.

SKILLS

● As each race usually only lasts 5 or 6 secs, the start is very important. Quick reactions to the green 'go' lights are imperative.

● Various tricks are used by drivers to get a quick getaway. The tyres have no tread on them and without treatment they would simply spin on the spot at the start of a race. So, before a race, the wheels are covered with household bleach which helps to soften the rubber. When the tyres spin at the start, the rubber melts and sticks to the track, so giving better traction. Throttle control is then important so the car does not rear up.

● Because the acceleration forces are so great, drivers must be prepared for the shock — the fear of most drivers is of passing out due to the gravitational forces put upon them.

EQUIPMENT

● Fire-proof clothing, helmets, gloves and boots are obligatory for drivers regardless of what category of car they are driving. Special breathing equipment is carried by some people who tend to resemble fighter pilots more than car drivers.

TECHNICAL TERMS

Christmas tree the set of coloured lights that start a race
funny car a hot rod car modified with garish colours and exaggerated displays of chrome
rail another name for a high-speed drag racing car
slicks bald tyres
strip the track
wheelie when the front wheels rear up off the ground due to the acceleration of the car

MOTORCYCLE RACING

DID YOU KNOW?

The Isle of Man TT current course is 61 km (38 miles) long and winds all over the tiny island, up hills and down valleys. For many years the course has been condemned by critics who fear it is too dangerous. They have a valid point as it has accounted for many deaths. Nevertheless, the annual TT races continue to attract riders and spectators and they appear to be lasting fixtures.

The course plays host to several races, but the most prestigious one is the 'senior', which is reserved for big machines and experienced riders.

Motorcycle racing which takes place on asphalt tracks is usually referred to as 'road racing' to differentiate it from the many other motorcycle sports which are competed on other surfaces. Few major races actually take place on ordinary roads these days and the majority of road racing events are held on prepared circuits. The first road races were competed as far back as the end of the last century both in France and in England. Today, road racing is an international sport and major races are held all over the world: regular competitions attract riders to European cities as well as to the United States and Japan.

For periods throughout its history, motorcycle road racing has earned a reputation for being a poor man's motor sport and many car racing enthusiasts have viewed it with disdain. It is true to say that road racing gets far less media coverage than, say, Grand Prix car racing, but it has its own devoted following, its own sense of glamour and it can generate drama and excitement unknown in car racing.

Up until the mid-1960s German, Italian and British motorcycle manufacturers tended to produce the bulk of winning machines. But since then road racing has been dominated by Japanese-made motorcycles which have proved superior in both speed and reliability. This dominance comes as a direct result of Japanese firms seeing road racing as an ideal way of promoting their products. They have invested colossal amounts of money in developing racing cycles and they are now reaping the rewards — sales of European and American motorcycles are very small when compared with those of the Japanese.

The World Championships (there are several championships for the various categories of motorcycle) are the most important challenges although one-off events such as the Isle of Man TT are also highly prestigious. The bulk of riders are professionals hired by manufacturers and teams. Motorcycling is a sport for both men and women at all levels.

AIMS OF THE GAME

COMPETITION
● There are essentially 3 different types of road racing:
- Grand Prix racing which takes place on circuits;
- TT (Tourist Trophy) racing which is held on public roads;
- endurance racing.
● Grand Prix races are organized and run like those for Grand Prix car racing. There is a starting grid marked on the track and a certain number of laps of the circuit have to be completed before the finish. The simple object is to beat the opposition and win. Many of the circuits used also host car racing — for example, Donington Park, Silverstone and Brands Hatch, the best-known racing circuits in England.
● The different classes of Grand Prix racing are defined below (see For the Record).
● In any one year there are about 15 Grand Prix races for each of the

▲ *Motorcycles have a streamlined covering that curves around the engine and gear unit. Riders crouch low to reduce drag further.*

different classes. Points are awarded according to how riders finish in each race — 20 for first spot, 17 for second, 15 for third and so on. At the end of a season, these points are accumulated and the riders with the highest totals win the respective World Championships for their class of machine.
● TT races are few and far between and, as a rule, they are considered less prestigious than Grand Prix events (the Isle of Man TT race is the exception).
● TT races are held on public roads that are contrived to form 'circuits' (the roads are cordoned off while a race is in progress). These circuits are often long and include climbs and descents as well as uneven road surfaces and everyday bends. A number of laps of a circuit have to be completed.

- A TT World Coupe exists and is won on the points system.
- Endurance races are a comparatively new innovation. They have come into being because manufacturers wanted to prove that their machines could survive long distances as well as just travelling fast. This commercial incentive should ensure the survival of these races.
- Races are necessarily lengthy — 1000 km (620 miles) on average — and are designed to test both machines and riders to the limit.

SKILLS
- Grand Prix races are not always won by the fastest machines — cornering techniques frequently decide who wins and who loses. Various skills can be employed at corners. Some riders let their machines 'slide' round corners but this demands the greatest finesse if tragedy is not to occur. Others take a more traditional approach to bends.

Motorcycles are rarely manoeuvred by twisting the handlebars, as they are in recreational use. More often, they are controlled by shifting body weight from one side of the saddle to the other and by leaning right over into a curve. Sometimes riders come perilously close to shaving off their knee pads. Precise judgement is needed — when to lean into a bend and when to accelerate out of it. In all classes of Grand Prix racing, speed is balanced by cornering skill.

In sidecar racing, the weight transference is largely up to the 'passengers' who invariably appear to invite certain death as they lean into corners.
- On straight sections of a course, riders tuck down behind their windscreens to reduce wind resistance.
- TT racing demands all of the skills needed in Grand Prix racing but riders must also be prepared for additional hazards — bumpy road surfaces, slick conditions, narrow lanes and so on.
- Endurance riders nurture skills all of their own. Speed is important but maintaining the will to keep going is just as imperative.

▼ *The driver of a sidecar motor-cycle lies low on his stomach while the passenger swings his body to the left or right to balance the vehicle round corners.*

▲ *Motorcyclists lean into curves on a Grand Prix racetrack at speeds of more than 160 km/h (100 mph).*

EQUIPMENT

● In most forms of road racing, the tyres are roughly V-shaped — when travelling along a straight section a machine is balanced on something of a knife edge, but when cornering, the width of the tyre comes into play for better traction.

● Riders wear leather overalls (leather is the best material for dispersing heat while not ripping should an accident happen) as well as gloves, boots and helmets. Plastic or leather knee pads are worn because knees often touch the ground around corners.

● Racing helmets use an aerodynamic design to lessen wind resistance. Tinted visors shield racers' eyes from glare and particles thrown up by other motorcycles.

FOR THE RECORD

World Championship Grand Prix classes are as shown:
- 125 cc
- 250 cc
- 500 cc
- sidecar

The 'blue ribbon' class is considered to be 500 cc. A 500 cc machine can develop approximately twice the power of an average saloon car and can travel at speeds of up to 320 km/h (200 mph). Even highly tuned 125 cc motorcycles can move at 190 km/h (120 mph) or more depending on the gearing.

Other classes include 100 cc (2 cylinder) motorcycles and the so-called superbikes, which have an engine capacity of 750 cc (4 cylinders). The Superbike World Championship is separate from the Grand Prix but follows a similar system of accumulating points.

DID YOU KNOW?

Bikes have no brakes, so control comes from skilful use of the throttle and clutch. The 'no-brake' rule prevents a frontrunner from braking suddenly and causing a pile-up.

SPEEDWAY RACING

Speedway, or 'dirt track' racing, dates back to the very beginning of the 20th century. From the United States it spread to Australia, New Zealand and Britain. Ironically, it is not a popular sport these days in the United States.

In Europe, Britain and Denmark in particular, it has a substantial following although it has never quite caught the imagination of the public at large. Events are usually held in the evening in uncovered stadia. Spectators new to the sport often sit in the ringside seats, only to get a dousing of dust and dirt every time the competitors complete a circuit; those who know better, sit further back.

At its best, speedway is an exhilarating sport to watch, full of drama, noise and excitement. There are annual World Championship events for individuals, pairs and teams. In Britain, a league system operates in which teams compete against each other for trophies and prize money. Speedway is a professional motor sport, although it does not compare in terms of prestige with motorcycle road racing.

AIMS OF THE GAME

COMPETITION

• The majority of speedway races are held over 4 laps of a circuit. In each race there are only 4 competitors who start shoulder-to-shoulder from a line. During the course of a meeting, in which 30 or so riders may be involved, a series of heats are usually held. At the end of each race 3 points are awarded to the winner, 2 to the second rider and one to the third. Each competitor is usually given a certain number of rides during the course of a meeting. At the end of the meeting the person with the highest total of points is the overall winner. In team and pairs competitions, individuals claim points not for themselves but for their team or partnership.

• Circuits are oval in shape and vary in length from 275 m (300 yd) to 460 m (500 yd). The surface of the track is usually covered with loose cinders or ash. This type of surface permits sliding and skidding — very much part of the sport. This loose surface reflects the sport's rural, informal origins in the American south. The first races were held along dusty farm roads. Speedway's alternative name is 'dirt track' racing.

• The motorcycles used in speedway usually have 500 cc engines which run on special high-octane fuel. Throttle-control is important because of the finely tuned engines and the powerful fuel used. They do not have gearboxes but can nevertheless accelerate fast and reach speeds of around 130 km/h (80 mph).

SKILLS

● As races are short — they only last for a minute or so — getting a clean start is important. The competitor who reaches the first corner in the lead has a huge advantage as he can 'block' those behind him who try to overtake. However, cornering in speedway requires tremendous control and balance, and over-enthusiastic riders often slide out too wide, thus giving space for an opponent to overtake on the inside.

● While cornering, a speedway driver allows the rear tyre of his machine to slide outwards. If he does this successfully and with sufficient control, he will be able to accelerate at full throttle down the following straight. Most races are won and lost on cornering technique.

▼ *A combination of speed, skill and balance is required for cornering quickly and safely.*

EQUIPMENT

● In addition to standard protective clothing common to many recreational motorcycle enthusiasts, such as 'leathers' and helmets, riders wear studded boots which allow them to put their feet down, if necessary, whilst cornering. They also wear special visors and face masks to protect their eyes, faces and lungs from any flying dust and grit.

FOR THE RECORD

In Scandinavia and in northern parts of the Soviet Union, dirt track speedway is practically unheard of, but ice speedway is something of a passion. In ice speedway, the wheels on the motorcycles are studded with gruesome-looking spikes which enable them to grip the icy tracks. Ice speedway is dramatic, exciting and potentially lethal.

MOTOCROSS

DID YOU KNOW?

Motocross bikes rely on careful engine tuning and lightweight frames for their renowned handling ability. Too much engine power would make it almost impossible for the rider to negotiate the rougher sections of a circuit.

Motocross, which also goes by the name of 'scrambling', is a specialized form of motor-cycling in which participants ride machines up, over and down dirt tracks. The first motocross races were held in the mid-1920s. Initially, motocross was an entirely British sport but it soon acquired a following and it was duly adopted as an international sport in the 1940s.

Motocross is massively popular in Britain and in certain parts of Europe, and has now achieved appreciable status in North America and other continents. This is not surprising because it is a thrilling sport for spectators and even more so for participants. It would appear to have all the credentials for popular worldwide appeal — excitement, mud, smell and speed. Above all else, it tests the personal stamina, courage and skill of the riders.

Although a few top riders are professionals, it is largely an amateur or semi-professional sport. Many of the best riders build (and re-build) their own machines. However, motocross is beginning to attract more world media cover-age, and sponsorship is increasing. Most of the

AIMS OF THE GAME

COMPETITION
● To win in motocross, a rider usually has to compete solidly for a given period of time (often 40 min) before going for a finishing 2 or 3 laps of the course. The winner is the person who laps the circuit most times within the time period. An alternative method of motocross competition uses a knockout system — the first half dozen or so of each heat go through to a deciding eliminator.
● Circuits vary considerably and there are no definitive rules regarding distance and what should be included on each course. Most courses, however, are about 800 m (½ mile) long and include sharp climbs, steep

descents, assorted jumps and, preferably, a great deal of soft mud and dirt.
● Competitors are started from a line and, once they have been given the signal to go, they negotiate the course as quickly as possible.

SKILLS
● Riding through dirt and mud at speed, up and down hills and over jumps, is extremely demanding. All riders must be fit and willing to take a few knocks and bruises.
● On steep, muddy climbs, maintaining the right amount of traction with the rear wheel is essential. If the engine is given too much throttle, the wheel will spin and the machine will slide down the hill out of control. If not

▶ *A motocross rider assumes a crouched position, with knees flexed, in mid-jump. The knees absorb part of the impact, as does the outsized suspension system of the machine's front wheel.*

sponsorship tends to come from small, local companies, although cases of sponsorship from international concerns are increasing.

Motocross is virtually a totally male preserve. The ultimate goal for a rider is to win one of the annual World Championships which are held for various classes of cycle. In addition to the World Championships, there are number of lesser competitions for individuals and teams.

enough throttle is applied, the motorcycle will not make the top of the incline. Subtle throttle control is therefore very important.

● On jumps, competitors try to keep the front wheel high off the ground but this can be risky as if it is slightly out of line on landing, a machine will fall over. On multiple jumps, experienced riders often try to clear the lot with one huge leap. Riders are usually out of the saddle until well after landing.

EQUIPMENT

● The only attire that riders tend to wear in addition to a helmet, goggles and protective clothing, is a face mask which prevents mud and dust from entering their lungs.

FOR THE RECORD

All motocross machines are finely tuned and have modified suspension units that can yield to the rough riding. The fine tuning gives them their characteristic high-pitched sound. Mud shields are obligatory — the one over the front wheel is often raised higher than normal to allow for the considerable movement in the suspension. Tyres are thick and knobbly so that they can maintain a grip in the usually muddy conditions.

World Championship categories include:
- 500 cc
- 250 cc
- 125 cc
- sidecar.

TRIALS RIDING

DID YOU KNOW?

The International Six-Days Trial, which began in 1913, is staged in a different country each year. It is organized so that riders are awarded individual medals, but more important are the awards for national teams — the Premier World Trophy (for six-man teams) and the Silver Vase (for four-man teams).

Trials riding is a highly specialized form of motorcycling but is not just enjoyed by eccentric trailblazers, as its popular image would have it. It has an interesting history, different from that of any other form of motorcycling.

In 1885, soon after motorcycles were invented, a few enthusiasts saw their potential, not as 'speed machines', but as substitutes for horses which could be ridden over ditches, hedges and other countryside obstacles. Gradually interest in the idea of driving tough vehicles across rough terrain grew. Motorcycles had the advantage over cars in that they were narrow and relatively easy to manoeuvre, so a new sport came into being — trials riding.

Motorcycle trials are held in various parts of the world and there is even a World Championship. But trials riding is perhaps unique in all motor racing, in that taking part in an event is genuinely considered more important than winning it; the sheer joy of 'rough riding', albeit in a competitive way, tends to eclipse the fanatical desire to win. The vast majority of trials riders are keen amateurs, although a select few can earn a living as professionals.

AIMS OF THE GAME

COMPETITION
● Trials riding is entirely concerned with testing a rider's ability to negotiate rough terrain. In most competitions, the objective of each rider is to complete an obstacle course on a motorcycle within a given time limit; failure at an obstacle (putting a foot down on the ground to gain balance, for example) results in penalty points. Rules of competition do vary, however, and in some competitions, a fast finishing time is the most important thing.
● Categories exist in trials riding according to the age and type of a motorcycle — experts, twin shock, pre-65 and so on. 'Junior' events are often held to encourage youngsters but the majority of competitions are for adults who ride larger machines.
● There is literally no end to the types of obstacles that can be presented in a trial, and course lengths can also vary. It is unusual for a course to be lapped; more often courses are long and have to be negotiated only once.

Some courses are man-made and include obstacles like tree trunks piled 2 m (6½ ft) high on top of each other, narrow bridges, and artificial lakes. Others rely entirely upon natural obstacles which can be even more hazardous — fast-flowing streams, muddy banks, man-size rocks, felled trees and so on.

All courses are outlined with flags or barriers so the only navigating a competitor has to do is through, over or under the obstacles. At pertinent points throughout the length of a course, marshals keep a wary eye out for faults made by riders. Putting a foot to the ground to maintain balance constitutes a fault just as much as a fall.

● The motorcycle machines used for trials riding are not fast but they are powerful — most obstacles have to be taken cautiously but instant energy is essential if steep inclines are to be tackled without incurring a fault and penalty points.

● Trials are most frequently decided on faults and the person who rides 'cleanest' — with the fewest penalties — is the winner.

SKILLS

● If trials riding is not about speed then it is certainly all about control: the essence of the sport is to control a motorcycle to the utmost degree. To take a machine over a pile of huge logs is not easy — too fast and an accident is inevitable, too slow and a foot down will gain penalties. Judging pace, and therefore the throttle, while maintaining a knife-edge balance is crucial.

● When negotiating an obstacle at a snail's pace, riders tend to stand up on their foot supports to control their balance more acutely. At the same time they also have one hand on the brake lever and another on the throttle.

EQUIPMENT

● Standard equipment for trials riding includes a crash helmet and waterproof overalls, boots and gloves. Fire is not a major hazard, so few competitors wear special fire-proof clothing.

FOR THE RECORD

THE SCOTTISH SIX DAYS TRIAL
Possibly the most important of all trials riding events, the 'Scottish' has been held annually since 1909. The course encompasses every conceivable type of terrain — rivers, forests, beaches, rocks and snowfalls in the Highlands. It provides a great challenge for both machine and rider.

▶ *A trial rider may get up off the saddle and stand on the foot supports as a way of balancing when riding over rough terrain.*

KARTING

DID YOU KNOW?

At least 2 of the world's greatest Grand Prix drivers started in karting. Nelson Piquet has won the World Championship in karting 3 times (1981, 1983 and 1987).

Likewise, Ayrton Senna, began his meteoric rise to success in karting. He was lucky enough to be given a custom-made kart by his father before he even went to school. He has subsequently become World Champion in karting twice (1988 and 1990).

Karting, or 'go-karting' as it is sometimes called, originated in the United States, where racing enthusiasts were determined to let their off-spring gain a feel for motor racing. The first karts, built in the mid-1950s, were relatively simple machines, often constructed from whatever came to hand — lawn mower engines, small wheels and basic steering gear. However, from these elementary machines a whole new sport arose and, although karting is generally engineered to suit young drivers, it should not be underestimated. It is an intensely exciting motor sport. Karting, incidentally, should not be confused with CART racing, which is a totally different sport altogether (see page 164).

Soon after karting was established in the United States, it spread to Europe and Japan, and now events are held worldwide. The main reason for its massive following is that it permits young people to race competitively before they are old enough to drive legally on the roads. At least two World Championship racing drivers started their careers in karting. There is even an annual Karting World Championship which is governed by the FIA (see page 160).

AIMS OF THE GAME

COMPETITION
- The simple object of karting is to win races. In major competitions there are often several heats with the first 10 or so in each heat going through to a final which can contain up to 60 entries.
- Karting is divided into 3 essential categories:
- 100 cc karts which have no gears;
- 125 cc and 210 cc which have gear-boxes and relatively sophisticated engines;
- 250 cc 'superkarts' which are similar to those in the second category except that they have cockpits for the drivers and are appreciably faster than other karts.

- Racing circuits range in length, and the number of laps per race also varies according the category of kart. 'Junior' races (which involve 100 cc karts only) are usually held on 'short' circuits that comprise no more than a few hundred metres (yards). 'Senior' races (for karts above 100 cc) are frequently held on recognized racing circuits, with lap lengths of up to 5 km (3 miles).
- Age limits for the various categories of kart fluctuate from country to country. An international ruling states that it is illegal for anybody younger than 8 years old to take part in junior events, and those who compete in senior events usually have to be over 16 years old.

▲ *In sprint races competitors sit upright as they nip around the track.*

● The racing procedure is much the same as for any other track motor racing sport. Competitors are lined up on a grid at the start and have to complete a given number of laps. Pit stops are not necessary as the races are seldom very long.

● To ensure the well-being of the drivers, strict regulations are always enforced. These include restrictions on the tuning of engines, the type of tyres used, and the length of the races which seldom exceed more than a few laps of a circuit. Safety features such as barricades of straw soften landings should an accident happen.

SKILLS

● Karts have a limited speed capacity — around 250 km/h (150 mph) for senior classes, so drivers must learn driving skills rather than just how to open the throttle. The drivers are low to the ground which tends to accentuate the sense of pace. Accurate steering, accelerating techniques and codes of conduct are all learnt in karting.

EQUIPMENT

● Safety equipment is always worn by drivers, even those in the junior categories. Helmets are essential and most drivers wear flame-retardant outfits like those used by automobile racers.

GOAL SPORTS

Some of the most popular games in the world, as well as some of the most obscure, are goal sports. Many of these games are ancient in origin, but others are barely a hundred years old.

▼ Polo demands masterly riding ability from the player and considerable courage and stamina from the horse or 'pony'. Both horse and rider must be able to take the knocks and jolts. Essential teamwork underlies the partnership between the 4 players.

POLO

Polo, the only major goal sport to be played on horseback, originated in Persia (Iran). A reference to the sport was made by the Persian poet, Firausi, in 600 BC, but the game is thought to be even older.

From Persia, the sport spread eastwards, but by the turn of the 18th century, it was played only in remote regions of northern India. Polo became popular with British army officers in India; they established the first polo club, in Calcutta, in 1862.

AIMS OF THE GAME

COMPETITION
● Polo is played between 2 teams of 4 people in which all the participants are mounted on horses. The object of the game is for players to hit a ball with a mallet into the opposition's goal.
● The playing area is up to 300 yd (275 m) long by 200 yd (183 m) wide. At each end of the 'ground' stands a goal which is 8 yd (7.3 m) wide.
● Play begins when a mounted umpire bowls the ball underarm between the 2 teams, which are lined up on their respective sides of the centre 'T', facing the umpire.
● Players then try to strike the ball towards the opposition's goal. They can use only their right hands to strike the ball with the mallet. Players can intercept the ball or 'ride off' the opposition's players.
● Fouls are awarded for dangerous play. When a foul is committed, a free hit is awarded to the other side.

The first matches to be held in Britain took place in about 1870, and soon afterwards the Hurlingham Polo Association was founded in London. It drafted a set of rules for the game. The Hurlingham Rules are still the basis for all national rules.

Polo is now played in countries all round the world, particularly in South America, the United States, Australia and Europe; it is still played in India, but not in Iran.

Polo is played both by wealthy amateurs and by professional players. There are a number of female players. Polo is an exclusive game, mainly because a player has to maintain a large number of horses in order to participate. The best known players include members of the British royal family, Indian maharajahs and some of the wealthiest men in the world. In recent years most of the world's greatest players have come from Argentina.

> **DID YOU KNOW?**
>
> Argentina has more polo players than any other nation and boasts more than 150 civilian and military clubs. The sport gained popularity with the arrival of British trade representatives in the 19th century.

● A goal is scored when a player hits the ball between the opposition's goal posts. A handicapping system exists, under which players are handicapped from 2 to 10 goals; thus weaker teams can play on level terms with superior ones.

● Matches are usually divided up into 4, 6 or 8 'chukkas' (periods) which last 7 min each. There is a 3-min interval between each period. The winning team is the one which scores the most goals after handicap goals have been taken into consideration.

SKILLS

● The sport of polo demands a combination of good horsemanship and accurate ball-playing ability. A player must be able to make his horse stop quickly and turn and resume its stride at any instant so that he can strike a ball with a long mallet at speed. The difference between good and bad players comes mostly from the speed at which they can play.

EQUIPMENT

● Mallets have wooden heads about 9 in (23 cm) long and 2 in (5 cm) in diameter. The shaft is usually made of cane and is 51 in (130 cm) long.
● The ball, made of compressed plastic, is 3½ in (9 cm) in diameter.
● Polo is an exhausting sport, not only for the riders, but also for the horses. Therefore players may ride a fresh pony in each chukka or ride them in 2 chukkas each, but not more.
● Players wear helmets, kneepads and gloves in addition to standard riding gear.

TECHNICAL TERMS

pony a horse used for polo; a group of ponies make up a 'string'
ride off to use your horse to push an opponent away from the ball
stick a mallet
web the strong cloth loop on the handle of a polo mallet

LACROSSE

The Indians of what is now Canada had been playing a ball game called baggataway for centuries before the French arrived. Matches were more like battles, fought out over huge tracts of land with thousands of players on each side. A baggataway stick included a basket — reminding French missionaries of a bishop's crozier ('la crosse' in French).

Towards the end of the last century, Canada regulated the game into an organized sport for men. Touring teams travelled to England where it was welcomed as a game which demanded skill as well as aggression. Lacrosse is now played by men in Canada, Australia, Britain, the United States and Japan. A separate game for women evolved in the late 1800s.

For men, the ruling body is the International Lacrosse Federation and the most important competition is the four-yearly World Championships. Women have the World Cup, with its own ruling organization — the International Federation of Women's Lacrosse Associations.

▼ Men's lacrosse is a fiercely competitive sport. Players wear safety helmets and sturdy gloves. Here, as one player leaps to catch the ball (left) he is tackled by an opponent. Another team-mate runs down the pitch (right) to be in a good position to receive a pass.

AIMS OF THE GAME

COMPETITION
Men's lacrosse
● The game is played between two 10-a-side teams who aim to score points by slinging the ball into opposition goals. All players use a 'stick' to manoeuvre the small, hard ball about the 'pitch'.
● The pitch has a number of markings on it but is essentially divided into thirds. In the centre of the 2 'end thirds' lie the goals, which measure 6 ft (1.8 m) high and 6 ft (1.8 m) across. A goalkeeper guards each goal.
● Play begins in the middle of the pitch with a 'face-off' in which 2 opposing players vie to gain possession of the ball once it has been put in play by the referee.
● While the ball is in play, players are allowed to carry the ball in their sticks and they can also pass it to team-mates. Legitimate tackling includes challenging for a 'running ball', knocking the ball out of an opponent's stick and barging. Fouls include outright violence and dangerous play.
● Most matches are divided into four 25-min quarters and the side that scores the most goals wins.

Women's lacrosse
● The game is played between two 12-a-side teams.
● In principle the game is much like the men's version but certain rules ensure that it is not so violent.
● The pitch and goals are smaller. Women's pitches are measured in metres and not yards.

SKILLS
● Lacrosse is often underrated as a sport. Great skill is needed in catching and throwing the ball — a crosse is an unwieldy weapon at the best of times. Tackling, however, is comparatively easy — nudging a 'carrier' is enough to throw all but the best out of balance.
● Team members adopt field positions similar to those found in soccer or field hockey.

EQUIPMENT

● For men, standard attire includes a protective helmet and face guard, gauntlets, and a crosse that is no more than 72 in (183 cm) long with a basket no wider than 10 in (25 cm). Smaller sticks, with shorter handles and narrower baskets, are common in North American men's lacrosse. These make for a faster game, with quicker passing.
● For women, the sticks have the traditional dimensions, but special protective clothing is rarely worn, except by goal keepers.
● The ball used in both men's and women's lacrosse games is hard and has a diameter of around 3 in (7.5 cm).

TECHNICAL TERMS

box lacrosse an indoor version of the game, popular in Canada
crozier another name for a crosse
lax a common term for the game in British public schools

▼ *The modern stick or crosse is usually made of reinforced plastic.*

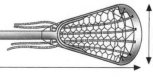

10 in (25 cm)

72 in (183 m)

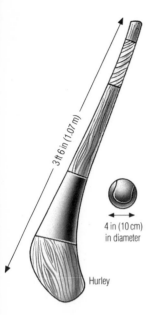

3 ft 6 in (1.07 m)

4 in (10 cm) in diameter

Hurley

▲ *Hurleys are made from ash wood using techniques that have remained unchanged for centuries. A ball struck squarely on the broad base can travel nearly the length of the 150 yd (137 m) pitch.*

HURLING

Hurling, the national game of Ireland, is one of the fastest of all goal sports. It is an ancient game, first mentioned in a 13th-century document called the Irish Annals when two clans had a violent game of hurling to determine which clan should rule Ireland! Throughout Irish history, hurling matches were used to settle feuds between clans. Hurling even became a gambling game and huge wagers were placed on individual teams.

Until the founding of the Gaelic Athletic Association (GAA) in 1884, hurling had few rules. As many as 300 players would play in village-versus-village contests. In such matches the winning team was the one that succeeded in hurling the ball back to its own village. The GAA standardized the laws and instituted the All-Ireland Championships — annual, inter-county competitions. The GAA remains the ruling body of the sport.

The traditional stronghold for hurling is in the southern counties of Ireland where skills are learned during childhood. Although hurling is played exclusively by Irishmen, emigrants to England and the United States have formed teams which have challenged for the McCarthy Cup, the trophy awarded to the All-Ireland champions.

► *Charging an opponent shoulder-to-shoulder is a legitimate tackle in hurling.*

AIMS OF THE GAME

COMPETITION
● The modern game is played between 2 teams of 15 players on a field or 'pitch'. Each team tries to score points by hitting a hard ball over or under crossbars on goals at each end of the pitch. Each player uses a broad-bladed stick or 'hurley' to hit the ball.
● A standard playing field measures 150 yd (137 m) by 90 yd (82 m). Features and markings are listed below.
- The goals are sited centrally on 'end lines', and each has 2 uprights, 21 ft (6.4 m) high, which are 21 ft (6.4 m) apart. The uprights are straddled by a crossbar 8 ft (2.4 m) from the ground.
- In front of each goal there is a 'goal area', 15 yd by 5 yd (13.7 m by 4.6 m).
- A centre line divides the pitch.
- In each half, '70 yd' (64 m), '21 yd' (19.2 m) and '14 yd' (12.8 m) lines are spaced accordingly from the end lines.
● The game starts in the middle of the pitch and is governed by a referee. A player is entitled to hit the ball with his hurley in order to pass it to a team-mate or to score. He may also run with the ball balanced or bouncing on the end of his hurley. Although he is allowed to catch the ball and kick it, he may not throw it or carry it in his hand for more than 3 paces. A player may not lift the ball from the ground using his hand — he has to use his hurley.
● If the ball goes out of play, a 'free hit' is awarded to the side that was not responsible for it crossing a line. Depending on which boundary line it crossed and which team was responsible, free hits are taken from the 70-yd, 21-yd, or 14-yd lines. (These rules are broadly similar to those in soccer — corner kicks, goal kicks etc.)
● Players are allowed to barge each other to gain possession of the ball but fouls include tripping and pulling.
● No attacking player is allowed to shoot at goal from within the defending goal area. Three points are given if the ball is driven between the posts and under the crossbar; one point is awarded when it is hit over the crossbar and between the uprights.
● Matches usually last for two 30-min halves, but in major competitions, 40-min halves are normal. The winning team is the one with the most points.

SKILLS
● There are 3 essential skills in hurling: to control the ball with a hurley, to hit the ball hard and accurately, and to tackle by flicking the ball away from an opponent's stick.
● Players inevitably adopt specialist positions — goalkeeper, backs, halfbacks and forwards.

EQUIPMENT

● A hurling ball is hard and about 4 in (10 cm) in diameter; like a cricket ball it has a stitched seam.
● Hurleys are usually made from ash wood and measure about 3 ft 6 in (1.07 m) in length with a blade that is about 3 in (7.6 cm) across.
● Players wear studded (cleated) boots. The only players at top level to wear additional protection are the goalkeepers, who don protective helmets and face masks. At lower levels, such as school leagues, all players must wear helmets.

TECHNICAL TERMS

caman Gaelic for a 'hurley'
parallelogram the goal area
puck to hit the ball with a hurley
sliothar Gaelic for 'the ball'

DID YOU KNOW?

There are two explanations of the origin of the word Shinty (Shinny in North America). One suggestion is that it is derived from the 17th-century match cry 'shin-ye'. Alternatively it could come from the gaelic word 'sinteag' meaning 'a bound'.

SHINTY

An almost exclusively Scottish sport, the modern game of shinty is a derivative of the ancient game of camanachd which was taken to Scotland by invading Gaels from Ireland some 1500 years ago. Camanachd was originally played with two types of stick — a broad-bladed one and a narrow one. The broad-stick version, most favoured in the south of Ireland, became hurling (see page 194), and the narrow-stick game, a favourite pastime in the north of Ireland, was exported to Scotland and became known as shinty.

For centuries, shinty was played with great fervour in Scotland and the game was even used to sort out feuds between clans. On such occasions, bands of bagpipers and supporters waving banners would turn out to boost the morale of clansmen.

Towards the end of the 19th century, however, shinty became a more organized sport and the Camanachd Association — still the ruling body of the game — was formed in 1893.

Today, shinty is only played seriously in the Highlands and Islands of Scotland, although from time to time international matches are arranged between Irish hurling clubs and Scottish shinty clubs. Most shinty competitions are confined to inter-club affairs, but to keep the game alive with younger players, competitions are also arranged between schools.

▼ *A shinty pitch is very large. Defending against quick attacks is hard, given the amount of field open for long passes.*

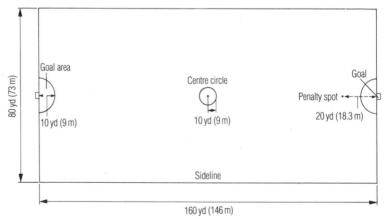

Goal area
10 yd (9 m)
80 yd (73 m)
Centre circle
10 yd (9 m)
Goal
Penalty spot
20 yd (18.3 m)
Sideline
160 yd (146 m)

AIMS OF THE GAME

COMPETITION
- Shinty is a men-only game played between two 12-a-side teams. Each team tries to score goals by hitting a hard ball with curved sticks through goals sited at the ends of a pitch.
- The pitch measures 160 yd (146 m) by 80 yd (73 m). Centrally positioned at each end stands a goal, which measures 12 ft (3.7 m) across and 10 ft (3 m) high. Markings on the pitch include:
  - a centre circle 10 yd (9 m) in diameter;
  - penalty spots 20 yd (18.3 m) in front of each goal;
  - 10 yd (9 m) hemispherical goal areas.
- After a game has been started from the centre circle, players can use their sticks to carry, dribble and hit the ball. Handling the ball is allowed only by goalkeepers while within their respective goal areas. Players are not allowed to kick the ball, as in hurling.
- To gain possession of the ball, players can tackle each other by knocking the ball from another's stick or by intercepting a pass. Barging from the side or front is also allowed.
- Fouls are penalized by free hits and, should a defender foul within his own goal area, a penalty is awarded.
- Games have two 45-min halves. The winning team is the one that scores the most goals.

SKILLS
- A fast and aggressive game, shinty requires stamina and courage. Because the pitch is so large, accurate passing is an important skill. As in soccer or field hockey, most of the tackling is done by defenders and most of the running by attackers.

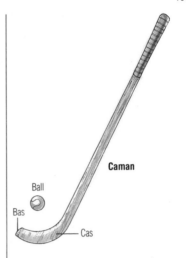

Caman

Ball

Bas

Cas

▲ *A well hit ball in shinty can travel nearly 100 yd (90 m). Hitting the ball cleanly is difficult because of the narrow stick.*

EQUIPMENT

- Balls have worsted and cork cores and are bound with leather. They measure roughly 8 in (20 cm) in circumference and weigh about 3 oz (85 g).
- Shinty sticks are made of wood. The head must be able to pass through a 2 ½ in (6.3 cm) diameter ring. The stick resembles a field hockey stick, but the head is angled rather like that of a golf club to give lift to the ball. Sticks must not stand higher than the hip.

TECHNICAL TERMS

caman a stick
camanachd the game from which shinty evolved. In some regions of Scotland, shinty is still called camanachd which means 'curved stick game'
hail a goal; traditionally, scores are given in 'hails', not goals

GAELIC FOOTBALL

DID YOU KNOW?

Gaelic football is one of the very few goal sports that does not have an offside rule; players can receive the ball regardless of their position on the field in relation to their opponents.

Gaelic football is an Irish game with a long pedigree. The first mention of a type of football being played in Ireland dates back to 1527, but it was not until 200 years later that a game resembling the current sport was played. Early in the last century a form of the game was played with an oblong ball, and entire villages would turn out to represent their side. In those days wrestling for the ball was permitted and 'fouls' were not recognized as such — aggression and ferocity were an integral part of the game. However, the Gaelic Athletic Association (still the ruling body of the sport) was formed in 1884 and it formalized rules and standards of play. These put an end to the blood feuds that were fought, literally and metaphorically, on playing fields. Over the years the GAA reduced the number of players per side from 21 to 15.

Gaelic football is still played mainly in Ireland, where it is considered a major sport, rivalled only by hurling. However, Irishmen the world over play in the game. In Australia, Gaelic football is especially appreciated, as it gave rise to the uniquely antipodean sport of Australian Rules football (see page 206).

Many clubs exist in Ireland. The most important competitions are the All-Ireland Championships which are contested every year.

▼ *At first glance a Gaelic football pitch resembles a rugby ground. However, the goal nets beneath the crossbars at each end give the sport its goal-scoring dimension.*

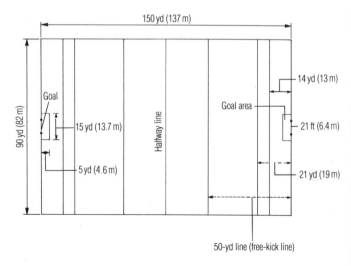

150 yd (137 m)

90 yd (82 m)

Goal

15 yd (13.7 m)

5 yd (4.6 m)

Halfway line

Goal area

14 yd (13 m)

21 ft (6.4 m)

21 yd (19 m)

50-yd line (free-kick line)

AIMS OF THE GAME

COMPETITION
● The game is played between two 15-a-side teams. Three substitutes are allowed per side per game. The game is played on a 'pitch' and the main objective is to score points by getting the ball over or under the goals at each end of the playing area.
● The pitch is 150 yd (137 m) long and 90 yd (82 m) wide. Markings and features on the pitch include:
- a halfway line;
- two '50 yd' lines ('free-kick lines') which run across the pitch — each is 50 yd (46 m) from the goal lines;
- two '14yd' (13 m) and two '21 yd' (19 m) lines which run across the pitch at the appropriate distances from the goal lines;
- H-shaped goals at each end — the width of a goal is 21 ft (6.4 m) and the crossbar is 8ft (2.44m) from the ground;
- a rectangular 'goal area' which measures 15 yd (13.7 m) by 5 yd (4.6 m) in front of each goal.
● Play begins with a kick-off from the centre spot. Players are allowed to run with the ball, provided they either bounce it on the ground every 3 strides or tap it on a foot every 4 strides. Alternatively, a player can pass the ball by kicking or punching it — throwing is not allowed. Players can tackle each other for the ball by virtually any means, within reason.
● One of the crucial rules of Gaelic football is that a player cannot lift the ball off the ground with a hand — he has to use a foot to scoop it into his hands. Intercepting a high ball with the hands is, however, permitted.
● Various rules prescribe where free kicks can be taken — either for fouls or as a result of the ball going out of play.

▲ *A player prepares to pass the ball by punching it with his fist – throwing it is prohibited.*

● Scoring is simple: 3 points are awarded if the ball goes into the net under the crossbar; 1 point if it goes over the crossbar.
● Games usually last for two 30-min halves (40-min halves are played for important matches).

SKILLS
● Gaelic football is a physical game, so all players have to be prepared to receive bruises and jolts. Ball-handling is hard to learn but the best players can bounce it while almost sprinting.

EQUIPMENT

● The ball is spherical and weighs around 15 oz (425 g); it has a diameter of about 28 in (71 cm).
● Players wear studded (cleated) boots, and shorts and shirts. Shirts bear the colours of the team or county. Few players bother with the niceties of protective padding.

DID YOU KNOW?

The highest price paid for a professional soccer player was £8.7 million when Fiorentina bought the Italian Roberto Baggio from Juventus in May 1990.

SOCCER

Soccer, also called Association Football or just plain football, is the most popular sport in the world, being played in one form or another by virtually every nation. A forerunner of the modern game was played more than 2000 years ago in China but it was in England that the sport took root. Various references to a 'ball-kicking' game appear in English history, but soccer did not become an organized sport until the mid-19th century when the first set of rules were drawn up at Cambridge University. These original rules were modified slightly over the years and in 1863, the Football Association (FA) was founded in England. The FA first allowed professionals to play the game in 1885 and three years later the English Football League was established.

The game rapidly became popular all over the world and in 1904, the current ruling body — the Fédération Internationale de Football Association (FIFA) — was formed.

Soccer is largely a male sport, although some women also play. It is usually played outside but a modified version — 5-a-side soccer — is played indoors on wooden floors. In 5-a-side soccer, the rules are broadly similar to the outdoor game but the pitch and goals are smaller. The indoor game is extremely fast and exciting to watch. There is even a professional version, played in the United States and Canada.

The vast majority of top soccer players are professionals, but the game is also played to a high standard by amateurs. The most important amateur competition is held at the Olympic Games and the chief international competition for professionals is the four-yearly World Cup.

European and Latin American countries have traditionally dominated soccer. Between them they have won every World Cup Championship since the competition began in 1930. In recent years, African teams have acquitted themselves well at international football. Cameroon, for example, beat the World Cup holder, Argentina, in the opening round of the 1990 World Cup Championships, which were held in Italy.

DID YOU KNOW?

Soccer teams, both professional and national, inspire enormous loyalty from their followers, although this support can sometimes be menacing to rival supporters. The most extreme example of soccer-related violence came in 1969, when a match between El Salvador and Honduras triggered a war between the two countries.

AIMS OF THE GAME

COMPETITION

● Soccer is played on a pitch by 2 teams comprising 11 players each. A maximum of 2 substitutions is allowed per side per game. The object of the game is for teams to score goals by getting the ball into nets located at each end of the pitch, and defended by a goalkeeper.

● The standard pitch for international matches is 110 yd (100 m) long and 70 yd (64 m) wide. Some pitches for English matches are smaller.

At each end of the field are sited 2 goals which are 8 yd (7.3 m) wide and 8 ft (2.44 m) high. Markings on the pitch include:

- touch lines and goal lines which define the playing area;
- a 20 yd (18.3 m) by 6 yd (5.5 m) 'goal area' at each end;
- a 44 yd (40 m) by 18 yd (16.5 m) 'penalty area' at each end;
- a 'penalty spot' which is centred in each penalty area, 12 yd (11 m) from each goal line;
- a halfway line which divides the pitch;
- a centre circle which has a radius of 10 yd (9 m).

The majority of pitches are grass-covered but some are made of artificial turf.

● Before a match begins, the 2 team captains toss a coin and the winner can elect to defend a particular goal for the first half or to start the match by 'kicking off'.

At the start of a game, the 2 sides must be in their respective halves of the pitch. The kick-off takes place in the centre circle on the halfway line; no members of the opposition team can enter the circle until the ball has been kicked.

▲ The ball is 'headed' on the top of the forehead so it can be angled accurately. The force comes from the torso pushing forwards.

- After the kick-off, the object of each team is to gain possession of the ball — they can run with it or kick it to a team-mate — with the ultimate aim of scoring a goal. Any part of the body can be used to propel the ball apart from the arms and hands. The exception to this rule is for the goalkeepers, who are allowed to handle the ball provided they are inside their respective penalty areas.

- A player is allowed to tackle an opponent who is in possession of the ball provided he does so fairly (for example barging is allowed but deliberate tripping is not). If the referee spots a deliberate foul, a 'free kick', taken from where the foul occurred, is awarded. There are 2 types of free kick. With an indirect free kick, a goal cannot be scored until another player has touched the ball; with a direct free kick, a goal can be scored without another player being involved. Minor infringements lead to indirect free kicks, with direct free kicks being reserved for serious violations of the rules.

If a defending player commits an offence inside his own penalty area, a 'penalty kick' is taken by a member of the attacking side. When a penalty kick is awarded, only 2 players are allowed inside the penalty area — the player taking the kick from the penalty spot and the goalkeeper, who has to remain stationary until the kick is taken. The player taking the penalty kick need not be the one who was fouled. Some team members are penalty specialists, spending hours of practice time honing their skills.

- If the ball is knocked out of play across a sideline, a 'throw-in' is taken from the sideline by the team who did not touch the ball last before it went out. Both hands have to hold the ball in a throw-in, and the ball has to be delivered from over the head.

If the ball is knocked over a goal line by an attacker, a 'goal kick' is awarded. This has to be taken, usually by the goalkeeper, from inside the goal area. If a defender hits the ball over the goal line, an attacker takes a 'corner' kick from within a 1 yd (1 m) quarter circle marked at the corner of the pitch nearer to where the ball crossed the goal line.

- The most complicated rule in soccer is the 'offside' rule. This rule is aimed at preventing attacking players from waiting for a pass while standing near the opposition's goal. Generally, a player is deemed offside if he receives the ball from a team-mate while being in the opposition's half of the field when there are fewer than 2 defenders between him and the goal. However, a player can legitimately receive the ball, when he would otherwise be offside, if he gets it directly from a corner kick, goal kick or throw in. A free kick is awarded against an offside player.

- After a goal has been scored, play starts again from the centre circle, with the team that conceded the goal kicking off.

- A match usually lasts for 90 min and is played in two 45-min halves. A referee can add on 'injury time' to compensate for time lost due to injuries. In major matches, 'extra time' can be played if the teams are level on scores at the end of 90 min. Extra time comprises two 15-min halves.

- Penalty shoot-outs, a controversial way of deciding matches that are still level after extra time, have been introduced in the World Cup and in many national competitions. The teams take 5 penalty kicks each, in turn, the winning team being the one with more goals scored in the shoot-out. Additional penalties are taken if the

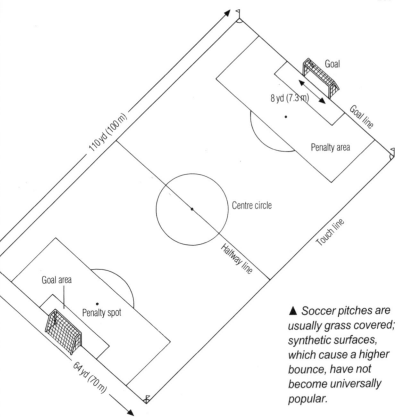

Goal

8 yd (7.3 m)

Goal line

Penalty area

110 yd (100 m)

Centre circle

Halfway line

Touch line

Goal area

Penalty spot

64 yd (70 m)

▲ *Soccer pitches are usually grass covered; synthetic surfaces, which cause a higher bounce, have not become universally popular.*

score is still level after the first 5 penalty kicks.

● A match is won by the team that scores more goals.

SKILLS

● Managers and coaches are the men who plan a team's strategy and tactics. They decide which players to include in a side and in what 'formation' they should play. The traditional formation was to have a goalkeeper, 2 defenders, 3 'midfield' players and 5 attackers. However, it is usual now to have more players in defence and midfield, and fewer attackers.

● Goalkeepers are the most specialized players on the field as they are the only ones allowed to use their hands. They are often tall and must be agile enough to leap up or dive for the ball — often in quick succession.

● Defenders are usually tough, strong men whose main job is to tackle opposing attackers.

● Midfield players are all-rounders, capable of both defending and attacking. They must be able to control the ball well, pass it accurately — both in the air and along the ground — and occasionally fire it fiercely at the goal. They are often the team's strategists.

● Attackers are quick and must be able to 'dribble' the ball well at their feet. A solitary attacker often finds himself surrounded by defenders so he must have the confidence and the ability to find a way through the ranks.

EQUIPMENT

- A soccer ball measures about 9 in (22½ cm) in diameter and weighs about 15 oz (425 g). They are usually faced with leather but plastic balls can also be used. The usual markings on the ball are alternate black and white pentagons, but a white ball is used in most matches in Britain.
- Shorts and coloured jerseys are worn by most players. Each team has its own colours but it wears a second kit with different colours for away games if the home team sports similar colours. Goalkeepers are obliged to wear different-coloured clothing from the rest of the members of their team. Goalkeepers may wear gloves.
- Boots have studs (cleats) on the underside which give them grip.

TECHNICAL TERMS

banana kick a kick that makes the ball swerve through the air; the ball is struck by the side of the foot

bench the seats, where a team's manager, coach and substitutes sit

booking when a player commits a serious foul, the referee enters his name in a book (see 'yellow card')

centre a kick struck from the edge of the pitch towards the penalty area; often in the air so that an attacker can head it towards the goal. (Also called a 'cross')

red card when a player is sent off the field for violent play, arguing with the referee or for continually flouting the rules, he is shown a red card by the referee

sending off a referee can order a player off the pitch, to take no further part in the game, for major fouls (see 'red card')

striker an attacker

sweeper a defensive player with a 'free' role who therefore does not have to mark any particular attacking player

winger an outside attacker

yellow card if a player commits a dangerous foul, causes dissension or continually breaks the laws, his name is written down in a book by the referee and he is also cautioned and shown a yellow card; 2 yellow cards in a match result in a player being sent off. In most major tournaments a player shown 2 yellow cards will be suspended from the following match or matches as well

◀ A throw-in has to be delivered over the head. Feet must stay on the ground behind or on the sideline. A throw-in taken near the opposing team's goalline can be as effective as a corner kick if the ball is landed near strikers positioned inside the penalty area.

FOR THE RECORD

MAJOR CLUB COMPETITIONS

The most famous English club competition is for the FA Cup. This knockout competition is held between English clubs (professional and amateur). After a number of rounds, only 2 teams are left in the competition and they compete for the cup at Wembley Stadium in London in mid-May, towards the end of the winter soccer season. The competition was first held in 1872 and a number of now obscure teams (including the Old Etonians, Oxford University and the Royal Engineers) won the trophy before the professional clubs dominated English football.

Many European nations also hold a knockout challenge series for a cup. Every year the winning teams compete against each other for the European Cup Winners' Cup.

▼ *In the 1990 World Cup match in Italy, Cameroon scored an unexpected 1-0 win over the cup-holding team, Argentina.*

Most major footballing nations operate a league system for professional clubs. The English Football League is divided into 4 'divisions', with the First Division containing the best clubs. (Scotland's top teams play in the Scottish Premier Division.) At the end of every season top teams from lower divisions can be promoted to superior ones, and conversely, weak teams can be demoted. In a league, each team plays the others who constitute the league twice — once 'at home' and once 'away' (on the opposition's pitch). Points are awarded according to the results — 3 for a win, 1 for a draw. When all the teams have completed their rota of matches, the team with the highest number of points wins the 'league title'.

The various league champions in Europe can play for the European Cup.

The UEFA Cup (Union of European Football Associations' Cup) is open to leading European teams that have not won either the national knockout competition or league.

Similar tournaments are held elsewhere in the world.

AUSTRALIAN RULES FOOTBALL

DID YOU KNOW?

The most famous teams are as follows:
Hawthorn Hawks
Melbourne Demons
North Melbourne Kangaroos
Richmond Tigers
St Kilda Saints
Sydney Swans
West Coast Eagles
Brisbane Bears
Carlton Blues
Collingwood Magpies
Essendon Bombers
Fitzroy Lions
Footscray Bulldogs
Geelong Cats
Adelaide Crows

Australian rules football, often simply called Australian or 'Aussie' rules, is a surprisingly old game which has a curious history. It evolved during the mid-19th century from Gaelic football and rugby, which had been taken to the 'new continent' by voluntary or involuntary expatriates. The earliest versions of the current sport were informal games played by Irish gold miners and farmers. In 1858, a man named Thomas Wills saw the potential of the game as a means of keeping cricketers fit and active during the winter season. Together with his cousin, Henry Harrison, he organized the first official games which were held on open parklands and soon became very popular. He also drafted the first code of rules, most of which are still valid today.

▶ *The playing area is oval in shape. The symbols indicate the position of team members at the start of play.*

Key to diagram

FB	Full back
FF	Full forward
BP	Back pocket
FP	Forward pocket
HBF	Half back flanker
HFF	Half forward flanker
CHB	Centre half back
CHF	Centre half forward
W	Wing
C	Centre
F	Follower
R	Rover

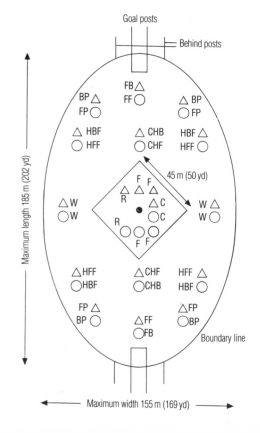

Australian rules football is a male sport, and physical conflict is encouraged, if not always condoned. It is fast, exciting and occasionally spectacular. For these reasons it is by far the most popular goal sport in Australia, easily eclipsing enthusiasm for rugby, soccer and American football. Few other countries play the game, although it is gaining a following in England, Canada, New Zealand and Denmark.

The game is played by amateurs at schools and colleges, but it is the professional teams that make the headlines. The ruling body of the sport is the National Football League. The main professional league is the Australian Football League, the bulk of whose teams come from the state of Victoria. The climax to the season is the Grand Final, a match held between the two top teams in the country and always held at the Melbourne Cricket Ground.

DID YOU KNOW?

The Brownlow medal is awarded annually to the player who is considered the fairest and best. The adjudicators are none other than the umpires who, after each game, secretly award Brownlow 'points' to players. At the end of a season, all the umpires' marks are added together and a winner is announced. Although the honour of winning a Brownlow medal counts for little overseas, in Australia it is considered a major achievement.

◀ *Defenders in Australian rules rely on a mixture of boldness and intimidation. Here, a player uses his hands to smother a kick, knocking it away from its intended path.*

AIMS OF THE GAME

COMPETITION
- A match is held between 2 teams comprising 18 players each. Two substitutions are allowed. The objective of the team is to score points by slotting the ball between posts at the end of the field.
- The playing field can be anything between 135 and 185 m (148 and 202 yd) long and 110 and 155 m (120 and 169 yd) wide. It is normally oval in shape and there is a boundary line marked around the outside perimeter.

  At each end of the field stand 4 posts, spaced 6.4 m (7 yd) apart. The 2 innermost posts are called 'goal' posts, and the outer ones are termed 'behind' posts.

  In the centre of the field a circle 3 m (3 yd) in diameter is marked in the middle of a 45-m (50-yd) square.
- After a toss for ends, players may go anywhere on the field. At the start of a game only 4 players from each side are allowed to stand inside the central square. The 'field umpire' then bounces the ball into the circle and team members try to gain possession of it.
- Once the ball is in play, the teams attempt to manoeuvre the ball between team-mates with the aim of scoring. A player can pass the ball only by kicking it or hitting it with a clenched fist. If a player elects to run with the ball, he must bounce it on the ground every 10 m (11 yd).
- Play is continuous, so to wrestle a ball from an opponent, a player can either intercept a pass or tackle the man with the ball. If the ball should run loose, anybody can pick it up and try and pass, kick or run with it.
- If a player catches the ball cleanly from the kick of another player, he can usually call for a 'mark'. Once a mark has been awarded, the player who caught the ball can take an unhindered kick in any direction.
- To score, a team member must either kick the ball between the opposition's goal posts (6 points) or between a behind post and a goal post (1 point). If it touches a goal post, it scores only 1 point; if it touches a behind post, the ball is ruled out of bounds.
- Matches last for 100 minutes, this period being divided into four 25-min quarters, with additional time added for stoppages. If scores are level (extremely rare) after the full period, no extra time is permitted.
- The winning team in a game is the one that scores the most points — points for behinds and goals being added together. A typical score sheet for a team score might read: 14-16, referring to the amounts of 6-point and 1-point scores. The 14-16 score would total 100 points.
- Occasionally a select team of Australian rules players will play an Irish team of Gaelic football players. Over a series of matches the teams usually play at least one game by Australian rules, one with Gaelic rules and one 'compromise' version incorporating elements of both sports.

SKILLS
- Australian rules football imposes fewer limits on positioning than other goal sports, but players tend to be either natural attackers or defenders.
- Attackers, or front field players, are fast sprinters who seek out positions for passes and punts. Midfield players often dominate the game and are all-rounders, able to catch, kick and run with the ball. Defenders are the strong men of the game — tackling and harassing are their forte, although a

strong kicking leg is invaluable as a hefty punt up field can regain lost territory.

● Australian footballers are perhaps some of the fittest sportsmen around. Regardless of which position they take on the field, they have to be able to jump for marks as well as being able to run with the ball whilst bouncing it on the ground. Hitting the ball with the fist or hand is not easy either, considering that the ball is oval in shape.

● There is no offside rule in Australian rules football. This means that players — defenders in particular — must be extra-vigilant to guard against attacks being mounted 'behind their backs'.

● Australian rules football is an outwardly aggressive game but it is not all thuggery — skill tends to win over brute force.

▶ *A player holding the ball must kick or punch it away if he is impeded or tackled by members of the opposing team. This feature of Australian rules maintains the flow of the game while reducing the risk of injuries caused by tackles.*

EQUIPMENT

● The ball is oval in shape and resembles that used in rugby or American football. It is an air-filled bladder covered with leather and measures about 47 cm (19 in) long with a diameter at its widest point of about 35 cm (14½ in).

● Players wear shorts and shirts which can carry insignia. Boots similar to those worn in soccer are normally worn as they ensure grip on grass.

FOOTBALL

Football, or American football outside North America to differentiate it from soccer, developed from rugby and soccer towards the end of the 19th century. It was first played by college teams along the east coast of the United States. To start with, the game was immensely violent and there were many serious injuries and even fatalities. Bit by bit the rules were amended to ensure fair play and to open the game up. After World War I, football was being played all over the United States and it began to rival baseball as the national game.

In 1922, the first professional league, the American Football Association, was formed. Two years later this became the National Football League (NFL), which remains the ruling body for the professional game. The Super Bowl, an annual match to decide the NFL champions, is one of the most popular televised events in the United States, eclipsing the Olympics in viewing figures. The Super Bowl certainly lives up to its reputation for razzmatazz.

▼ *Bulky linemen 'block' defenders to clear a path for their team-mate, who tries to gain precious yards on a running play. The 2 teams will line up again along the line where he is finally brought down.*

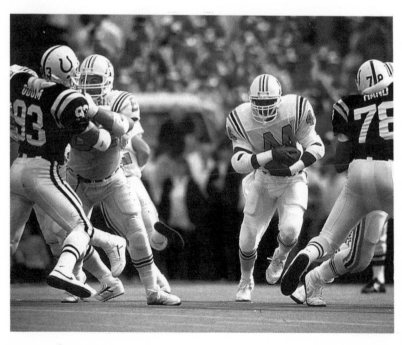

The amateur version of the sport (there are minor differences in the rules) is governed by the National Collegiate Athletic Association (NCAA). Amateur football is widely played by schools and colleges.

Professional Canadian football is governed by the Canadian Football League. The game is similar to the American one but is played on a bigger pitch and allows more players on the field. An amateur version is also played.

Until the 1970s, football was almost exclusively played in North America, but there has been a huge surge of interest in the sport in Europe, largely due to a massive publicity campaign by the NFL, which has been accompanied by television broadcasts of games. Britain now boasts its own football league and there are annual European Championships. In 1991, ten teams from ten cities began competing in the NFL-backed World League of American Football. Seven of the represented cities are in the United States, but Europe is represented by teams in Frankfurt, Barcelona and London. The London team is known as the Monarchs.

▲ *The oval ball is usually coloured dark red and measures around 28cm (11in) in length. Quarterbacks grip the stitching when throwing the ball.*

AIMS OF THE GAME

COMPETITION
An outline of the professional version of the American game follows.

● A match ('game') is held between 2 teams which can have as many as 45 players each, but only 11 of these are allowed to be on the field during play. (Regular substitutions are allowed.) The basic objective of the game is for a team to try and score points by carrying the ball over the opposition's goal line either by running with it or by passing it. The teams are like armies which, by various means, try to keep possession of the ball and move it towards the opposition's goal line.

● The playing field is 360 ft (110 m) long and 160 ft (48.8 m) wide. At each end of the field there is a 30 ft (9.1 m) wide strip called the 'end zone'. The field is also marked with 'yard lines', spaced 5 yd (4.6 m approx.) apart. Smaller 'hash marks' show the individual yards between yard lines. These help the referee judge where play has stopped. Goal posts are centrally situated at each end of the field.

● After the toss of a coin, one team elects to kick off or receive the kick. The ball is placed upright on a 'tee' on the attacking team's 35-yd line and is kicked up the field. This gives the possession of the ball to the opposition and the catcher of the ball will try to run as far as possible to gain territory. His team-mates help by blocking opponents who try to tackle him. He can run the length of the field to score, but in most cases he is tackled and the referee calls a temporary halt to the action.

● In football, the team that has possession of the ball — the 'offensive' team — is allowed 4 attempts (called 'downs') to move the ball 10 yd (9.1 m) up the field. If they succeed in doing this, they are allowed another 4 downs; if they fail, the possession of the ball moves to the opposing team, which tries to gain territory in a similar fashion.

● After a player carrying the ball has been stopped, play also stops, as does the official clock. After a short break the 2 teams line up on either side of an imaginary line (the 'line of scrimmage') indicating where play had stopped. As they face each other, the teams adopt formations: the defensive formation is usually fairly standard but the offensive formation is decided by the quarterback who plans the next tactic or 'play'. All plays in football are worked out by coaches and practised by players beforehand, so for every play each member of a team knows exactly what to do and where to go.

● When the players are ready, the centre — the man in the middle of the offensive front line — holds the ball on the ground between his legs. Standing behind the centre, the quarterback shouts out a series of commands — sometimes meaningful, sometimes bluffs to confuse the opposition — ending with the yell, 'hut!'. At that point, the centre pulls (snaps) the ball back into the hands of the quarterback. The quarterback then has a few seconds to set a running play in motion or to pass or throw the ball to a team-mate before the defensive team tackles him for a loss of yards.

● The type of play chosen by the quarterback will depend on the state of the game. One option is for him to pass the ball up the field to a 'receiver' who will then try and run for the goal line.

▲ Specialist kickers are used for kick-offs at the start of a game and for field goals.

This is a good move because, even if the receiver fails to reach the goal line, the chances are that more than 10 yd (9.1 m) will have been gained so the offensive team will maintain possession of the ball for 4 more downs. If the ball is not caught, the pass is termed 'incomplete' and the next play takes place along the original line of scrimmage.

The quarterback can also give the ball to a team-mate who will try and bulldoze his way through the defensive line to gain a few yards, or evade defenders altogether. On the fourth down the offensive team often tries a 'field goal' — a place kick sent through the goal posts. If the goal posts are out of range the team usually 'punts' the ball by kicking it towards the goal, well into the other team's territory.

▲ *A player runs with the ball, looking for an opportunity to pass it to a team-mate.*

● Players are allowed to block opponents even if they are nowhere near the ball — a tactic virtually exclusive to football. Heavy offensive players stand in the way of charging defensive players to protect the man with the ball — in the first instance usually the quarterback. Sometimes a man running with the ball will follow a team-mate whose job it is to clear a path, in the most literal sense, through the opposition.

● Rules concerning holding, clipping (blocking an opponent's back) and fouling (punches, eye-gouging and so on) result in the culprit team automatically losing territory.

● Scoring in football is as follows:
- 6 points are given for a 'touchdown' (when a team takes the ball over the opposition goal line into the end zone);
- 3 points are awarded for a 'field goal';
- 2 points are given for a 'safety' (when a player with the ball is tackled in his own end zone);
- 1 point is given for a 'conversion' (when the ball is kicked between the goal posts after a touchdown). A 2-point conversion is possible by running the ball into the end zone, but most teams opt for the single 'point-after'.

● A game has 4 'quarters' which last 15 min each. If, at the end of 60 min play, the teams are level on points, 'sudden death' extra time is played and the first side to score is the winner.

SKILLS
● Coaches play an important part in planning the team's plays, as well as organizing training sessions. It is a team's coach who decides the general strategy, and often patrols the sidelines screaming orders to his quarterback, who handles tactics. In short, the coach is the boss off the field; the quarterback is the boss on the field.

● Each playing member of a football side has a specific role to play, either in offence or defence; it is rare for a player to play in more than one position. As multiple substitutions are allowed, coaches make appropriate decisions as to who should come off and who should go on the field according to the state of the game. Some of the most important positions are the following:
- quarterbacks are the tacticians who start offensive moves. They are invariably impressive, all-round athletes with strong throwing arms and keen eyes. They must also be fearless, and strong enough to withstand ferocious tackles. They must be quick and prepared to run themselves if no other choice is available.

- linemen are the giants of football — many stand at least 2 m (6 ft 6 in) tall. When defending, linemen rush the opposition in an attempt to reach and 'sack the quarterback' (tackle him for a loss of territory). Offensive linemen oppose the rushing defenders.
- running backs are offensive runners who can also receive passes.
- receivers are pass-receiving specialists. Wide receivers run down the sides of the field in order to catch a throw. Speed is paramount for running backs and receivers, so professional football teams often lure sprinters from the ranks of amateur athletics.
- linebackers are quick but heavy men who play in defence. Their task is to catch or block receivers; they form a second line of defence behind the linemen.
- ends stand in the front row of an offensive line-up and are often prepared to receive short forward passes from the quarterback.
- safeties form the last line of defence. Their job is to intercept passes or to tackle opposing receivers.

EQUIPMENT

● The ball itself is a sharp oblong measuring around 28 cm (11 in) in length with a girth at its widest point of around 55 cm (21½ in). It is leather, with an inflated rubber bladder, and usually coloured dark red.
● Players have to wear helmets that include face masks. In addition they usually don thigh, shoulder, knee and hip pads. Loose jerseys with clear number markings are worn over the shoulder pads, and tight trousers (pants) cover the legs. Although special shoes are compulsory for most players, specialist kickers are allowed to kick the ball barefoot.

TECHNICAL TERMS

first down when an offensive team gains 10 yd or more to ensure 4 more downs
fumble when a player drops the ball or has it knocked away from him
gridiron a football field; also used to describe the game (gridiron football)
huddle when a team groups around the quarterback to discuss tactics
state of play before each down, a state of play is announced — this denotes how many (out of 4) downs are left available for the offensive team and how many yards it has to progress to gain a first down; an example might be '2nd and 6' which means 'second down, 6 yards to go'
time out periods taken off while the ball is not in play so that a team can discuss tactics and manoeuvres with its coach

FOR THE RECORD

NFL TEAMS
The NFL teams are divided into 2 'conferences' — the American Football Conference (AFC) and the National Football Conference (NFC).

AFC teams
Eastern division

Buffalo Bills
Indianapolis Colts
Miami Dolphins
New England Patriots
New York Jets

Central division

Cincinnati Bengals
Cleveland Browns
Houston Oilers
Pittsburgh Steelers

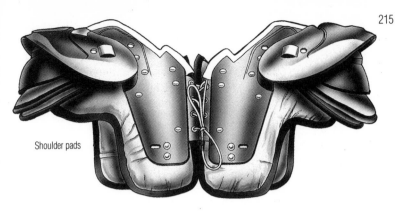

Shoulder pads

▲ *All players wear extensive protective clothing to minimize injury.*

Western division

Denver Broncos
Kansas City Chiefs
Los Angeles Raiders
San Diego Chargers
Seattle Seahawks

NFC teams

Eastern division

Dallas Cowboys
New York Giants
Philadelphia Eagles
Phoenix Cardinals
Washington Redskins

Central division

Chicago Bears
Detroit Lions
Green Bay Packers
Minnesota Vikings
Tampa Bay Buccaneers

Western division

Atlanta Falcons
Los Angeles Rams
New Orleans Saints
San Francisco 49ers

Helmet

Face mask

Rib pads

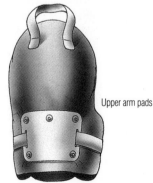

Upper arm pads

PERSONALITY PROFILE

Bo Jackson

Considered by many to be America's greatest professional athlete, Bo Jackson has achieved a status in the United States that no one has ever done before. Not only does he play as a running back for the Los Angeles Raiders, but he also plays baseball as a left fielder for the Kansas City Royals. Several men have played simultaneously in the America's most celebrated sports, but no one has been able to play both extremely well. In baseball, Jackson is considered an awesome slugger (he is the first member of the Royals to hit 25 or more home runs in consecutive seasons). In football, he has topped the NFL charts for yards gained.

A knee injury sustained in early 1991 threatened Jackson's 2 careers.

PERSONALITY PROFILE

Joe Montana

Statisticians and pundits endlessly argue over who is, or was, the greatest of all quarterbacks. Most, if not all, reckon that Joe Montana is the best of all time.

Born to a humble family in Pennsylvania, Montana played football for Notre Dame University after turning down a basketball scholarship to North Carolina State University. In 1979 he was scooped up by the San Francisco 49ers and has never looked back.

He led the 49ers to 4 Super Bowl victories and took them to the semi-finals in 1991.

He maintains a composure that inspires his team. With a right throwing arm that is unerringly accurate, he is an exceptionally good player leading an exceptionally good team.

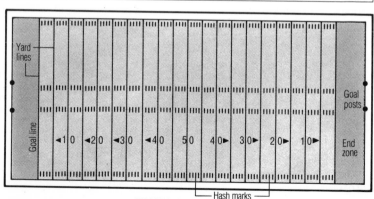

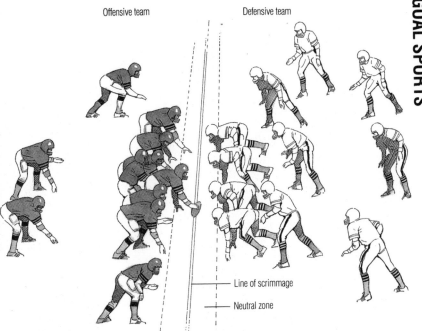

Offensive team   Defensive team

Line of scrimmage

Neutral zone

FOR THE RECORD

The annual highlight for professional American football is the Super Bowl, a challenge match that first took place in 1966. The contest is held at different venues and pits the champions of the American Football Conference against the champions of the National Football Conference. The Super Bowl is an event as much as a match, a gaudy extravaganza, the like of which cannot be seen anywhere else in the world. The host city can earn hundreds of millions of dollars in extra tourist and media spending. The game is televised around the world.

◀ *Football is a game of possession and precise 'yardage'. Yard lines and hash marks help the referee tell exactly where to mark the ball at the end of each play.*

▲ *Before each play the teams line up against each other on either side of a 'neutral' zone defined by the line of scrimmage. Each team member has a role to play in either offence (the team on the left) or defence.*

The team that has dominated recent Super Bowl confrontations is the San Francisco 49ers, victorious in 1982, 1985, 1989 and 1990.

Highly prestigious matches are held in amateur football between colleges (universities). These traditional 'bowl' games — named after famous bowl-shaped grounds — usually take place on New Year's Day. The most famous are the Rose Bowl, Orange Bowl, Sugar Bowl and Cotton Bowl. Star players in a team that competes in one of these events can expect handsome financial rewards in professional football.

BANDY

DID YOU KNOW?

The well known English phrase 'to bandy about' is a direct reference to the game of bandy.

Bandy is practically unheard of outside northern Europe. It is, however, an important and influential winter game, for it is thanks to bandy that ice hockey exists today.

Bandy originated in England between 1790 and 1820. Originally it was a popular sport in the flat, low-lying areas in the east of England but it gradually spread north. In 1865 the Nottingham Forest Football and Bandy Club was founded. (Bandy has subsequently been dropped from the name of the well-known soccer club.) From England, the game spread to other European countries and in the winter of 1890 the first international match took place — between the Dutch team, Harlem, and the English club, Buzu-Fen-Bandy. The National Bandy Association was founded in England in 1891, but the sport went into decline in Britain at the beginning of the 20th century, largely due to the fact that mild winters did not provide enough ice for the game to be played.

If there was not enough ice in England, there was plenty to be found in countries further north, and the game flourished in colder climates, particularly in the Baltic region of Europe. Today, bandy is a popular sport in Scandinavia,

▲ *A bandy stick and ball.*

AIMS OF THE GAME

COMPETITION
● The game is played on an ice rink between two 11-a-side teams who use sticks to try and hit a ball into goals sited at each end of the playing area. All the players wear ice skates. Most matches are played outdoors, but a modified version of the game is played on indoor rinks.
● A standard outdoor rink measures from 90 to 110 m (100 to 120 yd approx.) in length and from 45 to 65 m (50 to 71 yd approx.) in width. Markings (see diagram) include:
- a halfway line that has a circle 10 m (11 yd) in diameter at its centre point;

- semi-circular penalty areas at each end that have radii of 17 m (18 ft 6 in);
- 'free stroke points' that are marked on the penalty area lines (2 on each line);
- 'penalty points' (one at each end) that are sited 12 m (13 yd) directly in front of each goal;
- 2 goals (one at each end) that are 2.1 m (7 ft) high and 3.5 m (11 ft 6 in) wide.
● The game starts in the centre of the rink and players try to pass, dribble or score goals by hitting the ball with their sticks only. The ball cannot be handled (except by the goalkeeper within his own penalty area) and players are not allowed to raise their sticks above shoulder height. Players can use their

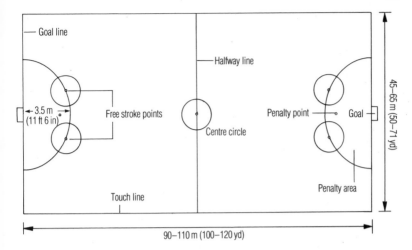

the Soviet Union, and as far afield as Mongolia. In these countries it rivals ice hockey, skiing and soccer in terms of participants; it is estimated that at least 100,000 Scandinavians regularly play the game.

The ruling body of the sport is the International Bandy Federation and the major international competition is the biennial World Championship. Bandy is an amateur game, played by men. It was once included as a demonstration sport in the Winter Olympic Games of 1952.

▲ *One factor limiting the popularity of bandy is the size of ice rink needed — nearly twice the size of that used in ice hockey and too large to be housed indoors. The scale of the bandy rink puts a premium on stamina.*

skates to stop and position the ball but are not allowed to kick it (goalkeepers excepted).
● Free strokes, taken from the free stroke points, are awarded for minor infringements, but fouls committed by defenders within their own penalty areas are penalized by penalty strokes, taken from the penalty points.
● A bandy match lasts for two 45-min halves and the winning team is the one that scores the most goals.

SKILLS

● Players adopt positions similar to those of soccer or field hockey players — defenders are adept at tackling, while attackers are faster and more

able to control and dribble the ball while skating at speed.
● Bandy is extremely fast and, as the ball can bounce, it takes great skill to control it.
● Goalkeepers have no sticks, so they must have quick hands and keen anticipation.

EQUIPMENT

● The ball is hard and coloured red; it is about 6 cm (2½ in) in diameter.
● Bandy sticks are similar in shape and size to field hockey sticks but may not be more than 1.2 m (4 ft) in length.
● Players wear protective padding, especially the goalkeeper.

▲ *Rugby balls are air-filled bladders with a covering of leather or similar material. This can be treated so the ball is easier to grip.*

▼ *The black and white dots on the pitch below represent 2 teams lined up for a scrummage. The black team is in a defensive position, while the backs on the white team are positioned so they can run, passing the ball along the line.*

RUGBY UNION

According to legend the game of rugby started in 1823 when William Webb Ellis, a pupil at Rugby School in England, flouted the rules of soccer by picking up the ball and running with it. The new handling game was later adopted by Cambridge and Oxford Universities (where it was called 'rugger') and a number of London hospitals established clubs. Until the rules were clarified by the Rugby Football Union in 1871, the laws were haphazard and there were no restrictions as to the number of people who could play on a side.

Unlike rugby league (see page 226), rugby union is only played by amateurs. It is a rough game played by men and women, but its reputation for being an outrageously dangerous sport is not wholly justified. As many, if not more, serious injuries are sustained by soccer players or by well-padded American football players.

The current ruling body, the International Rugby Football Board (IRFB), was formed in 1886. There are many important international competitions, which are contested by nations from all over the world. Each country has its own Rugby Union, or governing body.

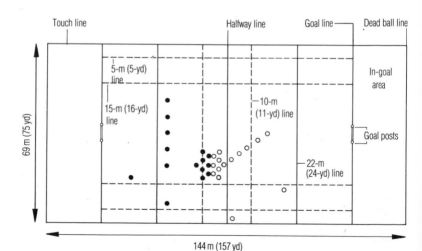

AIMS OF THE GAME

COMPETITION
● Rugby union is a 15-a-side team game played with an oval ball on a large pitch. The object of the game is for teams to score points and there are several ways in which this can be done.
● The pitch is always grass-covered and, for international matches, measures 144 m (157 yd) long by 69 m (75 yd) wide. Some club pitches are notably smaller. Markings and features on pitches include the following:
- 'goal lines' at each end — the distance between the goal lines should be 100 m (110 yd);
- 'touch lines' which run down both sides of the pitch;
- two 'dead ball' lines which are at the extreme ends of the pitch — the areas between the goal lines and the dead ball lines are called 'in-goal' areas;
- a 'halfway' line which divides the pitch;
- two '10-m' lines cross the pitch parallel to the halfway line and 10 m (11 yd) from it;

- two '22-m' lines which are 22 m (24 yd) from the goal lines;
- pairs of '5-m' and '15-m' lines which run parallel to the touch lines.
- The H-shaped goal posts are sited centrally along the 2 goal lines. Each has a crossbar 3 m (3 yd) high and measures 5.6 m (6 yd) across.
● The laws of rugby are complicated and are continually being updated. A match starts when a player from one team kicks the ball from the central spot on the halfway line into the opposition's half of the field. The ball must travel 10 m (11 yd) before touching the ground, and all of the opposition team must stand behind the 10-m line on their side of the pitch. At the same time the whole of the kicker's team must stand behind the ball until it is kicked. This procedure is repeated after each score, with the scored-against side kicking.
● Players are allowed to pick up the ball and run with it, pass it and kick it. The one essential rule in rugby is that the ball must be passed backwards or sideways, never forwards.

▲ In a scrummage, the 2 teams' forwards lock together and push against each other. A scrum half tosses the ball into the 'tunnel' between the 2 teams who try to heel it backwards while moving the scrummage forwards.

● Defending players are allowed to tackle opposition players who are carrying the ball by pulling them to the ground. As soon as a player is tackled, he must release the ball. In such a situation, it is normal for a 'ruck' to follow — team members clash together in a bid to gain possession of the ball. In a ruck, players are not allowed to touch the ball with their hands so they try to 'back-heel' it to another team member who waits to receive it outside the ruck.

● For minor misdemeanours, or if a ruck becomes a stalemate with no team gaining advantage, a 'scrummage' is ordered by the referee. In a scrummage, 8 'forwards' from each team bind together and clash against each other in a formal manner. There has to be a 'tunnel' between the front rows of the 2 teams and a person from the team that was not responsible for stopping play, throws the ball down the centre of it. Thereafter, the forwards try to back-heel the ball to team members waiting behind the scrummage.

● If the ball crosses one of the touch lines, a 'line-out' follows. Players (usually the forwards) line up side by side, 5 m from the touch line, facing the point where the ball went out of play. A player from the side which was not responsible for knocking or kicking the ball out of play, throws the ball into the gap between the rows of forwards who then try and manoeuvre it back to waiting team members.

● There are several ways of scoring:
- a try (4 points) is scored when a player grounds the ball in the opposition's in-goal area. After a try has been scored, a player from the scoring side has a chance to 'convert' it (2 points) by 'place kicking' or 'drop kicking' the ball between the uprights and over the crossbar on the goal post. The conversion kick has to be taken at a point opposite the spot on the goal line where the try was scored.
- a 'drop' goal (3 points) can be taken by a player when the ball is 'in play'. The player has to drop the ball and kick it as it touches the earth. To score, the ball has to go over the crossbar and between the uprights of the goal.
- a 'penalty' kick (3 points), which is awarded against a team for committing a foul, can be either a drop kick or a place kick over the crossbar and between the uprights of the goal.

● Matches last for two 40-min halves.

SKILLS

- A rugby team can be split into 2 distinct groups - the 'forwards' and the 'backs'. Forwards are invariably big, strong men and it is their job to gain possession of the ball from rucks, scrummages and line-outs. The backs are usually smaller and faster men who are adept at handling and kicking the ball. In scrummages, line-outs and rucks, the backs stand behind the forwards. Consequently, they have a better view of the opposition and are called upon to dictate strategy and tactics.

- Rugby Union positions are as follows:

- Forwards — each team has 2 props, tall men who are in the front row of a scrummage and who support a hooker between them. The hooker is usually shorter and it is his task to 'hook' the ball backwards in a scrummage. In a scrummage, 2 locks, usually the heaviest and biggest men, push behind the props and hooker. Two flankers and a No 8 form the 'back row' of a scrummage. They tend to be the lightest and fastest of the forwards and play crucial roles in defence as well as in attack.

▲ *A line-out takes place when the ball is kicked out of play. The forwards, lined up beside their opposite numbers, leap up to try to win possession of the ball, which is thrown down the line, and to pass it to the backs on their team.*

- Backs — the scrum half has to be fast — he forms the link between the forwards and the rest of the backs. It is the scrum half who receives the ball from rucks, line-outs and scrummages. Next to the scrum half is the fly half, who is usually the tactician of the side; he decides whether to pass the ball to his fastest men or to kick the ball forwards to gain territory. Two centre three-quarters lie outside the fly half. They have to be swift at handling the ball in attack and sure tacklers in defence. The fastest men on a pitch are the two wingers — playing on either side. A mark of a good winger is his ability to swerve round defenders or simply to out-pace them. The last line of defence is the fullback who must be a sound tackler as well as a sure kicker and catcher of the ball. In attack, a fullback can play a crucial role as an 'extra' man.

• The tactics employed by a rugby side often depend on the weather. In wet conditions, the ball tends to be slippery and hard to handle, so the forwards do much of the work and gain territory by forcing their way up field. In dry conditions, when the ball is easier to catch while moving, the speedy backs are more likely to have a chance to show their paces.

• Kicking for territory can play a vital role in rugby, and the fly half is often the man to do it. Sometimes the ball is merely punted up the field to be chased by the kicker's team-mates, but this can lead to the opposition gaining possession. Kicks can also be used to put the ball 'in touch' (out of play along one of the touch lines). This results in the opposition having the advantage of throwing the ball in at the ensuing line-out, but nevertheless massive gains in territory can be made. However, for territory to be gained, a kicker has to make the ball bounce at least once before it goes into touch, so punting has to be accurate. The exception to this is if a player kicks the ball from inside his own 22-m line, when it need not bounce before going into touch.

EQUIPMENT

• Rugby balls are oval in shape and measure about 30 cm (12 in) long.

• Rugby players wear strong shorts and jerseys, and boots with studs (cleats) on the soles. Some forwards wear protective bandaging around their heads and ears.

▼ *Backs are chosen for their speed and agility. If tackled by one or more players in a 'maul', from which they cannot free themselves, they must release the ball.*

TECHNICAL TERMS

blind side when a scrummage (or ruck) forms by the edge of the pitch, the blind side is the narrow gap between the scrummage and the touch line

drop out if a defending team touches the ball down in its own in-goal area after it has been carried or kicked over the goal line by an attacker, play is restarted with a drop kick up the field, taken by a defender from the appropriate 22-m line

dummy when a player runs with the ball and fakes a pass to a team-mate

grubber (grub kick) a kick that makes the ball bounce along the ground

knock on when a player fails to catch the ball and knocks it forwards; the penalty is a scrummage

Mark! if a player catches the ball while standing with both feet on the ground behind his own 22-m line, he can shout 'Mark!' and be awarded a free kick

pack the forwards

three-quarter line the backs (the centres and the wings) who usually form a diagonal line across the pitch behind the forwards

FOR THE RECORD

FAMOUS TEAMS
The British Lions is a team which comprises members from Scotland, Ireland, England and Wales. It goes on periodic tours to play series of 'test matches' against rugby-playing countries.

The All Blacks is the New Zealand national side which is so called because the players wear black. It is probably the most consistently good rugby side in the world.

The Barbarians is a club team which is unique in that players of any nationality can be invited to play for it and so it has a different set of players every time it takes to the pitch. Barbarian sides often play against national teams and traditionally contain at least one un-capped player (a person who has not played for his country). By tradition, the last match a visiting side plays in Britain is against the Barbarians, who have earned a reputation for fast, open play. The Barbarians celebrated their centenary in 1990.

FOR THE RECORD

FAMOUS COMPETITIONS
The first World Cup competition was held in 1987 between 16 nations:
Australia
Japan
England
United States
Canada
Ireland
Scotland
Tonga
Wales
New Zealand
Argentina
Italy
France
Romania
Zimbabwe
Fiji
New Zealand was the winning team.

The Home International Championship (the Five Nations' Championship) is held every year between England, Ireland, Scotland, Wales and France, who play each other once. It is possible for teams to tie as champions.

The Calcutta Cup match, which takes place during the Home International Championship, is between England and Scotland.

DID YOU KNOW?

Rugby league arrived in New Zealand in 1905. The first team was ironically called the 'All Golds' because they accepted payment for games.

RUGBY LEAGUE

Towards the end of the last century, the Rugby Football Union refused to allow clubs in the north of England to compensate their players for earnings lost while taking time off to play in matches. This ruling so infuriated certain players and clubs that they formed their own union — the Northern Rugby Union League — which did permit players to receive money for playing the game. In 1906, the new union adopted their own rules which included a reduction in the number of players per side from 15 to 13. In 1922, the Northern Rugby Union League changed its name to the Northern Rugby League and later dropped the tag of 'Northern'. Today, the 'new' game of rugby league is played almost entirely by professionals, some of whom have joined from the amateur ranks of rugby union — occasionally incurring resentment from rugby union supporters. Perhaps the most famous player who has changed codes in recent years is Jonathan Davies, who used to captain Wales (rugby union), but now plays for Great Britain, in the British national team (rugby league).

As with rugby union, the league game is played almost exclusively by men and is extremely tough and physically demanding. It is a more open game than the union version, with more running and less time taken up with rucks and scrummages.

The first international rugby league match took place in 1906. The game is now played in many

▼ *Rugby league pitches are usually smaller than those used for rugby union. The 10-m lines are similar to the 10-yd lines of American football.*

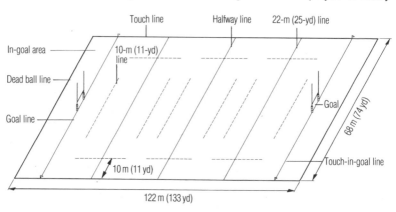

Touch line · Halfway line · 22-m (25-yd) line

In-goal area

10-m (11-yd) line

Dead ball line

Goal line

Goal

68 m (74 yd)

10 m (11 yd)

Touch-in-goal line

122 m (133 yd)

countries, including New Zealand, France and Australia, where it is far more popular than the union game.

The ruling body of the sport is the Rugby League International Board, which was founded in 1948. The most important international competition is the World Cup, which was won by Australia in 1988.

AIMS OF THE GAME

COMPETITION
● In many respects the game is very similar to rugby union (see page 220). The main differences are as follows.
● The pitch is somewhat smaller, measuring 122 m (133 yd) by 68 m (74 yd) with narrower 'in-goal' areas at each end. Additional markings on the pitch include '22-m' lines, which run parallel to the goal lines right across the width of the pitch.
● As there are only 13 men per side, there are only 6 forwards, not 8, but a team is allowed to substitute 2 players at any time.
● Each team is allowed to keep possession of the ball for 5 'tackles'. If a man is brought down while carrying the ball, he gets up and usually 'plays the ball back' to a man standing behind him who either runs with it or passes it to a team-mate. Playing the ball back simply means tapping the ball backwards with a foot. It is permitted for a player to play (tap) the ball to himself and then run with it or pass it. After 6 plays have been used up by a team, a scrummage of 6 players per side follows and the team that gains possession has the chance to make the most of the next 6 tackles.
● If the ball is kicked into touch without bouncing first, a scrummage takes place at the point where the ball was kicked. If the ball bounces into touch, a scrummage takes place at

least 10 m (11 yd) in from the touch line, opposite the point where it crossed the line.
● Players score in the same way in rugby league as they do in rugby union. In rugby league the points are as follows:
- 3 points for a try;
- 2 points for a conversion;
- 2 points for a penalty goal;
- 1 point for a drop goal.
● Games last for 2 halves of 40 min and the winning team is the one that scores the most points.

SKILLS
● Rugby league is a faster game than rugby union so players have to be continually on the look-out for breaks and subtle tactics. The backs in particular have to be fast runners.

EQUIPMENT

● The ball is marginally smaller than a rugby union ball but is the same shape.
● Most players wear shoulder pads for additional protection against tackling.

TECHNICAL TERMS

bench where a team's manager and substitutes sit near the touch lines
up and under a high kick that enables the kicker and forwards to run up the field while the ball is still in the air and to repossess it when it lands (also used in rugby union)

ICE HOCKEY

The fastest of all team games is ice hockey — usually just called 'hockey' in North America where field hockey is seldom played. The sport is thought to have originated in Canada during the winter of 1860 when English garrison soldiers introduced a disc-shaped 'puck', instead of a ball, whilst playing bandy (see page 218) on frozen lakes. It was soon taken up by players in the United States, USSR, and the Scandinavian countries, all of which had natural ice on which to participate.

Today ice hockey is played by amateurs and professionals on indoor and, when it is cold enough, outdoor rinks. It is an exciting, fast, and occasionally violent sport. It is rapidly gaining, or regaining, popularity in Britain, where dozens of clubs — and a professional league — have been established.

The ruling body is the International Ice Hockey Federation (IIHF) which was founded in 1908 and is based in London. The professional game, as played by North American club teams, is ruled by the National Hockey League (NHL) which was established in 1917. For amateurs, the premier events are the Winter Olympic Games, the annual World Championships and the European Championships.

▼ *Standard ice rinks are usually painted white with blue and red lines added. A sheet of clear ice covers the surface.*

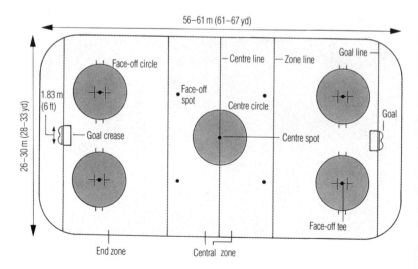

End zone   Central zone

AIMS OF THE GAME

COMPETITION

● The game is played on ice between two 6-a-side teams. Substitutions are allowed. Each team tries to score goals by manoeuvring a puck about the rink using 'sticks'.

● For major competitions, the rink must be 56-61 m (61-67 yd approx.) long and 26-30 m (28-33 yd approx.) wide. In junior competitions, smaller rinks are permitted.

The corners of the rink have to be rounded and the entire playing area has to be surrounded by a barrier that stands 1.22 m (4 ft) high. Markings and features on the rink include:

- 2 'goal' lines, marked in red at each end, sited 4 m (13 ft) from the edges of the rink;

- 2 'zone' lines, marked in blue, dividing the rink into 3 equal areas — 2 'end zones' and a 'central zone';

- a red 'centre' line dividing the rink into halves;

- a 'centre spot', in the middle of the centre line surrounded by a blue 'centre circle' 4.5 m (15 ft approx.) in diameter;

- 4 red 'face-off' spots marked within the centre zone;

- 2 red 'face-off' circles 4.5 m (15 ft approx.) in diameter in each end zone which have red 'face-off tees' sited in the middle of them;

- the goals, painted red, centrally placed on the goal lines at each end. They are 1.22 m (4 ft) high, 1.83 m (6 ft) wide and have nets that are not more than 1 m (3 ft approx.) deep. In front of each goal there is a shallow 'goal crease'.

● Play begins when the referee drops the puck between 2 face-off players at the centre spot who then vie to gain possession; all other players must be stationed outside the centre circle.

● After the initial face-off, team members can pass the puck amongst themselves. A number of rules determine when a player can pass to

▼ *A battle behind the net for the puck. Attacking forwards try to get the puck and pass it to their centre in front of the goal. Defenders can turn the tables by starting an attack from behind their own goal.*

another from one zone to another but the ultimate aim is to get the puck into the opposition's goal. Players can 'check' (tackle) for the puck by directly, and physically, going for the man who has it or by intercepting passes.

● Fouls and minor infringements occur all the time in ice hockey. When this happens, it is usual for face-offs to be taken in the nearest face-off spot. However a referee will play advantage to the team offended against until the offending team gains possession. If the offended team scores during such 'delayed penalties', the offence is forgotten. Players that foul the opposition are sent to the 'sin bin' — a side bench — for a period of time. For minor offences (like hooking another player's stick), a 2-min penalty is usual; for major offences (outright violence or for abusing the referee) penalties can last from 5 to 10 mins. When a player is sent to the sin bin, a team plays 'one man short' and substitution is not allowed. On minor penalties, if the opposition scores, then the offending player immediately rejoins the action.

● Individual points are awarded for goals and assists. A goal is scored when the puck crosses the goal line and goes into the goal; assists are awarded by the referee to players who take part in an attacking movement before a goal is scored. Both goals and assists equal 1 point.

● Ice hockey games are divided into three 20-min 'periods'. The team with more goals is the winner.

▶ *Ice hockey is a fast and aggressive game. Players should be able to keep their heads up as they skate at top speed, even when they are controlling the puck. In this way they can see opportunities to pass and shoot.*

SKILLS

● Ice hockey players have to be able to skate in all directions, including backwards. At the same time they must also be able to control a puck. Most teams contain:

- a net minder (goalie) whose job it is to keep the puck out of the goal;
- defencemen who specialize in tackling and defending;
- wingers who are fast skaters who patrol the perimeters of the rink with the aim of either scoring or passing to the centre who is invariably an all-round player with a talent for scoring goals.

● Ice hockey is a frantic and gruelling sport, so many substitutions and re-substitutions may take place during a game — 18 players plus 2 net minders are permitted per team.

● A team coach decides when his players should come off and when a fresh one should go on. He is also responsible for relaying tactics to his team members.

EQUIPMENT

● Most ice hockey sticks are made from laminated wood although some synthetic materials are permitted. A stick may not measure more than 147 cm (32 in) in length. The blades on net minders' sticks can be slightly longer and broader than those for other players, but no blade can be longer than 39 cm (15 in approx.).

● The black puck is made of vulcanized rubber and has a diameter of 7.63 cm (3 in), a thickness of 2.54 cm (1 in) and a weight of around 170 g (6 oz).

● In addition to superficial gear, all players wear helmets, gloves, and pads on the shins and elbows. The skates used are specially designed and do not carry rasps on the leading edges. Net minders wear heavy pads, chest protectors, gauntlets, face protectors, and special boots and skates.

TECHNICAL TERMS

poke check when one player stops another by blocking the puck
slap shot a full-blooded hit of the puck; neither a flick nor a push

FOR THE RECORD

The National Hockey League is fought out between 21 North American teams which are divided into 2 'conferences' - the Wales Conference and the Campbell Conference. Each conference has 2 divisions. The top teams in each division play off for the Stanley Cup each year. A best-of-seven series of games is played in the finals. New franchises have been awarded recently enabling 3 new teams to join the NHL.

PERSONALITY PROFILE

Wayne Gretzky
Without doubt the greatest ice hockey player of all time is Wayne Gretzky, who has earned more points for his teams than any other professional in the sport — nearly 2000 in under 850 games. He also has broken virtually every scoring record there is — goals in a season, points in a season, assists in a season etc. Gretzky even won the trophy for the NHL's 'most gentlemanly player' in 1980.

Gretzky was born in Brantford, Canada, in 1961 and after a precocious start with amateur teams, he joined the Indianapolis Racers before transferring to the Edmonton Oilers in 1977. In 1988, he led the Oilers to a fourth victory in the Stanley Cup before signing up with the Los Angeles Kings for a record fee of $15 million.

Quiet and unassuming both on the ice and off it, Gretzky does not behave like most 'superstars'. He is always able to 'read' a game like no other — in the right place at the right time, ready to pass as well as shoot. He is a true hockey genius.

DID YOU KNOW?

There is another game which is called court handball but which differs totally from the handball described above. It originated in Ireland and was then taken to the United States. It is played in a court and in many respects is similar to racketball, except that the hands are used instead of a racket.

HANDBALL

Handball is thought to have ancient origins, but the modern team game was devised in Germany towards the end of the last century. Originally an outdoor game, it failed to become very popular. Then, in the 1920s, it also became an indoor game, although it could obviously still be played outside. The rules were radically modified to incorporate many of the basic laws of soccer.

Handball is an amateur sport and can be played by either men or women. It is particularly popular in the Soviet Union, Continental Europe and the Far East. It is a fast, energetic and exciting game, that is simple to understand.

The International Handball Federation, the ruling body of the sport, was established in 1946 and the most important competitions for both men and women are held at the Olympic Games. There is also a four-yearly World Championship (for both men and women) and a European Cup — an annual team competition.

▼ *The markings on a handball court are shown below.*

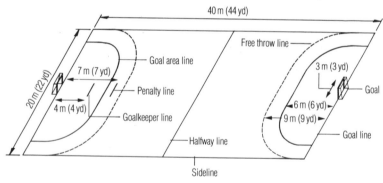

AIMS OF THE GAME

COMPETITION
● Although 11-a-side handball is still played outdoors, the most common version is a 7-a-side sport (with up to 5 substitutions normally allowed per side, per game) which is played indoors on a wooden 'court'. The essential object of the game is for a side to score more goals than its opponents.

● The standard indoor court is 40 m (44 yd approx.) long and 20 m (22 yd approx.) wide. The markings and features on the court include:
- a halfway line running across the court and dividing it;
- a goal at each end measuring 3 m (3 yd approx.) wide by 2 m (2 yd approx.) high;
- D-shaped goal area lines which are 6 m (6 yd approx.) from the goals;

- two D-shaped 'free throw lines' 9 m (9 yd approx.) from the goals;
- 'penalty' lines located 7 m (7 yd approx.) from the centre of each goal;
- 'goalkeeper' lines which are 4 m (4 yd approx.) in front of the goals.

● After winning the toss, a team captain can decide which goal to defend or can elect to 'throw off'. At the throw-off, which takes place in the middle of the court, players are obliged to be in their respective halves.

● Players can carry the ball for 3 steps before having to bounce it off the floor, but they have to pass it or throw it at the goal before advancing a further 2 steps. Players are not allowed to shoot at the goal from within the goal area line.

● Any part of the body, except the feet, can be used to propel the ball. Players can tackle each other for possession of the ball but must not infringe the rules (which do not allow tripping, hitting etc.).

● Most of handball's rules follow those of soccer — penalty throws are awarded for fouling a person who might otherwise have scored a goal, and throw-ins are taken from the sidelines. Goals are scored when a player manages to hurl the ball, past the goalkeeper, into the 'net'.

● For men, matches last 60 min, with two 30-min halves; women usually play two 25-min halves.

● The winning side is the one that scores more goals.

SKILLS

● Players usually specialize in being 'defenders' or 'attackers'. Defenders have to communicate with each other and one of their tasks is to close ranks around their goal area line to prevent an attacker having a shot at goal. Defenders must also be prepared to

▲ *An attacker leans forward so that the momentum of her body weight will add power to her shot.*

block and clear hard shots away from the goal (only the goalkeeper is allowed to use his or her feet to clear the ball).

● Attackers aim to score goals, so most of them are tall with strong throwing arms. The most spectacular shots in handball are made by players who throw the ball in mid-air while leaping over the goal area line.

EQUIPMENT

● The ball must be spherical. For men's matches it weighs around 450 g (16 oz) and has a circumference of about 60 cm (24 in); for women's games the ball is smaller and lighter — weighing 430 g (15 oz) and measuring 55 cm (22 in) in circumference.

● Players wear numbered shorts and T-shirts.

FIELD HOCKEY

DID YOU KNOW?

Roller hockey is becoming increasingly popular, in the UK and Europe. It is a variation on the field game but played indoors on roller skates.

In roller hockey, two 5-a-side teams try to score goals at an incredible pace — ace skaters sprint to 48 km/h (30 mph) in seconds. Fast, dangerous, but ultimately exciting, roller hockey seems destined to become a major sport.

Field hockey, so called to differentiate it from ice hockey, has origins dating back to the Ancient Egyptians, Greeks and Romans, who all played games which involved hitting a ball with a curved stick. Closer to modern times, similar games were played in medieval Europe but it was not until the middle of the last century that the game began to take the form in which we know it today. In 1875, the English Hockey Association devised a set of rules which helped to unify the game. From England, the game spread to other parts of the world, including the rest of Europe, Australia, and, most notably, to India and Pakistan, where it is played with a fervour unknown in other countries.

Initially hockey was a game for men, but women's clubs took root after World War II and now it is played by amateurs of both sexes. The current ruling body, the Fédération Internationale de Hockey, was not formed until 1924 and did not take responsibility for the women's game until as recently as 1982.

Hockey for men has been an Olympic sport since 1908 and women first played at the Games in 1980. Olympic gold medals are still the most coveted prizes, but the four-yearly World Cup and European Championships are also considered prestigious. A form of field hockey is played indoors and competitions include the European Indoor Cup.

▼ *Field hockey pitches have less variation than those used in other goal sports. Dimensions are standard around the world.*

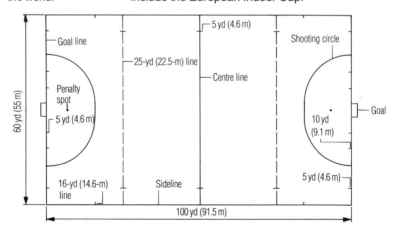

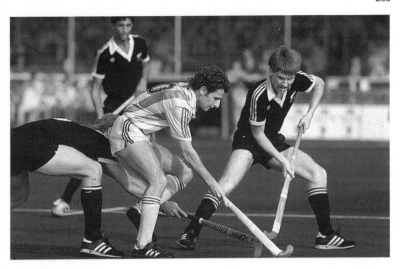

AIMS OF THE GAME

COMPETITION
● Field hockey is played between two 11-a-side teams whose objective is to win matches by hitting a hard ball with a curved stick into the opponents' goal. The goals are situated at each end of the hockey 'field'.
● A standard field measures 100 yd (91.5 m) by 60 yd (55 m). Markings and features include:
- a dividing centre line;
- two 25-yd (22.5-m) lines which divide the halves into quarters;
- two 5-yd (4.6-m approx.) markers on the goal lines, 25-yd (22.5-m) lines and centre line;
- a goal at each end which measures 4 yd (3.7 m approx.) wide and 7 ft (2 m approx.) high;
- in front of each goal a 'shooting circle' which is 16 yd (14.6 m) from the goal itself;
- a 'penalty spot' spaced 7 yd (6.4 m) centrally in front of each goal.
   The majority of fields are grass-covered but artificially turfed fields are becoming common.

▲ *Field hockey relies on accurate passing and tackling. International matches, such as the World Championship shown here, are supervised by referees, and defenders know they can go only so far before being booked for tripping or obstruction.*

● Play starts with each team positioned on its designated side of the field. At the 'pass back', which takes place in the middle of the centre line, a player uses a stick to knock the ball backwards to a team member. [Note: A 'bully-off' used to be the standard way of starting a game but the pass back is now favoured. Bully-offs still take place when fouls are committed simultaneously by opposing team members. In a bully-off, 2 opposing players stand face to face with the ball sited between them. Each player then has to tap the ground and his opponent's stick, above the ball, 3 times before challenging for possession.]
● When the ball is in play, the majority of players are only allowed to hit,

dribble and pass the ball using their sticks. Kicking and handling the ball is only permitted by the specialist goalkeepers who, if they choose to kick or handle the ball, have to do so within their respective shooting areas. To wrestle the ball from the opposition, players can tackle (going for the ball only with their sticks) or they can intercept passes.

Strict rules govern how the ball can be struck or passed: it can be
- 'hit', so long as the stick is not raised dangerously high in the swing;
- 'flicked', which means that it can be whipped up from the ground in an arc;
- 'pushed', shoved along the ground;
- 'scooped', which is similar to a flick, except that the ball is hoisted into the air, usually from a near-stationary position.
● If the ball goes out of play, across a side line, a team member from the side that was not responsible for knocking the ball out of play is entitled to take a 'hit' or 'push-in' from the point where the ball went out. All players have to stand at least 5 yd (4.6 m) from the ball.

● When the ball goes over the goal line, several different types of 'hit' can be awarded. These include:
- a '16-yd hit' (taken by a defender) if an attacker commits a foul within 16 yd (14.6m) of the goal line;
- a 16-yd hit (taken by a defender) if a defender accidentally knocks the ball over his own goal line while being more than 25 yd (22.9 m) in front of his own goal.
- a 'corner' (taken from the appropriate corner of the field by an attacker) if a defender knocks or hits the ball over his own goal line while behind his own 25 yd line;
- a 'penalty corner' (taken by an attacker) from one of the 2 points 10 yd (9.2 m) along the goal line from the goal post when a defender deliberately knocks the ball over his own goal line while within his own shooting area.

With penalty corners, defenders have to stand behind the goal line and the attackers are obliged to stay beyond the shooting area. The player taking the penalty corner pushes it to a designated team member who first

◀ A neutral bully-off takes place after 2 fouls have been committed simultaneously or after an injury. Team-mates have to stand 5 yd (4.5 m) or more away until the ball has been hit.

▲ *Only the goalkeeper is allowed to kick the ball or stop it with a hand. Goalkeepers wear protective clothing and helmets.*

stops the ball and then launches a shot at the goal.

● For major misdemeanours 'free hits' are given, but if a foul is committed within the defenders' shooting area, a 'penalty stroke' is awarded and this has to be a flick from the penalty spot.

● Field hockey shots have to be taken from within the shooting circles; apparently successful goals struck from outside these areas result in a 'free hit' from the 16-yd line to the other side.

● Most games last for two 35-min halves, with a 10-min interval.

SKILLS

● Positions are similar to those found in soccer — forwards, half-backs, backs and goalkeeper. Forwards tend to be fast and able at dribbling the ball with their sticks; defenders are more aggressive in tackling, but run the risk of fouling, which includes 'obstruction' and tripping. Goalkeepers have to be prepared to stop the ball with any part of their bodies.

EQUIPMENT

● Field hockey sticks are made of wood and are about 3 ft (91 cm) in length. The shaft is usually fairly flexible and the hooked end must have a flat face. The overriding rule is that it must be able to pass through a ring 2 in (5.10 cm) in diameter.

● The ball is white and hard, measuring about 9 in (23 cm) in circumference and weighing around 5½ oz (156 g).

● Most players wear studded (cleated) boots and kit similar to that worn in soccer. The exception is reserved for the goalkeepers, who are obliged to wear pads, gloves, helmets, 'kickers' (kicking boots) and abdominal and/or breast protectors.

TECHNICAL TERMS

reverse stick a player is only allowed to propel the ball using the flat edge of the stick — **reverse stick** means turning the stick the 'wrong way round' to play the ball

sticks when two players' sticks are interlocked during play; usually results in a bully-off

BAT AND BALL GAMES

Many hundreds of bat and ball games exist today, just as they did thousands of years ago. Bat-a-ball, French cricket and 'who's a fool' are played in playgrounds, in various forms and with various rules, in many countries. There are, however, just four bat and ball games that are of any consequence.

DID YOU KNOW?

The most famous cricket ground in the world, Lord's Cricket Ground, is named after Thomas Lord, a Yorkshireman who was devoted to cricket. He opened his first cricket ground in 1787 on the site of what is now Dorset Square in the heart of London. In 1811, the ground was moved to where Marylebone station now stands. Three years later it had to be moved again — to St John's Wood, where it has remained ever since.

CRICKET

Bat and ball games were played in England as far back as the 13th century and from these evolved the game of cricket. The first official rules for the game were written down in 1744. The headquarters of cricket is the Marylebone Cricket Club (MCC), which was founded in 1787 and is based at Lord's Cricket Ground in London.

During the 19th century, cricket was taken to British colonies and the first international ('Test') match was played in 1877 between England and Australia.

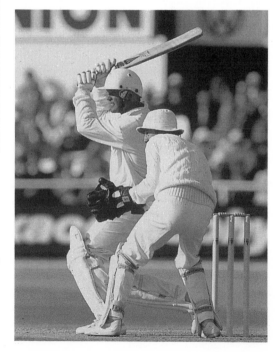

▶ The wicket-keeper often positions himself perilously close to the stumps in order to intimidate the batsman or to make a quick catch.

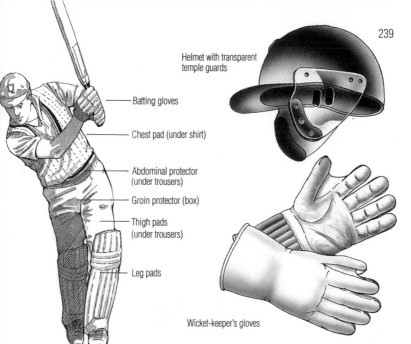

Helmet with transparent temple guards

Batting gloves

Chest pad (under shirt)

Abdominal protector (under trousers)

Groin protector (box)

Thigh pads (under trousers)

Leg pads

Wicket-keeper's gloves

Although some women play cricket to a high standard, the game is dominated largely by men. It is played by both amateurs and professionals at a variety of levels. The highest level of the game, 'first-class' cricket, is played only by professionals.

Cricket is a summer game but at international level it is played virtually all year round with nations hosting competitions and Test matches for touring sides. It is an immensely complicated and subtle game which many find hard to understand: some fail to see the attraction of a sport that can last for five days and can still end up as a draw!

Leading cricketing nations include Australia, New Zealand, the West Indies (former British colonies in the Caribbean), India, Pakistan, Sri Lanka, South Africa and England. Cricket is also played to a lesser degree in many other countries, such as Holland, Scotland, Zimbabwe and Canada.

The MCC is still responsible for the laws of cricket, but the International Cricket Conference (ICC), which has numerous nations as members or associate members, is the effective international ruling body.

▲ *The ball is very hard, so batsmen, wicket-keepers and some fielders wear special protective clothing.*

AIMS OF THE GAME

COMPETITION

• The game is played between two sides of 11 players each. The teams take it in turns to bat and field — the batting side tries to score runs and the fielding side tries to get the batsmen out.

• Cricket is played on a large grass field, about 150 yd (137 m approx.) across, which is surrounded by a white line or rope called a 'boundary'. In the middle of the field is a well-tended strip, or 'pitch', which is 22 yd (20 m approx.) long and 3 yd (3 m approx.) wide. The pitch is defined at each end by 'bowling creases' and in the middle of these are positioned 3 wooden 'stumps' which are topped by 2 'bails'. Each set of 3 stumps and 2 bails is called a 'wicket'. Another white line known as the 'popping crease' lies 4 ft (1.22 m) in front of each wicket.

• The captain of a team that wins the toss of a coin has the right to choose which team should bat first (an innings). This is an important decision, and the captain must consider the weather and the conditions of the pitch.

After all 11 of the fielding side have taken up their positions on the field, one of them — the 'bowler' — prepares to deliver the ball to one of the 'batsmen'. Two batsmen play at the same time. One stands in front of one wicket, on the popping crease and ready to receive the ball; the other waits at the popping crease at the other wicket.

• Two umpires adjudicate a cricket match. It is their responsibility to judge when someone is out and to see that play is fair.

• Once a bowler has bowled the ball 6 times (an over) from one wicket, another bowler takes over and bowls from the other wicket towards the batsman at the other end. When the bowlers change, all the fielders change positions as well.

• To score a run, the facing batsman has to strike the ball bowled at him by the bowler and run to the popping crease at the other wicket. At the same time, the non-striking batsman has to run to exchange places. The 2 batsmen can run once, twice or more times from one end of the pitch to the other; each time they do so, the facing batsman's score goes up accordingly, as well as his team's total. If the facing batsman scores an odd number of runs, his partner will have to face the bowler's next delivery.

If a ball is hit past the boundary line, the facing batsman automatically scores runs — 4 if it touches the ground before crossing the line or 6 if it goes over cleanly.

Other runs can be scored in a variety of ways. If the facing batsman fails to make contact with the ball, the 2 batsmen can still run a 'bye'; similarly if the ball strikes the facing batsman, the 2 batsmen can notch up a run for their side by running a 'leg bye'. If the bowler delivers the ball unlawfully (see Skills) — (a no ball), or if he bowls the ball beyond the reach of the batsman (a wide), a run is gained by the batting side.

• During the course of a game, the fielding side tries to get the batsmen out. There are many ways they can do this. These are the ways that happen most frequently:

- the bowler can bowl the batsman out — that is, bowl so that the facing batsman misses the ball and it hits his wicket;
- the batsman can be caught by a fielder after he has hit the ball, but before the ball hits the ground;
- the 'wicket-keeper', the fielder who

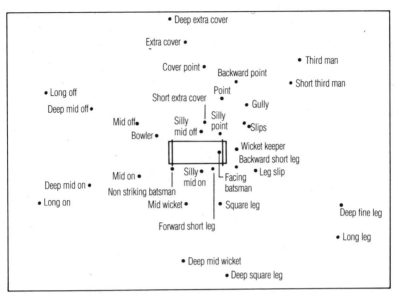

▲ *Cricket is renowned for its rather eccentrically named fielding positions, some of which are given in the above diagram.*

stays behind the wicket, can 'stump' the batsman. To do this he hits the wicket with the ball in his gloves while the batsman is standing beyond the popping crease;

- the bowler can bowl the facing batsman out 'leg before wicket' (lbw) — that is, when the ball hits the batsman's legs and the umpire reckons that it would otherwise have hit the stumps;

- any fielder can 'run out' either of the 2 batsmen. To do this, a fielder has to hit the wicket, usually with an accurate throw, before a batsman reaches the relevant popping crease.

● An innings usually ends when 10 out of the 11 batsmen are out or have retired through injury. The side is then 'all out'. However, if a captain reckons that his team has scored enough runs to beat the opposition at any time during the course of an innings, he has the right to 'declare' or end the innings prematurely.

Once an innings is over, the fielding side has its chance to bat. Its aim is to score more runs than the opposition.

● In first-class matches, games last for either 3 or 4 days and each team has a chance to bat twice; in Test matches, games last for up to 5 days and similarly, each team has 2 innings. To win one of these games, the side batting last has to gain a total number of runs greater than that already set by the opposition. For the fielding side to win, it has to get 10 of the batsmen out in their second innings before their own total number of runs is beaten. If the target is not achieved in the number of days allocated, but the batting side is not 'all out', a draw is declared.

In one-day matches, which are played at all levels, the number of overs bowled in the game is limited — usually to either 40 or 60 per side. There is virtually always a result in these games as the side with the highest total of runs at the end of the day wins.

SKILLS

Batting

The task of a batsman is usually just to score as many runs as possible. He must have a quick eye and be able to judge how the ball has been bowled. Some attacking shots are played with the batsman leaning forward as he hits the ball. However, many more subtle shots (strokes) are played with the batsman stepping backwards.

Batsmen do not always simply try to score, however — there are occasions when they are required to play defensively so as not to get out. A good batsman should be able to play a range of strokes to counter every conceivable type of delivery from the bowler.

Bowling

Bowling requires special skills. For a delivery to be legal, the bowling arm has to be straight as the ball is released. A ball bowled to the batsman that does not bounce usually provides an easy target; the skill is to make the ball bounce in front of the batsman. Bowlers fall into 3 categories — fast, medium and slow. Fast bowlers build up momentum by running up to the wicket before delivering the ball. They rely on sheer speed to confuse the facing batsman. Medium bowlers are more subtle. The batsman has more time to hit the ball, but most medium bowlers are able to make the ball swerve through the air or can make it bounce awkwardly by making it land on its seam. Slow bowlers' balls look easy to hit but rarely are. These bowlers spin the ball so that it bewilders the batsman by bouncing to the left or the right.

Fielding

Most cricketers play in favourite positions on the field. The wicket-keeper is the most specialized fielder

▲ *The batsman plays a defensive shot off the back foot. He points his bat down and uses a back stroke to protect the wicket.*

and he wears the most protective gear. He takes catches from the facing batsman, to receive bowled balls, and to catch throws from other fielders.

Some fielders prefer to be close to the facing batsman to take catches — quick reactions are essential. Others have strong throwing arms and prefer to stay further back.

Captaincy

The captain of a side plays a very important role. In cricket, the slightest change in the weather or the condition of the ground can alter the character of a game. A good captain will be able to use these changes to his team's advantage. For example, heavy cloud

▲ *Fast bowlers are permitted a long run-up to gain momentum, and then deliver the ball with a straight arm over the shoulder.*

cover and a slight breeze will mean that a medium bowler should be able to swerve the ball; if the ground is hard and dusty, a slow bowler will probably be more effective than a fast one. It is the captain's decision to choose which bowlers to use. In addition, a captain decides where to place the fielders. When batting, he can decide to declare if he thinks his team is in a winning position.

A captain must also be prepared to lead by example — on and off the field. This is important in rebuilding batting confidence if the side has lost several wickets in quick succession, or if personality clashes threaten the team-spirit.

TECHNICAL TERMS

all-rounder a cricketer who is good at bowling, batting and fielding

bouncer a fast delivery from a bowler that bounces halfway down the pitch so that it flies up to head height

century 100 runs scored by a batsman

collapse when a succession of batsmen are out in rapid order

duck when a batsman is out without scoring a run

googly a slow delivery from a bowler that is designed to look like a leg-break, but is in fact an off-break

guard the position a batsman takes relative to the stumps behind him; he can ask an umpire to help him find a position before marking the ground

leg (to a right-handed batsman) the left side of the field

leg-break a slow delivery from a bowler that makes the ball turn from leg to off when it bounces

length the point at which a bowler's delivery bounces

line the right or left aim of a bowler's delivery

maiden over an over during which no runs are scored

night watchman a defensive batsman put in towards the end of the day's play

off (to a right-handed batsman) the right side of the field

off-break the opposite to a leg break

Owzat? (How's that?) an appeal to the umpires from fielders when they think a batsman is out

pace bowler a fast bowler

seamer a bowler who makes the ball bounce off its seam

tail the weaker batsmen at the end of the batting order

tie when both sides finish with the same number of runs (rare)

yorker a bowler's delivery that pitches underneath the batsman's bat

EQUIPMENT

● Cricket bats are traditionally made from willow. Their weight can vary but they cannot exceed 38 in (96.5 cm) in length or 4½ in (11.5 cm) in width.

● Cricket balls are red and shiny with a stitched seam that goes right the way round. Balls have to weigh between 5½ and 5¾ oz (156 and 163 g) and have a circumference of not more than 9 in (23 cm). In most matches, a new ball is introduced every 85 overs.

● Test cricketers wear white clothes, but coloured caps are permitted. When batting, protective clothing is worn — thigh pads, pads around the legs, gloves, a groin protector (box), and occasionally a helmet and visor.
As a rule, the only fielder to don special gear is the wicket-keeper who wears pads, a box and heavy gloves. Sometimes fielders close to the batsman put on helmets. Bowlers wear woollen sweaters to remain supple when they are not bowling.

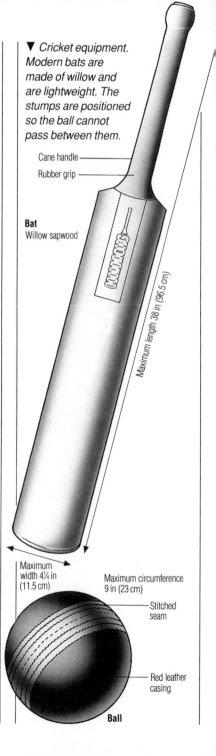

▼ *Cricket equipment. Modern bats are made of willow and are lightweight. The stumps are positioned so the ball cannot pass between them.*

Cane handle
Rubber grip

Bat
Willow sapwood

Maximum length 38 in (96.5 cm)

Maximum width 4¼ in (11.5 cm)

Maximum circumference 9 in (23 cm)

Stitched seam

Red leather casing

Ball

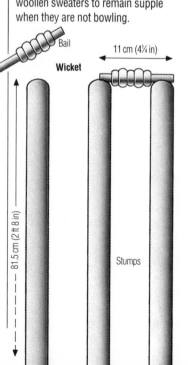

Bail

11 cm (4¼ in)

Wicket

81.5 cm (2 ft 8 in)

Stumps

FOR THE RECORD

NATIONAL TROPHIES
Most of the Test-playing countries have trophies or titles which are contested in 3 or 4 day matches by state teams or, as in England, by county teams. These are the main ones.

County Championship	England
Sheffield Shield	Australia
Quaid-e-Azam Trophy	Pakistan
Currie Cup	South Africa
Red Stripe Cup	West Indies
Ranji Trophy	India
Shell Trophy	New Zealand

In addition many countries hold one-day championships of various kinds.

FOR THE RECORD

TEST MATCH RECORDS
Most Tests played Sunil Gavaskar (India) - 125
Most runs scored in Test matches Sunil Gavaskar (India) - 10,122
Most Test centuries scored Sunil Gavaskar (India) - 34
Highest individual score Garfield Sobers (West Indies) - 365*
Best average score in Test matches Donald Bradman (Australia) - 99.94
Most wickets in Test matches Richard Hadlee (New Zealand) - 431
Most wickets in a single Test match Jim Laker (England) - 19
Most dismissals by a wicket-keeper Rodney Marsh (Australia) - 355
Highest test match innings total 903 for 7 wickets (declared) – England v Australia, the Oval 1938
Lowest test match innings total 26 – New Zealand v England, Auckland 1954–55

* not out

FOR THE RECORD

THE ASHES
In 1882, an Australian team under the captaincy of W. L. Murdoch became the first side to beat England on English soil. The Test match was held at the Oval cricket ground in London and *The Sporting Times* placed a joke obituary in its report of the match:

In Affectionate Remembrance
of
ENGLISH CRICKET
which died at the Oval on
29th August, 1882,
deeply lamented by a large circle
of sorrowing friends and
acquaintances.
RIP.

NB. - The body will be cremated and the Ashes taken to Australia.

Soon after, an English team set sail to Australia and succeeded in 'recovering the Ashes'. After the final Test, some Australian ladies burned a bail, collected the ashes and placed them in a small urn which they presented to the English team captain. The urn was brought back to London and is on public display at Lord's Cricket Ground where it is always kept. Ever since, England and Australia have played Test matches 'for the Ashes'.

Passions can run high when the Ashes are at stake. In 1933, the England side provoked a controversy in Australia. The English devised a 'bodyline' strategy — their fast bowlers aimed directly at the Australian batsmen's bodies. This restricted Australian stroke play but was seen as 'not cricket' after several Australians were hit by bouncers. England won the Ashes, but the team tactics have been a source of dispute to this day.

ROUNDERS

The first written reference to rounders occurs in *A Little Pretty Pocket Book*, which was published in 1744. In this volume, there is an illustration of rounders being played and a poem entitled 'Base Ball'. There is little doubt that one of America's favourite sports is a derivative of the English game of rounders and they still have much in common.

Rounders today is played in Britain and Ireland but there are no competitions at international level apart from an annual match between Wales and England. It is, however, hugely popular in schools and clubs.

▲ *The rounders bat is light and easy to handle, making the sport popular in schools.*

The governing body of rounders is the National Rounders Association, which has its headquarters in Nottingham, England.

AIMS OF THE GAME

● Rounders is a game played between 2 teams; the minimum number of players per side is 6, and 9 is the maximum. In mixed teams a maximum of 5 males is allowed. Each team has 2 turns at batting and 2 at fielding (innings). The batsmen try to score rounders while the fielding side tries to prevent this by getting batsmen out.

● The playing area is similar in layout to a baseball field but is considerably smaller and should be about 50 m (55 yd) square. A straight line on the ground separates the 'forward' and 'backward' areas; the forward area should equal about two thirds of the total playing area. In the forward area, a line is drawn from the batting square to the first post; the posts stand 1.2 m (4 ft approx.) high and are spaced 12 m (39½ ft) apart. The exception is the fourth post, which is 8.5 m (28 ft) from the third post.

● One member of the fielding side is nominated a bowler and delivers the ball towards a batsman from a 2.5 m-

(8 ft-) square box sited centrally in the forward area. Bowlers can be changed only after a correctly bowled ball. The rest of the fielders spread out in the forward area: one normally stands at first post; one acts as a backstop behind the batsman; and the others take up positions outside the square formed by the 4 posts.

● The bowler must bowl the ball underarm so that when it reaches the batsman it is within reach and between the head and the knee. An illegal throw is called a 'no-ball' — a batsman can score off a no-ball but cannot be caught out. When the batsman receives a good ball he must run whether he hits it or not.

● Every member of the batting side has a chance to bat. A batsman stands in a 2-m-(6½-ft-) square box marked in the backward area opposite the bowler and tries to hit the ball, delivered to him by the bowler, as far as possible. He then tries to run round all 4 posts to score a rounder. A 'live' batsman is allowed to stop at the first, second and third posts or can continue

in his bid to reach and touch the fourth post, thus scoring a rounder, before the next ball is bowled and without being put out. One batsman may not overtake another as he runs round, nor may 2 batsmen stop at the same post. A batsman who has stopped at a post may run on when the ball leaves the bowler's hand. If he reaches fourth post having stopped, but without being out, he does not score but rejoins the other batsmen. When all the batsmen are out, the batting side takes to the field and the fielders take turn to bat.

● A batsman can get himself out if he steps out of the batting box before hitting the ball or if he runs inside the posts. A fielder can get a batsman out in 2 ways: either by catching a ball which has been hit by the batsman before it hits the ground or by touching the post to which the batsman is running with the ball or with the hand holding the ball.

● Two umpires oversee the game — one stands near the batsman and the other near the second post.

▲ *A player is out if she reaches the base to which she is running after a fielder has touched that base with the ball in her hand.*

● When both teams have completed 2 innings, the side with the highest total of rounders is the winner.

EQUIPMENT

● Rounders requires very little special equipment — it is often played with a small cricket bat and a tennis ball. However, officially, the ball should be hard and weigh between 70 g and 85 g (2½ and 3 oz) and the bat should be round and should not be longer than 46 cm (18 in). The posts should be 1.2 m (3 ft 11 in) high.

TECHNICAL TERMS

half-rounder awarded when the bowler delivers 2 'no-balls' in succession or if a batsman runs round all 4 posts without hitting the ball.
stick a rounders bat

DID YOU KNOW?

The phrase 'to take a raincheck' comes from baseball. When a game was rained off, spectators were told to hold on to their tickets so that they would be allowed to see a replay of the game at a later date.

BASEBALL

America's national game — baseball — is thought to have developed from the old British game of rounders, which was introduced to North America in the 18th century and became known as 'town ball'. In 1854, a New Yorker called Alexander J. Cartwright drew up a standard set of rules for town ball, which then became known as baseball. The first game of baseball played according to Cartwright's rules took place in 1856. From then on the popularity of the game spread across the United States and to other countries.

Baseball is played by both professionals and amateurs and mostly by men. There are several professional leagues in the United States but the most important of these are the American League and the National League, which together make up Major League Baseball, and organize the professional game. During the six-month season, American League and National

▼ *The catcher wears more protective equipment than any other player.*

League teams do not play against each other, but after the season ends officially, usually in October, the best teams from each league meet in the so-called World Series — a best-of-seven games contest.

Amateur baseball is ruled by the International Baseball Association (IBA). One of the IBA's intentions is to make baseball an international game and to some extent it has succeeded: baseball is now enjoyed in many countries other than the United States and Canada, including South Korea, Japan, Italy, Venezuela and even Cuba. So far baseball has not attained much popularity in Britain, although there are clusters of devotees.

Baseball has been included as a demonstration sport in many Olympic Games, but it is due to gain full status for the first time at the 1992 Barcelona Games.

▼ *The playing area is divided into 2 parts, the outfield and the infield. The infield is a 90 ft (27.5 m) square called the 'diamond' and has a base at each corner. The 'base paths' are between the bases and a 'crescent' extending from the foul lines.*

The outfield can vary in size and is defined by the foul lines and a curved boundary fence. It is usually grassed.

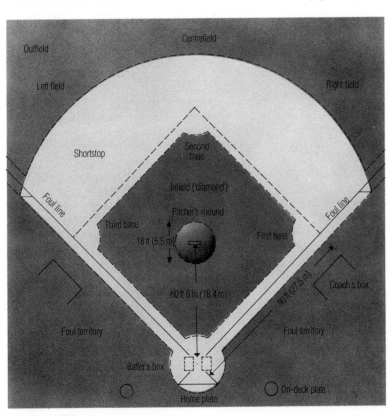

AIMS OF THE GAME

COMPETITION

● The game is played between 2 teams of 9 players each. Substitutions are allowed, but replaced players cannot return. The teams take it in turns to bat and to field; the visiting side always bats first and faces the home side's pitcher (bowler). A side batting tries to score runs, a run being scored when a batter advances to all 4 bases without being put out. The fielding side tries to get batters out; when 3 batters are out, the 2 teams swap roles.

Each team has 9 turns to bat; an 'inning' is when both teams have batted once. The team with the highest number of runs at the end of a game wins. If the scores are level after 9 innings, extra innings can be played until one side wins — there are no draws in baseball.

● A baseball field is divided into 2 specific areas — the infield and the outfield. The infield is a square (called a 'diamond') with a 'base' at each corner — home base (called 'home plate'), first base, second base and third base. The first, second and third bases are marked with 15-in (38-cm) square canvas bags which are pinned to the ground. Home plate is a five-sided piece of whitened rubber. The distance between the bases is 90 ft (27.5 m approx.). In the centre of the diamond, 60 ft 6 in (18.4 m) from home plate, is the pitcher's rubber — a piece of rubber 24 in by 6 in (61 cm by 15 cm). The pitcher's rubber is on a mound 16 in (40 cm) above the ground and is centred in a circle 18 ft (5.5 m) in diameter.

The outfield varies in size from stadium to stadium. It is the area defined by the 2 foul lines which extend outward from home plate and a perimeter fence which is usually about

▲ *A pitcher must keep a foot on the 'rubber' until he releases the ball. He can gain momentum by 'winding up' his other leg and then swinging it forward in time with his throwing delivery. He can rub his hands with resin to get a firm grip on the ball but he cannot polish it on his clothing.*

10 ft (3 m) high. The foul lines average about 330 ft (100 m) in length but because the outfield has a curved edge the fence in deep centre field can be as far away as 480 ft (150 m) from home plate.

The pitcher's mound is usually surrounded by grass or artificial turf and the outfield is also green, but the stretches between the bases and a curved area between the infield and the outfield (the base path) are covered with dirt. This allows players to slide into bases.

● When a batter is 'at bat', he stands to one side of home plate, ready to hit the ball when he receives it from the pitcher. If the pitcher pitches the ball over home plate at a height between the batter's armpits and his knees and the batter does not attempt to swing, it is called a 'strike'. (A swing that misses the ball is also judged a strike.) If, however, it goes high, low or wide, it is called a 'ball'. An umpire behind the batter adjudicates. If a batter receives 4 'balls' or if he is hit by the ball, he is allowed 'a walk' — to first base. Conversely, if he receives 3 'strikes', he is 'struck out' and has to retire.

● If the batter hits the ball into 'fair territory' — the fan-shaped area comprising the infield and outfield — he is obliged to run to first base, or further if he chooses. If he hits the ball over the fence or into such a position that allows him time to round all the bases, he scores a 'home run'.

If he only gets as far as a base, he can stay there safely, progressing to other bases either by running when the fielders seem ill-prepared to put him out or by being 'forced' along by another batter's hit. (Only one runner is allowed to stay on a base.) If the batter reaches home plate without being got out, he scores a run.

A batter can be out in 3 ways:
- by being struck out;
- by being caught — if he hits the ball in the air and a fielder catches it before it lands;
- by being put out — if a fielder receives the ball while touching the base to which the batter is running (a force-out) or if a fielder touches him with the ball while he is running between bases.

● The task of the fielders is to catch the ball or to retrieve it after it has been hit and to throw it hard and fast to a team-mate who is covering one of the bases, preferably one for which a batter is heading. The exception is the pitcher, who always remains near his mound and whose primary object is to pitch the ball at batters.

● The finer rules of baseball are exhaustive and complex but some of the most important ones include:
- a pitcher must keep one foot in contact with the rubber while delivering the ball;
- a batter cannot interfere with a fielder who is trying to retrieve the ball;
- a fielder cannot impede a batter running for a base, unless of course he is holding the ball and tries to touch him in an attempt to get him out.

● An umpire is stationed at each base to judge whether or not a batter reaches a base 'safely' (before the ball).

SKILLS
Fielding
Fielders can be divided into two distinct groups — infielders and outfielders. As the names suggest, infielders operate in or near the diamond and outfielders patrol the further reaches of the playing area. Most players have specialized roles when fielding. For example, a 'first baseman' must have an extremely quick eye for the ball and he must be

prepared for a lot of work since most batters are put out in trying to reach first base. The 'catcher' (like a cricket wicket-keeper) is one of the most important of all fielders. He has to catch high-speed throws and pitches, and organize all the other fielders as he is the only person with the entire field in front of him.

Pitching

There is a range of techniques a pitcher can use to confuse the batter. A good pitcher can make the ball swerve through the air (a 'curveball') or he can try pitching the ball more slowly when the batter is expecting a fast one (a 'change of pace'). He should be able to disguise what he is going to do next.

Batting

A batter must decide which pitches to hit and which to leave. Some 'sluggers' try to hit the ball as far as possible and run the risk of being out often. More subtle batters ('place hitters') try to place the ball into an area of the field where there is a gap between fielders. This requires great control.

Batters slide into bases. If they did not slide, batters would overrun and risk being put out.

▲ *A runner on his way towards a base is out if a fielder touches (tags) the base with any part of his body while holding the ball. A fielder can also tag the runner himself with a hand holding the ball.*

EQUIPMENT

● A baseball is hard and covered with white-coloured horsehide. It weighs between 5 and 5¼ oz (142 and 149 g) and has a circumference of between 9 and 9¼ in (22.9 and 23.5 cm). A bat is about 42 in (107 cm) long and has a diameter of about 2½ in (6.35 cm) at its thickest part. Bats are usually made of hardwood, but aluminium bats are often used for practice as they rarely snap.

● A batter wears a helmet. A large glove (mitt) is always worn by each fielder. The mitt is worn on the left hand by right-handed players and vice versa. It is used for fielding the ball.

● A catcher's equipment includes a heavy mitt, a mask, and pads that protect the chest, shins and knees.

● Baseball players traditionally wear tight-fitting trousers (pants) that finish halfway down the calves. Team-mates wear identical clothing.

TECHNICAL TERMS

at bat a player or team that is batting
base hit a hit that allows a batter to advance to first base
bases loaded runners on first, second and third bases
batter a team member who is batting
bunt to bat a ball gently forwards so that the batter can advance to first base; the shot often confuses fielders who are expecting a more powerful hit
designated hitter a specialist batter who does not field but takes the place of the pitcher in a side's batting line-up (American League only)
double a hit that allows a batter to advance to second base
fly ball a ball that flies high into the air after it has been hit
foul ball a ball that lands behind the foul lines after it has been hit
hit when a ball is struck safely and allows a batter to advance to first base or further
home plate home base
pinch hitter a substitute batter who replaces someone in the batting line-up — usually a pitcher — at a crucial moment in a game
runs batted in the number of runs scored while a batter is at bat (a season-long statistic)
sacrifice a tactic where a batter allows himself to be out so that a team-mate can advance one or more bases
single a hit that allows the batter to advance to first base
stealing when a batter on a base advances to another without waiting for a batter to hit a pitch; usually done when the pitcher's back is turned
triple a hit that allows a batter to advance to third base
walk if 4 pitches are deemed 'balls' by the umpire a batter can move on to first base

FOR THE RECORD

BASEBALL'S HALL OF FAME
In 1934, a Hall of Fame was established at Cooperstown in New York State. Its aim is to exhibit baseball memorabilia. Every year a select few players are elected to the Hall of Fame, where information on their careers is displayed.

FOR THE RECORD

MAJOR LEAGUE TEAMS
The American League
East Division:
Baltimore Orioles
Boston Red Sox
Cleveland Indians
Detroit Tigers
Milwaukee Brewers
New York Yankees
Toronto Blue Jays
West Division:
California Angels
Chicago White Sox
Kansas City Royals
Minnesota Twins
Oakland Athletics
Seattle Mariners
Texas Rangers

The National League
East Division:
Chicago Cubs
Montreal Expos
New York Mets
Philadelphia Phillies
Pittsburgh Pirates
St. Louis Cardinals
West Division:
Atlanta Braves
Cincinnati Reds
Houston Astros
Los Angeles Dodgers
San Diego Padres
San Francisco Giants

DID YOU KNOW?

Softball developed from the desire to play baseball indoors. The limited space led to the smaller playing field as well as to the softer ball. The reduced distance from pitcher to batter gave the pitcher an advantage, so the rules changed to only allow underarm pitching.

SOFTBALL

Softball was developed in Chicago as an indoor version of baseball at the end of the last century. It proved to be immensely popular and was soon played all over the United States, but under widely differing rules in various parts of the country. It was not until 1923 that a standard set of rules was published.

Softball is today the most popular recreational team sport in North America and is played at all levels by both men and women, young and old. It is also enjoyed by millions of people in other countries such as Britain, Australia, Japan and New Zealand. One reason for its popularity is that it can be played informally in parks and playgrounds.

The ruling body of the sport is the International Softball Federation and the most important international fixture is the World Championships. The first World Championships for women were held in 1965 and those for men followed a year later. In addition, various national championships are held in the United States for both women and men.

▼ *In the soft-pitch version the pitcher stands with one foot on the rubber and lobs the ball towards the batter.*

AIMS OF THE GAME

COMPETITION
● Softball is very similar to baseball
but there are several important
differences to the rules. The most
important differences are outlined
below:
- teams — Each team comprises 9
players but only 7 innings are played.
- the field — The diamond is
comparatively small — the distances
between the bases being 60 ft (18.3 m).
For men, the distance from the
pitcher's rubber to home plate is 46 ft
(14 m) and for women, 40 ft (12 m).
Unlike in baseball, the pitcher's rubber
is level with the ground and is not
placed on a mound.
- pitching — There are 2 forms of
softball — fast-pitch and slow-pitch. In
the fast-pitch game, a pitcher has to
throw the ball underarm but it can be
delivered hard and flat. (Some fast-
pitchers have been known to throw the

ball faster than a baseball pitcher.) In
the soft-pitch version, the ball has to be
lobbed — the pitcher must arc it
upwards so that when it reaches the
batter it is descending. The soft-pitch
game is most frequently used in
informal games, and one of its
advantages is that it allows more runs
to be scored, which makes the game
more interesting.

SKILLS
● A softball is easier to hit than a
baseball so scores tend to be higher.
But in the more serious fast-pitch
game, the pitcher plays a crucial role in
minimizing the number of hits.
● Being able to throw accurately is
important, especially for fielders in the
outfield. Throwing a comparatively
large softball a long distance takes
practice.

EQUIPMENT

● A softball is considerably larger and
softer than a baseball. It is usually
made from cork bound with hide and
should weigh about 6½ oz (184 g)
and measure about 4 in (10 cm) in
diameter.
● Apart from the ball, the equipment is
much the same as for baseball
although bats tend to be lighter. In fast-
pitch games, batters usually wear
protective helmets.

TECHNICAL TERMS

kitten ball (also mush ball and
diamond ball) names originally given to
softball
tag when a fielder holding the ball
touches a base to which a batter is
running, or while holding the ball
touches the batter with the ball in
between bases, to gain an out

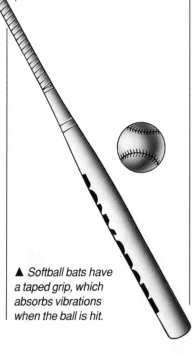

▲ Softball bats have
a taped grip, which
absorbs vibrations
when the ball is hit.

EQUESTRIAN EVENTS

Horses have been raced in various ways for thousands of years, but it was not until the 17th century that people fully appreciated their potential in other fields of competition. Sports where horses are used in ways other than racing are collectively called equestrian events. They combine artistry with horsemanship and stamina.

DRESSAGE

Dressage is often referred to as the art-form of horsemanship. It involves a rider directing and controlling a well schooled horse to the utmost degree, making it move backwards, sideways and in pirouettes, to the brink of perfection.

The sport was first developed in 16th-century Europe, where Italian, Austrian and French horse academies were established. The aim of

▼ *Competitors and their mounts are always immaculately turned out for events to give a good impression to the judges. Dressage is a supreme test of discipline and restraint in both horse and rider.*

AIMS OF THE GAME

COMPETITION
● Each competitor (horse and rider) must complete a number of specific movements within an arena which measures 60 x 20 m (66 x 22 yd). Five marking posts are positioned equally along the sides of the arena, and down the centre line there are at least 3 marked 'staging posts'. The sand on the floor of the arena is raked before each competitor performs.
● There are 5 categories of dressage, the most advanced being the Grand Prix Special. In the Grand Prix Special, each competitor is permitted 8 min 45 sec to complete a routine.
● A competitor is judged (usually by 5 judges) as soon as he or she enters the arena. But, before embarking on the prescribed set of movements, each rider has to 'present' to the judges — this involves halting the horse and saluting. After this formality, the competitor must perform a complex series of movements which can be

these academies was to teach riders how to manage horses until they were completely under control and would do virtually any manoeuvre asked of them.

The aims of modern dressage hardly differ from those laid down by the Renaissance horse schools, but current rules are governed by the Fédération Equestre Internationale (FEI) which was founded in 1921. The most important dressage events are held at the Olympic Games, where both individual and team competitions are included. Many European and national competitions are also held; the most prestigious of these is the four-yearly World Championship. Dressage is also one of the three categories of horsemanship included in eventing (see page 262) which together probably make up the most rigorous tests for both horse and rider.

▲ *A top hat is always worn with a black jacket. If a dark coat is favoured, a bowler hat completes the dress. Military uniforms and caps are also permissible.*

divided into the following general categories:
- paces — walks, trots, canters, counter-canters, flying changes and transitions;
- movements — halts, half-halts, reinbacks and a variety of different trots and walks;
- lateral movements — assorted walks and trots sideways and forwards;
- figures — circles, pirouettes and loops.
● Each judge marks a performance and the total number of points is added together. Before a result is given, penalty points (for moving the wrong way or for taking too long etc.) are deducted. The winner is the competitor who gains the highest number of points.

SKILLS
● The skills of dressage riding cannot be overemphasized, but much depends on the horse and its ability to accept commands. The best riders have a good understanding with their horses, often acquired over many years of partnership. For example, a light pull on the reins from one rider might mean 'trot' to a certain horse; from another rider, it might be translated as meaning 'slow canter to the right'.

EQUIPMENT

● Dress and overall neatness are extremely important to dressage riders. A top hat, hunting stock, breeches and tailcoat are always worn, regardless of sex. The horse also has to be groomed immaculately.

TECHNICAL TERMS

passage a slow, elegant trot in which a horse exaggerates its leg movements
piaffer a slow, exaggerated trot done on the spot; no forward movement is acceptable
pirouette a movement where a horse's hindquarters stay in one spot while its head and fore-limbs move in a circle (part of the 'figures' section)

▲ *All competitors must wear headgear to comply with safety rules. The most favoured hat is a hunting cap, complete with chin strap.*

▼ *British rider, Michael Whitaker, encourages his mount over a jump. A good rapport between horse and rider is essential.*

SHOW JUMPING

The first recognized show jumping competition was held in London in the middle of the last century, although informal competitions in which horse and rider jumped over obstacles had already been held for many years. The sport is thought to have derived from jumping skills developed by riders while out fox-hunting, but unlike steeplechasing, which also developed from hunting, it is less concerned with racing and more concerned with the type and quality of the jumps that the competitors have to negotiate.

Show jumping has always been a popular spectator sport, especially with rural people, but it has recently gained a huge following of television viewers, particularly in Britain, where several of the most important competitions are held. This is not surprising since show jumping can be very exciting to watch.

One of the attractions of show jumping is that, as in dressage and eventing, men and women compete on equal terms. Although fewer women take part in major competitions, many lady riders have proved worthy champions.

The governing body of show jumping in England, Scotland and Wales is the British Show Jumping Association. The international governing body is the Fédération Equestre Internationale. It is both an amateur and a professional sport, with substantial prize money being awarded to winners of professional competitions. For amateurs, the most important events are held at the Olympic Games and at the World Championships which are also held every four years. The Royal International Horse Show, staged every year at the National Exhibition Centre in Birmingham, includes two of the most prestigious prizes open to competitors — the King George V Gold Cup (male riders only) and the Queen Elizabeth II Cup (female riders only). The annual Horse of the Year Show, held in Wembley Arena in London, includes many different categories of competition — from those for children on ponies to some for star riders competing for significant prizes. It helps to generate and maintain interest in the sport. The Olympia International Show Jumping Championships are held in London at the Olympia Stadium each year just before Christmas.

DID YOU KNOW?

Each show jumping course is laid out differently, so the ability of a rider to 'read' a course is often the factor that wins a contest. The sport has been likened to a test in which the course designer is the examiner and the competitors are the examinees.

AIMS OF THE GAME

COMPETITION

● There are literally thousands of different events open to show jumpers but, in the main, these fall into the following three categories:

- jump contests, designed to test jumping ability. In these events each competitor (horse and rider) tackles a course with the aim of clearing all the fences cleanly. If more than one competitor clears the course without scoring any penalties (see below), or if more than 2 competitors finish with equal scores, it is usual for them to be asked to compete again to find the ultimate winner. In this second round, competitors usually jump against the clock and over a higher course — the person who has the lowest score after

penalties in the fastest time is the winner.

- high jump or 'puissance' contests, conducted in a series of rounds similar to an athletics high jump contest. Usually, 2 or 3 fences are presented to contestants. The first 2 are comparatively low, 'warm up' fences designed to prepare the horse for what lies ahead. No penalties are administered for the warm up fences. The puissance jump itself is usually a wall (made of polystyrene or wooden bricks) which is built higher and higher in succeeding rounds until the eventual winner is found.

- speed jumping contests, designed to test both the agility and the pace of each competitor. In these competitions, jumping penalties are converted into time penalties. The horse and rider who finish in the lowest time (after any time penalties have been added) are the winners.

• Courses vary from competition to competition, but there is always a defined arena. Indoor arenas should cover a minimum area of 2500 sq m (3000 sq yd) but most are larger and outdoor arenas are greater still. Depending on the type of competition, courses are designed to test rider and horse not to the limit, but near to the limit (if all competitors were eliminated at one go, the competition would fail). A good course design ensures that each competitor has to do sharp turns as well as slow manoeuvres before jumping the obstacles. The distance between obstacles is crucial as a horse's stride has to be taken into account. Obstacles (fences) invariably have to be taken in a specific order by competitors so they have to be mapped out carefully in order to be fair and reasonable. Fence categories include the following:

- 'uprights', where gaining height is more important than length (e.g. post-and-rails, walls, fences);
- 'spreads', where both height and length are important (e.g. triple bars);
- 'combinations', where 2 or 3 fences have to be jumped immediately one after the other;
- 'water jumps', where length to clear the water is more important than height.

• Scoring procedure differs according to the type of competition and to specific rules laid down by the organizers — there are no hard and fast rules of scoring and the following is only a rough guide.

- Puissance competitions are the easiest to judge because the winner is the competitor who jumps the highest. Equal positions are permitted if riders opt out at the same final height for the benefit of their horses.

- In jumping competitions, 4 penalties are given for knocking down a fence or part of it and 3 penalties are given for a refusal (when a horse decides not to jump). The competitor with the least number of penalties wins. In timed rounds, a knocked-down fence sometimes means elimination and the competitor who finishes with a faultless round in the fastest time wins.

- In speed jumping contests, failed jumps are converted into time penalty points. A knocked fence can equal up to 15 sec in time penalty points.

• Show jumping can be both an individual and a team event. In team competitions, individual scores are added together to find the winning total. The team with the lowest penalty point score is the winner. Team show jumping is one of the most popular equestrian events of the Olympics.

SKILLS

• Above all else, show jumping relies upon an understanding between horse and rider. The horse must be able to jump well but the rider must know the course and be able to guide the horse effectively. Timing is crucial because to succeed in jumping an obstacle, a horse has to have a certain number of paces in which to 'run up' and prepare for take off. Conveying precise commands and maintaining a horse's rhythm are just 2 skills required of a show jumping rider.

• Show jumping horses take years to train; they have to be taught how to take both high and long jumps. This sort of instruction is a rarely mastered skill. Training a horse to jump against the clock is not really a consideration for trainers. The best jumpers usually win provided they are ridden well.

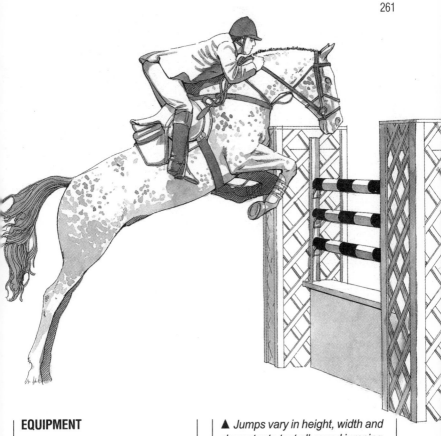

EQUIPMENT

● Strict etiquette is maintained at most show jumping events. At international level, men must wear a red hunting coat (known as 'pink'), while ladies wear blue or black show jackets. Military jackets are also permitted. Black or tweed jackets are acceptable in national events. A riding hat with a chin strap fastened at 3 points, white or buff breeches, and riding boots must be worn.

TECHNICAL TERMS

combination an obstacle that comprises 2 or 3 fences to be jumped in succession with a set of measured strides in between (usually 2 or 3)

▲ *Jumps vary in height, width and character to test all-round jumping ability. Post-and-rail fences are often arranged as 'combinations'.*

jump-off a final round of a jump contest to decide a winner; usually contested against the clock and some times leading to yet another round if no winner has been decided

kickback some horses flash their hind legs while jumping, often to one side only (skew kick)

lady a female rider is never called a woman

refusal when a horse suddenly declines to jump a fence, often landing the rider on the floor

spread a fence that incorporates length as well as height

DID YOU KNOW?

The gruelling cross-country stage of eventing grew out of horse trials, or hunter trials as they are sometimes called, which are practised all over the British Isles. In these trials, horses that are traditionally used for hunting are put through their paces over a course that contains natural and man-made jumps. The natural obstacles include streams, steep banks, stone walls, fallen trees and hedges — the same types of obstacles that are to be found on cross-country courses.

EVENTING

Eventing or three day eventing, as it is sometimes called, developed in the 19th century when cavalry horses were tested for obedience, speed, endurance and bravery by being ridden over long, arduous courses. It grew to become a popular sport, and eventing was first included in the Olympic Games in 1912.

A strictly amateur sport, eventing has a dedicated following of supporters. It is not as easy to understand and follow as show jumping, for example, but it is the most rigorous of all tests for horse and rider, and both have to be supremely fit. Women riders compete on completely equal terms with male competitors and some of the greatest riders in the sport have been women — HRH Princess Anne and Lucinda Green to name just two.

Several major competitions rival the Olympic Games in importance. These include the annual Badminton Horse Trials and the Burghley Horse Trials. The ruling body of the sport is the Fédération Equestre Internationale. Countries that have the strongest traditions in eventing include Great Britain, New Zealand, the United States and Germany as well as Sweden and the Netherlands.

▼ *In the dressage stage, horses trace exact figures. The diameter of the circle has to be more than 6 m (6½ yd).*

▼ *When cantering the figure of eight, a horse has to change its leading leg where the two circles join.*

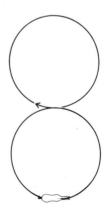

AIMS OF THE GAME

COMPETITION

● An eventing competition usually lasts 3 days although there are one-day events for which the rules are slightly modified. Competitions can be held between individuals or teams.

● On Day 1, there is the dressage section and each competitor has to perform set moves in an arena for about 10 min. It is run like a standard dressage competition (see page 256) and final marks form part of the intricate calculations eventually used to decide the overall winner of the competition. The leader after the dressage phase is the person with the lowest penalty score. Equal placings are permissible in eventing.

● Day 2 is divided into 4 parts, or phases, and is carefully designed to test the stamina, speed and jumping ability of each horse. Day 2 is often called the endurance day. The 4 phases, which have to be completed in order, are:
- roads and tracks;
- steeplechase;
- roads and tracks;
- cross-country.

In the roads and tracks phases competitors have to trot or canter a combined distance of 16 to 20 km (10 to 12½ miles) at a pace of around 220 m per min (240 yd per min). The course for this section is marked out along meandering lanes and roads and each competitor is timed from start to finish.

◀ The show jumping stage takes place in an arena and up to 12 jumps have to be taken in order. Penalties are given for refusals, fences knocked down and time faults.

The steeplechase section usually comprises 12 fences along a course that is about 4 km (2½ miles) long and has to be carried out at a pace of around 690 m per min (755 yd per min). Each competitor is timed.

Before the final cross-country phase, competitors and their horses are obliged to take a 10 min break during which the horses are checked for fitness by a veterinary surgeon. (Vets are present for the duration of the 3-day event.) The cross-country phase is the most gruelling of all. It is about 8 km (5 miles) long and has to be galloped at a pace of around 570 m per min (620 yd per min). Along the cross-country course, a number of obstacles and jumps have to be negotiated — there are usually about 30. The obstacles can vary enormously in shape and character. Some are solid walls, others are steep banks with severe drops and several usually contain water. Some obstacles are built to test a rider's judgment and can be either taken with one huge leap or tackled by 2 more modest jumps.

Each of the 4 Day-2 phases has a time allowance and competitors that exceed this allowance receive penalty points. In addition penalties are given for falling at a fence or if a horse refuses to jump. At the end of Day 2, penalties are added up and the person with the least is the leader.

● Day 3 is comparatively straight forward and consists of a show jumping contest which takes place in an arena. The main aim of this stage is to test a horse's suppleness and its reactions to a new environment. Each competitor has to tackle 10 or 12 jumps in a specific order and penalty points are given for knocking down a fence or part of a fence, for falls and refusals. As with the other sections, time is important and anyone who exceeds the time limit is given extra penalties.

● At the end of the show jumping stage, penalties for all of the 3 days' events are added up and the winner is the person with the lowest score. In team competitions, the best 3 scores are taken into account (there are normally 4 members to a team) and the team with the lowest total score wins.

● As this book goes to press, a new scoring system is being prepared, to take effect in 1992. At stake is the relative importance given to the 3 events.

SKILLS

● The best rider and horse combinations have usually been together for years and have established a rapport. Both have to be in peak physical condition and have to be able to trust each other. Each relies on the other for success and safety at some of the more daunting obstacles — particularly during the steeplechase and cross-country sections of Day 2.

● Horses have to be trained in 3 distinct disciplines so they have to be intelligent as well as strong. Training usually starts when the horse is young but can take many years to reach competition standard.

● Riders must be able to pace both themselves and their horses efficiently, especially in the Day-2 phases. If a horse goes too fast in the initial stages, it is bound to flag towards the end. The cross-country stage is where many competitions are won and lost and a rider's sense of judgment is always being tested. For example, many obstacles have an easy way and a difficult way in which they can be approached. The difficult way could save seconds but could result in a fall and lead to a few more penalty points.

EQUIPMENT

- Different clothing is worn at each of the different events. For the dressage, hunting dress — usually with a top hat — or a military uniform has to be worn. In addition it is compulsory for all competitors to wear blunt spurs. For Day 2, the clothes can be more practical than formal — the 2 compulsory pieces of equipment are a crash helmet and riding boots. For the show jumping, hunting dress or a military uniform is usually worn.
- Stopwatches are permitted and they allow competitors to judge pace accurately.
- On Days 2 and 3, horses frequently wear protective bandages on their legs to protect them from being damaged should they hit a fence.

TECHNICAL TERMS

competition ratio the relative importance of the 3 different eventing competitions is expressed as ratios: dressage 3, endurance 12, show jumping 1

multiplying factor this is a figure between 0.5 and 2.5 which is used to adjust marks given for the dressage section; the idea is that once the dressage marks have been multiplied by this figure, the Day 1 competition will have 'the correct influence on the whole competition'

penalty zone the marked areas around fences and obstacles in the steeplechase and cross-country phases in which penalties can be given for falls or refusals

running out when a horse refuses to jump and instead runs to the side and past an obstacle

FOR THE RECORD

BADMINTON HORSE TRIALS
The world-famous Badminton Horse Trials take place every year in the extensive grounds of Badminton House in Gloucestershire, the home of the Duke of Beaufort. The first trials were held in 1949 and have been held each May ever since.

▲ *The cross-country phase is the most testing of all. The obstacles are often large and awkward to jump. A horse senses its rider's confidence or apprehension as they near an obstacle.*

DID YOU KNOW?

The word 'bronco' comes from a 19th-century Mexican-Spanish phrase 'potro bronco', meaning wild colt. Cowhands refer to mustangs, small wild horses from the western United States, by this name. Mustangs are descended from the horses of early Spanish explorers.

RODEO

During the 19th century, cowboys of the Wild West orchestrated events where they could demonstrate their skills to an audience. These events became known as rodeos, and they became such entertaining spectacles that they rapidly spread south to Mexico and north to Canada. Towards the end of the last century, rodeo became big business and Colonel William Cody — otherwise known as Buffalo Bill — brought a rodeo show to Europe in 1877. Among his star attractions was the fabled sharpshooter, Annie Oakley.

Since those heady days, interest in rodeo has dwindled in Europe, but its popularity continues to flourish in North America, where professionals earn huge sums for competing in several different and apparently dangerous sports. Some of today's rodeo stars are city dwellers who have been to special rodeo schools.

The ruling body of the sport is the Professional Rodeo Cowboy Association and the main annual fiesta is the National Finals Rodeo, which is held in Las Vegas.

AIMS OF THE GAME

COMPETITION
● Rodeos are held in an enclosed area, something like a large circus ring, with sawdust on the ground and spectator seats all around. Some are held indoors but the majority are held outside.
● Five main events are usually held at a rodeo. These are as follows:
- saddle bronco riding, in which a rider tries to maintain his seat while riding a bucking horse for 10 sec. Two judges award marks out of 25 — one judge marks the ability of the rider, the other marks the spirit of the horse (some can be docile). The winner is the person who gains the most points from these 2 sources.
- bareback bronco riding, in which a cowboy rides bareback on a bucking horse for 8 sec; he has to keep one hand free while hanging onto a strap around the horse's neck with the other. Marks are awarded as for saddle bronco riding.
- bull riding, the most feared event. A rider has to sit bareback for 8 sec on a Brahma bull which can turn vicious after it has unseated its rider. Once off the animal, riders dive into protective barrels for safety.
- calf roping, in which a rider lassoes a calf, and throws the animal to the ground by hand. This event is timed against the clock and the winner is the fastest to tie up 3 of a calf's feet.
- steer wrestling, also a potentially dangerous activity. A rider has to gallop alongside a steer, catch its horns and, sliding from his horse, bring the steer to a halt on its side. Time is crucial and the winner is the quickest to bring a steer to a halt.
● Many additional events, such as barrel racing and team roping, are also held at rodeos.

SKILLS
● Courage, horsemanship, stamina and a tough backside are all required.
● A good sense of timing and co-ordination are essential in the roping events, where rushing a throw can actually lose time.

EQUIPMENT

● Surprisingly little equipment is essential. Bronco riders wear spurs on their boots and 'chaps', leather coverings, around their legs. Rodeo performers have favourite lassoes, on which they come to depend as much as golfers depend on their clubs.

TECHNICAL TERMS

barrel man a man, usually dressed as a clown, who positions a hollow barrel near where he thinks a rider will need shelter after riding a bull
bronco an untrained, or half-trained, horse
buck when a horse arches its back in an attempt to shed its rider
cinch the handle attached to a bare back bronco via a leather strap; it allows a rider to hold on to something as he struggles to stay on top
hang-up when a rider who falls off a horse or bull is caught by a stirrup
lariat another name for a lasso
shute box the gate on the side of the ring from which riders are let out at the start of an event.

◀ *Calf roping is a favourite rodeo event. A rider first lassoes a calf in traditional cowboy fashion and then jumps off his mount to tie up three of the animal's legs. Calf ropers compete against the clock.*

HORSE-RACING

Racing horses dates back to Ancient Egyptian times and the Ancient Greeks also raced horses at the original Olympic Games. Today racing in its various forms is to be found all over the world.

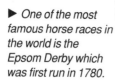
► *One of the most famous horse races in the world is the Epsom Derby which was first run in 1780.*

DID YOU KNOW?

Virtually all the world's best race horses are descendants of 3 Arabian horses that were introduced to Britain in the 18th century — Byerly Turk, Darley Arabian and Godolphin Arabian. These 3 stallions were crossed with English livestock to produce thoroughbreds which have been exported all over the globe to be crossed with local horses.

Ironically, camel-racing is now more popular in Arab countries than horse-racing.

FLAT RACING

Although racing horses over flat tracks is an extremely old pastime, it did not become an organized sport until the 12th century, when the first regular race meetings were held in London. Ever since it has been a favourite sport of the British aristocracy, which has patronized and encouraged it.

Horse-racing was introduced to America in 1644 by Colonel Richard Nicholls, who commanded the English forces that invaded New Amsterdam (New York). Since then it has become an international sport.

In Europe, the flat racing season runs from March to November. In Britain there is no racing on Sundays, when gambling is illegal, but in continental Europe Sundays are traditionally reserved for the most important races. In the United States and other countries, flat racing is a year-round institution.

The Jockey Club of Great Britain, established in 1751, is the ruling body of flat racing in Britain. Other countries have their own governing bodies, sometimes many of them, as in the United States where there is no solitary ruling organization. In Australia, the Australian Jockey Club governs the sport.

AIMS OF THE GAME

• Horses must be at least 2 years old before they can be raced. This can lead to confusion as all horses are allocated a birthday — 1 January of the year in which they are born in the Northern Hemisphere and 1 August in the Southern Hemisphere.

• Courses vary greatly in length and shape. They are rarely absolutely flat and straight. Most have shallow rises and dips as well as curves. Courses in Europe are usually grassed but dirt tracks are more common in the United States.

• The races held on the same courses also vary in length: some can be as short as 4 furlongs (800 m approx.), others are as long as 2½ miles (4 km approx.) [Note: In Britain and North America, races are measured in furlongs and miles and not in metric equivalents].

• The jockeys wear identifying colours on their shirts and helmets. The colours are the property of the horse-owners who hire jockeys to ride their steeds.

• The horses start from stalls, the gates of which are opened at the same time. Starting stalls were introduced to make starts fairer but on certain tracks where there is a tight curve, inside stalls can be an advantage.

• The winner is the horse and jockey who pass the finishing post first.

SKILLS

• Jockeys must be light, but strong enough to contain and steer a lively horse galloping flat out. They ride with short stirrups in which they stand up so that weight is taken off the horse's back. Slightly different techniques are used by jockeys in various parts of the world. In the United States, where races tend to be short sprints, jockeys usually hold the reins short and crouch right behind the horse's neck; in Europe, where the longest races are held, they usually hold the reins longer which helps to relax the horse.

▼ *Leaving the exit stalls at the start of the St Leger 'classic'.*

• A good jockey will take the trouble to find out the character of a horse before a race. A nervous, highly-strung horse will need careful, sympathetic riding, whereas a stubborn one will need maximum coaxing. Similarly, some horses like to be out in front, while others prefer to remain in the bunch. Jockeys are allowed to use whips in most countries, but their use is strictly governed; a jockey who thrashes a beaten horse will be severely reprimanded. In fact, a good jockey rarely uses a whip to hit a horse; it is usually used in glancing blows to encourage or maintain the rhythm of the gallop.

• The trainer is often the person who is most responsible for a horse's success. It is the trainer who keeps the horse fit and decides how it should be raced by the jockey.

▼ *Jockeys crouch on short stirrups with the reins held tight.*

EQUIPMENT

• In addition to wearing identifying colours, a jockey also wears thin, white breeches, black leather boots, a back protector, a crash helmet and goggles which protect the eyes from mud or dirt thrown up by other horses.

TECHNICAL TERMS

colt a male horse that is less than 4 years old
filly a female horse that is less than 4 years old
going the state of the track or turf which can be described as 'hard', 'firm', 'good to firm', 'good', 'good to soft', 'soft' and 'heavy'
handicap a race in which horses carry various amounts of lead weights according to their ability. The most able horses carry the most weight (the maximum weight a horse is allowed to carry is 10 stone (63.5 kg) including

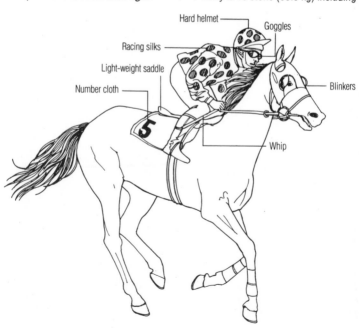

Hard helmet
Goggles
Racing silks
Light-weight saddle
Number cloth
Blinkers
Whip

jockey, saddle and additional weights); the theory behind handicapping is that all the horses in a race should have an equal chance of winning

head a winning margin, roughly equivalent to the width of a horse's head; the shortest possible winning margin is a 'short head', something less than a head

length a term used to describe the distance between 2 horses at the finish; a length is equivalent to the distance between a horse's head and its tail

maiden a horse that has never won a race

objection a jockey can complain to the stewards who oversee a race if he feels that he or his horse has been impeded in some way during a race; the stewards then hold an inquiry and view a video of the race to see if the objection is valid; if it is, the guilty horse can be disqualified and the jockey suspended

paddock the ring where horses and jockeys parade before a race

photo-finish in close finishes between 2 or more horses, photographs taken at the line are studied to determine the winner

silks the shirts worn by jockeys

starters orders when the starter of a race announces that he is about to open the starting stalls; usually signalled by the starter raising a flag

weigh-in after a race all jockeys are required to sit on scales while carrying their saddles and weightcloths, to check that they weigh as much as they did before the race — a jockey that has lost a lead weight, for example, will be disqualified

▶ *A jockey who steers his horse into the path of another may end up being the subject of a steward's inquiry and could be disqualified.*

FOR THE RECORD

FAMOUS RACES

Name	Where run
The English Classics	
The Derby	Epsom
The Oaks	Epsom
1,000 Guineas	Newmarket
2,000 Guineas	Newmarket
St Leger	Doncaster
The American Triple Crown races	
Kentucky Derby	Louisville, Kentucky
Preakness Stakes	Pimlico, Maryland
Belmont Stakes	New York
Other major races	
Prix de L'Arc de Triomphe	Longchamps, France
Melbourne Cup	Flemington, Australia
The Irish Derby	The Curragh, Co. Kildare, Ireland

DID YOU KNOW?

Point-to-point racing is a form of steeplechasing which is enjoyed by amateurs. The race meetings are organized by local hunts and the courses are laid out over local terrain.

STEEPLECHASING AND HURDLING

Steeplechasing developed from fox hunting in the 18th century. During a hunt, followers on horses were required to jump over hedges and ditches and it was a simple step to turn a hunt into a race. The first official race is thought to have taken place in Ireland in 1752. Hurdling is slightly different from steeplechasing in that the horses jump over stuffed wooden hurdles that were originally used for herding sheep. Steeplechasing and hurdling are widely enjoyed in Great Britain, Ireland and France, and they are becoming popular in the United States.

The season for jump racing — steeplechasing and hurdling — runs roughly from August to May with the majority of the most important races being run from October to April. Most jockeys are professionals, but it is not unusual for steeplechase horses to be ridden by amateurs.

Both steeplechasing and hurdling are governed by rules laid down by the Jockey Club, the same organization that runs flat racing.

AIMS OF THE GAME

COMPETITION

● Steeplechase horses have to be at least 4 years old before they can take part in a race but, unlike flat race horses, they carry on racing until they are quite old — anything up to 15. They are bred for jumping and are heavier and stronger than their flat race counterparts. Hurdlers, on the other hand, are not always bred to jump — many flat race horses have moved on to hurdling but they have to be at least 3 years old.

● Courses vary greatly, both in length and design. Steeplechases can vary from between 2 to 4½ miles (3 to 7 km approx.) long while the majority of hurdle races are from 2 to 3¼ miles (3 to 5 km) long.

● Steeplechase jumps, or fences, are made from birch twigs which are bound together and cropped into shape. They are usually about 4½ ft (1.35 m) high; the side facing the horses is sheer but the far side is sloped downwards to help horses land. Most courses have at least 2 or 3 modified jumps, often including a water jump which has a shallow pond about 15 ft (5 m) long on the far side of a low fence, and possibly several 'open ditches' which have a 3 ft (1-m approx.) ditch in front of the fence. The number of fences on a course can vary but there are usually about a dozen in a 2-mile (3-km) race.

▶ *Desert Orchid's brave finishes and string of victories have made him a favourite with British crowds and bookmakers alike.*

Hurdles are less substantial than fences. They are made from woven birch twigs and are about 3½ ft (1 m approx.) high. Horses can easily knock down hurdles but they are nearly always jumped if possible. There are usually about 8 hurdles in a 2-mile (3-km) race.

● As in flat racing, jockeys wear the colours of the horses' owners.

● No starting stalls are used in steeplechasing and hurdling. Instead, lengths of tape are suspended in front of the horses at the starting line and are quickly released when all the horses have assembled in a line. There are no draws for the order in which the horses should line up — it is a matter of preference for the jockeys.

● At the finish, the first horse carrying a jockey past the post is the winner. As with flat racing, a jockey can complain to the officiating stewards if he thinks that he or his horse has been hindered by another.

SKILLS

● In steeplechasing, it is not always the fastest horse that wins — a good jumper can gain significant distance over each obstacle and this is often the most telling factor. The trainer is the person who coaches a horse to jump but a good steeplechaser will have a natural ability to take fences. Because the longer races can be extremely gruelling, stamina is all-important, and a trainer will spend months getting a horse completely fit.

Hurdle races are generally shorter and less tiring than steeplechases but a horse must still be fit and be able to jump. Although a horse could run through all the hurdles in a race, it is much more efficient if it jumps them.

● Riding a horse over jumps requires considerable skill from the jockey. As most races take place in the winter when the ground can be soft and muddy, the jockey must decide how he is going to tackle the course — in the thick of it where the ground will be sticky or the 'long way round' on the outside where the earth will be firmer and faster. A jockey always tries to let his horse have a good view of a fence or hurdle — if the timing is bad, horse and jockey could fall.

A jockey must have a sound knowledge of his horse's ability. Some horses are good jumpers but do not have a strong finishing sprint, others are highly strung and have to be held back until the final dash for the post. If a jockey misjudges his horse, he is doomed to failure.

EQUIPMENT

● Jockeys dress in a similar way to their flat racing counterparts except that they tend to wear woollen jerseys instead of thin shirts. An essential piece of additional equipment that all jockeys wear is a back protector. This protects the back in the case of a bad fall.

TECHNICAL TERMS

brought down when a horse is knocked or tripped by another while jumping and falls
flight a hurdle
loose horse a horse that has lost its jockey but still continues to run in a race; this is potentially dangerous as it could run into other horses or trip on the reins dangling from its neck
sticks a fence or hurdle
weight as in flat racing, horses are handicapped by carrying lead weights in weightcloths under the saddle; the maximum weight a horse is allowed to carry is 12 stone 7 lb (80 kg).

FOR THE RECORD

The most famous steeplechase in the world, the Grand National, provides the toughest of all tests for both horse and rider. First run in 1936, the 'National' is run at Aintree, near Liverpool. Horses and riders have to negotiate 30 fences over 2 circuits of the track — over 4½ miles (7 km) in all.

Because the course is so long and the fences so high, the outcome of the race is never easy to predict — which is one reason why it such a popular race. In 1967, a rank outsider, Foinavon, came through to win after trailing far behind because all the leaders came to grief at a fence. However, the most famous winner, and possibly the most famous horse in the world, Red Rum, was a favourite and won the race 3 times — in 1973, 1974 and 1977.

Some of the most notorious fences — Beecher's Brook, Valentine's Brook and the Chair — have been modified since a number of horses lost their lives at them. The ditches on the far side of the two brook fences have now been partially filled in so that the landing is less dangerous.

Grand National day is always one of the busiest for British bookmakers.

FOR THE RECORD

FAMOUS RACES

Name	Where Run
Cheltenham Gold Cup	Cheltenham
Champion Hurdle	Cheltenham
Whitbread Gold Cup	Sandown Park
Hennessy Gold Cup	Newbury
King George VI Chase	Kempton Park

▼ *Hurdle races are usually shorter than steeplechases, and the jumps are less substantial, being made from woven birch branches. Many successful hurdle horses are trained originally to race on flat courses where there are no jumps.*

DID YOU KNOW?

The Hambletonian is a prestigious one-mile (1.6-km) race for three-year-old trotters run each year in the United States. It takes its name from a famous stallion which, from 1851 to 1874, sired 1331 horses. Most successful pacers and trotters are descendants of Hambletonian.

▼ *A horse wears a light, leather harness to pull the sulky. The harness allows the driver to control and guide the horse, a skill more difficult than it may at first appear.*

HARNESS RACING

Harness racing is a type of horse-racing in which a driver is pulled along in a cart behind a horse. The sport can be traced back more than 2000 years to Roman chariot races.

The modern form of harness racing started in America during the late 18th century when an English thoroughbred stallion called Messenger was taken there. Descendants of Messenger became formidable harness horses over the years, and many horses today still bear his name on their pedigrees.

In the United States harness racing is, if anything, more popular than flat racing, with huge crowds turning up to meetings. It is also has a vast following in continental Europe, New Zealand and Australia. In the past it was ignored in Britain and Ireland, although it is gradually beginning to gain favour. The French Trotting Authority and the Jockey Club arranged for a courtesy 'visit' in 1990 to test a proposed track surface.

The World Trotting Conference is the international authority, but different countries have marginally different rules. In Britain all races are governed by rules laid down by the British Harness Racing Club.

AIMS OF THE GAME

COMPETITION

● Harness horses are trained to move their legs in one of 2 ways. 'Trotting' horses move their legs so that when a right front leg steps forwards, the left hind leg also moves forwards. 'Pacing' horses are trained so that both left legs and both right legs move together. Trotters and pacers rarely compete against each other — separate events are normally held for the 2 styles.

● Drivers sit on lightweight carts attached to the horses via shafts and harnesses; horses are steered with long reins.

● Courses are usually oval dirt tracks and can range in length from ½ mile (800 m approx.) to 1 mile (1.5 km approx.).

● If a horse — either a trotter or a pacer — starts to gallop during a race, the driver is obliged to move to one side until the horse starts to trot or pace again; if the driver continues, he will be disqualified.

● The first horse, cart and rider past the winning post wins.

SKILLS

● Driving a harnessed horse is not easy as the temptation for the driver is to let the horse move too quickly and allow it to start galloping. Skilled drivers know exactly how fast they can push their horses. A familiar technique used by drivers is to keep a horse's head high by using a 'check' to maintain the horse's balance. If the check breaks, the animal usually breaks stride.

● Training a horse to trot or pace fast takes great skill. Pacers, slightly faster than trotters, can move at nearly 50 km/h (30 mph approx.) without starting to gallop.

EQUIPMENT

● The cart, or sulky, is extremely light, no more than 18 kg (40 lb) and rides on bicycle-type wheels. Carts are designed so that when a driver sits on one, it is perfectly balanced with the pull of the horse.

● Drivers wear coloured 'silks', just as in flat racing.

TECHNICAL TERMS

boots protection wrapped or strapped to a horse's legs so that they are not injured
break gallop
gait the movement of a horse
hobbles leather straps worn by pacers around the legs to help balance and maintain the stride
offstride when a horse breaks into a gallop
sulky cart towed behind the horse

Trotting

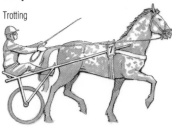

Pacing

▲ *Trotting, above, is the older form of harness racing. Pacing, below, was introduced in the United States during the 1860s and has since become very popular.*

GOLF

Golf is a game like no other and historians disagree about its origins. Some reckon that a forerunner to the game was played by the Chinese some 2000 years ago, others claim that the Romans were first to knock balls into holes. The game as it is played today, however, is a mere 250 years old.

GOLF

▼ *Bunker shots are played with a 'wedge', a club with an angled face which scoops the ball up and over the overhanging edge of the bunker. A dramatic spray of sand accompanies the ball on its flight.*

Scotland is considered to be the spiritual home of modern golf. During the 14th century, a primitive form of the game was played there by herdsmen who used roughly hewn clubs to knock balls into small holes that were dug into the ground. Over the years, golf became fashionable for the upper classes and James IV of Scotland is known to have played a version of the game. In the middle of the 18th century, a standard set of rules was drawn up and was accepted by the Royal and Ancient Club in 1754. The Royal and Ancient (R&A), which is based at St Andrews in Scotland, is still one of the two most important ruling bodies of the sport. Its Old Course often plays host to the Open Championships — the premier golf tournament.

During the course of the 19th century, golf became a popular sport worldwide and is now played in most countries of the world by both men and women, young and old. One reason for its popularity is that it guarantees light exercise in the open air and also demands considerable mental concentration. The majority of players are amateurs, the best of whom compete to enter the professional game. Top competitors can earn fabulous amounts of money. The US professional 'tour' is a series of tournaments open to professionals who have attained a certain standard. Commercial sponsors organize the tournaments, which are held nearly every week from January to early October. Similar tours take place in Europe and Asia.

The R&A and the United States Golfing Association (USGA) co-operate to produce the Rules of Golf and the Rules of Amateur Status. The governing of the game in any country — seeing that these rules are applied — is undertaken by the national federation or union. There are many important competitions for individual men and women at both amateur and professional level. In addition, there are also team competitions — usually played for national pride rather than for cash.

DID YOU KNOW?

Early golf balls were stitched leather pouches stuffed tightly with feathers. These balls continued to be used right up until the middle of the 19th century when they lost favour to solid balls made from gum.

AIMS OF THE GAME

COMPETITION
● Golf is essentially a simple game, the object being to hit a small ball into a series of holes in as few strokes as possible using a variety of clubs.
● A full-size course comprises 18 'holes', each of which can be divided up into 4 distinct areas. First there is the flat area — the 'tee' — where a golfer makes his first shot. The hole itself is situated on a smooth, grassy area called a 'green'. In between the tee and the green lies a stretch of mown grass called a 'fairway'; and beside that is the 'rough', ground from which it is difficult to play. The fairway can be undulating terrain and it can also contain a number of obstacles and hazards. Hazards are such things as sand-filled 'bunkers' which are designed to trap the ball, and water hazards such as a stream or lake.
● Each 'hole' — from tee to green — varies in length but most are between 100 and 500 m (110 and 550 yd) long. The greens can also vary greatly in size and shape and need not be perfectly flat. The grass on them is always tightly cropped. The holes themselves are 10.8 cm (4¼ in) in diameter and must be at least 10 cm (4 in) deep. A flag is usually placed in the hole to mark where it lies on the green. The position of the hole is changed regularly so that every part of the surface of the green wears evenly.

● When starting from a tee, a golfer is allowed to place the ball on a small, cup-shaped tee peg (called a 'tee') which makes it easier to hit. This is the only time a tee peg can be used — thereafter, the ball must be struck onwards towards the green from where it lands. If, however, the ball should land in such a position that it is impossible to hit — in a lake for example — the player may be allowed to reposition the ball or use a new one subject to a penalty stroke being added to his or her total score. Strict and exhaustive rules govern how and when a ball can be repositioned. Penalty strokes do not apply to certain 'man-made' obstacles such as hosepipes.

● Once a player's ball has landed on the green, usually after a number of strokes off the fairway, he or she can mark its position with a disc in case an opponent's ball should hit it or the wind blow it away. Similarly, a player can be asked to mark and remove a ball if it is in the line of play for opponents.

● When a player succeeds in getting his or her ball into the hole, or 'holing out', he or she moves on to try and do the same at the next hole. This continues until 18 holes have been completed (a 'round').

● Courses are usually par-72, meaning that a scratch golfer should complete a round in that score. Most holes are par-4, with longer par-5 holes matched by the same number of par-3 holes.

● There are 2 main types of competition — strokeplay and matchplay. The more common form is strokeplay where the number of strokes that each player takes to complete a round of the course is noted. In major championships, 4 rounds are played over 4 successive days, the winner being the person with the lowest overall score. Matchplay is used in knockout tournaments and can be played by either individuals or teams. In matchplay, golfers try to win individual

▼ *Undulations on a green can make the ball roll in a curve so it has to be aimed to one side of the hole. A club dangled vertically can help a golfer to judge the correct line that a putt should take.*

holes in the fewest number of strokes. So, a person who takes 4 shots to hole out will beat an opponent who takes 5 shots. Matches end when one player has a lead of more holes than there are holes still left to play. For example if a player has a 3-hole lead and there are only 2 left, the opponent cannot possibly win. The winning margin for such a game would be termed 3 and 2 (3 up and 2 to play).

▲ *Modern golf balls comprise long strips of rubber wound around a core. The dimples on the outer casing help the ball to fly smoothly.*

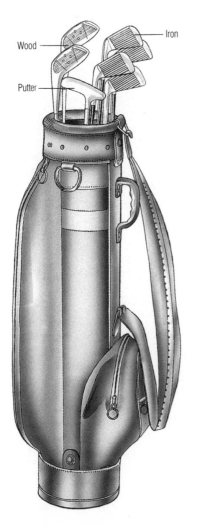

Wood — Iron

Putter —

SKILLS

● Golf is a great deal more than just hitting a ball hard and far with a club. Achieving distance is important when starting from the tee — 'driving off' as it is called — but it is also crucial to a golfer that the ball ends up in a good position for the next shot. Skilled golfers will take into account the condition of the fairway as well as any wind that might catch the ball and make it end up in an awkward position. For example, in hot, dry weather, the fairway may be hard, which will cause the ball to bounce and roll, perhaps further than intended. Conversely, if the fairway is damp, the ball may hardly move at all once it has landed.
● A key decision for a golfer is which club to use; some make the ball fly high and short, others low and long.
● Playing the ball off the fairway and on to the green may take several shots. Again, a golfer will try not to over-hit or under-hit and will be anxious to avoid any bunkers that 'guard' the green.

◄ *Everything that a golfer needs can be put in a golf bag — umbrella, score card and spare balls, as well as a selection of up to 14 clubs. Bags are often carried by hired caddies.*

• Once on the green, different skills are brought into play. A flat-faced putter is usually used to play the ball along the ground and into the hole. This sounds simple but greens usually undulate and good players can judge in which direction the ball is likely to stray.

• Some of the most spectacular shots in golf are made from bunkers when the ball is lodged in sand. In most cases, a special club is used to loft the ball out of the sand and over the lip of the bunker.

• Golfers try endlessly to perfect their 'swing' — or method of hitting the ball. Ideally, the head should be kept steady with the eyes on the ball. The swing of the club should be rhythmical with the minimum of movement in the legs. When playing on the green a cool temperament and a steady head count for a lot.

• There are several ways to grip a golf club. Perhaps the best known is the Vardon grip — named after the great English golfer Harry Vardon — where the index finger of the top hand interlocks with the little finger of the bottom hand.

EQUIPMENT

• Golf clubs come in a staggering variety of designs but there are just 3 general categories — 'woods','irons' and 'putters'. The most important part of a club is the head — the part that actually hits the ball. It is attached to a steel or graphite shaft with a hand grip. Heads have slanted faces: the greater the slant upwards, the higher the ball will fly.

The heads on woods are made from wood, metal or plastic. Because they are relatively heavy, woods are used for hitting the ball long distances. There are 4 basic types of wood. A No.1 is usually used for driving off a tee; No. 2 and 3 have slightly more angled faces and are handy on long fairways; the No. 4 wood is sometimes used to get the ball out of rough grass.

▼ Four stages of a golf swing: the takeaway (1), the backswing (2), the downswing (3) and contact (4). The eyes focus on the ball throughout.

Golf ball — Tee

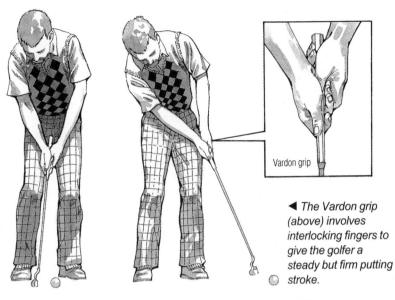

Vardon grip

◀ *The Vardon grip (above) involves interlocking fingers to give the golfer a steady but firm putting stroke.*

Irons have heads made of steel and other materials and the shafts are shorter than those on woods. Irons are numbered from 1 to 10 and are usually used to play shots off the fairway. The higher the number, the more the face is angled — a No.1 iron will send the ball lower but further than a No.9 iron. The No.10 iron is sometimes referred to as a 'wedge' because it has such an angled face. A wedge is used to loft the ball out of bunkers.

Putters come in any number of shapes and sizes but they all have flat faces so that they do not lift the ball off the ground at all. They are only used on greens.

● Golf balls have a diameter of 4.2 cm (1.65 in). All golf balls have a dimpled surface to make them more aerodynamically efficient.

● Players carry all their equipment around in specially designed golf bags which can be slung over a shoulder or pulled in a cart. Electric golf carts are often available for older or handicapped players.

TECHNICAL TERMS

address the stance a golfer takes before striking the ball
albatross 3 strokes under par (also called a double eagle)
birdie one stroke under par
bogey one shot over par
caddie a person hired by a golfer to carry the golf bag; a good caddie can also advise with the choice of clubs
divot a chunk of earth that is lifted when playing a shot with an iron
dogleg a fairway that incorporates a sharp bend, either to left or right
drive the first shot off the tee
driver a No.1 wood
eagle 2 shots under par
Fore! a traditional warning yell shouted before a shot is taken
handicap a stroke or shot allowance given to a player so that he or she can play on equal terms with a superior opponent; not used in professional tournaments
links a golf course situated close to the sea

open a tournament or championship open to anybody, professional or amateur, provided they are up to the specified standard

par a stroke rating for each hole; the number of shots it should take a scratch golfer to complete the hole or round

pin the flag in a hole

rough the rough grass that lines the sides of a fairway

sudden death play-off if 2 or more players have equal scores at the end of a given number of rounds, they can play extra holes and the first person to win a hole wins the tournament. Some play-offs are not sudden death; the winner is the competitor with the lowest score after a specified number of extra holes

FOR THE RECORD

THE MAJORS

The 4 most important golf tournaments are collectively known as the 'majors'. They are all played annually.

The Open, played on a British links, is the oldest and most prestigious of the 4 and was first played in 1860. In addition to prize money, a silver claret jug is awarded to the winner of the tournament. Several courses are used for the Open, including the one at St Andrews, Scotland.

The US Open was first held in 1895 and is also played over several different courses.

The US PGA Championship was first held in 1916. Originally it was a matchplay competition but switched to strokeplay in 1958. Various courses play host to the championship.

The US Masters is unique among the majors in that it is always held at the Augusta National course in Georgia. Competition is between invited players only and each year the winner is presented with a green jacket as well as a substantial cheque.

FOR THE RECORD

IMPORTANT TOURS AND COMPETITIONS

Hundreds of important golfing tournaments are held each year — France, Sweden, Australia, Zimbabwe and numerous other countries all host open competitions. These tournaments are divided into so-called 'tours' and the person who wins the most money on a tour is awarded a bonus prize of yet more money. The best known and most lucrative tours are the US and the European, but others include the African and the Asian.

The most famous team competition is the Ryder Cup tournament, which was first held in 1927 between teams of 12 from the United States and Britain. The competition is held every 2 years but in 1979 the rules were changed and the British team became a European team. Although the players in the 2 teams are professional, no prize money is awarded to Ryder Cup champions. Instead, players compete for honour.

The Walker Cup is a team competition for British and American amateurs. It is also held every 2 years.

The premier tournaments for professional women golfers are the US Women's Open, the US Ladies Professional Golf Association Championship and the British Women's Open Championship. Important amateur contests include the US Women's Amateur Championship and the Ladies' British Open Amateur Championship. The Curtis Cup is a biennial team competition held between the United States and Great Britain and Ireland.

PERSONALITY PROFILE

Nick Faldo

One of the most successful golfers in recent years is Nick Faldo of Great Britain, who won 2 of the 4 majors in 1990.

Born in 1957, Faldo took up golf after watching Jack Nicklaus playing in the US Masters on television. He has a long way to go to catch the majors' record set by his hero, but time is on his side. In all, Faldo has won the US Masters twice and the Open twice. Faldo came close to winning the US Open — which is won rarely by a non-American — in 1988. He was even with Curtis Strange after 72 holes but lost the 18-hole playoff to decide the championship the next day.

Faldo has a reputation for being a perfectionist in his sport. Even after achieving his childhood ambition by winning the Open in 1987 he decided that there were faults in his swing. He took more than six months off to 'rebuild' his swing, and came back to a string of tournament victories. He was rated the world's No.1 golfer in 1990, but ended the year with an injured shoulder.

PERSONALITY PROFILE

Jack Nicklaus

Probably the most famous golfer in the world, Jack Nicklaus was born in 1940 in Columbus, Ohio. He took up golf in his early teens and won his first important tournament — the Ohio State Open — when he was 16. Since then, he has achieved a record second to none, winning 4 US Opens, 6 US Masters, 5 US PGA Championships and 3 British Opens. His nickname is the Golden Bear — a reference to his reddish-blond hair and powerful build. Rivals must wonder if the 'Golden' refers to the prize money he has won over the years.

A multi-millionaire who heads a financial empire he built up himself, Nicklaus still plays in the majors and is one of the most popular of all players. Nicklaus is one of the many professionals who have gone on to compete regularly in the Senior Circuit of tournaments in the United States. Entry to the circuit is confined to players over 50 years of age, but the playing standard — and prize money — often matches those of normal professional tournaments.

One of his new money-making ventures is designing golf courses at more than one million dollars a time.

LAWN GAMES

Bowls, croquet and pétanque can appear to be sedate, slow games but they are actually very sophisticated. In all three games tactics play an important part, and games can become aggressive.

DID YOU KNOW?

Crown Green bowls is a popular form of the traditional game and is played in the north of England. The green has a slight rise in the middle which provides an extra hazard. Bowlers have to play across the green and over the rise.

BOWLS

Bowls has been a popular outdoor game since the 13th century. The first purpose-made bowling green was constructed at Southampton in 1299 but before then various forms of the game had been played in many parts of England on any stretch of suitable turf.

The first official rules for bowls were drawn up in the middle of the 19th century and since then the sport has had a steadily growing following. Although bowls is traditionally considered an old-persons' game, many young men and women also enjoy it.

A recent innovation has been the building of indoor bowling 'greens' which are laid with artificial turf which is not susceptible to changes in the weather. So what was once a traditionally summer sport can now be played all year round.

The ruling body of the game is the International Bowling Board, formed in 1905. The premier events are the World Outdoor Championships which are held every four years and bowling competitions at the Commonwealth Games. Countries that have the keenest bowlers include Britain, Australia, South Africa, New Zealand and Hong Kong.

▼ *A bowling green is usually divided into strips, or 'rinks'. These are marked by green threads which are attached to pegs at the corners.*

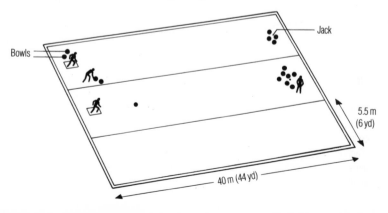

Jack

Bowls

5.5 m (6 yd)

40 m (44 yd)

AIMS OF THE GAME

COMPETITION

● Outdoor bowls is played on a flat area of closely mown grass called a 'green'. The green is 40 m (44 yd) long and is divided up into strips that are about 5.55 m (6 yd approx.) wide so that several games can be played at the same time.

● The object of the game is for competitors to roll their bowls along the green so that they end up as close as possible to a 'jack' or target ball. At the beginning of a round, or 'end', the jack is rolled down the green from a mat. Players then take it in turns to deliver their bowls from the mat. When all the bowls have been delivered, single points are awarded for each bowl that finishes closer to the jack than the nearest ball of an opponent. After an end finishes, the players play back down the green in the opposite direction.

● Competitions can be held for singles (one against one), pairs (2 against 2), triples (3 against 3) and fours (4 against 4). In singles, each player has 4 bowls and the first to reach 21 points wins. In pairs, each player also has 4 bowls but the winning side is the one that gains the most points after 21 ends. In triples, players have 3 bowls each and bowl 18 ends. In fours, only 2 bowls each are permitted and play lasts for 21 ends.

SKILLS

● Bowls are slightly biased which means they are heavier on one side. Delivery is not simple as the bowl will tend to move in a curve. A good bowler can judge curve as well as distance.

● Tactics include knocking opponents' bowls out of the way or alternatively moving the jack.

▼ *A player has to keep at least one foot on or above the mat when delivering a bowl towards the target ball ('jack'). Judging the distance of the jack accurately is an essential skill. Delivery is made more difficult because the bowl is biased and will tend to move in a curve. A bowler must be able to judge curve as well.*

EQUIPMENT

● Bowls were traditionally made from wood but they are now usually moulded from solid rubber and weigh about 1.5 kg (3½ lb approx.). Bowls are bought as sets of 4 so that they all have an identical bias. Jacks are wooden and weigh just 227 g (8 oz).

● Bowlers traditionally wear white jackets, and shoes must have flat soles.

TECHNICAL TERMS

draw the line a bowl takes as it is delivered
rink the playing strips on a green
shot the bowl closest to the jack
weight the power with which a bowl is delivered
wood a bowl — they used to be made from lignum vitae, the heaviest wood known

DID YOU KNOW?

Although boules are now made of steel, they were at one time made of box wood and were studded with hundreds of tiny nail heads.

PÉTANQUE

Pétanque is a comparatively new game and only became a recognized sport in 1910. However, its parent game, 'jeu provençal' is much older. Both games originated in France where they are still enormously popular and are played by people of all ages and both sexes. The main difference between jeu provençal and pétanque is that in the older game, players are allowed a run before delivering their bowls, or 'boules'; in pétanque, the boules have to be delivered while the player is stationary.

One of the attractions of pétanque is that it can be played on virtually any gravel surface. Although it is most popular in France, it is widely played all over Europe as well as in the United States and Australia.

Pétanque is usually played for fun, but there are also competitions that are taken with deadly seriousness. The French national championships are held every year and winners are fêted as national heroes. World Championships between 34 national teams are also organized every year and, although France has won more titles than any other nation, Switzerland, Italy and even Morocco have also been champions. The ruling body of the sport is the Fédération Française de Pétanque et Jeu Provençal, which has its headquarters in Marseille.

▼ *Although pétanque is usually played for fun, many French players carry a measuring tape to ensure accuracy down to the last millimetre.*

AIMS OF THE GAME

● The object of the game is for a player to throw or lob bowls — 'boules' — at a wooden jack from a stationary position. It can be played as singles, doubles or triples. In singles, each player uses either 3 or 4 boules, in doubles each player has 3 boules and in triples, 2. After all the boules have been thrown, the boule or boules from one player or team that lie closer to the jack than those of the opponent (or opponents) score one point. The first person or team to reach 13 points wins.

COMPETITION
● In serious competitions, a piste is marked out: it should be at least 4 m (4 yd approx.) wide and 15 m (16 yd approx.) long. The winner of a tossed coin has the right to choose a starting point which is marked out by a 35-50 cm (14-20 in approx.) circle. Standing in the circle, the person throws the jack on to the piste; it must land between 6 and 10 m (6½ and 11 yd approx.) away.
● Once the jack has been thrown, players take it in turns to deliver their boules towards it from within the circle — the object being to end up with as many boules as possible close to the jack.

SKILLS
● There are several techniques that can be used to deliver a boule. One is to roll it along the ground towards the jack. Another is to lob the boule so that when it lands it hardly moves forwards at all. The most spectacular technique is to try and hit an opponent's boule out of the way with a fiery shot; if such a delivery lands as intended, it will not only knock the opponent's boule flying but will end up in its place.

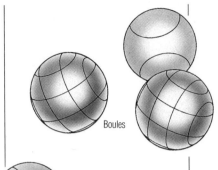

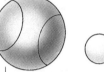

Boules

Jack

▲ *Boules are made from steel and marked with specially patterned grooves so that players can identify which are theirs during the course of a game. The smaller jack, or cochonnet, is made from wood.*

EQUIPMENT

● Boules are made from steel and are between 7 and 8 cm (2¾ and 3 in approx.) in diameter; they weigh between 620 and 800 gm (22 and 28 oz approx.) The jack is made from wood and is 30 mm (1¼ in approx.) in diameter. Boules are usually sold as sets, complete with a jack.

TECHNICAL TERMS

baguette metal rod used for tracing lines and measuring distances
cochonnet (also petit bois and ministre) the French name for the wooden jack
plomber to lob a boule high into the air so it virtually stops on landing
tirer the fast way to deliver a boule so that if it hits another it will scatter it out of the way

DID YOU KNOW?

Croquet was once played at the Olympic Games — in Paris, 1900. The French picked up all the available medals — 6 in total.

CROQUET

Croquet is thought to have originated in France sometime during the 12th or 13th centuries. The name is supposed to have derived from the French word *croche* (crooked stick). From France the game spread to England and Ireland where it was called Pall Mall, from the Latin *palla mallens*, which means 'ball and mallet'. Croquet quickly became popular because it could be played on almost every lawn. In 1867 the first Open Championships were organized in England.

From England and Ireland, croquet spread to Australia, South Africa and the United States of America, where it was called 'rogue' croquet or lawn croquet.

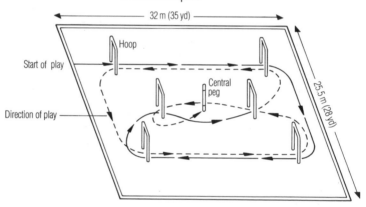

▲ *Players have to knock their balls through the hoops in a specific sequence. The sequence for the English game is shown here but other versions of the game adopt a different layout.*

Croquet is largely an amateur game, but there are a few professionals, mainly in the United States. The sport is increasingly played worldwide. In Britain alone there are between 350,000 and 400,000 croquet players — from back-garden players to those involved in international competitions. Many leading players began playing croquet on the simple sets familiar to most garden players.

There are 180 tournaments a year to cover all types of player. The leading competition is the World Championship, first played in 1989.

The ruling body of the sport is the Croquet Association, whose headquarters are at the Hurlingham Club in London.

AIMS OF THE GAME

COMPETITION
● Croquet can be played between individuals or pairs. The object is to use a wooden mallet to drive balls through a series of 6 hoops — first clockwise and then anti-clockwise — and to finish by hitting a central peg. Individuals have 2 balls each; pairs players have one ball each.
● The game is played on a lawn measuring 32 m (35 yd) long and 25.5 m (28 yd) wide. The grass is cut very short. Hoops are not less than 10.7 cm (3¾ in) wide; balls are 10.4 cm (3⅝ in) in diameter.
● Play starts from the edge of the lawn and competitors attempt to hit their balls through the hoops in a prescribed sequence. Extra shots are gained by hitting an opponent's ball or by going through a hoop. The winner is the first person or pair to hit the central peg after going through the hoops in both directions.

SKILLS
● Two techniques are used to wield the mallet — either swinging it to the side (as a golfer would putt) or through the legs. The through-the-legs method is more accurate but is less powerful than the swinging method.
● Accuracy in striking the ball is everything in croquet — the extremely narrow clearance between ball and hoop means that shots must be lined up with great precision.
● Croquet is very much a tactical game. As in snooker, a player tries to have a run of shots, while at the same time putting an opponent's balls in awkward positions. Patience is often a virtue, but well-timed boldness is necessary for success in major competitions.

▲ *Two bonus shots are awarded to a player if his or her ball hits an opponent's ball. The first of these shots is usually used to knock the opponent's ball out of the way as illustrated here.*

EQUIPMENT

● The croquet mallets used in competitions are made of hardwood and have a handle about 1 m (3 ft approx.) long. Some have a 22 cm (9 in) square-faced head which helps give a better aim.
● The balls are made of a composite with a hard plastic cover. They weigh 0.5 kg (1 lb).

TECHNICAL TERMS

roquet hitting an opponent's ball and therefore gaining an extra shot
wicket alternative word for a hoop, used in the United States

ATHLETICS

Some of the sports that go to make up athletics are almost as old as civilization and date back to the Ancient Greeks and beyond. Athletics can be broadly divided into two categories — running, or 'track', events and 'field' events such as throwing and jumping.

DID YOU KNOW?

According to legend, a messenger named Pheidippides ran to Athens to tell of the Greek defeat of the Persians at the battle of Marathon in 490 BC and then dropped down dead.

The event may not have happened, but it inspired the organizers of the modern Olympics to include a 'marathon' race.

The first 4 marathons to be held at the modern games were about 40 km (25 miles) long, but at the 1908 games, the race started at Windsor Castle and ended at the White City stadium in west London — a distance of exactly 26 miles 385 yd (42.2 km). This was to become the standard length of a 'marathon'.

TRACK AND FIELD

Running races of various kinds have been held for thousands of years, but the Ancient Greeks were among the first to organize regular competitions for specific events. They also initiated the idea of special running tracks. The Greeks are, of course, famed for the original Olympic Games which were first held at Olympia in 776 BC.

Wrestling, boxing and chariot racing were included alongside running and throwing events at the original Olympics. No women were allowed to watch, let alone compete, in the four-yearly games which were at first open only to people of Hellenic descent. However, before the games were abolished in AD 394, Romans were allowed to take part. In addition to the Olympics, the Greeks held athletics competitions between men from rival cities, but the stadia in which these events took place were not always of a standard size. The tracks were frequently straight and not at all like the familiar ovals of today. The track at Delphi, for example, which can still be seen, is dead straight.

Although running races and other athletics events took place informally in various parts of the world in the intervening centuries, it was not until the 19th century that recognized national and international competitions were re-instituted. In 1894, a Frenchman, Baron Pierre de Courbetin, resurrected the idea of organizing a modern version of the Olympic Games. The first 'modern' Olympics were held in Athens in 1896. The Olympic Games have been staged every four years since then, with only three interruptions — 1916 (World War I) and 1940 and 1944 (World War II). Medals are awarded, national pride is boosted by victories, but no money is offered.

Many other events are held at the Olympics but 'the Games' are still considered to be the most prestigious showcase for both track and field events. Other important competitions now include the four-yearly World Championships, the Pan-American Games, the Asian Games, the Commonwealth Games and the European Championships. In addition to these competitions, leading athletes take part in a series of prestigious 'Grand Prix' meetings which are held at a number of locations around the world every year. Indoor athletics meetings are held in the winter, or 'off', season, and the most important international competition in this sphere is the World Indoor Championship.

Athletics is, by and large, a sport for amateur men and women only. Attempts to organize competitions for professional athletes have usually failed. However, in recent years, the dividing line between professional status and amateur status has become increasingly vague and leading athletes do indeed earn money. Athletics has also been dogged by doping scandals which have proved that a few athletes have taken drugs to improve performance. The International Amateur Athletics Federation, the ruling body of the sport, has tightened up testing procedures and it is hoped that drug abuse is now on the decline.

▼ *Athletics is a sport for all ages and levels. These young women sprinters are dashing for the line at an international schools meeting.*

AIMS OF THE GAME

TRACK EVENTS

COMPETITION

• The simple object of track running is to win races. All events are run anti-clockwise on (or at least finished on) a track. The events can be split into 6 categories:
- sprint races;
- middle distance races;
- long distance races;
- hurdle races;
- steeplechases;
- and road races.

• A standard outdoor track is oval in shape and divided into 8 lanes, each 1.22 m (1.3 yd) wide. The inside lane is exactly 400 m (437 yd) around. As the outside lanes are necessarily longer, a number of staggered starting lines are marked on them (see diagram). The shortest sprint and hurdle races are run on a 'straight' which extends slightly beyond the curve of the track. All races finish at one line. Competitors in long races may have to complete several laps of the circuit.

• Most modern tracks have an artificial, 'all weather', surface which is usually made from a special rubber compound.

• At major outdoor competitions the wind speed is measured, and if it exceeds 2 m (2.2 yd) per second, any records that might be broken in the shorter sprints will not be made official, as the competitors will be deemed to have been 'wind assisted', that is, pushed along by the wind.

• Indoor tracks are only 200 m (218 yd) around and, because the curves are tighter, they are banked

▶ *Modern stadia have all-weather tracks. Most field events take place in the middle of the circuit.*

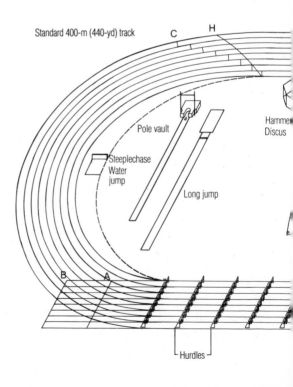

Standard 400-m (440-yd) track

Pole vault

Steeplechase
Water jump

Long jump

Hammer
Discus

Hurdles

Key for diagram

A 100 m and 100 m hurdles (100 yd)
B 110 m hurdles
C 200 m (220 yd)
D 400 m (440 yd)
E 800 m (880 yd)
F 1,500 m (1,650 yd)
G 3,000 m steeplechase
H 5,000 m (5,500 yd)
I 10,000 m (11,000 yd)

to make running safer and easier. The curves call for different tactics from those used in outdoor competitions. The shortest indoor sprint and hurdle races are run on a special track positioned inside the circuit. Indoor tracks are usually made of wood.

● Races are started by an official 'starter' who before each race gives commands to the athletes before firing a harmless, but noisy, starting gun. In all major competitions, every track event is electronically timed from the moment the gun goes off to the end of the race, marked by a thin tape stretched across the track. Sophisticated photographic equipment is used to decide 'photo finishes' — referees will study a photograph taken at the exact moment the competitors cross the line to decide on the winner.

Sprint races
● Races included as sprints are 60 m (indoors only), 100 m, 200 m and 400 m (approx. 65 yd, 110 yd, 220 yd and 440 yd). Competitors run in lanes for the duration of the race.

● Competitors are allowed to use starting blocks and the commands given by the starter are 'to your marks' and 'set' before he fires the gun. If a competitor starts before the gun is fired, the race is restarted; a second offence leads to disqualification.

● There are 2 common relay races:
- 4 x 100 m;
- and 4 x 400 m.
The shorter race is run entirely in lanes, using the staggered start. In the longer relay, runners from each team have to stay in lanes until after the first corner of the second lap; after that they are allowed to cut in to the inside lane.

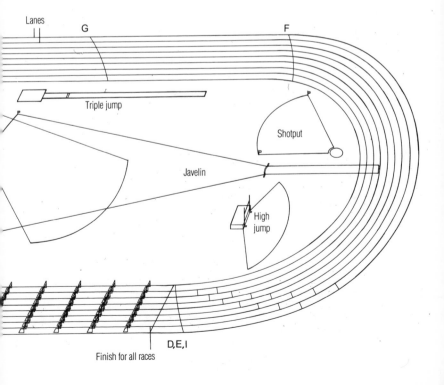

Lanes
G
F
Triple jump
Shotput
Javelin
High jump
D,E,I
Finish for all races

Middle distance races
● Included in this category are 800 m (880 yd), 1500 m (1650 yd) and the mile (1.6 km). In 800 m races, competitors start from staggered marks in lanes, but after the first corner they are allowed to break out of their lanes and run on the inside of the track. The 1500 m and mile races are started with athletes lined up across the track; they do not have to stay in lanes.
● Athletes are not allowed to use starting blocks and the sole command before the gun is fired is 'to your marks'.

Long distance races
● These include 3000 m (women only; 3300 yd), 5000 m (5500 yd) and 10,000 m (11,000 yd). The starting procedure is as for the longer middle distance races.

Hurdle races
● These include 60 m hurdles (indoors; men only), 100 m hurdles (women only), 110 m hurdles and 400 m hurdles (65, 110, 120 and 440 yd respectively). All the races are run in lanes and, with the exception of the 400 m hurdles, all of them are along straights.
● Hurdles range in height from 0.84 m (2 ft 9 in) for women to 1.067 m (3 ft 6 in) for men, and they are specially constructed so that they can only fall one way. In the 60 m race, six flights (hurdles) are positioned in each lane; in all the other races, there are 10. Competitors are not penalized for hitting or knocking over hurdles, but it is in their interest to save time by clearing them cleanly.
● The starting procedure for hurdle races is the same as for sprint races.

Steeplechases
- The most common steeplechase (men only) is run over 3000 m (approx. a 2-mile steeplechase). During such a race, which is not run in lanes, athletes have to negotiate 28 barriers and 7 water jumps.
- Steeplechase barriers are sturdy and stand 0.914 m (3 ft) high. Athletes are permitted to jump over them or, if they prefer, step on them. The water jump is set just by the inside lane of the track. It comprises a barrier and a pool of water which measures 3.66 m (12 ft) square. All runners land in the water after jumping the barrier. The water is deepest near the barrier so athletes have an incentive to jump longer and try to land in the shallower water.

Road races
- These races include the longest of all races, the marathon, 42.2 km (26 miles 385 yd), and men's walking races, the most common of which are 20 km (12½ miles) and 50 km (31 miles) long. In these races, it is usual for competitors to start and finish on the track, but the bulk of the running or walking takes place on cordoned-off roads.
- During these races, athletes are permitted to sponge themselves down or take water at regular intervals.
- In the walking events, competitors are obliged to keep unbroken contact with the ground at all times — a competitor who breaks into a run will be disqualified.

◄ *Hurdlers work to achieve a measured stride pattern between flights in the shorter events. If the pattern is not achieved, the take-off leg will be too near, or too far away from each hurdle and the athlete will fail to clear them cleanly.*

SKILLS
- In sprinting, an explosive getaway off the starting blocks is imperative, as races are won or lost by fractions of a second. Athletes, especially those who specialize in the shortest races like the sprint races 100 m (110 yd) and 200 m (220 yd), rehearse starts repeatedly until their reactions are needle-sharp.

Most coaches believe that strong chest and arm muscles are nearly as important as powerful legs when it comes to sprinting. Certainly, a fast, rhythmic arm action is needed to maintain speed. Consequently, most sprinters spend a great deal of time weight-training in gyms to improve muscle tone.

When they approach the finishing tape, sprinters tend to 'dip' their bodies forward to gain a few hundredths of a second. To do this successfully, timing is crucial — a dip too late will make no difference, a dip too soon will make an athlete lose balance.

- Tactics play a huge part in middle distance running. Most middle distance runners are able to put on a finishing burst towards the end of a race, but choosing the time to make a break is crucial — too early and the athlete may flag and get overhauled at the end; too late and the race will already be lost. The best middle distance runners can judge their own ability to perfection and will instinctively know when to sprint for the line, but even the greatest have been caught because they have been carefully watched and shadowed by a wily opponent.
- Long distance runners must have stamina above all else and they must also be able to judge pace. They must be willing to put in countless hours of training, covering up to 150 km (90 miles) a week.

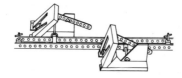

▲ *Starting blocks must not incorporate springs or other mechanisms which could give sprinters artificial help.*

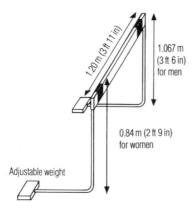

1.20 m (3 ft 11 in)

1.067 m (3 ft 6 in) for men

0.84 m (2 ft 9 in) for women

Adjustable weight

▲ *Hurdles have metal stands and wooden crossbars.*

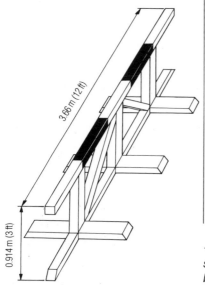

3.66 m (12 ft)

0.914 m (3 ft)

When racing, some like to lead from the front with the aim of breaking the will of those behind. This can lead to disaster if they are the ones who cannot keep going. Other long distance specialists are able to put in a burst of speed perhaps a lap from the end of a race to 'shake off' opponents. To do this effectively, an athlete has to be supremely confident, as others are bound to follow this example.

● Short hurdle races demand sprinting speed as well as the ability to leap the hurdles. Without a supple body, a hurdler will get nowhere and much depends on technique — leaning into the hurdle, keeping the leading leg straight, keeping the trailing leg high and so on. Maintaining a rhythm is also important because hurdlers usually have a favoured take-off leg, and if they take too many, or too few, strides between flights, they will surely fail.

The 400 m hurdles event is commonly known as the 'killer' and is one of the most gruelling of all races. The most important thing of all is to keep strides as long as possible. If they get shorter and shorter, a hurdler will lose rhythm and go 'out of sync', running the risk of stumbling when taking the last few flights.

● The steeplechase is another energy-sapping race. The race is so long that athletes have little hope of maintaining a steady rhythm throughout. Every time they go over a barrier, especially the water jump, their pace is upset and they have to regain their composure all over again. Steeplechasing demands strength, stamina, timing and skill in negotiating the obstacles.

◄ *The obstacles used in steeplechasing include sturdy barriers (left) and water jumps.*

● The toughest part of a marathon race comes about 10 km (6 miles) from the end when runners 'hit the wall'. This expression describes the effects when all the body's readily available energy resources have been used up and it has to resort to using fat reserves as fuel. The pain felt by athletes can be excruciating and many cannot continue.

Marathon runners must be well prepared but, because the race is so long, it is still possible for a runner right at the back to progress to the front of the race.

● Walking requires special skills and disciplines. To maintain a steady rhythm and pace, walkers adopt a curious movement in which their hips swivel and sway from side to side. A good walker can often move as fast as a mediocre runner over a long distance.

Walkers frequently experience the urge to break into a run, but if they do, they will be disqualified. To quell this urge takes self-discipline — which not everybody has.

FIELD EVENTS

COMPETITION
● In most athletics meetings, the field events take place in prepared areas or pits in the middle of a track circuit. The most commonly contested field events are:
- high jump;
- long jump;
- triple jump (men only);
- javelin;
- shot put;
- discus;
- hammer (men only);
- pole vault (men only).

◀ *The shot put requires concentration and explosive energy in the legs and arms. Most putters start by adopting a crouched position and then work their way around the whole throwing circle to gain momentum for a powerful launch.*

High jump

● In the high jump, competitors attempt to leap over a horizontal bar supported on uprights. There are a series of eliminating rounds; after each round the height of the bar is increased. Each athlete has 3 opportunities to jump the bar at a given height and is eliminated if not successful in any of them. The winner is the person who jumps highest.

● The crossbar and uprights are placed at the focal point of a fan-shaped run-up area which is usually faced with an artificial surface. Beyond the jump itself is a cushioned landing mat.

● Athletes can take as long or as short a run up to the jump as they like. If they knock the crossbar off the up-rights, they 'fail' the jump, but if they just nudge it and it stays in place, a successful jump is conceded.

Long jump

● In this event, athletes run down a wide track and launch themselves into a long sandpit from a 'take-off' board. In major competitions, each competitor is allowed 3 jumps and the best 8 competitors are then allowed 3 more. The person who jumps farthest is the winner.

● The track, or 'runway', is 1.22 (4 ft) wide and usually has an artificial surface. The white take-off board, often a plank of wood, is the same width as the runway and is about 20 cm (7½ in) wide; it is sunk into the ground so that it is flush with the track and is sited about 1 m (1 yd) from the front of the pit. Beyond the take-off board there is a fine line of putty which reveals an impression if a jumper puts a foot over the board — if a person takes off before the board, the jump is legal, but if a foot treads beyond the board, the jump is not allowed. A judge will raise a white flag if the jump is good or a red flag if the jump is not allowed. The sand in the pit is raked to the same level as the runway after each jump.

● Jumps are measured from the edge of the take-off board to the closest mark left in the sand by any part of a jumper's body. Long jumpers use their momentum to carry their body past their feet on landing.

Triple jump

● This event is organized along similar lines to the long jump, except that competitors have to take a hop (from one foot to the same foot), a step (a leap onto the other foot) and a jump from the take-off board into the sand.

Hop   Step

Javelin

● The javelin, which looks like a spear, is thrown overarm from behind a curved white line marked at the end of a runway. For a throw to be valid, an athlete must not step over the line and the javelin must land, point first, in a large fan-shaped area or 'sector'. If a large number of competitors are taking part in a javelin event, each athlete has 3 initial throws and those who throw farthest are allowed 3 more. The winner is the person who throws the javelin the farthest distance.

● The 4 m (4 yd) wide runway is usually made of synthetic material, but the fan-shaped landing sector is always grass covered.

● Men use longer and heavier javelins than women, but there has been recent controversy concerning designs. It has been discovered that by tampering with the shafts in certain ways, albeit innocently, aerodynamic efficiency can be improved, so greater distances can be achieved. Athletes are allowed to coat their hands with resin to ensure a good hold on the grip of the javelin, but a glove on the throwing hand is not allowed.

● Distances are measured from the throwing line to the nearest mark made on the ground by the javelin.

Shot put

● In this event a heavy spherical weight, or 'shot', is pushed, or 'put' from a throwing circle into a fairly narrow, fan-shaped landing area which is usually covered with grass or cinders. As with many throwing competitions, it is the competitor who achieves the greatest distance who wins. Competitors are allowed 6 attempts.

● The throwing circle is 2.14 m (7 ft) in diameter and has a hard surface, usually concrete. A curved 'stop board' along the edge of the throwing circle that abuts the landing area stands about 10 cm (4 in) high. If a shotputter steps out of the circle onto the stop board, a put is automatically declared invalid.

● The shots can be made from any metal provided it is not softer than brass. Men's shots must not be greater than 13 cm (5 in approx.) in diameter and must weigh at least 7.26 kg (16 lb). Women's shots are smaller and lighter: 11 cm (4½ in approx.) in diameter with a weight of 4 kg (8¾ lb approx.).

● Distances are measured from the edge of the throwing circle to the closest point where a shot makes a dent in the ground after it has been thrown.

Jump

▼ *This illustration shows why the triple jump was formerly called the 'hop, skip and jump'.*

Discus

● Like the shot, the discus is launched from a throwing circle into a landing sector. Competitors get extra force by spinning several times before releasing the discus. The athlete who achieves the greatest distance after 6 throws is the winner.

● The discus throwing circle measures 2.5 m (8 ft 4 in) in diameter and has a hard, non-slip surface. The throwing circle is surrounded by a wire mesh cage on 3 sides as a safety precaution in case a discus should be hurled in the wrong direction after a spin.

● For a discus throw to be valid, it must land in the designated area, and the athlete must not step out of the circle until it has landed.

● Most discuses are made of wood but have rounded metal rims. A discus is thicker in the middle than at the edges. Men's discuses weigh at least 2 kg (4½ lb approx.) and have a diameter of about 20 cm (8½ in). Women's discuses weigh 1 kg (2¼ lb) with a diameter of about 18 cm (7 in).

● Throws are measured from the edge of the circle to where the discus first hits the ground.

▼ *The discus has a smooth, convex surface with a weight in the centre.*

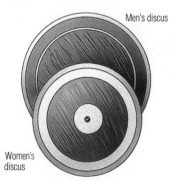

Men's discus

Women's discus

Hammer

● The rules for throwing the hammer are broadly similar to those for the discus. The throwing circle is smaller — 2.14 m (7 ft) in diameter. It, too, has a safety net on 3 sides.

● The hammer comprises a heavy, spherical metal weight attached to a handle via a strong wire. It weighs 7.26 kg (16 lb) and is about 1.2 m (4 ft approx.) long.

Pole vault

● In pole vault competitions, athletes use a pole to power themselves over a horizontal bar mounted on 2 tall up-rights. Rules are similar to those found in high jumping and competitors are eliminated if they fail on 3 consecutive vaults.

● The runway is usually 45 m (50 yd) long and at one end there is a 20-cm- (7¾-in-) deep, metal box sunk into the ground. The box has sloping sides. Above the box stand the uprights and the crossbar and beyond it there is a soft, 1 m (3 ft) thick, landing mattress. The object is for a competitor to sprint up the runway, place the tip of his pole into the box and lever himself up and over the crossbar.

● Poles are usually made from glass fibre and they are flexible. They vary in length according to each competitor's preference and can be bound with tape to provide a hand grip. The tip of a pole can also be bound to protect it from getting damaged in the box.

▶ *Successful javelin throwing requires a combination of power, speed, balance and accuracy. The well known British national record holder, Fatima Whitbread, (opposite) prepares to launch her javelin into the air with a powerful overarm throwing action.*

SKILLS

● In the high jump athletes are only allowed to take off from one foot. Traditionally, high jumpers ran directly at the jump and leapt forwards, 'rolling' one shoulder over the bar first, and letting the rest of the body follow. Most people, both men and women, now adopt the 'Fosbury Flop' way of jumping (named after the 1968 Olympic champion, Dick Fosbury). In this, a jumper runs up sideways to the jump and attempts to leap over the bar backwards with the head and shoulders going over first. At the mid-point in such a jump, the body should 'drape' over the bar — head and shoulders on one side, legs on the other. The Fosbury Flop apparently defies the laws of science — the body's centre of gravity actually goes under the bar when in fact the body goes over it!

High jumpers are tall, lean people who have a springy running action. As with all jumping competitions, high jumpers are allowed to mark the measured start of their run-ups alongside the runway.

● Long jumpers have to be able to sprint as well as jump, for without speed and momentum they will not be able to achieve any great distance. Jumpers spend hours practising run-ups until they achieve a consistent stride pattern: until they do this, they will worry about landing on the take-off board as they sprint down the runway, and this will affect their speed.

Long jumpers always try to gain height when jumping, with the idea that if they are travelling fast and jump high, they must go far.

● Triple jumpers are less concerned about gaining height than long jumpers and for them balance and momentum are more important.

● Javelin throwers have to be careful how they launch their weapons, not just because they might hit somebody. If a javelin is launched in a shallow trajectory, it will not 'float' on the air; if it goes too high, the chances are that it will come down tail first, and so will not count as a legal throw. A well thrown javelin follows a smooth arc on its flight and does not wobble in the air at all.

▲ *To execute the Fosbury flop an athlete twists as she takes off. Bending backwards, she clears the bar head-first. A powerful and carefully timed kick completes the jump.*

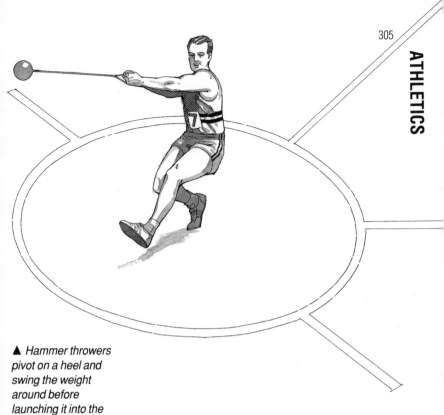

▲ *Hammer throwers pivot on a heel and swing the weight around before launching it into the throwing area.*

● Putting the shot any worthwhile distance requires great skill because the small throwing circle limits momentum. Some athletes use a technique which involves facing away from the landing sector while holding the shot underneath the chin and bending low down. Then with a swift, explosive movement, the body is swivelled round and the shot is launched high as well as far.

Shot putters have to have strong legs and arms in order to wield the heavy weights. The best shot putters undergo rigorous training involving diet and weightlifting drills. They must ensure that any extra power thus gained does not hamper their throwing technique. Muscle-bound arms do not allow for proper extension.

● To gain momentum in discus throwing, athletes grip the discus in one outstretched hand and swivel round within the circle before launching it high into the air. If a discus is to fly far, it must not wobble in the air, so the launching procedure must be smooth with a long follow-through.
● Hammers are also swung round and round before being launched.
● Pole vaulting requires both technique and courage. Although poles are designed to bend, they can snap or shatter with potentially nasty consequences. As a pole vaulter sticks the end of his pole into the box, he leans backwards to make the pole bend and then, as it straightens up, he raises his legs high above his head and pushes himself up and over the bar.

EQUIPMENT

- Sprinters, jumpers and javelin throwers wear spiked shoes to grip the track. The spikes, or metal prongs, vary in length according to the nature of the track but they cannot be more than 12 mm (½ in) long. For other events, competitors wear trainers or, if they prefer, no shoes at all.
- Lightweight, and occasionally skin-tight, clothing is worn. In major events numbers, as allocated by the organizers, are compulsory.
- Sprinters use blocks to get off to good starts. These are adjustable foot plates which are fixed to the track. The sprinter places his or her feet on the angled plates and consequently cannot slip backwards when pushing off explosively.

FOR THE RECORD

DECATHLON/HEPTATHLON
There are 2 'multi-discipline' athletics competitions designed to test all-round ability in track and field events.

The decathlon is only for men and includes 10 different events held over 2 days:
- Day 1: 100 m, long jump, shot put, high jump and 400 m;
- and Day 2: 110 m hurdles, discus, pole vault, javelin and 1500 m.

A scoring table is used to convert times, distances and heights into points. The person with the highest final total of points wins the competition.

The heptathlon, which has superseded the pentathlon (5 events), is contested only by women; 7 events are included:
- Day 1: 100 m hurdles, shot put, high jump and 200 m;
- Day 2: long jump, javelin and 800 m.

FOR THE RECORD

Cross-country running is an important branch of athletics and used to be an Olympic event until 1924. Many national and international competitions are still held; the most important of these are the annual World Cross-country Championships which include events for men, women and national teams.

Cross-country courses vary enormously, but a good course will include a variety of gradients and different types of terrain. As races are usually run during the winter, weather conditions can provide an extra challenge to runners. Races for men are usually about 15 km (9 miles) long and women's are shorter — about 5 km (3 miles).

Cross-country running is gruelling as it is hard for even the strongest of athletes to maintain a steady pace and rhythm on hilly and muddy circuits. Many middle and long distance specialists view cross-country running as an important part of their winter training schedule.

FOR THE RECORD

Many of the world's major cities now host annual marathon races, run over the traditional distance of 42.2 km (26 miles 385 yd). The first to do so was Boston, USA, and the others that have followed suit include Chicago, New York, Rotterdam and London. The largest marathon to date was the 1990 London Marathon, which had an entry of around 30,000 people.

Most people who enter city marathons take many hours to finish, but a select few runners make up 'elite' squads and complete the race in just over 2 hr.

TECHNICAL TERMS

boards slang for an indoor track

boxed in when a middle distance, or occasionally a long distance, runner is surrounded by other athletes and is consequently unable to make a move to take the lead

break when athletes, who started a race in lanes, move across to the inside of the track after passing a marker beyond which they are allowed to run where they want

▼ *Runners at the 1988 Seoul Olympics race the gruelling 42.2 km (26 miles 385 yd) of the marathon. Apart from the start and finish, the event is run on roads.*

off the bend runners often like to sprint or accelerate when completing the second half of a bend; it can catch other runners unawares

pacemaker in middle and long distance races, it is not unusual for an athlete to be invited to start off fast and so set a fast time for the opening laps while others follow behind; a pacemaker cannot usually keep up the pace but allows others to overtake. Pacemakers are frequently used when world record attempts are being made

pain barrier in middle and long distance races, runners usually reach a point when their bodies have used up adrenalin and the muscles begin to ache; courageous athletes run 'through' the pain barrier

GYMNASTIC SPORTS

The three gymnastic sports develop body suppleness and strength. Modern gymnasiums are equipped with high-technology training facilities — a far cry from the training halls of ancient times.

DID YOU KNOW?

Nadia Comaneci of Romania won the first of her 5 Olympic gold medals at the age of 14. She had already trained for 8 years. Soon afterwards her bones became brittle and her joints began to seize up.

The Olympic Committee now has minimum age limits for gymnasts — 16 for men and 15 for women.

GYMNASTICS

In Ancient Greece and Rome, athletes prepared for their events by performing physical exercises without clothes (*gymnos* means 'naked' in Ancient Greek). The disciplines and movements were considered to improve spiritual as well as physical development. When the Roman Empire went into decline, so did gymnastics, and it was not until the 18th century that the sport was revived in Europe.

A German, Friedrich Ludwig Jahn, was the most prominent teacher of gymnastics in the early 19th century. He introduced new equipment such as the parallel bars. Organized competitions were first held at around that time.

An amateur sport, gymnastics was included in the first modern Olympic Games. Other major competitions include the biennial World Championships and the annual European Championships. The ruling body of the sport is the Fédération Internationale de Gymnastique (FIG).

▼ *In addition to the mat exercises for men and women, gymnasts perform exercises on the different pieces of equipment shown below.*

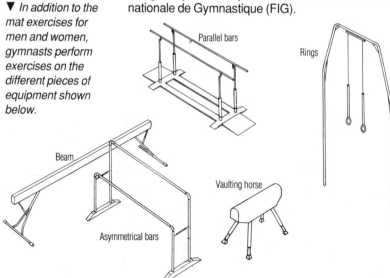

Parallel bars

Rings

Beam

Asymmetrical bars

Vaulting horse

▶ *The rings are the most physically demanding piece of apparatus. Immense strength in the legs, arms and chest is required to hold some of the positions perfectly still.*

AIMS OF THE GAME

COMPETITION

● There are separate competitions for men and women; with different sets of apparatus. Each individual is assessed by a panel of 4 judges who award marks out of 10 — the top and bottom marks are ignored and the other 2 are averaged. All exercises are graded according to difficulty — A, B and C (A being relatively easy, C being difficult). In voluntary or 'optional' routines, competitors have to include a certain number of B and C grade moves. Judges look for style of execution while acknowledging difficulty.

● International competitions are split into the following 3 parts:

- team competition — In the team section of a competition, 6 members from each country perform compulsory routines on each piece of apparatus. (Teams are notified as to what the 'compulsories' involve, months, if not years, beforehand.) Then the gymnasts carry out 'optional' exercises on each piece of equipment. The 5 best combined scores from each team are added together to decide the winner.

- individual competition — After the team event, the top 36 gymnasts challenge for the coveted individual all-round prize. In this, each competitor performs optional routines on every piece of apparatus. The winner is the person with the highest overall score.

- apparatus competition — The apparatus competition decides who is the best individual on each separate piece of equipment. The best 6 or 8 performers on each piece, as judged from the team competition, carry out voluntary exercises and winners are those with the highest scores.

● The men's apparatus includes the following:

- the parallel bars, 1.6 m (5 ft 3 in) above the ground, 42 cm (16½ in) apart and 3.5 m (11 ft 6 in) long. Exercises on the 'bars' include swinging movements, handstands and changing hand grips from one bar to the other.

- the horizontal bar, a 2.4-m (7ft 10-in) steel shaft mounted on two 2.55 m (8 ft 4 in) high uprights. Handstands and assorted swinging movements with the legs apart and together make up a standard routine.

- the 12 m (13 yd) square mat used for floor exercises. Competitors have to perform tumbles, somersaults and twists within the confines of the mat.
- the pommel horse, 1.2 m (47 in) high and 1.63 m (64 in) long with 2 raised handles in the centre. Gymnasts must use as much of the horse as possible while supporting themselves on their hands. Swinging movements to the side or over the horse are common, and so are scissors movements in which the legs straddle the horse.
- the rings supported on wires spaced 50 cm (20 in) apart and standing 2.5 m (8 ft 2 in) above the ground. Rolls, swings, 'pikes', tucks and handstands are all performed on the rings.
- the vaulting horse 1.35 m (53 in) high and 1.63 m (64 in) long. Men have to touch the horse as they vault over it, usually upside down. While in the air, they can perform twists and turns. In the men's competition, the horse is vaulted lengthways.
● The women's apparatus includes:
- the vaulting horse for women. It is the same length as the men's version but is lower — only 1.2 m (47 in) high. Unlike men, women vault across the horse, not along it.

▲ A typical women's vault might include a handspring followed by a full twist. Unlike women, men vault over the horse lengthways.

- the asymmetrical bars, sometimes called the uneven parallel bars — parallel but at different heights. Both are 3.5 m (11 ft 6 in) long but one is 1.5 m (59 in) off the floor while the other stands 2.3 m (7 ft 6 in) above the ground. The horizontal distance between the 2 supporting frames is 43 cm (17 in). Gymnasts swing from one bar to the other and incorporate a whole range of tucks, hand change-overs and pikes into their routines.
- the beam, a 5-m (16 ft 6-in) long piece of wood that is 10 cm (4 in) wide and supported horizontally 1.2 m (47 in) above the ground. Exercises on the beam include balancing moves such as somersaults, twists, jumps and handstands.
- the mat, exactly the same size as the men's but the movements carried out on it can be done to a musical accompaniment. Acrobatic tumbles, splits, and handstand swivels are just some of the movements that can be carried out on the mat.

SKILLS

● For men, gymnastics is a trial of strength as well as of suppleness and agility. Exercises on all of the pieces of apparatus demand powerful muscles, but none more so than on the rings, which demand immense strength as well as self-control.

● Although women gymnasts have to be strong, they have also to possess a suppleness that almost defies belief. This is most evident when, performing on the beam, gymnasts lean over backwards to touch their heels. But they have to be careful to maintain their sense of poise and not appear to be reducing the event to a contortionist spectacle. It also helps to have an acute sense of balance!

● Women's events demand more artistry than those for men. This is especially true for beam and floor routines, where elegance and style count for a great deal. As music is usually played for the women's floor exercises, a sense of rhythm is important, and a sense of humour can also prove valuable — a winning smile can attract critical appreciation as well as applause.

● Gymnasts have to be meticulous about their routines if they are to perfect them. They are aware that they get judged from the moment they step out to perform until they finish. This means that run-ups, mounts and dismounts are all taken into account. Any sloppiness could be costly.

● Competitors, or more usually their coaches, have to take important decisions about what movements to include in voluntary routines. For the very best gymnasts this is not a problem — they simply go for the most difficult moves. For others the choice is between doing difficult moves badly or easier ones well.

EQUIPMENT

● Men usually wear vests and long trousers (pants). The trousers must be tight-fitting but they should also be elastic so that the legs can be moved freely. Trousers are held up with braces and down with foot straps. In routines, bare feet are allowed, but most men prefer to wear lightweight gymnastic slippers with pointed toes.

● Women wear elasticated leotards and slippers.

● Before performing on rings or bars, gymnasts are allowed to dip their hands into a bowl of magnesium carbonate powder. This prevents the hands from sticking and also absorbs moisture. Similarly, the soles of shoes can be coated with resin immediately before a competitor takes to the beam or attempts a vault. This helps to prevent the feet from slipping.

● Safety equipment is compulsory at all events — even the most experienced competitors can come to grief. Rubber mats are placed under and alongside all pieces of apparatus with the exception of the mat.

TECHNICAL TERMS

crucifix when a competitor holds himself in a cross position with his arms outstretched while performing on the rings; possibly the most testing of all exercises, it demands great strength and self-control

dismount when a competitor has finished a routine, he or she adopts a 'dismount' position with feet together and hands held out straight above the head

flik-flak a backwards or forwards handspring in mat exercises

pike when the legs are brought forward, straight and together

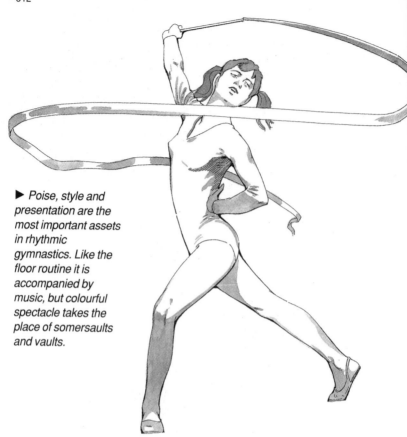

► *Poise, style and presentation are the most important assets in rhythmic gymnastics. Like the floor routine it is accompanied by music, but colourful spectacle takes the place of somersaults and vaults.*

FOR THE RECORD

RHYTHMIC GYMNASTICS
In the comparatively new discipline of rhythmic gymnastics, individuals or teams of women perform routines on a mat while juggling or waving balls, ribbons, hoops and clubs. The movements are carried out in time to music giving the performance a spectacular, choreographed look.

A rhythmic gymnastics competition first took place at Olympic level at the Los Angeles Olympic Games in 1984 and it proved so successful that a similar event was held in Seoul 4 years later.

FOR THE RECORD

TRAMPOLINING
The trampoline was invented by an American, George Nissen, in 1936. The first trampolining competitions took place 10 years later. The most prestigious international competitions are the biennial World Championships, which include events for men and women as well as for synchronized pairs and several other categories.

A standard trampoline comprises a steel frame supported 1 m (39 in) off the ground. The frame is around 4 m (13 ft) long and 2 m (19 in) wide. Hundreds of springs along the inside edges of the frame support a 'bed' which is made from a mesh of nylon straps.

In most competitions, trampolinists have to perform compulsory and optional routines which are carried out whilst bouncing about. In synchronized events, 2 trampolines are placed side by side and pairs perform movements in time with one another. Common routines include twists, turns, somersaults and pikes while bouncing as much as 6 m (20 ft) in the air.

Trampolining demands tight control of body movement because if a competitor should land slightly off balance, he or she will be catapulted to one side. For this reason, the rim and springs of the trampoline are covered with protective padding and it is normal for a person to stand at each corner so that a competitor can be stopped from bouncing off the bed on to the floor.

The clothing worn is similar to that used in gymnastics — vests and trousers or a leotard.

FOR THE RECORD

The nation that towers over all others in men's gymnastics is the USSR, but Bulgaria, Japan and China have also produced individual champions. In the 1988 Seoul Olympics, the USSR won the team competition. In addition 4, out of a possible 7, individual gold medals went to Soviet competitors.

The USSR also has a strong tradition in women's gymnastics, but Romania, Bulgaria and the United States have also produced outstanding competitors. In the 1988 Olympics, the USSR won the team competition, and 2 Soviet individuals captured gold medals. All the gold medals for the other individual routines — uneven parallel bars, balance beam and floor exercises — were taken by Daniela Silivas of Romania.

▼ *As part of an individual performance of aerial tumbles, this trampolinist holds a pike position in mid-air.*

WEIGHTLIFTING

Weightlifting is an ancient sport and dates back to at least the original Olympic Games, when men attempted to prove their strength by lifting lumps of stone. References to weightlifting continue throughout history, but it was not until the end of the 19th century that the sport evolved into its present form, with lifters of similar weight competing against each other.

The first World Championship took place in London in 1891 and the sport was re-adopted by the Olympic Games in 1896. These two competitions are still the most important contests.

Although weightlifting is practised mostly by men (amateurs only), there are a few competitions for women. The ruling body of the sport is the International Weightlifting Federation (IWF) which has its headquarters in Hungary, traditionally one of the strongest weightlifting countries. Other leading nations include the USSR, Bulgaria and Turkey.

▼ *In the clean-and-jerk, the lifter first raises the bar to his shoulders and then pushes it up above his head. To get his body weight underneath the bar, a lifter is allowed to squat down or to do a 'split'. After completing the movements needed to lift the bar, he must stand motionless, with his feet in line, while holding the weight in the air until the referee signals that the weight may be replaced.*

AIMS OF THE GAME

COMPETITION

● The simple object of the sport is to lift disc-shaped weights supported on either end of a 'barbell'. There are 2 types of competition, which are defined by the way the weights are lifted — the 'snatch' and the 'clean-and-jerk'. Lifters are separated into 10 weight categories, which range from 52 kg (115 lb) to over 110 kg (242 lb) (see For the Record).

● Competitions are run on a knockout basis. Weights are added to a barbell in successive rounds until there is only one person left in the competition able to lift the weight — the winner. Each lifter is given 3 chances to lift the barbell in each round.

● Weightlifting takes place on a 4 m (4 yd) square raised platform and a panel of 3 judges assesses each lift. The barbell is a 2.2 m (7 ft 2 in) steel bar. Weights, which come in the form of steel or rubber discs with holes in the middle, are added in equal quantities to each end and are kept in place by collars. The heaviest weight that can be added is 50 kg (110 lb) and the lightest is 0.25 kg (½ lb).

● In a snatch competition a lifter has to use both hands to lift a weighted barbell from the ground to above his head in one movement. He is allowed to 'split' his legs — 'stepping' forwards — in order to gain thrust from the legs but once the bar is above his head he must stand motionless for an instant if the lift is to be valid.

● In the clean-and-jerk a lifter first heaves the bar to shoulder height where it is brought to rest (the clean), and then with a lunging movement thrusts the bar above his head (the jerk). He must remain motionless until the judges give their decision.

SKILLS

● Weightlifting calls for formidable strength, balance and control. A sense of timing is also important.

EQUIPMENT

● Lifters wear leotards, boots and sometimes belts which protect the stomach muscles. Bandages are allowed around knee joints and the wrists, but not around the elbows.

● Powder is used to improve grip.

FOR THE RECORD

WEIGHT CLASSIFICATIONS
Weightlifters compete in the following strictly regulated groups:

Flyweight	to 52 kg (115 lb)
Bantamweight	to 56 kg (123 lb)
Featherweight	to 60 kg (132 lb)
Lightweight	to 67.5 kg (149 lb)
Middleweight	to 75 kg (165 lb)
Light-heavyweight	to 82.5 kg (182 lb)
Middle-heavyweight	to 90 kg (198 lb)
Heavyweight	to 100 kg (220 lb)
Heavyweight	to 110 kg (242 lb)
Super-heavyweight	over 110 kg (242 lb)

FOR THE RECORD

POWERLIFTING
There are 3 types of powerlifting — squat, bench press and deadlift.

In the squat a lifter takes a barbell off a stand onto his or her shoulders, then squats down until the thighs are parallel to the ground and stands up again and replaces the barbell.

In the bench press event, a lifter lies on a 45 cm (18 in) high bench. A barbell is lowered onto his or her chest and, gripping the bar, the lifter pushes it up until his arms are straight.

In the deadlift, a lifter raises a barbell from the floor to thigh level.

BODY-BUILDING

DID YOU KNOW?

The film *Pumping Iron*, made in 1977, launched Arnold Schwarzenegger as an international star and introduced the world of body-building to millions of viewers. The title of the film is body-builder's slang for lifting weights. Audiences marvelled at the discipline and dedication demanded by the sport which gained many converts in the body-building craze that followed.

For centuries there have been men who have striven to turn their bodies into replicas of the perfect male form by developing their muscles to an exaggerated degree. It is for this reason that body-building is sometimes referred to as 'body sculpture'.

In the 1950s, an American body-builder called Charles Atlas became a household name. He turned himself, and millions of disciples, into more muscular versions of themselves, using a technique called 'dynamic tension', which he patented. Charles Atlas made body-building a hugely popular pastime both in the United States and in Europe and it is largely thanks to him that it has become a recognizable, if not universally loved, sport. Another supreme body-builder is Arnold Schwarzenegger who, after winning numerous international body-building titles, became a movie star.

There are many national and international organizations and competitions open to body-builders of both sexes. The best known competitions are the Mr Universe, Miss Universe, and Mr Apollo contests.

AIMS OF THE GAME

COMPETITION

● In most competitions, body-builders are ushered onto a podium positioned on a stage. A spotlight is fixed on them and during the course of a given time limit, each competitor adopts a succession of 'poses' in which he flexes his muscles, and holds them flexed, for a few seconds. The poses are designed to show off every muscle that can be voluntarily manipulated.

● A panel of judges awards marks, assessing personal presentation and 'proportion' as well as 'bulk'.

● There are usually one or 2 eliminating rounds until just a half dozen or so are left in the contest. The winner is the person who accumulates the most marks.

SKILLS

● Body-builders necessarily train in the gym for hours on end but they train in a special way and, nowadays, on special equipment.

If a track athlete goes to 'work out' on 'weights', he or she usually uses comparatively light weights and repeats exercises in quick succession. Body-builders do the opposite — they work with extremely heavy weights and are not too concerned by the number of times that they perform an exercise. The reason for this is that if a person lifts an abnormally heavy weight, tissue within the carrying muscles will be torn and subsequently replaced with more tissue; if the muscles are worked in this way often and hard enough, the muscles will become huge, due to replacement tissue. They will not,

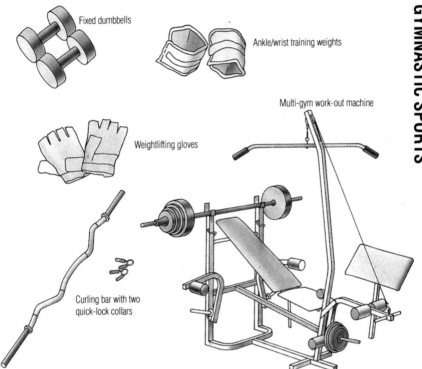

Fixed dumbbells

Ankle/wrist training weights

Multi-gym work-out machine

Weightlifting gloves

Curling bar with two
quick-lock collars

however, necessarily be stronger. But
to the body-builder, strength is less
important than bulk.
● Serious body-builders look to
develop all voluntary muscles, not just
specific ones; in a contest a person
with huge biceps and undeveloped
calves will not come near a person who
has moderately proportioned muscles
all over.
● Diet is important to body-builders
and they concentrate on eating food
that has a high protein content.
● Before a contest, body-builders
dehydrate themselves so that when
they flex their muscles the skin will be
taut, causing veins and sinews to stand
out even more than normal.
● Both men and women shave off
body hair before a competition and
cover themselves with glistening oil.

▲ *A selection of equipment used
by body-builders. Serious
contenders use extremely heavy
weights on work-out machines in
order to increase muscle bulk.*

EQUIPMENT

● Very little equipment is required in
body-building competitions. Men wear
trunks while women wear brief 2-piece
costumes like bikinis. No footwear is
worn.

TECHNICAL TERMS

multi-gym a special 'work-out'
machine on which a number of
different exercises can be performed
with varying weights
pecs pectoral (chest) muscles

CYCLING

The first pedal bicycle was invented in the mid-19th century, and it was not long before races took place. Today, there are three categories of cycle racing — road, track and cyclo-cross. There is one nominal ruling body — the Union Cycliste Internationale (UCI) — but, under the aegis of the UCI, two further bodies exist: the Fédération Internationale de Cyclisme Amateur (FICA) and the Fédération Internationale de Cyclisme Professional (FICP).

▲ *Cycling helmets must be worn in all amateur events. The heel-less shoes are clipped to the pedals, and padded shorts reduce the chances of getting saddle sores.*

ROAD RACING

Road racing developed in France and north-west Europe towards the end of the last century. The most prestigious and important annual cycle race in the world — the Tour de France — was held first in 1903. In road racing, individuals who are also members of a team, race from A to B, along roads, over cobbles, through narrow lanes, and up and over mountains. Some races last for just a day or less but others, called 'stage races', take weeks to complete. In these, 4000 kilometres (2500 miles) may be cycled.

The most famous road races are contested by professionals who ride for sponsored teams. Others, however, are for amateurs. In France, the Netherlands, Italy, Belgium and Spain cycling is considered a major sport, and winners of important races are fêted as heroes. In the United States and much of the rest of the world however, cycling is hardly considered an important sport at all. The three-time American winner of the Tour de France, Greg LeMond (also world champion twice), is barely known in his home country, but in Europe he is considered a great sporting champion. Two Frenchmen — Jacques Anquetil and Bernard Hinault — and Belgium's Eddy Merckx have each won the Tour de France five times.

Although men take the most lucrative and prestigious prizes, tour races are also held for women. Ladies' cycling is becoming increasingly popular, both with participants and with spectators. For example, a Tour de France Feminin, a replica of the men's race, is now contested by women cyclists.

AIMS OF THE GAME

COMPETITION

● In road races, the object is simple — the person who finishes in the fastest time wins. It is the intrigue, the team-work and the challenge for prizes that makes road cycling interesting.

● Races are over ordinary roads and paved tracks. Distances vary from 70 km (45 miles) for one-day amateur events, to over 4000 km (2500 miles) for 3-week professional contests.

● The winner of a race is the person who completes the course in the fastest time. However in long races trophies and prestige and possibly lucrative 'bonuses' are given to others who perform well. Apart from the winner's trophy, the most important titles to be gained in the Tour de France, for example, include:

- 'Points Champion', awarded to the person who achieves the best average placing in stages;

- 'King of the Mountains', given to the person who proves himself the best rider up mountains.

● In road cycling, riders are started in a 'bunch' — all the cyclists, sometimes more than 200, are released from a starting point together. In one-day races, the person who finishes first, wins. But in stage races, the person who finishes first at the end of a day's racing only wins the stage; the winner of the race is the person who has the fastest aggregate time for the whole course. It is possible for a person to win a long race without winning a stage.

● In long stage races, a number, perhaps 2 or 3, 'time trials' are held. In these, competitors are started individually at regular intervals and have to ride independently along a designated course against the clock. The time taken to complete the course is added, like any other stage, to a person's overall time. Time trials make riders compete without help from team-mates so that their racing ability is fully tested.

● Team-mates are usually allowed to help each other out, to the extent that a less talented rider may hand over his cycle to a senior member of a team who has crashed. However, cyclists are not allowed to be pushed or physically aided, and even if an enthusiastic spectator gives some 'help', a rider may have seconds docked off his time.

● In all major road races, prizes or awards go to the winning team — the team whose riders accrue the most points.

SKILLS

● All riders in major races are members of a team comprising 4 to 12 riders — without back-up from team-mates or from a following 'team car', a rider would be doomed to failure. Senior riders in a team expect, and always receive, assistance from juniors. This may involve 'pacing', in which a potential winner is led by a team-mate through a tricky part of a stage or race. Or, it might mean that a junior team-mate has to sacrifice his water bottle.

● Tactics play a huge part in tour cycling and the longer the race, the more manoeuvring goes on. Leading riders are perpetually on the lookout for breaks made by others. It is the duty of team-mates to make sure that leaders know exactly what is going on during the whole course of a race or stage. Sometimes a potential winner will stay back in order to conserve energy but if a leading rider from another team breaks away from the 'bunch', he will try and keep in touch.

- The greatest riders are all-rounders, able to race up long, arduous mountain lanes, as well as being able to compete effectively in time trials and along hot, dusty roads that apparently lead to nowhere. The vast majority of cyclists specialize — some prefer 'climbing' up mountains, others like sprinting. A metronome-like rhythm is all-important for the best time trialists. With no team-mates to pace them, they must know how to harness their reserves to the best effect.
- All tour cyclists have to be immensely fit with strong lungs and able legs.

EQUIPMENT

- Road-racing cycles are specialized machines, light but strong. The cycles used by top professional riders are extremely expensive and beyond the means of the average person. They can have up to 24 gears with the low ratios being used for climbing hills and mountains and the high ones being used for sprints. Teams always have a selection of spare cycles and hundreds of spare tyres and accessories. Amateur racing cycles are much less costly.
- Crash helmets have been compulsory for amateur cyclists since January 1991; they are especially useful when careering down steep mountain roads where speeds of up to 112 km/h (70 mph) can be achieved. In hot weather sunglasses and peaked hats are often worn.
- Most serious cyclists shave the hair off their legs to facilitate massage and for treatment of the 'gravel rash' gained in minor spills. They wear padded shorts to prevent 'saddle sore', an unamusing ailment that can lead to incapacity.

TECHNICAL TERMS

domestique a less experienced rider within a team who must always be prepared to sacrifice his race position, or even his cycle, in order to support his leader
jersey in stage races, coloured jerseys are worn by leading riders:
- a yellow jersey, *maillot jaune* in French, is worn by the race leader in most tours (a pink jersey is worn in the Tour of Italy);
- a green jersey is worn by the points leader;
- a red polka dot jersey is worn by the King of the Mountains
peloton the main field of riders
stage a stage can be as short as 40 km (25 miles) or more than 190 km (120 miles) long; they never take more than a day to complete

FOR THE RECORD

MAJOR TOURS
Tour de France
Tour of Italy (Giro d'Italia)
Tour of Spain (Vuelta de Espagna)
Tour of Britain
Cours Classic (United States)
Tour of Switzerland

MAJOR ONE-DAY RACES
World Championship Professional road race
World Championship Amateur road race

THE CLASSIC ROAD RACES
Milan-San Remo (Italy)
Tour of Flanders (Belgium)
Paris-Roubaix (France)
Flèche-Wallone (Belgium)
Liège-Bastogne (Belgium)
Paris-Brussels (France/Belgium)
Tour of Lombardy (Italy)

OTHER IMPORTANT RACES
Bordeaux-Paris (France)
Paris-Nice (France)
Criterium International (France)

FOR THE RECORD

The longest stage race in the world is
the Tour de France. The course
changes each year but it is usually
around 4000 km (2500 miles) long and
takes 21 days to complete.

Although most of the tour is cycled
in France, and always ends in Paris, it
does occasionally cross borders into
neighbouring countries — a stage was
even raced in Britain once.

There can be as many as a million
spectators watching the race along the
roadside every day of the race, so
hundreds of publicity cars precede the
riders through towns and villages.
Towns even pay to be put on the route.

▼ *The gruelling mountain stages
of the Tour de France can make or
break champion cyclists. Below,
cyclists on the 1990 Tour take on
the roads of the 17th stage, from
Lourdes to Pau in the Pyrenees.*

TRACK CYCLING

Track racing dates back to the first modern Olympic Games (1896) and since then a number of important competitions have evolved, the most prestigious of these being the annual World Championships which are held for professional riders and amateurs. In Olympic years, amateur World Championship races that clash with those on the Olympic programme are not contested, so Olympic and World Championship titles have equal status. Separate races are held for men and women.

▼ *Cycle tracks, or velodromes, can vary in length but all retain the same oval shape. Banked sides, especially at corners, prevent cyclists from flying off the edge.*

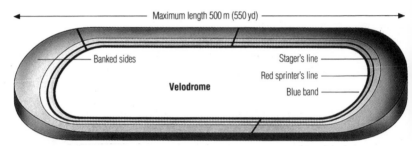

Maximum length 500 m (550 yd)

Banked sides

Velodrome

Stager's line

Red sprinter's line

Blue band

AIMS OF THE GAME

COMPETITION
● Track racing is divided up into a number of major events which vary in both length and character. Races take place on oval tracks which can vary in size. They should ideally not be more than 500 m (550 yd approx.) long and some are as short as 250 m (273 yd) long. The standard World Championship course lies in between the two and is 333 m (365 yd) long.

Tracks can be indoors or outdoors and are made of wood, asphalt or concrete. The surface is banked, especially at the corners, and three coloured lines run round the entire circuit.
- The blue band, 20 cm (8 in) wide on the inside of the track, marks the inner limit of where riders can cycle.
- The red line or 'sprinter's line', which

is 90 cm (1 yd) from the inside edge, marks a no overtaking area — no overtaking is allowed inside the line if the rider ahead is inside the line.
- Some steeper tracks have a thin blue line about a third of the way in. This is the 'stager's line' and is used to control overtaking in the motor-paced events. Starting and finishing lines are also marked across the track.
● The most important competitions are as follows:
Sprints In these, 2 or 4 riders compete against each other for 3 circuits of the track. Races are run on a knockout basis, with the winners of each heat progressing to a final. Sprints are also held for tandem cycles.
Pursuits In these, riders start on opposite sides of the track and race against the clock more than each other. Distances range from 2000 m (2200 yd) for junior riders to 5000

(5468 yd) for professional men. If one rider does not overtake the other, the winner is the person who completes the distance in the fastest time.

Team pursuits With these races 2 teams of 4 race against each other as in ordinary pursuits. The winning team is the one that gets 3 men past the finishing line in the fastest time.

Time trials In time trials there is only one person on the track at a time and he races over a specified distance — usually 1 km (1093 yd) — as fast as he can. The winner is the person who has the fastest time for the distance. Sometimes the trial is to achieve the maximum distance over a set time — 50 km (30 miles approx.) in one hour was a barrier for decades.

Motor pacing In these races, a motorcyclist leads a cyclist round the track. The winner is the person who rides fastest over a given distance or completes a greater distance in a given time period.

Points racing As many as 20 riders are started in a bunch. On specified lap numbers the leaders pick up points as they pass the finish line (a race can last for tens of circuits). The person with the most points at the end of the race wins — irrespective of that cyclist's position at the finishing line.

SKILLS
● Different disciplines are needed for each type of track racing. In sprint racing, for example, the first 2 laps of the track are taken as 'warm up' laps and riders vie against each other to get into a good position for the final lap; it is only in the last 200 m (220 yd) or so that they go flat out.

In the other races, however, riders have to pace themselves carefully, always conserving enough energy for the last lap.

EQUIPMENT

● Track cycles are very light and they have no gears or brakes. In recent years, 'solid' wheels and 'close grip' handlebars have proved successful in cutting down wind resistance.
● Riders wear extremely light clothing, usually made of lycra. Helmets are always worn and contemporary ones are shaped into a tail at the back so that they do not cause 'drag'.

TECHNICAL TERMS

tubs thin tubular tyres that are stuck on the rim of a wheel; if they are punctured, the whole wheel is replaced
velodrome a cycle track

▲ *Track cyclists participating in a points race, vying for position on the steeply sloped ends of the velodrome.*

DID YOU KNOW?

Most cyclo-cross obstacles are natural hazards such as deep mud, fallen trees or rocky outcroppings. Some cyclo-cross circuits go further and add man-made features such as fences and flights of stairs.

CYCLO-CROSS

Cyclo-cross is thought to have originated in France around the turn of the century. It is essentially cross-country cycling, and one theory has it that the sport developed from military manoeuvres in which army cyclists were obliged to ride across fields and over uneven terrain during 'battle training'.

The French were responsible for developing the sport, and the first World Championship was held in 1925. However, the World Championships were not recognized by the Union Cycliste Internationale until 1950. These World Championships are now the most important competitions and are divided into professional and amateur categories (senior and junior) — the professional class is open only to individuals, but there are trophies for both individuals and national teams in the amateur class. The World Championships are now held in a different country each year.

Today, cyclo-cross is a booming sport with a strong following in many parts of Europe including Britain. It is also popular in certain regions of North America, particularly around Chicago. It is largely a male sport and as yet there are no important competitions open to women.

▼ *Carrying rather than riding the bicycle often saves time along steep or muddy sections of a cyclo-cross course.*

AIMS OF THE GAME

COMPETITION

● The simple object of the sport is to win races over a number of laps along a treacherous course that is 1-2 km (½ - 1¼ miles long). The course includes all manner of different terrain — ordinary roads, ditches, woods, muddy hills and so on. If race organizers do not consider a course tough enough, they have the right to place obstacles along it, a 40-cm (16-in) fence for example. Races vary in length, but most are between 15 and 20 km (9 and 12½ miles) long.

● There are few specific rules in cyclo-cross and, after a massed start, it is up to individual riders as to how they tackle a course.

● Competitors are allowed to dismount from their cycles and carry them. Indeed, it would be a bad course that did not force riders to dismount from time to time. Downhill sections can be particularly treacherous.

● The first person to cross the finishing line is the winner, but he has to have his cycle with him; he does not have to ride over the line, he can carry his cycle if he wants.

SKILLS

● Riders always like to get away to a good start. After the broad starting area, the course invariably narrows and if a rider gets caught up in a bottleneck, he will lose precious time. A rider generally needs to be among the first 10 after 400 m (440 yd) in order to win.

● It is not always quicker to ride a cycle than to carry it — riders can stall while climbing a steep bank. Competitors have to judge which option is faster.

● Cyclo-cross riders have to be fit and strong. As well as being able to ride fast they must also have shoulders sturdy enough to take the weight of a cycle as they run uphill. A good sense of balance is important for jumping ditches and hopping over logs while carrying a cycle.

● Riding down a steep, slippery slope takes courage and, while some may prefer to play safe and get off, the best riders have nerves of steel.

EQUIPMENT

● Cycles are made as light as possible by using aluminium wherever feasible instead of heavier steel. However, they have to be strong enough to take rough treatment. Tyres are usually thick with deep treads, so that they can grip in muddy conditions. The chain is protected by a guard, so that it does not get clogged up, or jump off on rough descents. Most cycles have at least 12 gears arranged on a derailleur mechanism, which shifts the chain between sprockets of different sizes.

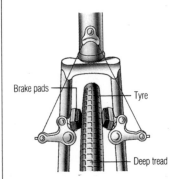

Brake pads

Tyre

Deep tread

▲ *The tyres on cyclo-cross bikes are much wider than those used on touring or road-racing bicycles. They have deep, knobbly treads to enable them to grip in slippery or muddy conditions. The brakes act evenly on either side of the tyre.*

MULTI-DISCIPLINE SPORTS

Three important sports are made up of two or more disciplines, so competitors have to be able athletes in more ways than one.

DID YOU KNOW?

At the 1976 Montreal Olympics, Major Boris Onischenko of the USSR was found to be using an épée that was rigged up so that when a button was pressed, a 'hit' was registered. Onischenko, the 1971 Individual World Champion, was immediately banished.

▼ *The pentathlon is a test of all-round sporting ability. The accuracy and nerve needed for the fencing, shooting and riding are balanced by the sheer speed called for in the swimming and running.*

MODERN PENTATHLON

Modern pentathlon — not to be confused with 'ordinary' pentathlon, an athletics event which has now been replaced by the heptathlon (see page 306) — dates back to before World War I. It is based on a military 'theory': a 'king's messenger' has to take a 'message' (no actual message is carried) across enemy territory. First, the person rides while carrying the message but his horse is incapacitated, so he must fight his way through enemy lines with sword and pistol. To make good his escape, he swims a river and finally runs to achieve his objective. Success!

The modern pentathlon — comprising the five sports of fencing, swimming, shooting, running and riding — was included in the 1912 Olympic Games at the insistence of Baron Pierre de Courbetin (the founder of the modern Games) who wished to include an event that truly tested all-round ability.

Today, the Olympics still provide the most prestigious competition, but only men compete in them. (Individual and team competitions are held.) In the annual World Championships, however, a women's event is included.

The ruling body is the Union Internationale du Pentathlon Moderne et Biathlon (UIPMB).

1 Fencing

2 Swimming

AIMS OF THE GAME

COMPETITION
- In the major competitions, 5 events take place on 3 or 4 consecutive days. Competitors score points in each event and winners are those that have the highest total after all 5 events have been completed. Team positions are worked out by adding up the scores of the 3 team members.

The 5 events are taken in the following order:

- fencing — In the fencing competition, each competitor uses an épée and has to duel against everybody else in the competition. A competitor who wins 70% of his or her bouts scores 1000 points. If a person wins more than 70% of the given number of bouts, extra points are gained; losses result in deducted points.

- swimming — Men swim 300 m (330 yd) and women 200 m (220 yd) against the clock. The optimum time for men is 3 min 45 sec and for women 2 min 40 sec. Four points are gained or lost for every ½ sec above or below these time allowances.

- shooting — 5.6 mm (.22 in) pistols are used in the shooting events which are held in a 25-m (27-yd) range. Each competitor fires 20 shots (5 shots in each of 4 rounds) at a turning target that is visible for 3 secs and concealed for 7. A score of 182 out of a possible 200 equals 1000 points and scores

above and below this mean that points are added or taken away.

- running — Men run cross-country for 4000 m (4374 yd) and women for 2000 m (2187 yd). The time target, worth 1000 points, for men is 14 min 15 sec and for women 7 min 30 sec. For every second faster or slower than the target times, 3 points (men) or 5 points (women) are gained or lost.

- riding — In the riding contest, competitors draw lots for horses. The course is a show jumping course, 600 m (660 yd) long, and includes 15 jumps. A clear round, completed within the time allowance, scores 1100 points. Time penalties are added for exceeding the time allowance, for knocking fences down and for refusals.

SKILLS
- A good competitor has to be competent in all 5 events but inevitably individuals are stronger in some events than in others. The most unpredictable event is the riding, because there is no way of telling what sort of horse a rider will pick — some are lucky and get a good horse, others are not.

EQUIPMENT

- All the clothes and pieces of equipment needed, apart from the horse, have to be supplied by the competitors themselves and all of them have to conform to standard rules.

3 Shooting

4 Cross-country running

5 Riding

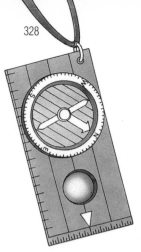

ORIENTEERING

Orienteering, cross-country running with the aid of a map, developed in Sweden at the beginning of the 20th century. It did not become internationally popular until the 1960s when the ruling body, the International Orienteering Federation, was founded. The first British orienteering clubs sprang up in the mid-1960s, and clubs were soon established in France, Belgium and Germany. The sport has not caught on in the United States, but there are several clubs in Canada, Australia and New Zealand.

▲ *The 'silva' compass used in orienteering takes its name from the Latin word for woodland.*

Orienteering is undertaken by both men and women. The most important competitions are the biennial World Championships. It is an amateur sport and is frequently used as a training exercise to sharpen up wits as well as to improve stamina.

Orienteering is normally done on foot but it has also been adapted for horse riders and cyclists. In Scandinavia, where cross-country skiing is a popular pastime, ski orienteering takes place during the winter months.

AIMS OF THE GAME

COMPETITION
● Orienteering is a sport in which competitors navigate their way at their own pace between features marked on a special, coloured map. These features are normally known as 'controls'. At each control, which is identified by a unique code, competitors use a patterned needle punch to clip their control card, which shows that they have visited that control.
● An orienteering course varies in length from about 2 km (1¼ miles approx.) with 6 to 10 control points for beginners and children, to over 12 km (7¼ miles approx.) for experienced adult orienteers. Orienteering takes place on a wide range of outdoor sites — from town parks to the countryside, forests and moorlands.

● Orienteering is a sport for everyone. The youngest recognized age class is 10 and under, the oldest 70 and over. Newcomers often tackle a course in pairs or groups. Most events offer a string course for younger children.
● Everyone has a separate start time and the winner is the person with the fastest time. A good course will offer a navigational challenge.
● Route choice is important and concentration on reading the special orienteering maps is essential. The map is only issued at the start so that none of the competitors is familiar with the course, as this would give an advantage over the others.
● Competitors are normally started individually with at least one-min intervals: this provision tries to ensure that people do not just follow each other round the course.

▶ A map in a waterproof wallet, a watch and a compass are all necessary in orienteering. As courses usually cover rough terrain, strong shoes are always worn.

SKILLS

● Orienteering requires a combination of physical and mental abilities. At the introductory level, concentration on map-reading is more important than fitness; a quick compass reading can save time and energy. At the higher levels an ability to read a map at the same time as running is needed. Advanced competitors must be in peak condition and have a keen knowledge of their own energy reserves as they make their way through unfamiliar terrain.

● The competitors' aim in orienteering is to navigate their way to features (e.g. a stream, path junction etc). A course is planned so that correct navigation will result in the feature being located. The duration of events varies. Some end only when the course is completed; others have a time limit.

EQUIPMENT

● Competitors wear sensible outdoor clothing and a good pair of walking or training shoes. Full leg cover is essential and special lightweight 'O' suits are used by the more competitive. Orienteering shoes have studded soles and are normally more sturdy than cross-country running shoes.

FOR THE RECORD

In score orienteering, various checkpoints are allocated different numbers of points — those in remote or inaccessible areas being more 'valuable' than those that are easy to reach. At the end of a given time limit, competitors return to the starting point. The person with the most points is the winner.

DID YOU KNOW?

The greatest number of people ever to compete in a triathlon was 3888 in Chicago in 1987.

TRIATHLON

Probably the most gruelling and physically demanding of all sporting events is the triathlon, which comprises a long swim, a cycle ride and a road-running race.

The concept for a 'super event' that would test an all-round athlete to the limit came from a group of Americans who organized the first triathlon event in 1978. The inaugural event was staged on the island of Hawaii and was dubbed the 'Ironman' contest.

Only a handful of men competed in the first triathlon, but these days some international events, of which there are now many, attract several thousand entrants. Women take part in triathlon contests, often over the same courses as men.

Although it cannot be termed a hugely popular sport for participants, contests or parts of contests are frequently televised, particularly in the United States, and the sport has a growing number of admirers.

The organization that rules over most triathlon contests is the Union Internationale de Triathlon. Apart from the Ironman contest (there is an Ironman for women, too), the most important competitions are the annual ones held at Nice in France and the regular World and European Championships, held over the 'shorter' distances (see Competition).

AIMS OF THE GAME

COMPETITION
● The object is simple — to complete the course in the fastest time. The 3 events are always taken in this order — swimming followed by cycling and running.
● Courses vary considerably, not just in character but also in length. The Ironman contest comprises a 3.8-km (2.4-mile approx.) swim in the Pacific Ocean, a 180-km (112-mile) cycle ride in the mountains and a marathon of 42 km (26 miles). However, most competitions are shorter and usually consist of a 1500-m (1-mile approx.) swim, a 40-km (25-mile) cycle race and just a 10-km (6-mile approx.) run.
● Contestants are usually started en masse from a beach and have to swim out to sea, sometimes through breaking waves. Once they have rounded a marker buoy, they return to the shore and start cycling and running. Breaks taken between events count against competitors. Doctors are always on hand to check a contestant's health. Pulse rates may be taken from each individual at each stage.

● The first person home to the finish line is the winner. It takes a little over 8 hr for the best male contestants to complete an Ironman and around 2 hr to finish the shorter courses.

SKILLS

● Entrants to triathlon contests have to be immensely fit and have an unbreakable will. Hours and hours of training are necessary on a daily basis to build up stamina.

● Tactics are few because the field quickly separates even during the swimming event. However, contestants must be able to pace themselves and anybody who starts too quickly will almost certainly fade later on. Most people favour one of the 3 events, but overall consistency is important.

EQUIPMENT

● If the swimming leg is in the sea, a special neoprene 5-mm (¼-in) wetsuit is worn when the water temperature is below 23 °C (73 °F). When the water is above this temperature wetsuits are not allowed.

● The cycles used are lightweight racers and standard cycling gear is worn — padded shorts, vests, shoes and helmets. Disc wheels (with no spokes) and special triathlon handle bars (Tri-bars) are also used. Tri-bars allow cyclists to crouch very low to cut wind resistance. Disc wheels also have reduced wind resistance but can become unstable in a cross-wind.

● Ordinary running clothes are worn in the marathon race.

▶ The triathlon is the toughest sporting test of physical endurance. The swimming element is longer than most competitive swimming races. The cycle race is as long as a day's ride in the Tour de France and the running race alone would exhaust many athletes.

MISCELLANEOUS SPORTS

Half a dozen sports do not readily fit into any specific category as they have little in common with others. For this reason, they have been grouped together.

GLIDING

Mankind has been fascinated by flying since the earliest of times. In Greek mythology, Daedalus and his son Icarus attempted to escape imprisonment on the island of Crete by flying with feathered wings attached to their arms; Daedalus was successful, Icarus was not. Much later, the great Renaissance engineer, Leonardo da Vinci designed gliders and helicopters but none of his contraptions got off the ground. In fact nobody actually succeeded in flying until the late 19th century when a man named Otto Lilienthal took off from a hilltop in Germany with light wings attached to his shoulders. Lilienthal made over 2000 flights with a variety of hang-gliders (see below) before being killed in an accident.

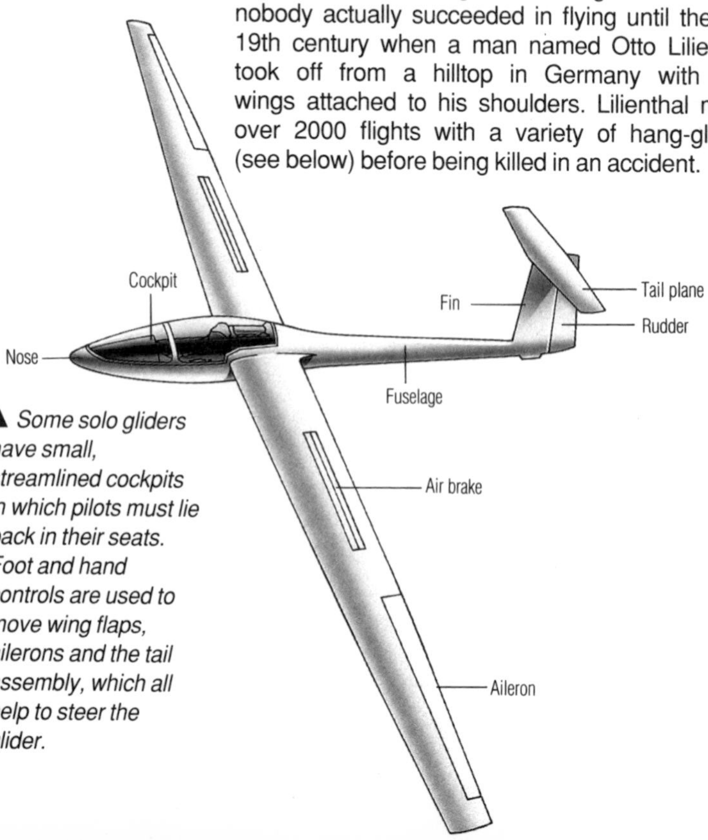

Cockpit

Fin — Tail plane

Rudder

Nose —

Fuselage

▲ *Some solo gliders have small, streamlined cockpits in which pilots must lie back in their seats. Foot and hand controls are used to move wing flaps, ailerons and the tail assembly, which all help to steer the glider.*

Air brake

Aileron

After the American Wright brothers had succeeded in developing the first aeroplane, interest in unpowered flight waned. However, after World War I, Germany was forbidden to build aircraft, and a few German engineers and pilots started to fly gliders once more. Initially, gliders were launched from the tops of hills and tended to have short flights. But it was not long before wind and thermal currents were exploited — which made it possible for gliders to stay in the air for hours. So began a new sport which spread to other parts of Europe, to Australasia and North America.

Men and women now glide in one- or two-seater craft known as sailplanes and there are hundreds of clubs scattered throughout the world. Although it is mainly a pleasure sport, there are a number of national and international competitions for various categories of glider, the most prominent being the biennial World Championships. Some pilots are also concerned with breaking height, speed, distance and soaring records.

The governing body of the sport is the Commission Internationale Vol à Voile (CIVV) which is affiliated to the Fédération Aéronautique Internationale, based in Paris.

DID YOU KNOW?

A German pilot, Hans Werner Grosse, established a straight-line glider-flight world record in 1972. He took his ASK 12 sailplane from Lübeck in Germany to the coastal resort of Biarritz in southwest France — a total of 1460 km (907 miles).

AIMS OF THE GAME

• Gliding is the sport of unpowered flight. Gliders have thin, sleek bodies with long, narrow wings.

• Beginners are usually launched by winch. A glider is attached to a long cable which is wound around a drum at high speed. As the glider is pulled along the runway, it gains lift, just like a kite, and is launched into the air. Car towing is similar in principle to winching. A car races along a runway pulling the glider behind it.

The most popular launching method used by experienced pilots is aerotowing in which a small aeroplane takes off while using a long cable to tow the glider. Once both aeroplane and glider have reached a height of approximately 650 m (2000 ft), the glider pilot then releases the tow-rope and is then free to soar.

COMPETITION

• The most common form of competition is speed racing over a triangular course. In this pilots are launched separately and have to glide round a triangular course back to the starting point. Courses range in length from 100 km (60 miles) to 1250 km (775 miles). Championships often last for 1 or 2 weeks and a different event is held each day. Points are awarded for each event and at the end, the person with the highest total is the overall winner.

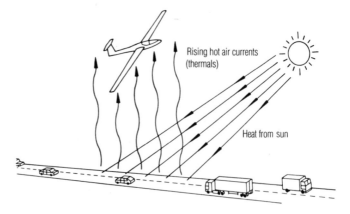

Rising hot air currents (thermals)

Heat from sun

National and international records are held for:
- straight distance;
- distance to a declared goal;
- distance to a declared goal and back;
- gain of height (the height reached from the release point);
- absolute height (above sea level);
- speed over a triangular course.

SKILLS
● Before a novice glider pilot is allowed to fly solo, he or she has to complete a number of flights with an instructor in a 2-seater glider during which all the essential skills are learned — take-off, turning, landing and so on. After perhaps 60 winch launches and 20 or 30 aerotows, a pilot will be permitted to go solo. In many countries a pilot does not need to hold a licence but certificates are awarded according to proficiency.
● Once in the air, a pilot has to search for rising air currents in order to remain aloft. Currents can be found when a breeze blows up against a hill and is forced upwards; but rising draughts can sometimes also be located on the leeward (downwind) side of hills. Strong lift can also be gained from isolated thermals — currents of hot air rising over towns and roads.

▲ *Lift is generally gained from thermals, currents of hot air that rise from land heated by the sun.*

● Gliders usually only have one wheel under the cockpit so landing has to be on smooth, level ground. If this is not a runway, the pilot has to judge from the air whether a field or other open space is suitable and he has to bear in mind that he only has one chance at landing — once on an approach, it is impossible to take off again.

EQUIPMENT

● A single-seater glider weighs around 200 kg (440 lb) and wingspans can range from 15 m (50 ft) to 30 m (100 ft). Most gliders are made from glass fibre and the wings can be dismantled so that they can be stowed alongside the fuselage in a trailer.
● No special clothing is required but in sunny weather, when most gliding takes place, sunglasses and a hat are useful. Loose clothing allows unrestricted movement.
● Parachutes are usually worn in case of emergency, and for pilots who intend to soar above 3000 m (10,000 ft) for any length of time, oxygen may be necessary.

FOR THE RECORD

HANG-GLIDING

In the 1970s the sport of hang-gliding took on a new lease of life. Following the example of Otto Lilienthal, who had first pioneered the sport in the 1890s, people exploited the proliferation of new, ultra-light materials and constructed 'wings'. These comprised an arrow-shaped metal frame over which a fabric was stretched. Underneath the frame there was a handbar and a body sling. Hang-gliders today come in a huge variety of shapes, sizes and designs — a typical one might weigh around 15 kg (33 lb).

In hang-gliding, a pilot runs down a hill (or leaps off a cliff) holding onto the handbar of the glider. Wind keeps the craft in the air and manoeuvres are carried out by shifting body weight from the supporting sling, or by pulling or pushing the handbar which alters the angle of the glider.

Despite its obvious dangers, hang-gliding has become an increasingly popular sport and there are a number of national and international championships for men, women and teams.

Many of the skills used are similar to those in gliding — manipulating thermals to gain lift and so on.

Safety equipment, such as a parachute, is seldom worn by pilots, but warm clothing and goggles are essential as the wind can be extremely cold, even in warm climates.

Microlights are similar to hang-gliders in appearance except that they are powered by small engines. Separate records are kept for microlights.

▼ *When flying high, hang-gliders stretch their bodies out flat to reduce wind resistance; when turning (below), they swing their legs below the handbar and shift their weight to steer.*

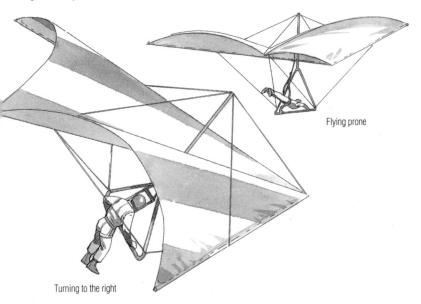

Flying prone

Turning to the right

DID YOU KNOW?

The late American millionaire publisher, Malcolm Forbes, had 2 passions — motorcycles and balloons. Every year he hosted a balloon festival at his château in France where he launched his latest creations — monstrous balloons in the shape of his château, the Sphinx, the Taj Mahal, motorcycles and many others.

▼ *Balloons from a rally in Gstaad float above the Swiss ski resort. Updraughts of mountain air help keep the balloons aloft.*

BALLOONING

Man first took to the air in 1783 when two Frenchmen, de Rozier and the Marquis d'Arlandes, went aloft for 25 minutes in a balloon designed by the Montgolfier brothers. This flight was in a hot-air balloon but 10 days later a hydrogen-filled balloon took off and ascended some 600 m (2000 ft) and flew for more than two hours. This second flight was so impressive that the Montgolfiers' achievements were eclipsed and for nearly two centuries, the vast majority of balloons were hydrogen-filled.

During the last century, ballooning became a fashionable sport and many impressive records were achieved. There were flights over the English Channel and the Alps and a distance record of 1300 km (800 miles) was gained in the United States. Ballooning remained popular well into the beginning of this century but the advent of the powered aircraft temporarily quelled enthusiasm for lighter-than-air flight. However, a few stalwarts persisted in the sport which they considered to be infinitely more pleasing than flying an aircraft.

It was not until after World War II that ballooning again became a popular pastime for those that could afford it. Until the mid-1960s, most

balloons were still filled with hydrogen but as the gas was relatively expensive, hot-air ballooning began to take over. Nowadays, most balloons are hot-air and hydrogen is seldom used.

Today, ballooning is largely a fun sport although some people continue to compete for distance, or chase records for height. Balloon 'fiestas' are held all over Europe and the United States. The ruling body of ballooning, which is mainly concerned with regulations, is the British Balloon and Airship Club (BBAC).

AIMS OF THE GAME

FLYING FOR FUN

● Competition is a secondary consideration for most balloonists, who derive more satisfaction from the sense of exhiliration shared with their fellows. Most flights are for fun and take off from a local field or at an organized meet.

Balloons are classified according to their cubic capacity.

SKILLS

● The person who actually flies a balloon (the pilot) is dependent on a ground crew who help him or her to fill the balloon with gas (usually hot air) while keeping it on the ground with ropes. Several people can accompany a pilot on a flight — the number depends on the size of the balloon, the size of the basket and weather conditions.

● Steering is necessarily haphazard as it relies entirely on wind and air currents. However, a knowing pilot will acquaint himself with detailed weather forecasts before take-off and will be able to catch different currents at different altitudes. To gain altitude in a hot-air balloon, a pilot heats up the air captured in the balloon by means of a burner underneath it; to descend, air is expelled by means of a flap at the top of the balloon. In a hydrogen balloon, the traditional way of gaining height is to discard heavy sandbags from the basket; to come down, gas can be released by opening the flap at the top of the balloon.

● Take-off and landing are always somewhat hazardous. At a launch there should be very little wind. When landing, a pilot has to choose a wide open area and essentially hopes for the best — some landings can be extremely bumpy. On landing, a pilot immediately collapses a balloon by opening the flap at the top of the balloon to release hot air.

EQUIPMENT

● All balloons have a basket or 'gondola' suspended beneath them to accommodate the pilot and his crew. Baskets are usually made of woven wicker — a strong, lightweight material that makes a good shock absorber in rough landings. In hot-air balloons a propane gas burner is sited above the basket and this can be made to produce a sheet of flame that heats the air in the balloon through an aperture at its base.

● Safety equipment includes crash helmets; parachutes are generally carried. High-altitude balloonists often use enclosed — and even pressurized — gondolas.

DID YOU KNOW?

Skateboards were developed in California during the surfing boom of the 1960s. Surfers would test their skateboard skills in beach car parks when there were no waves. Skateboarding was known briefly as 'skurfing' because of the surfing connection.

ROLLER SKATING

The first roller skate, or wheeled boot, was created by a Belgian named Joseph Merlin in 1760 but unfortunately for the inventor, his innovatory contraptions did not receive popular acclaim. If he were alive today, he would have the pleasure of seeing millions of children, as well as competitive adults, riding on skates not too dissimilar to his own creations.

Just over a hundred years after Merlin had patented his device, an American called Everett Plimpton created the first four-wheel skates. Plimpton's intention was to provide ice skaters with an alternative means of practice when there was no ice available. However, being an observant business-man, he saw a successful future in creating a whole new sport and opened a public roller skating rink in the US state of Rhode Island, in 1866.

The new sport gained wide approval and, before World War I, many major cities on both sides of the Atlantic boasted roller skating rinks. Ever since, roller skating has been a favourite pastime of children who skate on the pavements, or indoors to music. However, roller skating is not confined to children — adults compete at the highest level in a variety of disciplines but in most cases the sport has yet to overcome the stigma of 'copying' ice skating which tends to be more elegant.

The ruling body of roller skating is the Fédération Internationale de Roller Skating (FIRS). The most prestigious competitions are the World Artistic Skating Championships and the World Speed Skating Championships. Both are held annually.

▼ *The development of skateboards has reflected some of the advances in roller skate design. Synthetic rubber wheels replaced the early metal ones, and boards made out of fibreglass rather than wood have helped to increase stability.*

◀ *Speed skaters crouch low on turns to reduce drag. Sleek helmets and skin-tight outfits are also designed to offset wind resistance.*

AIMS OF THE GAME

COMPETITION

● Competitive roller skating can be divided into 3 categories, rather like ice skating: speed skating, free (figure) skating and dancing.

● Outdoor tracks are usually made of concrete, asphalt or a similar material. Indoor rinks are usually made of wood.

● Speed skating usually takes place on oval tracks and races can be as short as 300 m (330 yd) or as long as 50,000 m (55,000 yd). Competitions are usually held on a 'heats' basis with the first 3 or 4 going through to subsequent rounds.

● Free skating and dancing, which is often performed by pairs of dancers, take place on an oval rink and routines are carried out to music. Figure skating takes place around lines traced on the floor. The scoring system is similar, if not identical, to that used in the ice equivalents of figure skating and ice dancing.

SKILLS

● Roller skating originated as a warm-weather version of ice skating, so it is not surprising that many of the competitions, and indeed skills, are similar. However, roller skaters have an extra burden to carry — their skates can weigh up to 3 kg (6½ lb). For this reason alone roller skating is slower and can often appear more cumbersome.

● As there are often massed starts for speed skaters, an aggressive technique usually prevails throughout the race.

● Pirouettes and spins, such as those on display at the Artistic Skating Championships, can be extremely delicate. They can seem even more dramatic than those seen in ice skating simply because the roller skates are so heavy.

EQUIPMENT

● The synthetic plastic wheels of modern skates (metal wheels used to be 'de rigueur' but are now frowned upon) are screwed to lightweight boots. The wheel format is usually 2 pairs side-by-side, as in a car. Boots lace up past the ankles, as they do on ice skates.

● In speed events, racers wear helmets and protective elbow and knee pads.

▲ *The pins are arranged in a triangular formation at the bottom of a lane.*

TENPIN BOWLING

Bowling a ball at target 'pins' is often assumed to be a modern game, but its origins date back a long way. The 6000-year-old tomb of an Ancient Egyptian prince revealed the rules of a game in which a stone ball was rolled at nine target pins. Similar games have been played all over the world for centuries. The game of skittles, a popular pastime in pubs and taverns in parts of England, is also an old game but, again, only nine pins were or are used as targets. In the Netherlands 'Dutch pins', another version of the game, was played.

'Ninepins', as the game was often called, was a popular gambling game. It caught on in the United States when it was taken there by immigrants in the 18th and 19th centuries. However, ninepins was banned in certain states because of its gambling overtones. So, according to legend, bowlers added a tenth pin, apparently legitimately, and gave birth to the modern game.

Tenpin bowling is now a highly mechanized and sophisticated game, played by both amateurs and professionals, men and women. It

AIMS OF THE GAME

COMPETITION

• The object of tenpin bowling is to topple over pins by rolling a ball at them down a 'lane'. A game comprises 10 turns (frames) attempting to knock down 10 sets of tenpins, with a possible bonus of 2 more sets in the tenth frame. Players are allowed 2 attempts to knock over all the pins within one frame. Matches are usually decided over 3 games.

• A lane is made of oiled wood and is 60 ft (18.24 m) from the foul-line (point of delivery) to the front pin. The pins are set with 12 in (30 cm) between the centre of each pin.

• A player must not step beyond the foul-line.

• Scoring in tenpin bowling is surprisingly difficult, but all modern bowling centres have computer scoring. If a player knocks all 10 pins down (a 'strike') with his first bowl in a frame, he scores 10 points (1 for each pin) and gains 2 additional attempts to score 'bonus points'. If he or she knocks all 10 pins down with 2 bowls (a 'spare'), one extra throw is awarded. At the end of a game, the maximum score is 300.

SKILLS

• Few tenpin bowlers would pretend to be great athletes, but skill is required in delivering the ball with consistent accuracy. If a ball is hurled down the centre of a lane towards the centremost pin, not all of the pins will necessarily topple. So, experienced bowlers have

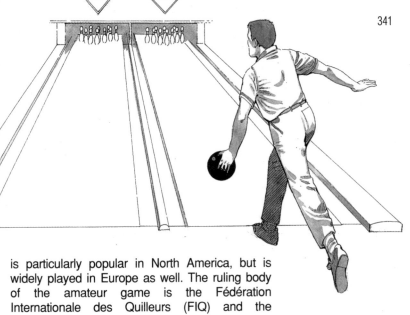

is particularly popular in North America, but is widely played in Europe as well. The ruling body of the amateur game is the Fédération Internationale des Quilleurs (FIQ) and the leading professional organization is the Professional Bowlers Association (PBA). Many amateur and professional contests are held. Those organized by the American Bowling Congress are some of the most prestigious. The British counterpart is the British Tenpin Bowling Association.

▲ *Skilled players can 'swing' the ball so that it makes a slightly oblique contact with the pins.*

developed techniques to 'hook' or spin the ball in such a way that if the ball enters the 'pocket' between the headpin and the adjacent pin, all the others will fall.

EQUIPMENT

● Bowling centres are packed with machinery. A machine automatically delivers each ball back to the delivery area after it has been bowled and simultaneously resets all the pins in their correct positions.
● The balls, originally made from lignum vitae wood, were later made of hardened rubber, but urethane is now used. They must not weigh more than 16 lb (7.26 kg) nor have a circumference greater than 27 in

(67 cm). Each ball has three holes drilled into it — one for the thumb and the others for fingers; balls are gripped using these holes.
● Special shoes are worn when tenpin bowling to avoid marking the approach. They have slippery soles with white rubber heels, suitable for sliding and braking during the conventional 4-step approach.

TECHNICAL TERMS

gutters channels on either side of a lane which catch badly bowled balls
pin-spotter the machine that automatically picks up and replaces pins after each bowl, repositioning those that are standing and clearing those that have toppled

DID YOU KNOW?

The 1990 Sand Yachting World Championships were held in the United States. Competitors had to contend with the searing heat of the Nevada desert floor.

SAND YACHTING

Sand yachting is a comparatively new sport, developed in the last 50 years. It is a derivative of sailing, but it has also a great deal in common with ice yachting.

The practice of sailing 'yachts' across land can possibly be dated back to Ancient Egyptian times and, even before then, to China. Old manuscripts and stone engravings depict boats being sailed, but it is not always clear whether this was across land or across sea. What is certain is that both the Ancient Chinese and Egyptian cultures knew how to harness wind power with sails. These people were also familiar with the wheel. Consequently, it is not unreasonable to assume that they rigged up huge land craft to transport the monumental pieces of stone that they used to build their lasting masterpieces. The forerunner to the trans-continental truck could well have been a wind-driven yacht on wheels.

In the 17th century, the Dutch used wind-driven wagons to ferry goods from one region to another. Holland's flat terrain, coupled with the constant onshore breeze from the North Sea, made wind-driven craft an obvious and efficient

▼ *A sand yachtsman lies on his back and controls the sail with ropes and pulleys. The wide wheel base gives the yacht stability.*

means of transporting goods. Ice yachting (see page 74) also developed in Holland, thanks to the canals, sometime after sand yachting.

The first land yachts had wooden wheels, which were mounted on primitive wooden frames. They were designed to carry heavy loads and consequently had wide chassis.

Today's sand yachts are often custom-made from whatever comes to hand — a canoe belly fixed to a roughly forged, triangular framework that is supported on three 'mini' car wheels. The sail and mast are often taken from a dinghy and welded onto the sub-frame.

However crude though the craft may appear, they are well constructed — a reflection of the single-minded devotion of most sand yachters.

The ruling body of the sport, which is essentially amateur by nature, is the International Federation of Sand and Land Yacht Clubs.

The sport, taken on by both women and men, is especially popular in the desert regions in the southwest of the United States (Utah, Arizona, California etc.) and in the flat, deserted areas of Europe and Australia. World Championships are held annually, either on disused airstrips or on dry mud flats.

> **DID YOU KNOW?**
>
> In the 19th century, repair parties along the Kansas Pacific Railway in the United States used a sailing car on the rails. These repair cars could average 50km/h (30mph) using only wind power.

AIMS OF THE GAME

COMPETITION
● Most competitions comprise a triangular course which tests both speed and manoeuvring skill. These are run on a knockout basis, with winners of each heat going through eliminating rounds to an ultimate final. There are several classes of 'boat' — determined by the sail area; some categories are for solo riders only, others for pairs.

SKILLS
● Sand yachting is akin to ice yachting and sailing but there is less margin for error. As the wheels are converted car tyres, skidding and sliding around markers requires great manoeuvring skill — too fast and the yacht will 'turn turtle', too slow and it will come to a standstill. Speeds in excess of 112 km/h (70 mph) can be achieved.
● Steering techniques are similar to those used in yachting; tacking ability (navigating a zig-zag course directly into the wind) is especially crucial as there is not normally a great area in which to move.

EQUIPMENT

● Sail area and rigging must conform to rules governing each category. Most yachts ride on 3 wheels (one 'up front', 2 behind).
● Yachtsmen wear goggles, gloves and helmets. Other attire depends on the weather conditions.

INDEX

In this index the figures in *italics* denote illustrations in the book. In a work of this kind it is not possible to index every entry. For entries not found in the index, look in the section on the relevant sport.

F

G

H

Acknowledgements

The publishers wish to thank the following for supplying photographs for this book:

ACTION PLUS Photographic   Page 52; 107
ALLSPORT   Page 29; 30; 38; 63; 67; 75; 82; 87; 96; 111; 122; 128; 145; 161; 172; 181; 205;
        229; 235; 238; 258; 269; 273; 278; 288; 307; 321; 336; 342
Hulton-Deutsch Collection   Page 40
Mansell Collection   Page 8
Supersport Photographs   Page 293; 303
Tennis and Rackets Association   Page 135
Bob Thomas Sports Photography   Page 90; 118; 224; 313

Picture Research: Su Alexander and Elaine Willis